Between Impunity and Imperialism

Between Impunity and Imperialism

The Regulation of Transnational Bribery

KEVIN E. DAVIS

OXFORD
UNIVERSITY PRESS

OXFORD
UNIVERSITY PRESS

Oxford University Press is a department of the University of Oxford. It furthers the University's objective of excellence in research, scholarship, and education by publishing worldwide. Oxford is a registered trademark of Oxford University Press in the UK and certain other countries.

Published in the United States of America by Oxford University Press
198 Madison Avenue, New York, NY 10016, United States of America.

Library of Congress Cataloging-in-Publication Data

Names: Davis, Kevin E., author.
Title: Between impunity and imperialism : the regulation of transnational bribery / Kevin E. Davis.
Description: New York : Oxford University Press, 2019. | Includes bibliographical references and index.
Identifiers: LCCN 2019007415 | ISBN 9780190070809 ((hardback) : alk. paper)
Subjects: LCSH: Bribery—Law and legislation. | International business enterprises—Law and legislation—Criminal provisions. | Corporations—Corrupt practices.
Classification: LCC K5216 .D38 2019 | DDC 345/.02323—dc23
LC record available at https://lccn.loc.gov/2019007415

3 5 7 9 8 6 4 2

Printed by Sheridan Books, Inc., United States of America

Note to Readers

This publication is designed to provide accurate and authoritative information in regard to the subject matter covered. It is based upon sources believed to be accurate and reliable and is intended to be current as of the time it was written. It is sold with the understanding that the publisher is not engaged in rendering legal, accounting, or other professional services. If legal advice or other expert assistance is required, the services of a competent professional person should be sought. Also, to confirm that the information has not been affected or changed by recent developments, traditional legal research techniques should be used, including checking primary sources where appropriate.

(Based on the Declaration of Principles jointly adopted by a Committee of the American Bar Association and a Committee of Publishers and Associations.)

To my parents, Claude and Marcia Davis.

Contents

Acknowledgments

A book like this is the product of years of reading and reflection. It is also the product of many, many conversations, with colleagues, students, and practitioners. I am particularly grateful to the anonymous reviewers and colleagues who went out of their way to provide detailed comments on earlier drafts: Jennifer Arlen, Samuel Buell, Alexander Cooley, Branislav Hock, James Jacobs, Daniel Sokol, Tina Søreide, Andrew Spalding, John Stinneford, Benjamin Straumann, Nicholas Wilson, and Nathan Yaffe. I have also benefited greatly from innumerable conversations with my collaborators and co-teachers Guillermo Jorge, Benedict Kingsbury, Maíra Machado, and Scott Muller. In addition, I owe a particular debt of gratitude to my research assistants, Rafaela Calcena, Maya Danaher, Deborah Kalu, Laura Kaufmann, Marissa Kibler, Mimi Powell, Stefan Rajiyah, and Mastewal Taddese, as well as to my faculty assistant, Ian Brydon. All errors remain my own.

The ideas in this book have been presented in earlier forms in many different fora, including: NYU Law School's Conference on Corporate Crime and Financial Misdealing, Faculty Workshop, History and Theory of International Law Workshop and Legal, Political and Social Philosophy Colloquium; HEC Paris; Max Planck Institute for International, Regulatory and European Procedural Law; the International Law and Foreign and Comparative Law Committees of the New York City Bar; University of Florida Levin School of Law, Marshall M. Criser Distinguished Lecture and Workshop Series; University of Toronto Faculty of Law, Law and Economics Workshop; University of Toronto, Munk School of Global and Political Affairs; Conference on Grand and Petty Corruption in Developing States: Business, Citizens, and the State, Yale University; The State of Anticorruption Efforts: Lessons from Latin America, Yale Law School; Fundação Getulio Vargas, São Paulo and Rio de Janeiro; University of San Andres; and the Symposium on Strengthening Global Leadership and Cooperation against Corruption, Anti-Corruption and Civil Rights Commission of Korea, Seoul. I am grateful to the participants in those sessions for their comments. I have also had the privilege of teaching and learning from students in courses on regulation of foreign corrupt practices at NYU, the University of Toronto, and Fundação Getulio Vargas, São Paulo.

My research has been generously supported by New York University School of Law, and in particular by funding from the Filomen D'Agostino and Max E. Greenberg Research Fund.

Finally, I am grateful to my wife, GuyLaine Charles, who lived with this project for so many years and whose encouragement is the main reason why I was able to complete it.

1
Introduction

> Okay. So my first reaction in reading this indictment is that your office is to be congratulated because, apparently, you have reduced crime in the Northern District of California, and indeed in the United States of America, to such a point that you are using resources of your office to go after criminal activity that occurs in foreign countries . . .[1]

The case was *U.S. v. Sidorenko*.[2] Judge Charles Breyer's sarcastic opening did not bode well for the two government lawyers arguing in front of him. The targets of the prosecution were two Ukrainians, living in Dubai, and a Venezuelan-Canadian who worked for the International Civil Aviation Organization (ICAO), an international organization based in Montreal. The Ukrainians allegedly bribed the Venezuelan-Canadian to use his position and influence to promote their company, which sold security and identity documents such as passports. None of the relevant conduct took place in the United States. The only apparent connection to the Northern District of California was that the United States was a member of the ICAO and supplied approximately 25 percent of the organization's annual budget, although there was no indication that programs funded by the United States were affected by the alleged bribery scheme.

Judge Breyer's feelings about the case were clear. Dropping the sarcasm, he said: "I never in my life, in 50 years of criminal practice, [*sic*] seen a more misguided prosecution as the one that you've brought. I just don't even get it. I don't get it, how you can—how you can use resources of the United States Attorney's Office to prosecute some foreign nationals involved in a foreign company, engaged in conduct which was foreign, on doing things that weren't directly related to the contribution of the United States to that entity."[3]

No one in the courtroom should have been surprised when Judge Breyer went on to dismiss the charges against the defendants.

* * *

Judge Breyer's ruling in *U.S. v. Sidorenko* was in line with recent U.S. Supreme Court decisions that are skeptical about the idea of applying U.S. laws outside of U.S. territory. Nonetheless, there is an important sense in which his decision was out of step with the times. Since the mid-1970s, U.S. prosecutors have taken up many cases involving corrupt practices with little connection to the United States: a German company that paid bribes to public officials in Argentina for a contract to provide identity cards;[4] a Japanese engineering company that paid bribes to Nigerian public officials to build a liquefied natural gas facility on an island off the coast of Nigeria;[5] a former Ukrainian prime minister who embezzled and extorted funds from both the state and various Ukrainian businesses;[6] a minister from Equatorial Guinea who misappropriated and extorted enormous sums from the treasury of his oil-rich country while the vast majority of his countrymen remained impoverished.[7] All of these cases involved public officials from countries other than the United States. In many of the cases the only connection to the United States was incidental, in the form of a transfer of funds into or through the United States. To the extent cases like these involve bribery of foreign public officials, they typically involve enforcement actions brought under the Foreign Corrupt Practices Act of 1977 (FCPA).[8] Also pressed into service are U.S. anti-money laundering laws, which generally are concerned with dealings with the proceeds of crime and can be triggered by either bribery or embezzlement.

At one point during the *U.S. v. Sidorenko* hearing, Judge Breyer worried that the prosecution was trying to "wipe out bribery . . . throughout the world."[9] He obviously thought that would be a quixotic enterprise. Based on its recent enforcement activities, it is not so clear that the U.S. Department of Justice agrees. In fact, the Department of Justice, as well as other members of the executive branch of the U.S. government, routinely portray the United States as the leader in a worldwide effort against corruption. That effort is often linked to promotion of economic development and respect for human rights. In President Barack Obama's words, "we are leading a global effort to combat corruption, which in many places is the single greatest barrier to prosperity, and which is a profound violation of human rights."[10]

The global effort to which President Obama referred has, to date, focused most intensely on transnational bribery of public officials, meaning transactions between public officials and foreign or multinational actors in which: (1) the official is offered or solicits a bribe, or (2) the official transfers proceeds of bribery to or with the assistance of the other actor. Regulation of these activities involves formulating prohibitions as well as all the steps involved in adjudicating and imposing sanctions for violation of those prohibitions. Legal institutions in the country served by the corrupt, or potentially corrupt, public officials obviously have an interest in regulating bribery and dealings in proceeds of crime involving those officials. What is distinctive about modern regulation of transnational bribery is that it is administered by legal institutions outside the country governed by the corrupt official. From the perspective of the official's country, this means foreign regulation of bribery. From the perspective of other countries, it entails regulation of foreign bribery.

We can refer to the legal substrate for regulation of transnational bribery as "transnational bribery law," which is itself a branch of "anti-corruption law," the body of law that regulates corrupt actions or events, including those that transcend national boundaries.[11] This body of law consists of a complex ensemble of legal instruments and enforcement practices. Most countries in the world have signed treaties committing them to prosecute firms for paying bribes to foreign public officials and to help other countries to recover proceeds of corrupt activity from corrupt officials. Those treaties include the Organisation for Economic Cooperation and Development's (OECD) extremely influential Convention on Combating Bribery of Foreign Public Officials in International Business Transactions (OECD Convention)[12] and the broad-ranging United Nations Convention against Corruption (UN Convention),[13] as well as several regional agreements. Many countries, along with the major international development banks, also have the power to "debar" firms that have engaged in corrupt practices, that is to say, refuse to do business with them in the future. Several countries have followed up on these formal commitments with meaningful enforcement actions. Finally, courts and arbitrators around the world are increasingly reluctant to enforce contracts tainted by bribery. We can call this global collection of laws and enforcement practices the "anti-bribery regime."[14]

The anti-bribery regime is now an established feature of the legal landscape, taking its place alongside established regimes such as competition/antitrust law as well as emerging bodies of law concerned with protection of privacy and intellectual property. Transnational bribery law is now a major source of legal risk for companies and individuals doing business across borders, and a promising new revenue stream for the professionals who advise them.

Defining Questions

Now that the legal structures associated with regulation of transnational bribery have become so prominent, hard questions are being asked about their foundations.

Suppose we got beyond Judge Breyer's question of whether the United States should ever regulate foreign corrupt practices before stamping out corruption at home. The next question would be, which practices deserve the attention of U.S. law? One of the allegations in *Sidorenko* was that the ICAO official had the ICAO endorse passports the Ukrainians produced for their home country (Ukraine) in order to aid in their pursuit of a contract to produce e-passports for Interpol. Corruption of the international organization that ensures the security of passports around the world seems like a matter of global concern, arguably worth the attention of U.S. authorities. Another allegation, however, was that the official helped the girlfriend of one of the Ukrainians to obtain a visa to visit Canada by writing a letter, on ICAO letterhead, indicating that she would participate in an ICAO event. It is far less clear that, taken on its own, this ought to be a matter of concern in the Northern District of California. It would be even less clear if this kind of behavior was commonplace in Canadian organizations and qualified as "the ways things are done" there.

Another challenge in many transnational bribery cases is that several people are complicit, and many of them act on behalf of organizations. The issue then is: How widely should the net of liability be cast? Was it appropriate to prosecute both the payers and the recipient of the bribes in *Sidorenko*? Should the company owned by the Ukrainians have been prosecuted as well? What about the banks that participated in the transfers of funds?

Next is the question of sanctions. Should people go to prison for this kind of conduct? If they do, should their prison terms be more like those of thieves (in Canada) or rapists (in the United States)? And what about firms whose employees or agents pay bribes; should their liability be measured in the millions, tens of millions, or hundreds of millions of dollars?

Finally, there is the question of how to allocate responsibility for enforcing prohibitions on transnational bribery. Almost by definition, transnational law potentially involves courts, prosecutors, police, and administrative agencies from multiple jurisdictions, not to mention bodies such as arbitral institutions that may have only nominal ties to any single jurisdiction. For instance, at the *Sidorenko* hearing, Judge Breyer wondered aloud why the United States couldn't simply rely on the Royal Canadian Mounted Police to pursue the case. And even if the Mounties could not have been counted on to get their men, enforcement agencies in the other member states of the ICAO could conceivably have taken up the case. In fact, one of the Ukrainians was at large in the United Arab Emirates while the other was in custody in Switzerland (on the basis of a U.S. warrant), so in principle either of those countries could have been a venue for a prosecution—not to mention the Ukraine or Venezuela. Moreover, most courts and arbitrators around the world would probably give the Ukrainians a hard time if they attempted to enforce contracts tainted by corruption. Last but not least, governments with which the Ukrainians hoped to do business in the future, as well as the international development banks that would fund those projects, would also be positioned to sanction the Ukrainians by way of debarment.

There are many outstanding questions about whether and how to coordinate the actions of multiple enforcement agencies in these sorts of cases. For instance, if more than one agency will act, which one should move first? This could be an important practical concern if both Canada and the United States were to request extradition of the Ukrainian detained in Switzerland. Then there are the questions that relate to whether agencies should act independently or in concert, and if in concert, how they ought to adjust their behavior to reflect one another's actions. If defendants are prosecuted in the United States, should they be immune from prosecution elsewhere? What if the Venezuelan-Canadian was given leniency in the United States as a reward for disclosing the Ukrainians' schemes? Should he be subject to prosecution in Canada on the basis of those disclosures?

Other questions of coordination involve allocating the economic burdens and the benefits of enforcement. Judge Breyer was obviously concerned about the economic burden of pursuing *U.S. v. Sidorenko*. It is difficult to know whether his concern was well founded. Corruption investigations and prosecutions can be expensive, and it is appropriate to ask whether and how the costs will be shared among enforcement agencies and the private actors involved in the case. But sometimes enforcement yields direct economic benefits, in the form of fines collected by and assets forfeited to enforcement agencies. In these circumstances the question becomes, how should the benefits be divvied up among the agencies?

The OECD Paradigm

To recapitulate, the questions that define regulation of transnational bribery are:

- What types of conduct should be targeted?
- Which actors ought to be considered complicit?
- What sanctions ought to be imposed?
- Who should bear the benefits and burdens of imposing those sanctions?

Judging by the current state of the anti-bribery regime, the accepted response to these questions is: "Every little bit helps." In other words, anything foreign legal institutions can do to help combat transnational bribery is likely to be worthwhile: they should prohibit a broader range of conduct, target more actors, impose more severe sanctions, and get more and more agencies involved in enforcement. This approach is advocated with particular force by the OECD Working Group on Bribery in International Business Transactions (Working Group), which is charged with monitoring implementation of the OECD Convention.[15] Moreover, law enforcement agencies, nongovernmental organizations, and commentators that endorse the every-little-bit-helps approach view the OECD Convention as a critical instrument in the fight against transnational bribery.[16] Accordingly, it seems apt to use the term "OECD paradigm" as shorthand for the combination of the every-little-bit-helps approach and the arguments commonly used to support it.[17]

"Every little bit helps" is an understandable reaction in light of the way in which contemporary scholars and policymakers tend to understand bribery and the more encompassing phenomenon of corruption. In the not-too-distant past, respectable social scientists argued seriously that bribery was an efficient way of cutting red tape generated by dysfunctional bureaucracies.[18] The views of these apologists have been challenged vigorously by more recent studies, and the balance of academic opinion now weighs strongly in favor of the view that bribery of public officials is a serious problem. Bribery is, among other things, believed to undermine governance, increase the cost of doing business, and, overall, serve as a drag on economic development. Multinational firms that participate in bribery are considered to be poorly managed, a potential source of embarrassment to their home countries, as well as sources of bad habits that threaten to contaminate the business environment wherever they operate. In other words, bribery causes economic, social, and political harms both inside and outside the borders of the country whose public officials have been bribed.[19] Nowadays, it is virtually taboo for a serious policymaker to defend bribery in polite company; the new consensus is that bribery of public officials is intolerable.

At the same time, bribery and other forms of corruption are perceived to be both pervasive and invisible; they are everywhere and nowhere at the same time. Anonymous surveys and public revelations prompted by audits, enforcement actions, whistleblowers, or media investigations leave the impression that corruption is widespread in many societies. There is also a sense that at least some corrupt actors profit enormously from their misconduct. Moreover, it is understood that most corruption will never be revealed. Typically, corrupt transactions can be conducted behind closed doors, often through intermediaries that can be located anywhere in the world, including secretive offshore financial centers. Even worse, although corruption is not a victimless crime, the victims often do not know who they are. In cases of bribery, the only visible product of the offense might be an official act that is only objectionable because it was done for the wrong reason, and that reason is unlikely to come to light. At the same time, the effects of the tainted action may be felt by a large group of people—potentially, the entire population of a country—and no individual victim is likely to notice or complain.

Anti-corruption activists and scholars complain that even when corruption comes to light it routinely goes unpunished because legal institutions are rarely capable of effectively enforcing anti-corruption laws. This seems especially plausible in the case of corruption in the highest echelons of the governments of desperately poor countries. Most troubling of all are cases in which corrupt public officials in poor countries collude with multinational enterprises or shadowy financiers based in wealthier countries. When high-level officials or powerful foreign actors are involved, the potential impunity of the perpetrators compounds the offensiveness of the underlying corrupt acts. Many, though not all, cases of transnational bribery fit this description.

The every-little-bit-helps approach to regulation of transnational bribery promises to overcome this problem of impunity. The hope is that legal sanctions will serve three main purposes: to condemn wrongful conduct, to prevent harm, and to compensate victims for harm that has occurred.

Having legal institutions from multiple jurisdictions impose harsh penalties expresses a particular form of moral condemnation. Harsh penalties underscore the fact that bribery is intolerable, not only because of the magnitude of the harm it causes but also because it represents a refusal to respect the role assigned to that official by the state, an act which represents a direct challenge to the authority of the state. Any state whose authority has been challenged ought to be entitled to participate in the expression of condemnation. Pushing this line of argument a bit further, bribery arguably represents a challenge to the very idea of state authority, suggesting that every state is entitled to condemn the perpetrators.

The every-little-bit-helps approach is also appealing as a means of preventing bribery. Prevention can be accomplished by making it physically impossible for bribery to occur (incapacitation), persuading actors not to engage in bribery (persuasion), or creating incentives to refrain from, and even combat, corrupt behavior (deterrence). In practice though, most attention focuses on deterrence. Sophisticated arguments have been developed to explain why deterrence of a practice like bribery demands the every-little-bit-helps approach to the issues of which conduct and which actors ought to be targeted, what penalties ought to be imposed, and which agencies ought to be involved in enforcement.

Let us start with the arguments for targeting a broad range of conduct. The pervasive-yet-invisible nature of bribery suggests that law enforcement agencies should react forcefully to even the slightest evidence of misconduct. The hope is that even if the dirty deeds that lead to actual social harm take place in the shadows, warning signs may be relatively easy to spot. Consorting with known wrongdoers, unexplained transfers of value, furtive behavior, and unexplained wealth—common sense suggests that these are all associated with an increased likelihood of corruption and its associated harms. In other words, they are risky behaviors. Moreover, risk is a function of both the magnitude and the likelihood of harm. Since bribery is understood to be extraordinarily harmful, conduct associated with a relatively low probability of impropriety can still be considered to present a substantial risk.

The implications for the scope of anti-bribery law are clear: if public officials cannot be caught in the course of their corrupt acts, they ought to be punished whenever the indicia of bribery are present and the risk is high. This explains, for instance, why the offense of "illicit enrichment" has found its way into the penal codes of many countries. It is also why the United States punishes companies for maintaining slush funds that can be used to hide bribes, with or without proof that bribes have actually been paid.

The arguments for targeting a broad range of actors follow a similar line of reasoning. The perception that bribery takes place largely in the shadows and that the principal perpetrators are beyond the direct reach of the legal system creates a felt need for additional conscripts in the battle. Fear of liability is used to motivate other actors to assist law enforcement agencies in the fight against bribery. It is now considered common sense that when an individual pays a bribe, the corporation that employs him should face punishment. Only slightly more debatable is the idea that the net of liability should extend to officers, directors, and other supervisory personnel in his company; his employer's auditors and bankers; and his employer's parent company. Similarly, when a public official receives a bribe, it is considered eminently reasonable to target her accountants and bankers, and anyone else who helps her either to keep or dispose of her ill-gotten gains. In fact, the same logic supports holding the state that employs the official legally responsible.

The perceived gravity of the problem of bribery also drives thinking about the appropriate level and kinds of sanctions. Bribery is a lucrative activity that causes grave social harms yet is difficult to detect. According to mainstream deterrence theory, this is exactly the kind of misconduct that should attract harsh punishment. This theory postulates that bribery ought to be deterred because it causes serious social harm and deterrence requires harsh sanctions in order to override incentives to pursue large corrupt rewards, especially when potential wrongdoers conclude they have a low chance of being punished and discount the value of sanctions accordingly.

Similar logic justifies the kinds of sanctions we see in transnational bribery law. Firms that engage in transnational bribery have been hit with large monetary penalties. We have already discussed the rationale for targeting corporate entities. The emphasis on monetary penalties for violations is partly a result of necessity: unlike natural-born individuals, corporations are not vulnerable to physical or spiritual sanctions. As lawyers like to say, a corporation "has no soul to be damned and no body to be kicked."[20] The hope is that even if a corporation is not concerned about threats to its body or soul, it will be concerned about, and respond to, threats to the economic resources that give its existence meaning.

This takes us to the question of which legal institutions should be involved in implementing transnational bribery law. The fact that a corrupt transaction involves actors in multiple jurisdictions does not necessarily mean that it has to be regulated by agencies from multiple jurisdictions. In principle, transnational bribery could be regulated solely by institutions located in the same jurisdiction as the corrupt public official. The every-little-bit-helps philosophy assumes that involvement of additional legal institutions—foreign legal institutions—is a valuable means of combating impunity on the part of corrupt actors because: (1) foreign actors are interested in combating transnational bribery, and (2) foreign actors bring to the table valuable resources that locals are unable to match. Under these conditions, foreign legal institutions will enhance the effectiveness of local anti-bribery law. In other words, local and foreign legal institutions will be complements.

In theory, anti-corruption law can serve not just to condemn and to prevent, but also as a way of securing compensation for victims. When it comes to regulation of transnational bribery, practice has not yet fully caught up to the theory. The practice of imposing substantial monetary sanctions on multinational enterprises that are complicit in transnational bribery is a useful step toward the goal of compensation. Those sanctions are especially likely to result in actual payments when imposed by states in a position to move against assets the firms value. In principle, the resulting funds could be channeled to victims of corruption. In fact, the UN Convention commits its signatories, which include most countries in the world, to cooperate in transferring confiscated proceeds of corruption, and awarding compensation, to victimized states. To date, however, the funds collected rarely have been used for the purpose of compensation. They typically are remitted to the Treasury of the United States or whichever other country has launched the relevant legal proceeding. This practice, which may be in the process of changing, is contrary to the spirit of the UN Convention. At the same time, defenders of the current practice point to the practical difficulties inherent in awarding compensation to victims of corruption. In many cases it is difficult to identify individual victims. The most plausible candidate for receiving compensation is typically the state whose officials have already been proven to be corrupt. The natural concern is that money given to such a state will go right back to the people who victimized it in the first place.

Critiques of the OECD Paradigm

The OECD paradigm has been tremendously influential in the development of transnational bribery law and is widely accepted by both practitioners and scholars. This does not, however, mean that it is invulnerable to criticism.

Past challenges to the OECD paradigm have targeted the background assumption that corruption in general, and bribery in particular, is intolerable by arguing that it is functional in various ways. Those arguments are generally unpersuasive. Perhaps the most plausible contention is that bribery can serve as a means of cutting unnecessary red tape that would otherwise stifle economic activity.[21] A major problem with this argument is that the hope of receiving a bribe operates as an incentive for officials to create unnecessary red tape.[22] On another tack, it was once in vogue to argue that bribery is morally acceptable in some societies, and so anti-bribery laws imposed and enforced by foreigners represent a form of moral imperialism in relation to those societies.[23] This argument has gained little traction because there does not seem to be much disagreement about the moral status of the kinds of high-level bribery that are the focus of transnational bribery law.[24]

There is, however, a twist on the moral imperialism argument that deserves more attention. Societies do in fact vary in terms of how much they condemn various types of low-level corruption. In the face of this kind of variation it makes sense to be concerned about any approach to transnational bribery law that leads to a one-size-fits-all approach. Rather than questioning whether bribery is a problem, perhaps we should question whether the OECD paradigm has embraced the right response.

Several interrelated criticisms focus on these issues.[25] One set scrutinize the outcomes associated with the OECD paradigm in terms of effectiveness, efficiency, and fairness. In other words: How well does it achieve its objectives relative to the associated costs, and are those costs distributed appropriately? Another set of criticisms question the processes associated with the OECD paradigm in terms of both due process and legitimacy. Due process is a synonym for procedural fairness. Legitimacy means simply whether or not a particular assertion of power is justifiable and may be a byproduct of perceptions of effectiveness, fairness, or due process. Legitimacy is important both as an end in itself and also because people tend to be more likely to comply with laws they perceive as legitimate.

Each component of the every-little-bit-helps approach is vulnerable to one or the other of these arguments. Take, for instance, the fact that the OECD paradigm focuses on transnational bribery as opposed to other forms of transnational corruption. This focus is the result of an improbable sequence of events in U.S. history rather than an inclusive and reasoned analysis of whether transnational bribery is the variety of corruption most suitable for transnational regulation. As a result, there is no guarantee that the overall orientation of the current regime is legitimate, effective, or efficient.

Individual features of the OECD paradigm's approach to transnational bribery law are also vulnerable to criticism. Take the idea of targeting transactions that are risky instead of only the ones that create verifiable harm. The more money, time, and other resources devoted to transactions that are merely risky, the fewer resources that will be available for transactions that result in actual harm. It is cost-effective to trade off depth for breadth if the costs of targeting the risky transactions are low, or the benefits are substantial. A lot turns, therefore, on the magnitude of the risk presented.

Every interaction between a public official and a private individual creates some level of risk. At one end of the spectrum is a multimillion dollar wire transfer to a head of state in exchange for the award of a government contract. At the other end of the spectrum is a cup of coffee or a holiday gift of a bottle of Scotch whisky. Campaign contributions fall somewhere between these poles. All of these transactions entail risk of harm, but some of them also have redeeming value. Beyond what point on the spectrum of risk is it worthwhile to engage the costly machinery of transnational bribery law? In the *Sidorenko* case, the Ukrainians offered a job to the ICAO official's son. Suppose this was the only "bribe" offered, and the only favor sought in return was help in securing a visa for the Ukrainian's girlfriend. Is this a risky transaction? Certainly. Is it risky enough to justify the invocation of U.S. law? As evidenced by colloquy between Judge Breyer and the prosecutors representing the government, reasonable people will probably disagree about that, particularly if they focus on whether the costs outweigh the benefits. "Every little bit helps" amounts to a bias toward engaging foreign law in these situations. That amounts to a bias toward overbreadth, in other words, laws that cover too much of the spectrum to be cost-effective.

A curious feature of the *Sidorenko* case is that the defendants were prosecuted for fraud, not bribery. It is not uncommon for enforcement agencies to rely on broadly worded prohibitions to target cases of suspected bribery. The best examples are the many cases in which U.S. enforcement agencies have sanctioned firms suspected of bribery for risky accounting practices. This tactic is consistent with the every-little-bit-helps approach because it allows enforcement agencies to capture an extremely broad range of conduct. For example, under U.S. law, liability is triggered by failure to keep records—not just accounts—that "in reasonable detail, accurately and fairly reflect" transactions.[26] Allowing enforcement agencies to impose severe penalties for violations of broadly worded prohibitions also raises concerns about procedural fairness—or to use a more lawyerly term, "due process"—specifically, citizens' entitlements to have notice of what conduct is prohibited.

The practice of targeting people beyond the immediate parties to corrupt transactions raises similar concerns about overbreadth. The most attention-grabbing applications of transnational bribery law have been the prosecutions of corporations whose employees or agents have engaged in bribery. In December 2008, Siemens, a German multinational enterprise, made headlines around the world when it agreed to pay approximately $1.6 billion in monetary penalties to enforcement agencies in the United States and Germany as part of an agreement settling charges stemming from a number of transnational bribery scandals. Fear of this kind of liability drives corporations to place strict controls on employees or agents who deal with public officials (as well as their friends, families, and associates) and even to refrain from doing business in countries where corruption is perceived to be widespread. Fear of liability is also supposed to drive firms implicated in wrongdoing to conduct exhaustive internal investigations, discipline employees, and, when appropriate, to report themselves to the authorities and cooperate in any ensuing investigation. Critics worry that if given the option of pursuing prominent organizations with deep pockets, law enforcement agencies will neglect their obligations to pursue individuals. They also worry that fear of liability will encourage organizations to cover up rather than publicize their misdeeds.

Another major source of concern is the cost of recruiting organizations into the fight against transnational bribery. Those costs are unquestionably high—Siemens spent more than $1 billion on its internal investigation.[27] Even more troubling, the costs of organizational liability do not fall only on the owners of the targeted companies. The costs also fall on employees, customers, suppliers, and, sometimes, even the people transnational bribery law is designed to protect—ordinary citizens in countries with endemic corruption who find themselves abandoned by the international business community. Here again, the OECD paradigm is open to the criticisms that it is insensitive both to whether the costs of expanding the net of legal liability outweigh the benefits, and to whether those costs fall disproportionately on some people and communities. Proposals to hold states legally responsible when their officials solicit or receive bribes raise similar concerns.

The harsh sanctions demanded by the OECD paradigm merit different forms of criticism. For starters, there are reasons to doubt whether harsh sanctions will have the predicted deterrent effects. Deterrence theory is premised on very specific and hotly contested assumptions about what drives people's behavior. The theory takes it as given that people respond to incentives. Alternative assumptions lead to different predictions about the impact of harsh sanctions. Suppose, for instance, potential defendants respond mainly to persuasion as opposed to incentives. Persuasion is a function of respect for perceived expertise and capacity for moral judgment, not power. An agency that imposes moderate and reasonable sanctions on defendants who have made genuine efforts to do the right thing might inspire more respect than one whose enforcement actions can be dismissed as efforts to bolster the reputations of individual prosecutors or to line the coffers of its political masters.

Even if we accept the motivational assumptions of deterrence theory, the deterrent effects anticipated by the OECD paradigm only arise if potential defendants know what will befall them if they violate the law. Enforcement agencies must make credible commitments to impose harsh penalties for future misconduct and then communicate those commitments to potential defendants. It is often doubtful whether enforcement agencies have the requisite credibility and communication skills. Western multinationals and their advisers undoubtedly pay close attention to legal developments like the *Siemens* case; it is less clear that Ukrainian firms like the one implicated in the *Sidorenko* case will be so attentive to these signals. And even if they get the message, they may not believe it matters to them. Why would anyone expect enforcement strategies to remain constant over time when it is apparent that governments and their priorities often change? In 2010, Barack Obama, the forty-fourth president of the United States, portrayed enforcement of the FCPA as a moral obligation that would promote economic development. Less than two years later, the man who would eventually become the forty-fifth president (before he announced his candidacy for the presidency), said the FCPA was a "horrible law and it should be changed" and that it was "absolutely crazy" for the United States to prosecute companies for FCPA violations in places like Mexico or India when that would put U.S. businesses at a "huge disadvantage" and prevent them from creating jobs.[28] Interestingly, after the first year of the new administration, U.S. enforcement policy appeared to be broadly consistent with past practice, but for the first few months its credibility was certainly in question.[29]

Even if enforcement agencies can shape incentives, there is no guarantee that harsh penalties will create the right incentives. For instance, individuals who would be willing to accept a moderate penalty might contest efforts to sentence them to prison, and the time and money spent on litigation might not be worth any incremental deterrent effect. To the extent they create incentives, harsh sanctions might also exacerbate concerns about overbreadth. The harsher the sanctions, the greater the costs borne by people who venture into the zone of liability, and, if that zone is defined too broadly, the greater the likelihood of deterring conduct that is risky but on balance socially desirable. A separate but related concern is that the costs of harsh sanctions and vigorous enforcement will be distributed unfairly. Proponents of the OECD paradigm expect it to deter corrupt practices that disproportionately hurt the poor. Critics worry that vigorous enforcement of anti-bribery laws will serve to deter investment in countries afflicted by corruption, which tend to be impoverished countries whose people would benefit from foreign investment. Some also worry that enforcement of anti-bribery laws will tend to have the greatest adverse impact on countries ruled by progressive governments that intervene extensively in the economy. Yet again the result will be to diminish the prospects for advancement of the most vulnerable members of society.

Finally, there is the most prominent feature of the OECD paradigm: reliance on foreign institutions to combat corruption of local officials. This practice is based largely on the idea that foreign anti-corruption law fills an "enforcement gap" caused by the ineffectiveness of local law. That presumption is contestable. In the first place, at present only a handful of OECD countries actively enforce prohibitions on transnational bribery. Several major exporters of capital, goods, and services—notably, China, India, and Russia—have shown little interest in joining the group of active enforcers. Moreover, even the most capable legal institutions are likely to be less effective when they try to operate across borders. No matter how well intentioned and competent they might be, foreign legal institutions typically can only deploy coercive force within their own territory. Everywhere else they require the cooperation of local authorities. This means that most countries will find it difficult to punish, and sometimes even investigate, foreign firms and individuals, including most foreign public officials. Even the long arm of U.S. law can find it difficult to reach corrupt actors who remain outside U.S. territory. A case in point is Yuri Sidorenko, who managed to remain at large until Judge Breyer dismissed the case against him.

Foreign institutions also will inevitably struggle with the challenges inherent in designing an effective anti-corruption regime. Institutions that operate outside of familiar environments may lack the inclination, expertise, or moral authority to decide which transactions present enough risk to be worthy of condemnation, what sorts of preventive and investigative measures are cost-effective for organizations, and what sorts of sanctions will induce compliance. What expertise does the U.S. Department of Justice have in determining whether to punish a Japanese firm for making illicit campaign contributions to a Nigerian political party? How does it know what types of sanctions will elicit compliance from other Japanese firms, whether through deterrence or persuasion? Shouldn't Japanese firms suspect that penalties will be crafted with a view to giving a competitive advantage to U.S. firms?

Even if foreign anti-corruption institutions are willing and able to combat impunity, there remain real questions about whether they are capable of doing so without undermining local institutions. It is quite possible that foreign and local anti-corruption institutions work as substitutes rather than complements, meaning that each reduces rather than enhances the effectiveness of the other.

For example, prosecuting multinational corporations for paying bribes or seizing proceeds of bribery that have been transferred overseas may be sufficient to deter a great deal of misconduct and thus may reduce the marginal benefits of prosecuting corrupt public officials locally. In this scenario, foreign intervention will undermine, rather than enhance, the effectiveness of the local institutions. At first glance, substitution of foreign for local institutions seems unproblematic; in the short term, a society might benefit from foreign interventions that serve as substitutes for local action. Substitution becomes a problem, however, if the displaced local institutions would have improved over time and eventually outperformed their foreign counterparts. In this scenario, the use of foreign institutions as substitutes for local anti-corruption entities will lead to a net decline in the effectiveness of all anti-corruption efforts.

Foreign institutions also face the inherent challenge of coordinating the activities of multiple enforcement agencies, especially when their efforts are combined with those of an array of private actors pressed into service as ersatz corruption fighters.

And then there are questions about due process, fairness, and legitimacy. Allowing foreign institutions to become involved in enforcement makes it possible for the same misconduct to be punished by multiple agencies, including agencies in countries with which the defendant has little connection. These conditions jeopardize some of the most fundamental attributes of due process, including: advance notice of what conduct will attract liability, advance notice of the forum in which liability will be adjudicated, timely adjudication of liability before an impartial tribunal, no more than one trial for each allegation of wrongdoing arising from the same transaction, and punishment proportionate to the harm or risk of harm created.

Foreign institutions also will be tempted to make self-interested and potentially unfair enforcement decisions. For instance, a foreign agency might retain the proceeds of bribery collected from wrongdoers instead of using them to make restitution to victimized states. Or, it might prosecute firms that compete with its own firms, even if the result is to raise the prices faced by the government of a poor country.

These concerns about potential violations of due process and unfairness combine with concerns about lack of accountability to generate deep concerns about legitimacy. Foreign anti-corruption institutions typically are not accountable to the public in the societies most affected by their activities. The local public generally has only the most indirect input into the drafting of multilateral anti-corruption treaties; little or no input into the formulation of policies adopted by the various international, intergovernmental, and nongovernmental organizations involved in transnational anti-corruption efforts; no input into the drafting of foreign legislation that is enforced extraterritorially; and no say in the appointment of foreign compliance officers, police officers, prosecutors, and judges who implement transnational anti-corruption law. These problems are exacerbated by the fact that many anti-corruption institutions are considered part of the criminal justice system.

Organizations and individuals charged with enforcing criminal law norms usually enjoy a significant amount of independence from political control. However, private actors conscripted into enforcing transnational bribery law do not necessarily enjoy any more legitimacy than their public counterparts. Corporations that adopt compliance programs and arbitrators who take it upon themselves to police corrupt agreements are even less accountable to affected members of the public than are foreign enforcement agencies. For all these reasons, foreign anti-corruption institutions will struggle to achieve legitimacy in the eyes of local actors.

Each of the individual criticisms of the OECD paradigm might be addressed through modest changes in the existing approaches to transnational bribery law, but their combined force suggests that more far-reaching changes are required. Taken together, these critiques represent a fundamental challenge to the OECD paradigm. That challenge hearkens back to the critiques of neo-imperialist practices of the late nineteenth and early twentieth centuries. Neo-imperialist interventions in Africa, Asia, and Latin America were defended as ways of bringing good governance to benighted peoples but were criticized for being ineffective, illegitimate, and unfair exercises of power by some groups of people over others. In recognition of that parallel, I refer to the collection of criticisms of the OECD paradigm as the "anti-imperialist critique."

Inclusive Experimentalism

Is there any response to the anti-imperialist critique of the OECD paradigm? At first glance, no satisfactory response seems possible. The anti-imperialist critique seems to strike at the very idea of a paradigm, that is to say, a widely shared commitment to a set of legal practices and accompanying theoretical justifications. The OECD paradigm embraces the every-little-bit-helps approach, supported by assumptions about the best ways of achieving condemnation, prevention, and compensation. The critique exposes disagreements about both objectives (or at least how to prioritize them) and ways to achieve them. Any satisfactory response has to acknowledge these disagreements.

Part of the solution is to make the paradigm more flexible; the other part of the solution is to temper the critique with realism. Although there is virtually infinite room for disagreement about the objectives of transnational bribery law, most stakeholders are likely to take positions that overlap with one another.

At the same time, the extent of possible disagreement about best practices is limited because no one can be truly confident about the merits of any particular practices. This means that the stakeholders interested in transnational bribery law have not only overlapping objectives but also common interests in exploring alternative ways of achieving those objectives. That exploration generally will involve experimentation, a term I use loosely to mean any systematic effort to identify causal relationships between legal interventions and social, economic, or political outcomes.

The common interest in experimentation will typically translate into an interest in coordinated experimentation, if only to avoid conflict and duplication of effort. For instance, several law enforcement agencies may have an interest in trying to figure out whether promises of leniency induce self-reporting, but any single agency's effort to test a leniency program will be thwarted if other agencies threaten to use self-reports as a basis for prosecution.

A body of transnational bribery laws organized around a set of overlapping objectives and a common interest in coordinated experimentation represents an intriguing alternative to one organized around the OECD paradigm. Such a regime would qualify as an example of what Gráinne De Búrca, Robert Keohane, and Charles Sabel call "Global Experimentalist Governance." In their words,

> [Global Experimentalist Governance] is an institutionalized process of participatory and multilevel collective problem solving, in which the problems (and the means of addressing them) are framed in an open-ended way, and subjected to periodic revision by various forms of peer review in the light of locally generated knowledge.[30]

There are already signs of experimentalism in transnational bribery law. Individual enforcement agencies in the United States and elsewhere seem to be genuinely committed to continuous improvement of their efforts to regulate transnational bribery. At the international level much of this activity is supported by the activities of the OECD Working Group, whose activities include periodic reviews of each member state's anti-bribery legislation by teams from peer countries; publication of reports from the country reviews as well as occasional research papers; and organization of conferences, workshops, and meetings, particularly among law enforcement agencies.

The status quo falls well short of an ideal global experimentalist regime. The OECD is "a club of mostly rich countries."[31] Its members make up less than 20 percent of the world's population.[32] Non-OECD members have been given a role in the OECD's anti-bribery activities, and there are noteworthy treaties and networks of policymakers outside the OECD, but nevertheless, regulation of transnational bribery clearly is dominated by the OECD's members, and especially the United States. Consequently, although transnational bribery law affects the entire world, it is shaped by people who represent only a small fraction of the world's population.

The missing voices disproportionately include people whose public officials solicit or receive bribes. Their absence from the discussion compromises the legitimacy of the regime. Unequal representation also is likely to undermine the effectiveness of the regime, to the extent the unrepresented people possess valuable information. Curing these defects ought to be at the top of the agenda for reform of transnational bribery law.

Outline of the Book

This book describes the defining features of modern regulation of transnational bribery and explains how those features reflect the tension between the OECD paradigm and the anti-imperialist critique.

Chapters 2 through 4 trace the history of regulation of transnational bribery, as a prelude to analysis of the contemporary regime. Chapter 5 sets out criteria for analyzing the merits of the regime. Chapter 6 kicks off that analysis with a detailed examination of how the law defines and ought to define bribery, followed by a brief discussion in chapter 7 of whether it is appropriate to use more expansively defined offenses, such as fraud or improper accounting, to target transnational bribery. Chapter 8 turns to the question of who besides the individual perpetrators of bribery ought to be targeted, with special attention to the private firms and states that employ the perpetrators. Chapter 9 asks how the law ought to be enforced, with emphasis on what sanctions ought to be employed, how much effort ought to be devoted to enforcement, and what sort of information about enforcement practices ought to be communicated to the public. Chapter 10 asks what roles different countries' enforcement agencies ought to play in regulating transnational bribery. Chapter 11 concludes by discussing an inclusive experimentalist alternative to the current approach to transnational bribery law.

2
Imperial Anti-corruption Law

Introduction

Norms against bribery date back to Biblical times. The Old Testament vividly warns that bribes blind those who see and pervert the words of the righteous.[1] But transnational bribery law is a more recent invention, if only because its obvious prerequisites took time to emerge. Nation-states. An accepted definition of bribery. An organized legal system. All of these appeared relatively recently in human history. Without them the concept of transnational bribery law is meaningless.

The Trial of Verres

Precursors to transnational bribery law date back at least as far as the Late Roman Republic. In fact, one of the most famous trials in ancient history was a corruption trial that was replete with allegations of bribery.

The case was prosecuted in 70 B.C. by Cicero, one of the most famous advocates in all of history. The defendant was a Roman aristocrat who went by the unfortunate name of Verres, literally, "the Hog." The charges were brought based on Verres's depredations while serving as governor of Sicily during the three preceding years. Cicero's speeches are the only surviving records of the trial. Known to generations of Latin students as "the Verrine Orations," Cicero's speeches show Verres in the worst possible light, setting out a litany of outrageous crimes against men, women, children, and gods alike. According to Cicero, during his three years in Sicily Verres swindled beneficiaries out of their legacies; took bribes in exchange for appointments to public offices, exemptions from military service, and favorable legal decisions; embezzled from tithes that should have been remitted to Rome; confiscated statues, ornaments, and jewelery from temples, public squares, private citizens, and visiting potentates; and executed Roman citizens, including one who was crucified at a spot chosen for its view across the strait to Italy in mockery of his claim that his citizenship guaranteed him protection from execution.[2]

The charges against Verres were brought on behalf of the people of Sicily. The claim was heard in the *quaestio de repetundis*, "the (court of) inquiry into

Between Impunity and Imperialism. Kevin E. Davis.

moneys claimed back," sometimes referred to as the "Extortion Court." This tribunal was established in 149 B.C. for the express purpose of hearing claims against Roman magistrates who oppressed or mismanaged provinces and allies. A convicted governor could be ordered to pay damages and would often go into exile. The establishment of the Extortion Court was followed by a long series of legal initiatives designed to protect Rome's allies from misgovernment and oppression, culminating in the *lex Julia de pecuniis repetundis* passed by Julius Caesar in 59 B.C., the last extortion law of the Roman Republic.[3] The *quaestio de repetundis* had a reasonably impressive conviction rate. Of the fifty-nine reported trials, forty-three resulted in a verdict, and nineteen of those verdicts were convictions.[4]

These efforts to reform provincial governance reflected a mix of cosmopolitan and self-interested motivations.[5] Stoics like Cato, a contemporary and political peer of Cicero's, believed that all human beings were members of a worldwide cosmopolis so that the same moral obligations were owed to foreigners and to citizens.[6] Stoics also believed that moral superiors had an obligation to govern in the interests of the governed. Self-interest was undoubtedly at work as well though. Roman politicians were well aware that dissatisfied allies were prone to rebel, or at least side with foreign invaders. In 88 B.C., Mithridates VI of Pontus was able to capture Asia Minor and massacre 88,000 Romans and Italians with the assistance of the locals. At the time of the trial of Verres this memory was still fresh in the minds of Roman leaders, especially because Mithradites' armies were still in the field threatening Rome's provinces.[7] In other writings Cicero himself drew causal connections between the efficacy of laws against corruption and the stability of the Republic.[8]

Despite its worthy mandate and record of convictions, the Extortion Court of Cicero's time was famously corrupt. Its members were known for turning a blind eye to oppression in the provinces so long as they were given a share of the spoils.[9] In fact, Cicero opened his first speech by acknowledging that Verres had bribed the court.[10] Perhaps this is why Cicero went on to appeal not only to the sense of justice of the judges but also their self-interest as Romans. He emphasized that Verres's crimes went beyond merely accepting bribes, which he acknowledged might have been tolerable. Cicero instead dwelled on the crimes Verres had committed against Roman citizens and the losses he had imposed on the Roman Treasury and hinted—perhaps ironically—at the risk that Verres would bring his corrupt practices to Rome.[11] Cicero was also careful to cite instances in which Verres's oppression had incited even normally peaceable allies to violent protest[12] and played on fears that allowing misdeeds such as Verres's to go unpunished would corrode the ties between Rome and its allies.[13] Last but certainly not least, Cicero appealed to the judges' political self-interest. At this point in Rome's history the Extortion Court was controlled exclusively by senators, but their position was being contested by the equestrian class. Cicero warned that failure to convict Verres would lead to control of the courts being taken away from the senators.[14]

When Cicero did focus on Verres's bribery, he stressed either the unjust consequences of the corrupted decisions or the exceptional wickedness of Verres's behavior. One such instance was the case of Sopater of Halicyae.[15] Sopater was a supposedly innocent man brought up on criminal charges before Verres. Sopater paid Verres's henchman a bribe in order to avoid conviction, only to be told later that Verres had accepted a larger bribe from Sopater's accusers. Sopater refused to pay any more money and was pronounced guilty. Worst of all, Verres did not even return Sopater's money. Cicero argued that although it was "a wicked thing" for a judge to accept a bribe, "there may now and then have been someone who did something of the same description."[16] What was much more wicked and vicious and shameful was for the judge to renege on his corrupt bargain and then refuse to give the money back.[17]

Verres fled before Cicero completed his first speech and was quickly condemned and ordered to pay damages. He died in exile in 43 B.C. The case catapulted Cicero into prominence in the Senate, and his subsequent literary and political accomplishments ensured that his speeches against Verres would be marked for posterity. For Romans, the Verrine Orations came to serve as exempla, stories of famous historical figures that both entertained and delivered moral instruction. For our purposes, the case stands as an early demonstration of how, given the right set of motivations, legal institutions can be used to deny prominent actors impunity for corrupt practices in far-off lands.

The Impeachment of Warren Hastings

Fast-forward almost two thousand years to eighteenth-century England, where the trial of Verres inspired another famous attempt to apply imperial anti-corruption law. Between 1788 and 1795, Warren Hastings was prosecuted before the English Parliament for oppressive and corrupt practices during his terms as Governor of Bengal and Governor-General of India from 1771 to 1785.[18] The outcome of the Hastings trial was very different from the outcome of the trial of Verres; Hastings was acquitted. If the trial of Verres demonstrated the potential of imperial anti-corruption law, the trial of Hastings demonstrated its limits.

The charges against Hastings resembled those against Verres. According to his prosecutors, Hastings ousted the rightful ruler of a province (known as a "nawab") without cause and replaced him with a usurper;[19] he took bribes in exchange for favorable decisions in disputes concerning inheritances[20] and the award of rights to collect taxes;[21] he circumvented the books and records of the East India Company;[22] he and his designates confiscated property and redistributed it arbitrarily;[23] and his tax collectors tortured people hideously, to the point where they were compelled to sell their bodies.[24]

Concerns about corruption in the East India Company predated Hastings' appointments as Governor and Governor-General.[25] In fact, Hastings' predecessor, Lord Clive, had become notorious for accepting lavish "presents" from the nawab of Bengal. Clive also expanded a system of "private trade," which allowed Company agents to secure monopolies over trade within India in various commodities, free of customs duties. The ensuing orgy of self-enrichment by the Company's agents was linked to a calamitous series of subsequent events, in both India and Britain. Most notably, the Great Bengal Famine of 1769–1770, in which an estimated ten million people perished, was caused in part by drought, taxation, and wars required to fund payments to the Company; but it was also caused by taxation required to fund presents for individual Company agents and those agents' mismanagement of the rice trade. Meanwhile, the Company's interests suffered not only because of the famine but also because presents that could have gone into its coffers were diverted into private hands, and its interventions in Indian politics and wars were crafted with an eye to furthering individual rather than collective interests. By the early 1770s, the Company was on the brink of insolvency. The government's eventual response had dramatic effects on British history. Parliament not only provided rescue financing but also passed the Tea Act of 1773. The Tea Act was intended to help bail out the Company by giving it more lucrative privileges over the export of tea to the British American Colonies. Unfortunately, this provoked American merchants into the protest now known as the Boston Tea Party, a precipitating event for the American Revolutionary War in which Britain lost the colonies.[26] Last but not least, Clive presided over the East India Company during a period in which the corruption of its servants in India introduced a new form of corruption into the British political system—agents who accepted lavish stipends from Indian nawabs then returned to England and represented the nawabs' interests in Parliament. According to Professor Dirks, "Between 1763 and 1792, at least a dozen Englishmen actually sat in Parliament with seats bought with nawabi money."[27]

Over the years there were several efforts to improve the governance of the East India Company. In 1765, Clive himself forced Company servants to sign covenants against taking presents. In 1773, two separate Parliamentary committees were charged with investigating Clive's affairs. Parliament ultimately voted to exonerate Clive, but a few months later, as a condition of providing rescue financing to the Company, it passed the Regulating Act of 1773. The overall purpose of the Regulating Act was to improve the governance of the

Company. Among other things, it prohibited the receipt of presents and placed restrictions on private trade.[28] The Regulating Act also specifically provided for the appointment of Warren Hastings as Governor-General of Bengal. Ironically, this was in part because he was viewed as "honest and incorruptible."[29]

Hastings failed to put an end to the corruption that prompted the Regulating Act, and his failure did not escape the attention of observers in Britain. The legal responses included a select committee established in 1780[30] and the East India Company Act 1784,[31] which brought the Company under direct Parliamentary control. The most dramatic response, however, was the impeachment proceeding launched against Hastings himself.

The impeachment was led by Edmund Burke, an Irish writer who also served as a colonial agent representing New York in Great Britain and then as a Member of Parliament. He is famous both for his advocacy on behalf of inhabitants of the British colonies—in both America and India—and as an intellectual father of conservatism. Over the course of the 1770s, Burke became an increasingly fervent critic of the East India Company and its activities in India. In Burke's eyes, Hastings created and encouraged a corrupt administration that not only caused tragic political and economic disruptions in India but also threatened to undermine the government of England itself. Burke was preoccupied with the risk that corrupt men like Hastings would bring their vices back to England and use their ill-gotten wealth to corrupt the political system at home.[32] He was determined to prevent "the breakers of law in India from becoming the makers of law for England."[33]

In arguing the case for the prosecution, Burke portrayed Hastings as Verres reincarnated, and modeled his own speeches after Cicero's.[34] Like Cicero, Burke claimed to be speaking on behalf of "whole tribes of suffering nations" harmed by oppression.[35] When Burke impeached Hastings, it was in the name of not just "the Commons of Great Britain" but also "the people of India" and "human nature itself."[36] Unlike Cicero, though, Burke was not actually retained by, or even in direct communication with, any of the alleged victims.

Burke's speeches against Hastings were remarkable for their eloquence and detail. They also were remarkable for insisting that British law should treat corruption overseas the same way it treated corruption in England. As a matter of law, this was a novel proposition. Prior to this case, the leading authorities agreed that the common law offenses of bribery and embezzlement did not apply outside of England, and that English statutes only applied in the colonies if they said so explicitly.[37] Following the traditional line, Hastings argued, at least in his initial defense before the House of Commons, that his actions had to be judged by the "Manners, Customs, Principles and Laws, peculiar to the Countries in which such Measures were adopted" rather than the laws of England.[38]

Burke contemptuously rejected this "geographical morality."

> But he has told your Lordships in his defence, that actions in Asia do not bear the same moral qualities as the same actions would bear in Europe. . . . we are to let your Lordships know that these Gentlemen have formed a plan of Geographical morality, by which the duties of men in public and in private situations are not to be governed by their relations to the Great Governor of the Universe, or by their relations to men, but by climates, degrees of longitude and latitude, parallels not of life but of latitudes. . . . This Geographical morality we do protest against. Mr. Hastings shall not screen himself under it. And I hope and trust not a great many words will be necessary to satisfy your Lordships. But we think it necessary in justification of ourselves to declare that the laws of morality are the same every where, and that there is no action which would pass for an action of extortion, of peculation, of bribery and of oppression in England, that is not an act of extortion, of peculation, of bribery and of oppression in Europe, Asia, Africa, and all the world over.[39]

Burke did not rest his case solely on abstract moral principles. He went to great pains to establish that Hastings violated explicit prohibitions on receiving presents, prohibitions set out in both Hastings' agreement with the East India Company and the Regulating Act of 1773 (neither of which specified whether violations amounted to crimes).[40] Burke went even further and provided extensive evidence that Hastings' conduct violated the laws of Asian societies as well; he went so far as to quote from the Institutes of Tamerlane, in addition to canvassing Hindu and Islamic law. Burke warned in his opening remarks:

> Let him fly where he will; from law to law. Law thank God meets him everywhere; and the practice of the most impious tyrants which he quotes cannot justify his conduct. I would as willingly have him tried upon the law of the Koran, or the Institutes of Tamerlane, as upon the Common Law or the Statute Law of this Kingdom.[41]

And,

> [L]et him have Eastern or Western Law; you find everywhere arbitrary power and peculation of Governors proscribed and horribly punished; more so than I should ever wish to punish any human creature.[42]

The process that Burke deployed against Hastings was as remarkable as the substance of the charges that he brought. Burke was convinced that Parliament rather than the courts or the Executive should supervise British government in

India.[43] The parliamentary process he chose to vindicate this philosophy, impeachment, involved a prosecution led by the House of Commons, represented by a team of "managers," before the House of Lords. Though ancient, impeachment had fallen into disuse by the end of the eighteenth century. When Burke launched his case against Hastings, the process had not been invoked in forty years.[44]

This particular impeachment was exceptionally prolonged.[45] Burke made his first speech advocating revival of the ancient process to the House of Commons in February 1786. On May 10, 1787, the House of Commons voted to impeach Hastings on twenty Articles of Impeachment. The trial before the House of Lords began in February 1788. Burke's opening speech stretched over four days. Burke and the other managers from the House of Commons took the remainder of the 1788 Parliamentary session to present evidence on the first two charges. Presentation of the evidence pertaining to the next two charges—the ones concerning presents—stretched across three more years, after which the prosecution abandoned the remaining charges. The sessions of 1792 and 1793 were devoted to Hastings' defense. In 1794, Burke replied on behalf of the prosecution, in a speech that lasted nine days. The House reassembled to give its verdict in 1795.

Why did Burke go to such lengths? Burke wanted to make an example of Hastings, in part to make a statement of moral principle—one that would echo the burgeoning movement to abolish slavery[46]—and in part to prevent the misdeeds that occurred during Hastings' administration from recurring.[47] Those misdeeds went well beyond the acts committed by Hastings himself. In Burke's telling, Hastings tolerated and encouraged corruption throughout the East India Company. He shared spoils of corruption with subordinates while simultaneously threatening them with punishment under the Company's strict anti-corruption regulations if they broke ranks and complained about him. And when the Company did try to discipline its agents for corruption, Hastings protected them and had the proceedings quashed. The result was a corporate culture—an "Esprit du Corps"—that promoted rather than condemned corruption and punished anyone who tried to report it.[48] Burke thought that targeting Hastings, "the head, the chief, the captain-general in iniquity," was the most effective way to address the situation.[49] He declaimed, ". . . if you strike at him you will not have need of a great many more examples; you strike at the whole corps if you strike at the head."[50]

So what defense did Hastings present to Burke's assault? In his own speech to the House of Lords, Hastings was much more concise than Burke, and his language was considerably less colorful. Nonetheless, it proved effective.

Hastings opened his speech by complaining bitterly about the length and cost of the proceedings. He argued that their unexpected—and unprecedented—

length made it difficult for him to mount a defense.[51] While waiting in vain to be called, several of his witnesses died, returned to India, or simply left the hearing. And then there was the cost. Hastings lamented, "every day's delay amounts to a fine."[52] He also pointed out that throughout the time that the prosecution took to present its case, he was being condemned in the court of public opinion.[53]

After raising these procedural objections, Hastings' defense turned to matters of substance. Though it was not reduced to a specific charge, Hastings responded to the sweeping claim that he had ruined the territories he governed by pointing to the substantial increase in revenue he generated for the Company.[54] He rebutted the allegation that he had oppressed the people under his rule by reminding the House that it had heard "testimonials of all ranks of people in India in my favour."[55] He denied that some of the atrocities alleged by Burke had ever occurred and argued that his decisions on how to intervene in local politics and rates of taxation were well within the discretion granted to him by the Directors of the East India Company.[56]

Most interestingly for present purposes, Hastings admitted to many of the facts underlying the two charges of having received presents. In response to one set of charges, Hastings argued that he had "no corruption intention" because he accepted the presents on behalf of the Company rather than himself—though the evidence in support of this assertion was shaky, to say the least—and it was impossible for him to know that this would be considered unlawful.[57]

In response to another set of charges, Hastings admitted to having accepted "the usual entertainments" given to visitors. This took place during a period before acceptance of presents was outlawed by Parliament but after Hastings swore an oath to the Company that he would not accept any more than 400 pounds sterling in rewards or gifts from any "Indian Prince." Hastings' defense was that his actions could not be unlawful because they were undertaken openly and in accordance with custom. He said, "It is usual in the country; and it is impossible for any person to read any oriental history without knowing that the custom has prevailed all over the East, from the most ancient times to the present."[58] Hastings pointed out that the Company followed this custom by providing gifts when the nawab of Bengal visited and that his highly regarded predecessors had accepted presents during their time in India as well. He also emphasized that his actions had been publicly known for fifteen years and neither the Company nor Parliament had previously associated them with criminality.[59]

Ultimately Hastings' arguments carried the day. Not only did the House of Lords vote to acquit him, they awarded him a backdated annuity that went a long way toward allowing him to recoup the expenses of the trial.[60]

Notwithstanding the outcome of the trial, Burke's speeches against Hastings were an intellectual breakthrough. The proposal that his country's legal system should treat corruption—broadly defined—in the course of governing a foreign territory as a "high crime or misdemeanour," and put the complaints of foreigners on the same footing as those of natives, foreshadowed the most noteworthy features of modern anti-corruption law. His supporting argument that even the people of less developed countries regarded corruption as pernicious and unlawful—as opposed to customary and lawful—challenged traditional European views. Burke's concern about widespread corruption in the East India Company, as opposed to just the misconduct of a few individuals, foreshadowed modern concerns about systemic wrongdoing on the part of multinational corporations. In many ways, Burke laid the intellectual foundation for the OECD paradigm that dominates contemporary transnational bribery law.[61]

And yet, Hastings survived Burke's attack. There is a popular American saying, "When you strike at a King, you must kill him."[62] Burke's failure to overcome Hastings' defenses ultimately only strengthened the ideas they embodied, namely, that English law would not, and perhaps should not, punish corrupt practices conducted in foreign territory.

In this sense, Burke's approach to anti-corruption law not only promised to deliver many of the potential benefits of modern transnational law but also demonstrated some of the same limitations. For instance, Hastings' acquittal suggested that some combination of indifference to the sufferings of foreigners, economic self-interest, and concern about whether anyone benefited from the extension of English moral standards overseas, would inevitably limit the motivation of English lawmakers to combat foreign corrupt practices.[63] The enormous cost of the proceeding certainly demonstrated the practical difficulty of regulating the foreign practices of a large commercial enterprise. Moreover, as Hastings argued, the trial brought to light the potential unfairness of prosecuting individuals when no social cues put them on notice that their conduct is illegal, the underlying transactions are so complex that sifting through the evidence requires a long and costly process, and much of the evidence is difficult to access because it must be obtained from overseas.

The impeachment of Warren Hastings also was shadowed by concerns about legitimacy. For one, the motives of the prosecutors went beyond simply putting an end to impunity for corruption. Burke was a politician, and his actions clearly had political motivations.[64] When Burke first took up the case, Hastings was aligned with Burke's political opponents. Moreover, Burke initially relied heavily on a partisan source, one Philip Francis, for incriminating information. Francis was one of Hastings' rivals within the Company and hoped to replace him as Governor-General. Burke's motivations were also political in a broader sense. Impeaching Hastings was a step toward his goal of persuading Parliament to strip the East India Company of responsibility for government of India.

Hastings' trial also hinted at reasons to be concerned about the legitimacy of attempting to regulate foreign corrupt practices in particular. Burke claimed to speak on behalf of Hastings' Indian subjects, much like Cicero claimed to speak on behalf of Verres's Sicilian subjects. Cicero, however, had served in Sicily, was retained by Sicilians, spent fifty days in Sicily investigating the allegations against Verres, and called over a dozen non-Roman witnesses.[65] Burke, by contrast, did not call any witnesses from India and may never have spoken to any Indians about his case.[66] The only testimony from natives of the subcontinent was introduced by Hastings. Both Burke and Hastings claimed to be concerned about the interests of people subject to the East India Company's rule. But it is far from clear which man was better suited to speak on the behalf of the Indians. Each of them certainly had his own biases and blind spots. Hastings claimed to be concerned about the welfare of Indians, but that concern was clearly limited by his sense of obligation to generate profit for his Company. Burke also had well-known biases. He was a cosmopolitan, but he was no democrat. He was sympathetic to the plight of Indians victimized by Hastings, but most of his sympathy was directed at disgraced Brahmins, disinherited nobles, and dispossessed landowners rather than more humble laborers.[67]

A final point to keep in mind is the limited scope of the precedent that Burke sought to establish by prosecuting Hastings. It is true that he sought to hold Hastings liable for corrupt practices undertaken on behalf of a private firm operating outside of England's borders. And he also seemed concerned about the extent to which the practices of Hastings and the East India Company undermined local political institutions in India. However, it was important to Burke's case that the East India Company was more than just an ordinary commercial enterprise. He took the position that the Company exercised a form of delegated sovereign authority and so was necessarily responsible to the sovereign from which it received its power.[68] This was the lynchpin of Burke's argument that the Company and its servants were accountable under English law; to Burke, Hastings was more like an English public official than an agent of a private company.

Moreover, Hastings was accused of misconduct in relation to people over whom he exercised sovereignty. Strictly speaking, the Mughal Emperor retained sovereignty over the territories controlled by the East India Company; the Company merely held a *Diwani* granted by the Emperor that permitted it to collect revenues in the territories. At the same time, there is no doubt that the Company was the de facto sovereign.[69] The Company's sovereignty was another critical component of Burke's case: many of his charges were based on the theory that Hastings had violated his duty as a British Governor to "pursue the good of the people as much as possible in the spirit of the Laws of this Country."[70] In this sense the Hastings impeachment was very much an exercise in imperial self-regulation, much like the prosecution of Verres. Modern anti-corruption law extends beyond imperial boundaries to true foreigners operating in truly foreign territories, including not only foreign public officials but also wholly private companies implicated in their misconduct.

Anti-corruption Law in the Postcolonial Era

The scope of anti-corruption law in the British Empire expanded somewhat as the colonies developed their own anti-corruption institutions. When Burke tried to impeach Hastings, English law was clearly serving as a substitute for local law. At that point in time there was no question of trying the former Governor-General under Indian law or before Indian courts. If the issue had come up two centuries later, the question certainly would have been asked. A case from Hong Kong suggests that the answer would not have been obvious.

In 1973, corruption was, by all accounts, rampant in Hong Kong. The police force was especially notorious, with syndicates of police officers banding together to extort payments from both legal and illegal enterprises. In the middle of that year, however, a senior police officer named Peter Godber fled to Britain while under investigation for having amassed large amounts of unexplained wealth. The ensuing outcry led to the creation of a new anti-corruption agency, the Independent Commission against Corruption (ICAC). The ICAC was independent of the police force and reported directly to the governor. The ICAC adopted a three-pronged approach to anti-corruption efforts, including public education and preventive initiatives, but the initial priority was enforcement of criminal prohibitions, beginning with a concerted effort to prosecute members of the police syndicates. The most high-profile case was the successful prosecution of Peter Godber after he was extradited by the United Kingdom. The impact of the ICAC was dramatic. Immediately after its establishment, the number of corruption incidents reported to the authorities more than doubled.[71] As for the police syndicates, by mid-1977 the head of the ICAC reported to the governor that "no major syndicates were known to exist."[72] Survey data suggests that "by the mid-1980s (or late 1980s, at worst) corruption in government was no longer a routine practice."[73]

The establishment of the ICAC and the eradication of corruption from the Hong Kong police force is one of the creation myths of the modern anti-corruption movement. The ICAC became the prototype for anti-corruption agencies around the world. Most interesting for present purposes, though, is the role that British actors played in Hong Kong's story. In 1974, Hong Kong was still a British colony. The prime mover behind the creation of the ICAC was the Governor of Hong Kong, Murray MacLehose, a Scottish career diplomat appointed by the Queen. Moreover, the prosecution of Peter Godber would not have been possible without the assistance of the U.K. police and courts, which extradited him to Hong Kong in 1975. Overall, therefore, British personnel and laws played a valuable contribution to combating corruption in Hong Kong, but they did it by serving as complements rather than substitutes for local institutions.

Britain was much less enthusiastic about combating corruption outside of the Empire. The limited available evidence suggests that until very recently, British companies routinely paid bribes to foreign public officials in order to secure contracts, concessions, and other favors.[74] Corruption was reported to be particularly common in the arms industry, where companies often worked closely with and received financial support from the British government.[75] Official investigations revealed that British banks were more than willing to hold funds on behalf of corrupt foreign officials.[76] Yet through much of the twentieth century, Britain did little to regulate foreign corrupt practices. For instance, prior to enactment of the Bribery Act 2010, there were no prosecutions for bribery of high-ranking foreign public officials under British law.[77]

The situation appears to have been similar in other developed countries. Until the turn of the century, only the United States and Sweden had explicit legal prohibitions on transnational bribery,[78] and in some countries bribes were tax deductible. It is difficult to know how prevalent transnational corruption was in the late twentieth century, but every once in a while evidence comes to light which suggests that it was widespread. In France, for instance, the Elf Scandal, which began with an investigation launched in 1994, revealed that Elf Aquitaine, which was a state-owned oil company at the time, had made large surreptitious payments to political leaders in France, Africa, and other countries.[79] The money sent overseas was paid not only to give Elf a competitive advantage over other oil companies but also to ensure that the leaders remained friendly to France. A striking feature of the *Elf* case was that no one was prosecuted for bribery of foreign officials. Rather, the prosecution was aimed at Elf executives who had appropriated corporate funds for their own benefit and French officials who allegedly received bribes. The chief executive officer of Elf, who was imprisoned for his role in the affair, and a former French foreign minister, who was accused of receiving bribes but ultimately cleared, both claimed that members of the French cabinet were aware of Elf's overseas payments and regarded them as an instrument of French foreign policy.[80]

Since the late 1990s there has been a sea-change in attitudes toward at least one form of transnational corruption, namely, transnational bribery. The remainder of this book will focus on that new regime.

3
The Birth of Modern Transnational Bribery Law

Introduction

Transnational bribery law in its modern form first emerged in the United States of America. The reasons appear to be historically contingent.

Concern about the issue of transnational bribery can be traced back to the country's founding, when the United States was an emerging nation whose political institutions were vulnerable to being corrupted by powerful foreign interests. This was a matter of grave concern to the U.S. founding fathers. In fact, at a time when it was commonplace for diplomats to be presented with expensive gifts from foreign officials, the very first constitutional document of the fledgling nation took the unusual step of barring public officers from receiving "any present, emolument, office, or title of any kind whatever, from any king, prince or foreign state."[1]

There is scant evidence of U.S. efforts to regulate corruption on the part of foreign public officials in the first two hundred years of the Republic. However, an 1880 decision of the Supreme Court of the United States suggests that in principle at least, U.S. law has long condemned bribery of foreign public officials.

The case was actually a contractual dispute. The plaintiff, Oscanyan, was the consul general in New York for the Ottoman Empire (aka Turkey). He sued Winchester Repeating Arms Co., manufacturer of the famous Winchester repeating rifle, for a commission he claimed to have earned by using his influence to persuade the Ottoman government to purchase Winchester rifles. The amount claimed was $136,000, 10 percent of the value of the rifles purchased. Oscanyan pointed out that his position as a consul was an unpaid honorary office and that the agent of the Ottoman government whom Oscanyan was said to have influenced was aware of the commission arrangement and made no objection. The U.S. courts refused to enforce the agreement nonetheless. The Supreme Court, in an opinion authored by Justice Field and labeled *Oscanyan v. Arms Co.* (it is unclear why the reference to Winchester was dropped),[2] cited several domestic cases which established that the agreement in question would

Between Impunity and Imperialism. Kevin E. Davis.

be unenforceable if it concerned influence over a domestic public official. Justice Field then went on to say:

> A contract to bribe or corruptly influence officers of a foreign government will not be enforced in the courts of this country,—not from any consideration of the interests of that government or any regard for its policy, but from the inherent viciousness of the transaction, its repugnance to our morality, and the pernicious effect which its enforcement by our courts would have upon our people.... In any view of the contract here, whether it would be valid or invalid according to Turkish law and customs, it is intrinsically so vicious in its character and tendency, and so repugnant to all our notions of right and morality, that it can have no countenance in the courts of the United States.[3]

This passage taps into a moral current that continues to propel U.S. transnational bribery law. Justice Field implicitly adopts Edmund Burke's view that foreign and domestic bribery should be treated consistently and echoes Burke's fear that overseas corruption might be morally contagious. Justice Field takes the added step of asserting that U.S. laws against corruption can be applied even when they conflict with the laws of the country whose officials allegedly have been corrupted. Recall that even Burke did not go this far; he went to great pains to establish that the laws he sought to enforce were consistent with the laws of India. In this sense Justice Field was ahead of his time. His decision in *Oscanyan v. Arms Co.* sketched out a theoretical foundation for a body of transnational bribery law that would take almost another century to emerge.

Evolution of Anti-bribery Law in the United States

Modern U.S. regulation of foreign corrupt practices either relies upon or has been influenced by laws originally enacted to target domestic corruption. Accordingly, a brief digression into domestic anti-bribery law is required to set the scene for our investigation of transnational law.

In his magisterial survey of the history of bribery, John T. Noonan Jr. claims that laws against corruption were rarely enforced against high-ranking officials in the United States before the latter part of the twentieth century, even though complaints about corruption were widespread in earlier periods.[4] The stage for increased enforcement was set in the 1960s by important changes in the scope of the laws in the statute books. At the state level, the Model Penal Code of 1962 expanded the scope of liability for bribery to preclude extortion as a defense to bribery[5] and, in many cases, to allow nonpecuniary as well as pecuniary favors to qualify as bribes.[6] The Model Penal Code also made it an offense for any person to sell political influence, regardless of whether they held a government appointment.[7] At the federal level, the federal bribery statute—which applies to officials of the federal government—was expanded in 1962 to include an "illegal gratuity" offense that did not require proof that the bribe was given "to influence" any official action.[8]

In addition to regulating interactions with officials of the federal government, the U.S. federal government also regulates corrupt practices under the auspices of its broad authority to regulate interstate and international commerce. Since the middle of the twentieth century it has used that authority to enact many criminal statutes that cover corrupt practices. The classic examples are the federal "mail fraud" and "wire fraud" offenses, which criminalize fraudulent use of the mails or of telecommunications services in connection with interstate or international commerce.[9] The federal power to regulate commerce has also been used to enact laws aimed at organized crime, many of which cover corrupt practices. The Hobbs Act of 1946—originally aimed at racketeering labor unions—outlawed extortion, defined to include "obtaining of property from another, with his consent . . . under color of official right."[10] This phrase was eventually interpreted to include the solicitation of a bribe or kickback by public officials.[11]

In the mid-twentieth century, fears of organized crime inspired new legislation that made it a federal crime to violate some other state or federal statute (the "predicate offense") in specified circumstances. This regulatory model would later be employed with predicate offenses defined by foreign law. Following this approach, the Travel Act of 1961 criminalizes the actions of anyone who "travels in interstate or foreign commerce or uses the mail or any facility in interstate or foreign commerce" in connection with extortion or bribery in violation of other state or federal law.[12] The Racketeering Influenced and Corrupt Organization Act, popularly known as RICO, has a similar, though more complex, structure.[13] RICO defines "racketeering" to mean any violation of one of a long list of state and federal offenses. These are RICO's predicate offenses. Committing more than two predicates within a ten-year period as part of a related series of activity counts as a "pattern or racketeering activity." RICO makes it an offense to engage in pattern of racketeering activity to infiltrate, control, or operate "a[n] enterprise which is engaged in, or the activities of which affect, interstate or foreign commerce."[14] RICO also permits either the government or private actors to sue for violations of its main prohibition and to recover treble damages.[15]

Anti-money laundering laws adopt a variant on this structure. "Money laundering" is the popular term for the practice of dealing in the proceeds of crime. Conventional anti-money laundering laws permit law enforcement agencies not only to prosecute money launderers but also to seek forfeiture of property that can be identified as proceeds of specified predicate offenses.[16] These laws also require financial institutions to take precautions against dealing in proceeds of crime and to report suspicious transactions.[17] Anti–money laundering laws have long been the principal legal weapons in the war on drugs.[18]

The Foreign Corrupt Practices Act of 1977

The genesis of modern transnational bribery law was a series of scandals which exposed prominent U.S. corporations making illicit payments to domestic and foreign public officials. Unlike previous scandals, high-level officials in not just one, but many, firms and countries were implicated. The revelations toppled leaders of major corporations and governments, drove at least two senior business executives to suicide, and sparked investigations by an array of public bodies, as well as many private firms. The sheer volume of disclosures, and the direct link between corruption overseas and an unprecedented domestic crisis, created a perception that transnational bribery was a pervasive and urgent problem that demanded a drastic response. As a result, instead of a single initiative led by a dynamic crusader in the mold of Cicero or Burke, there were multiple teams of prosecutors, as well as legislators, vying to draft legislation that would create structural changes in transnational bribery law. Ultimately, the confluence of these forces resulted in the passage of the FCPA, the single most important development in the history of transnational bribery law. This story has been recounted by many other scholars, including luminaries such as John T. Noonan Jr. and Stanley Sporkin, but we will review the highlights here because it is impossible to understand either the purpose or the content of modern transnational bribery law without understanding the events that led to the enactment of the FCPA.[19]

The domestic scandal was Watergate. A thwarted burglary at the Watergate hotel in June 1972 led to revelations that operatives in the campaign to re-elect Richard Nixon as president of the United States engaged in large-scale spying on and sabotage of political opponents. Shockingly, the president himself, who had been re-elected in a landslide, was involved. In August 1974, Nixon became the first U.S. president to resign. He was preceded by his vice president, who stepped down in 1973 to plead guilty to tax evasion charges stemming from his receipt of bribes while governor of Maryland. It was undoubtedly the biggest political scandal in the history of the United States.

Early in 1973, the Special Prosecutor appointed to investigate the Watergate affair uncovered evidence that major U.S. corporations—including household names like American Airlines, Ashland Oil, Braniff Airways, Goodyear Tire and Rubber, Gulf Oil, 3M, Northrop—had made illegal contributions to benefit Nixon and other political figures.[20] Several of the companies pled guilty to making illegal campaign contributions. These revelations about the country's leading business organizations, combined with the revelations about the Nixon administration, created a sense that corruption was pervasive in the upper echelons of U.S. society.

The mechanics of the illegal corporate payments were probably the least exciting features of the Watergate scandal, but they attracted the attention of the U.S. Securities and Exchange Commission (SEC). As it turned out, many of the payments came from secret "slush funds," often held by foreign subsidiaries. Moreover, the same slush funds were often used to pay foreign public officials bribes, or as the SEC referred to them, "questionable or illegal foreign payments."[21] The SEC, following the lead of its director of enforcement Stanley Sporkin (who happened to be a trained accountant), launched investigations into several of the companies identified by the Special Prosecutor.[22]

The SEC was concerned that the funds passing through these secret channels were not properly accounted for, in the sense of being either properly recorded in the companies' books and records or subject to the same degree of oversight as other disbursements. The SEC wanted to ensure that questionable or illegal foreign payments would come to the attention of companies' auditors, outside directors, and shareholders. The federal securities laws at the time required companies to make public disclosure of "material" information. The SEC took the position that information about questionable or illegal payments was always material, "regardless of whether the payments themselves were of material size or a material amount of business depended on their continuation."[23] The SEC's theory was that information about payments not authorized by senior management was relevant to the investing public because it said something about the quality of management, while information about payments approved by management had a bearing on the political and reputational risks facing the company.[24]

The SEC's investigation quickly snowballed. Beginning with companies caught up in the Watergate investigation, during a roughly two-year period ending in May 1976, the SEC investigated and then launched enforcement actions against fourteen companies that had failed to properly account for or disclose illegal and questionable foreign payments. The actions were all resolved consensually. As part of their settlements, thirteen of the companies agreed to establish independent special review committees mandated to conduct internal investigations and recommend remedial measures.[25] Sometimes the disclosures of foreign payments also led to criminal prosecution by the U.S. Department of Justice. The charges brought included mail or wire fraud, transporting currency into or out of the United States without proper reporting, or making false statements to U.S. government agencies such as the Export-Import Bank and the Agency for International Development.[26]

Meanwhile, the number of companies that merited investigation continued to grow. In the aftermath of Watergate there was a flurry of congressional hearings on the overseas activities of multinational enterprises, and in March 1976, President Gerald Ford created a special task force on the topic of questionable foreign payments.[27] Information turned up in one hearing sometimes led to further investigations. Lockheed Aircraft Corporation, for instance, escaped untarnished by the initial Watergate investigation—it apparently had a strong double standard when it came to domestic as opposed to foreign bribery. However, Lockheed's competitor Northrop was implicated in the domestic scandal, and this led to revelations of questionable foreign payments.[28] When called before a Senate subcommittee to testify about payments to Saudi and Swiss agents, Northrop agents explained that their payment structure was "based on the Lockheed model."[29] Within months Lockheed was the subject of hearings before two separate Senate subcommittees as well as an independently launched SEC investigation, and shortly afterward its treasurer shot himself to death.[30]

For United Brands Corporation the sequence of events operated in reverse. The suicide came first. Its chief executive Eli Black used his briefcase to smash away the glass in the window of his office on the forty-fourth floor of Manhattan's iconic Pan Am building, and then jumped out. The SEC investigated and discovered that United Brands, a major banana producer, had agreed to pay the president of Honduras $2,500,000 to reduce a tax on banana exports.[31]

With its resources stretched by the volume of revelations, the SEC shifted to a new enforcement model. In July 1975, it announced the creation of a voluntary disclosure program. The program invited companies to conduct internal investigations, adopt policies designed to prohibit improper accounting and establish appropriate internal controls, and finally, disclose the results of the investigation. Firms which participated in the voluntary disclosure program may have expected a measure of leniency,[32] but it is not clear that any was granted. Some companies that voluntarily disclosed found themselves the targets of SEC enforcement actions, and on a few occasions their cases were referred to the Department of Justice for criminal prosecution.[33]

With all of these disclosures, incriminating so many firms and so many countries, in the space of just three years, the informational snowball grew into an avalanche. The impacts were felt around the world. Gulf Oil, one of the companies identified by the Watergate Special Prosecutor, saw its confidential testimony before the SEC about payments in an unnamed country leaked to the press. Shortly afterward its assets in Peru were expropriated.[34] This was a curious turn of events because although Gulf eventually confessed to making questionable payments in Bolivia, Italy, and Korea (the unnamed country), it did not report any irregularities in Peru.[35] In Honduras, the scandal provoked by news of United Brands bribery became known as Bananagate. It led to the overthrow of President Oswaldo Enrique López Arellano's military government by one of his fellow generals, and the nationalization of United Brands' properties.[36]

The most far-reaching repercussions came from the revelations about Lockheed.[37] Lockheed was the nation's largest defense contractor and also earned large amounts of revenue from selling commercial and military aircraft to overseas customers, many of whom were public bodies. In 1971, Lockheed ran into difficulty developing a new wide-body commercial jet on time and on budget, around the same time it was weakened by losses on some major contracts with the U.S. Department of Defense. After a vigorous debate, Congress narrowly agreed to allow the U.S. government to bail out Lockheed with a $250 million loan guarantee. As part of the arrangement, Lockheed had to submit to monitoring by a government agency known as the Emergency Loan Guarantee Board. This extensive government oversight and support made the revelations about Lockheed's misconduct all the more embarrassing for the United States. There was an important sense in which the American people were implicated in Lockheed's corrupt actions, much as England was implicated in the activities of the East India Company.[38]

Lockheed eventually admitted to making between $30 million and $38 million in questionable payments during the period between 1970 and 1975, in fifty foreign countries.[39] Both Lockheed and the State Department tried to prevent details about the recipients of its payments from being publicized, but the Senate committee led by Idaho Senator Frank Church published enough details to allow several recipients to be identified.[40] The world was shocked to discover that the list of the great and the good who received money from Lockheed included high-profile figures in relatively prosperous and supposedly developed countries like Italy, Japan, and the Netherlands. In Italy, the former chief of staff of the air force and a former minister of defense were convicted.[41] In Japan, former Prime Minister Kakuei Tanaka was tried and found guilty of accepting bribes from Lockheed while he was in power.[42] In the Netherlands, His Royal Highness, Bernhard, Prince of the Netherlands, consort of Queen Juliana, was not prosecuted, but he was forced to resign from all his positions in businesses, charities—including the World Wildlife Fund, which he had founded— and the Armed Forces.[43]

In the United States, the direct product of the congressional hearings was the enactment of the FCPA. The statute represented an amalgam of provisions set out in proposals put forward by different members of Congress, the SEC, and the White House. The most prominent feature of the FCPA is a series of prohibitions—backed by stiff criminal and civil penalties—on payments to foreign public officials in order to assist in "obtaining or retaining business."[44] These are known as the FCPA's anti-bribery provisions. Just as important but somewhat less prominent are the FCPA's books and records provisions, which require firms with securities listed on U.S. exchanges to keep accurate records.[45] These record-keeping obligations are complemented by a separate obligation to maintain internal controls that ensure the integrity of corporate records.[46]

The FCPA is a U.S. statute, but as a result of its broad scope of application, which includes many firms with only tenuous connections to the United States, its effects are felt around the world. The scope of the FCPA is so broad because it is based on principles of both nationality and territoriality. To begin with, the current versions of the FCPA's anti-bribery provisions apply to corrupt practices committed anywhere in the world by U.S. citizens or permanent residents, or by corporations that are incorporated or headquartered in the United States.[47] In addition, both the anti-bribery provisions and the accounting provisions apply to firms that list their securities on U.S. markets.[48] Finally, the FCPA applies to anyone who violates the statute "while in the territory of the United States."[49] Strictly speaking, foreign individuals or corporations are only caught by the anti-bribery provisions if they act while in U.S. territory or make use of "the mails or any means or instrumentality of interstate commerce."[50] However, in recent cases, even a wire transfer involving the U.S. financial system or an email passing through U.S. servers has been deemed to satisfy this requirement.[51]

Many scholars characterize the FCPA as an expression of "post-Watergate morality,"[52] a self-conscious effort to restore confidence in American business and the free market system. The House Report on the bill that eventually became the FCPA made these moralistic motivations explicit:

> The payment of bribes to influence the acts or decisions of foreign officials, foreign political parties or candidates for foreign political office is unethical. It is counter to the moral expectations and values of the American public. But not only is it unethical, it is bad business as well. It erodes public confidence in the integrity of the free market system. . . . [I]t rewards corruption instead of efficiency and puts pressure on ethical enterprises to lower their standards or risk losing business.[53]

The moral statement embodied in the FCPA was clearly intended for foreign as well as domestic audiences.[54] At the time, the United States was still embroiled in the Cold War and had recently lost ground to the Communists in Vietnam and Angola.[55] Taking a stand against foreign corrupt practices was a step toward reclaiming the moral high ground in the battle for the hearts and minds of wavering nations. As the House Report put it:

> Corporate bribery also creates severe foreign policy problems for the United States. The revelation of improper payments invariably tends to embarrass friendly governments, lower the esteem for the United States among the citizens of foreign nations, and lend credence to the suspicions sown by foreign opponents of the United States that American enterprises exert a corrupting influence on the political processes of their nations.[56]

The idea that Congress intended the FCPA to make a moral statement is consistent with the fact that the drafters rejected the proposal backed by both President Ford and the SEC to eschew criminalization in favor of simply requiring disclosure of foreign bribery.[57] It also explains why proponents of the legislation were able to override claims that a criminal prohibition would be "essentially unenforceable."[58] Whatever its merits as a means of deterrence, a disclosure requirement does not make the same kind of moral statement as criminalization. Disclosure regimes deter by enabling embarrassment, by triggering naming and shaming. They work by exposing wrongdoers to condemnation by customers, suppliers, peers, and the public at large. What disclosure does not entail is explicit denunciation by the state; under a disclosure regime, denunciation is outsourced to society as a whole. By contrast, criminal prohibition is the most potent form of denunciation known to law,[59] regardless of whether the prohibition is enforced. To the extent that the purpose of the legislation that became the FCPA was to make an immediate moral statement, criminalization made much more sense than a simple disclosure requirement.

Although the primary motivation behind the enactment of the FCPA may have been moral condemnation, Congress was not completely oblivious to the FCPA's potential impact on U.S. economic interests. The House Report took the position that U.S. businesses would not be placed at a competitive disadvantage if they refused to pay bribes, citing evidence of firms that managed to compete successfully in export markets without paying bribes.[60] This view was consistent with the SEC's tentative finding (based on data provided by participants in its voluntary disclosure program) that cessation of questionable or illegal foreign payments "will not seriously affect the ability of American business to compete in world markets."[61] It is important to recall that at the time U.S. firms were dominant in many markets.[62]

There were even suggestions that the FCPA would have positive economic effects for the United States. The House Report noted evidence that "in a number of instances, 'payments have been made not to "outcompete" foreign competitors, but rather to gain an edge over other U.S. manufacturers.'"[63] In addition, the SEC made it clear that it viewed undisclosed questionable foreign payments as bad for business.[64] The SEC maintained its position that information about such payments was generally material to investors because it bore upon both the quality of the company's business and the attendant risks.[65]

The FCPA was amended in 1988 and 1999. The 1988 amendments were motivated by concerns about the burden the FCPA imposed on U.S. exporters and issuers of securities.[66] Tellingly, they were enacted as part of the "Omnibus Trade and Competitiveness Act of 1988."[67] The 1988 amendments limited the scope of criminal liability for violation of the accounting provisions by imposing a knowledge requirement.[68] They also created exceptions and affirmative defenses to liability for certain payments to foreign public officials, namely: reimbursements for expenses incurred in connection with promotional activities, payments that were lawful under the law of the foreign official's country, and payments for routine governmental action.[69] In addition, the 1988 amendments created a procedure for the Department of Justice to issue general guidelines and advisory opinions and directed it to provide guidance on its enforcement policy to "potential exporters and small businesses that are unable to obtain specialized counsel."[70] Consistent with the hypothesis that this reform was motivated by self-interest, the 1988 amendments only permitted firms with ties to the United States to request advisory opinions, even though the FCPA's prohibitions also apply to other actors who make payments to foreign officials while in U.S. territory.[71]

Enforcement of the FCPA received a boost in 2002 with the enactment of a federal statute called the Sarbanes-Oxley Act.[72] Sarbanes-Oxley ostensibly had little to do with corruption—it was enacted in response to a series of accounting scandals, including the spectacularly complicated shenanigans that led to the bankruptcy of Enron. Sarbanes-Oxley had a profound effect on the governance of publicly traded U.S. firms, mainly on account of two new requirements: (1) that companies and their auditors report on the scope, adequacy, and effectiveness of the company's internal control structure, and (2) that the chief executive officer and the chief financial officer of the company personally certify that they have evaluated the effectiveness of the company's internal controls.[73] The effect was to create strong personal incentives for the most senior leaders of corporations to beef up internal controls, including the ones that would serve to detect foreign bribery, and to report situations in which control structures fell short. Both these actions—improving controls and reporting deficient controls—tend to bring suspicious financial activity into the light, making it easier for enforcement agencies to detect foreign bribery.

4
The Modern Regime

Introduction

Since the enactment of the FCPA, U.S. transnational bribery law has grown from an idiosyncratic but weakly enforced branch of U.S. law into the lynchpin of a prominent and potent global regime. This transformation occurred at the beginning of the twenty-first century, after the members of the OECD agreed to adopt their own versions of the FCPA. Around the same time, a range of organizations, both public and private, began to monitor levels of both corruption and enforcement. Soon, the United States and a handful of other countries began to enforce their transnational bribery laws vigorously. Both the number of enforcement actions and the size of penalties skyrocketed. Not surprisingly, companies engaged in international business now devote significant amounts of time and money to compliance with transnational bribery law. Much of that expenditure finds its way into the pockets of lawyers; as a result, regulation of transnational bribery now represents a major area of practice for large law firms. In terms of impact on international business, transnational bribery law now rivals the better-established bodies of law governing topics such as competition and money laundering.

The "anti-bribery regime" is a useful way of referring collectively to the ensemble of domestic and international legal instruments, enforcement agencies, international or intergovernmental organizations, arbitrators, private providers of compliance services, and nonprofit organizations that implement transnational bribery law.[1] In strictly territorial terms, the regime is global in scope, but much of the impetus for its activities originates in the United States and a handful of OECD countries. In legal terms, the outer bounds of the regime are difficult to define with precision since they overlap with neighboring regimes, including those concerned with money laundering, competition, government procurement, and fiscal transparency.[2]

The Diffusion of Transnational Bribery Law

Almost as soon as the U.S. Congress began considering domestic legislation to regulate foreign bribery, the executive branch of the U.S. government began

Between Impunity and Imperialism. Kevin E. Davis.

to press for international agreements on criminalization of foreign bribery.[3] It was clear from the outset that unilateral action by the United States would not be able to deter all foreign bribery, simply because it would be impossible for U.S. law enforcement officials to obtain evidence from or sanction all the relevant actors.[4] There were also concerns that the FCPA placed U.S. firms at a competitive disadvantage relative to firms from countries without similar legislation.[5] In fact, the 1988 amendments directed the executive branch to negotiate with members of the Organisation for Economic Co-operation and Development (OECD) with a view to concluding an international agreement on foreign bribery.[6]

The idea that corruption might be a matter of more than local concern, and that corrupt practices might be regulated outside the community where the corrupt officials were based, took a while to catch on after the enactment of the FCPA. When it did begin to spread, there were several driving forces.[7]

One of those forces was pressure from firms subject to the FCPA, and the U.S. government speaking on their behalf. Firms subject to the FCPA shared an interest in seeing other countries adopt similar legislation in order to ensure that the FCPA's constraints would not place them at a competitive disadvantage. In other words, they were eager to level the playing field.[8]

Other factors came into play in the early 1990s. For instance, Mark Pieth, who eventually came to play a key role in the development of the regime, argues that the end of the Cold War may have made other countries more receptive to anti-corruption messages from U.S. actors. He claims that during the Cold War, the superpowers relied on corruption to secure influence, but with the fall of the Berlin Wall and the opening of Eastern Europe they developed a greater interest in removing obstacles to international trade and investment.[9]

The 1990s also saw widespread acceptance of the view that corruption tends to inhibit democratization and economic development. As a result, the anti-corruption movement attracted a range of human rights activists and development experts from both developed and developing countries who were concerned about the corrosive effects of corruption.[10] Prominent among the nongovernmental organizations was Transparency International, a nongovernmental organization established in 1993 and dedicated to combating corruption. Transparency International, both through its international organization and various national chapters, lobbied for the adoption of anti-corruption laws at both the domestic level and in international organizations.[11] The global anti-corruption campaign eventually became a mass movement, very much like the movements that campaigned for abolition of the slave trade around the beginning of the nineteenth century and which continue to campaign for initiatives such as fair trade, Third World debt relief, and respect for various sorts of human rights.[12] The U.S. State Department capitalized on these developments by deploying the argument that regulation of foreign bribery could serve as a tool for promoting political and economic development, alongside other moral and self-interested arguments, in urging other countries to enact their own legislation criminalizing foreign bribery.[13]

Pressure from the United States and the international anti-corruption movement began to produce visible legal results in the late 1990s. An important milestone was the endorsement of the anti-corruption movement by the leaders of the World Bank. In 1996, the president of the World Bank, James Wolfensohn, gave a widely noticed speech denouncing the "cancer of corruption,"[14] and in 1998 the World Bank adopted a formal anti-corruption policy.[15] The most notable success, however, was the signing in 1997 of the OECD Convention on Combating Bribery of Foreign Public Officials in International Business Transactions (OECD Convention).[16] Like the FCPA, the OECD Convention focuses on bribery in international business. It encourages states to prohibit bribery of foreign public officials, to prohibit dealing in (laundering) the proceeds of transnational bribery, to ensure that bribes are not tax deductible, and to cooperate with foreign governments in investigating and prosecuting bribery through both extradition and mutual legal assistance. The text of the Convention is supplemented by "recommendations" and "good practice guidance" issued periodically by the states that drafted the OECD Convention.

A body known as the Working Group on Bribery in International Business Transactions (OECD Working Group), made up of representatives from the parties to the Convention, is officially charged with monitoring the implementation and enforcement of the OECD Convention and its related instruments. The Working Group is assisted by a secretariat at OECD headquarters in Paris. Among other things, the OECD Working Group hosts biannual meetings of law enforcement officials. These meetings, which coincide with some of the Working Group's meetings, provide opportunities both for monitoring implementation of the Convention and networking. They include reviews of open enforcement actions in a practice known as the *tour de table*.[17]

The OECD Convention is now only one of several international anti-corruption agreements that require regulation of corruption. At the regional level, the Organization of American States actually beat the OECD to the punch by signing the Inter-American Convention against Corruption in 1996. Shortly afterward, anti-corruption conventions emerged from the Council of Europe and the African Union.[18] Finally came the UN Convention against Corruption, which entered into force in 2005 and by the end of 2018 had 186 parties. In 2017, members of the UN General Assembly, under the auspices of the United Nations' Sustainable Development Goals, resolved to "substantially reduce corruption and bribery in all their forms" (Goal 16, Target 16.5).[19]

The UN Convention pushes its signatories to adopt the state of the art in anti-corruption law. Among other things, this means prohibiting a wide range of corrupt practices such as payment or receipt of bribes, embezzlement, conflicts of interest, and illicit enrichment on the part of domestic public officials. A whole chapter is devoted to preventive measures such as transparency in public administration, codes of conduct for civil servants, and requirements that public procurement processes be open, competitive, and accountable. Again, this all points toward regulation of corrupt practices aimed at domestic public officials.[20]

More importantly for present purposes, the UN Convention makes it clear that the state of the art in anti-corruption law includes regulation of transnational bribery. Like the OECD Convention, the UN Convention requires states to adopt FCPA-style prohibitions on payment of bribes to foreign public officials, as well as prohibitions on associated forms of money laundering. But it goes beyond the OECD Convention by encouraging states to prohibit the solicitation or acceptance of bribes by foreign public officials as well as bribery of private actors.[21] The UN Convention also contains provisions requiring states to cooperate in the recovery of assets that qualify as either proceeds or instruments of corrupt practices, and in collecting compensatory damages for harm caused by corruption.[22] In other words, states seeking compensation from corrupt officials who have transferred their ill-gotten gains overseas are entitled to call on other parties to the UN Convention for assistance.

The specialized anti-corruption conventions are not the only international instruments that pressure countries to regulate transnational corruption. Among the most influential of the other international instruments are the recommendations of the Financial Action Task Force (FATF), an intergovernmental organization dedicated to fighting money laundering and terrorist finance. The FATF makes detailed recommendations on the design of anti–money laundering laws and intensively monitors countries' compliance with its recommendations. Although the FATF's recommendations are not legally binding on any country, it has the power to "recommend" that financial institutions from noncompliant countries be excluded from the global financial system. In 2003, the FATF recommended that countries include "corruption and bribery" among the predicate offenses to money laundering (Financial Action Task Force, 2003).[23] This had the effect of mobilizing every financial institution in the world, as well as a host of specialized law enforcement agencies, to join the fight against corruption. The FATF also recommends that countries become parties to the UN Convention.[24]

The pressure to regulate corruption from beyond the national level has also affected the multilateral development banks. The major development banks have all followed the World Bank's lead and adopted anti-corruption policies of one sort or another. The rationales are both to ensure that the proceeds of their grants or loans are not used for corrupt purposes and to fulfill their mandates to promote development. The anti-corruption policies include procedures for cancelling agreements with firms or governments found to have engaged in improper activity and debarring guilty firms.[25] The major development banks have also agreed to "cross-debar" firms debarred by their peers.[26] These are potent sanctions for firms that depend on revenues from development bank–funded projects.

Finally, the movement to regulate corruption across borders has reinforced courts' and arbitral tribunals' traditional distaste for enforcing contracts tainted with corruption. As far as the law of international contracts is concerned, the watershed was the decision in *World Duty Free v. Kenya*. The claimant was a firm incorporated in the Isle of Man and owned by a businessman from the United Arab Emirates. World Duty Free's agreement with the Republic of Kenya awarded it exclusive rights to run airport terminals in Mombasa and Nairobi. Its principal, Mr. Ali, appeared before an arbitral tribunal alleging that the agreement had been wrongfully terminated by the government of Kenya and sought either return of his stores or compensation "in the vicinity of US$500 million." He candidly admitted that he had obtained the contract by delivering a briefcase containing US$500,000 in cash to Daniel Moi, the president of Kenya at the time. This startling admission was devastating to Ali's case. In a ruling handed down in 2006, the tribunal dismissed Mr. Ali's claim entirely, concluding that Kenya was entitled to refuse to be bound by the contract. The tribunal cited the profusion of anti-corruption conventions as evidence of an international consensus to condemn corruption, even in particular countries or sectors in which it is widespread or customary.[27] In a similar vein, in *Metal-Tech v. Republic of Uzbekistan* (2013), an arbitral tribunal established pursuant to an investment treaty ruled that it could not even hear an Israeli investor's claim against the government of Uzbekistan because there was evidence that the investor had procured the contract upon which its claim was based through bribery.[28] By its terms, the treaty only covered investments "implemented in accordance with the laws and regulations" of the host state and the *Metal-Tech* tribunal ruled that this language did not cover a contract procured through bribery.

The decisions in *World Duty Free* and *Metal-Tech* cast considerable doubt upon the enforceability of government contracts procured through bribery. Both decisions have, however, been sharply criticized by commentators who believe that governments which permit their officials to solicit or accept bribes ought to be treated more harshly.[29]

Enforcement

The decades since the enactment of the FCPA have, for whatever reason, seen worldwide convergence on the general proposition that transnational bribery ought to be prohibited. There has been less convergence on ideas about how those laws ought to be enforced, meaning which wrongdoers should be targeted, what sanctions ought to be imposed, and which countries ought to be responsible for enforcement.

Before the adoption of the OECD Convention, the United States was the only country active in this arena, and it prosecuted only one or two foreign bribery cases each year, focusing on the bribe payers. The level of U.S. enforcement increased somewhat following the signing of the OECD Convention, perhaps because it encouraged governments of other OECD countries to assist rather than thwart U.S. agencies when they needed to collect evidence or target companies based overseas. The level of U.S. enforcement jumped even more dramatically in the mid-2000s once Sarbanes-Oxley came into effect. In the post–Sarbanes-Oxley period, a large proportion of corporate enforcement actions were initiated as a result of publicly traded firms stepping forward to self-report violations. Figure 4.1 shows the trend in U.S. FCPA enforcement over time.[30]

Outside the United States, only a handful of countries actively enforce laws against bribery of foreign public officials. Transparency International classified just seven countries—Germany, Israel, Italy, Norway, Switzerland, the United Kingdom, and the United States—as active enforcers in 2018. Those countries accounted for 27 percent of world exports. At the same time, Transparency International reported that countries representing 39.6 percent of world exports engaged in little or no enforcement, a list that included China, Hong Kong, India, and Singapore, which are not parties to the OECD Convention, as well as eighteen parties to the Convention.[31]

In the United States, individuals who are punished for paying bribes to foreign public officials face severe sanctions. At the high end of the range, one man was sentenced to fifteen years in prison for FCPA and money-laundering violations, and sentences of more than two years in prison are not uncommon in FCPA cases. Other countries also send people to prison for foreign bribery. According to the OECD Working Group, at least 115 individuals, in 11 parties to the OECD Convention, were sentenced to prison terms for foreign bribery between the time the OECD Convention entered into force and the end of 2015.[32]

Sanctions for corporate bribe payers have increased over time. The pace has been set by the U.S. enforcement agencies. In 1978, United Brands, whose pre-FCPA misconduct involved a $2.5 million bribe that brought down a

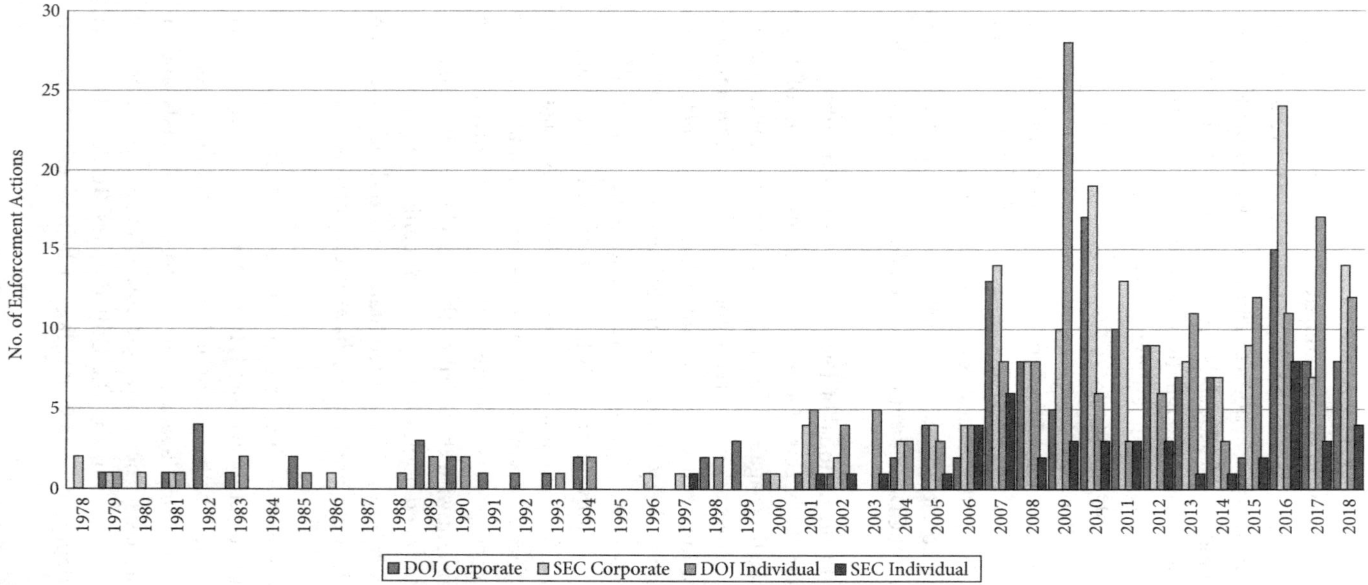

Figure 4.1 DOJ and SEC Enforcement Action by Years.

Figure 4.1 relies on data from the Foreign Corrupt Practices Act Clearinghouse database. Stanford Law School. Foreign Corrupt Practices Act Clearinghouse. Accessed February 5, 2018. https://www.fcpa.standford.edu/. For corporate defendants, all enforcement actions brought by the same enforcement agency against related companies, i.e. parent companies and any subsidiaries or affiliates, are treated as a single enforcement action. For individual defendants, each enforcement action against a natural person is counted separately. Therefore, if an individual is sanctioned in both civil and criminal proceedings, these cases are treated as separate enforcement actions. This methodology differs from both the OECD's methodology in collecting data regarding the enforcement of the OECD Convention and the approach used by the U.S. Department of Justice in its submissions to the OECD regarding compliance with the OECD Convention. For information regarding the methodologies of the OECD and U.S. Department of Justice, see OECD Working Group on Bribery, Methodology for data on enforcement of the Anti-Bribery Convention (OECD, 2017), 1–2, and U.S. Department of Justice, Appendix B of Response of the United States: Questions Concerning Phase 3 (Washington, D.C.: U.S. Department of Justice, 2010).

government, pleaded guilty and paid a fine of only $15,000.[33] Lockheed, whose misdeeds were more extensive in scale and scope, paid $647,000.[34] Companies prosecuted under the FCPA now face a very different enforcement regime. In 2008, Siemens paid $1.6 billion dollars to the United States and Germany. In 2016, Odebrecht, a Brazilian construction conglomerate, was ordered to pay at least $2.6 billion (an amount subsequently reduced because of the firm's financial difficulties) to resolve cases brought by authorities in the United States, Brazil, and Switzerland.[35] These headline-making cases are not representative though. From 2016 to 2018, the average corporate FCPA prosecution resulted in monetary sanctions ranging from $53.3 million to $98 million.[36] This is a lot more than $15,000, but far from $2.6 billion. In many countries, corporate sanctions are much lower. A 2016 OECD study, based on figures from an actual case prosecuted in the United States, compared the maximum monetary penalties provided by law to the benefits the defendant would have earned. In at least six parties to the OECD Convention, the penalties were insufficient to outweigh the gains.[37]

Although the focus of transnational bribery law has been on bribe payers, recipients have also felt its effects. Occasionally, investigations of bribe payers have led to proceedings against the recipients, or at least their assets. More commonly, proceedings against corrupt foreign officials have targeted deposed officials with a long history of corrupt behavior that includes but is not limited to foreign bribery. Most foreign bribery statutes, including the FCPA, only apply to bribe payers, not recipients—and that is all that is required by the OECD Convention and the UN Convention. In part for this reason, and in part for evidentiary reasons, proceedings against foreign officials typically focus on violations of anti–money laundering laws rather than the initial corrupt acts.[38] Some of these cases involve criminal prosecutions, but, consistent with the spirit of the UN Convention, the emphasis in recent years has been upon identifying and confiscating assets that represent proceeds of corruption. The United States, Switzerland, and, more recently, the United Kingdom and France have been fairly active on this front.[39]

Anti–money laundering laws also happen to be the principal legal weapons in the fight against embezzlement, the other major form of transnational corruption besides bribery. There have been notable efforts to enforce anti–money laundering against corrupt foreign officials and financial institutions that assist them in a few countries, including France, Switzerland, the United Kingdom, and the United States. To date, however, enforcement of "anti-kleptocracy" laws has lagged behind enforcement of anti-bribery laws.[40]

Monitoring of Enforcement

The OECD Working Group has played a critical role in collecting and disseminating information about regulation of transnational bribery, including both laws and enforcement actions. The centerpiece of its monitoring scheme is a peer review system in which each state party's performance is reviewed by a team of experts from other parties. The country reviews have proceeded in phases. Phase 1 was limited to evaluation of whether the country's legislation complied with the terms of the Convention. Subsequent phases have examined enforcement as well as follow-up on recommendations from previous phases. The reports resulting from these country reviews are all published on the OECD website.[41]

The Working Group's biannual meetings of law enforcement officials, including the *tour de table*, play an important role in both monitoring and promoting countries' enforcement of prohibitions on foreign bribery. However, those proceedings are confidential. As for published data, since 2010 the OECD Working Group has collected and published annual data on completed enforcement actions from the parties to the Convention. The 2016 edition of this report included for the first time data on the prevalence of international cooperation in enforcement. Curiously, the data on international cooperation only covered enforcement actions pursued to completion by the U.S. Department of Justice and the SEC; it was collected from press releases in which those agencies acknowledged assistance from foreign enforcement agencies.[42]

Since 2010, the UN Convention has used a peer review mechanism similar to the one employed by the OECD Working Group. So far the UN mechanism has been less successful. Fewer than half of the parties (82 out of 168) have allowed full versions of the reports on their first review to be published on the UN website.[43]

Another potentially useful source of data is the World Bank's Integrity Vice Presidency, which publishes an annual report on the steps it has taken to enforce its rules on fraud and corruption. The report includes information on whether cases have been referred to the national authorities for further investigation and whether the World Bank is aware of any further action by those authorities.[44] These data on referrals offer one of the few bases for insight into how national enforcement agencies respond when credible allegations of corruption are brought to their attention.

Private actors also participate in monitoring of enforcement, including representatives of business enterprises, organized labor, and nongovernmental organizations (NGOs). All of these actors are invited to participate in country reviews under the OECD Convention. In addition, the world's most prominent anti-corruption NGO, Transparency International, periodically produces a glossy report on the quality of countries' implementation of the OECD Convention.[45] However, private actors are excluded from the meetings of the Working Group, which seems to be conceptualized as a forum for collaboration among law enforcement officials. The situation is somewhat different under the UN Convention. Private actors have complained that they have been excluded from the review process, both by specific countries and the supranational bodies charged with overseeing the process.[46]

It is often useful to complement data on enforcement of laws against foreign bribery with information on the enforcement of domestic anti-corruption laws. The main sources that cover multiple countries are surveys conducted by multilateral development banks and various private actors. For example, as part of its Country Policy Institutional Assessment, the World Bank asks its staff to rate countries on, among other things, "the accountability of the executive and other top officials to effective oversight institutions."[47] Similar data are collected by other multilateral development banks, as well as private organizations such as the Bertelsmann Stiftung and the World Justice Project.[48]

Monitoring the Incidence of Bribery

What about data on the incidence of bribery?[49] There is now a consensus about the importance of collecting these data. Under the auspices of the project to establish Sustainable Development Goals, the members of the UN General Assembly have agreed to measure progress toward the goal of "substantially reducing corruption and bribery" with two indicators:

> 16.5.1 Proportion of persons who had at least one contact with a public official and who paid a bribe to a public official, or were asked for a bribe by those public officials, during the previous 12 months.
> 16.5.2 Proportion of businesses that had at least one contact with a public official and that paid a bribe to a public official, or were asked for a bribe by those public officials during the previous 12 months.[50]

These kinds of data on the incidence of bribery are typically collected using surveys, whether of individuals, firms, or experts.[51] Respondents are generally asked to provide information about either their own experiences—"in any of [your inspections or meetings with tax officials in the last year] was a gift or informal payment expected or received"—or their perceptions of other peoples' experiences—for example, "how pervasive is political corruption?" Sometimes surveys ask about the experiences of people "like" the respondent. It is not always clear whose experiences these questions are asking about. For example, one World Bank survey asks, "When establishments like this one do business with the government, what percent of the contract value would be typically paid in informal payments or gifts to secure the contract?"[52] A respondent might reasonably decide to answer based on their own experience, but if they believe their situation is atypical, they might report perceptions of other firms' experiences.

A wide range of public and private actors field surveys that ask about the incidence of bribery. We have already seen that the World Bank is active in this arena. The UN Office of Drugs and Crime Control, agencies of national governments, and various NGOs all also collect data on either experiences with or perceptions of bribery.[53] Among surveys conducted across multiple countries, the best known are probably Transparency International's Global Corruption Barometer and Bribe-Payer's Index.[54]

Some, but not all, of these surveys, make it possible to measure levels of transnational—as opposed to domestic—bribery or corruption. Transparency International's Bribe-Payer's Index, which is based on surveys of business executives who have business relationships with foreign firms, focuses exclusively on transnational bribery.[55] In addition, some enterprise surveys cover local subsidiaries of foreign companies and require them to identify themselves as such in their responses.[56] By contrast, surveys of the general population typically are unhelpful on this front, either because they cover only domestic corruption or they do not distinguish between domestic and transnational varieties.

The most famous cross-country measures of the level of corruption are Transparency International's Corruption Perceptions Index (CPI) and the World Bank's Control of Corruption Indicator. These measures are in a category of their own, not just because of their fame but on account of their methods of construction. Both indicators purport to measure perceptions of the level of corruption, broadly defined, by aggregating data from multiple sources. Transparency International says that the CPI aggregates data on "perceptions of business people and country experts of the level of corruption in the public sector."[57] The World Bank says, "Control of corruption captures perceptions of the extent to which public power is exercised for private gain, including both petty and grand forms of corruption, as well as 'capture' of the state by elites and private interests."[58] Confusingly, however, both the CPI and Control of Corruption incorporate data on perceptions of both levels of corruption and the quality of laws and law enforcement.

Investigations conducted by law enforcement agencies, naturally, collect information about transnational corruption. Some but not all of this information eventually makes its way into the public domain. A few agencies, like the U.S. Department of Justice, make detailed public disclosures about the cases they pursue. Journalists are another potentially valuable source of information, particularly in countries like Brazil, where the popular press aggressively investigates and reports on corruption cases.[59]

This book is a testament to the fact that cases brought to light by enforcement agencies and the media can provide vivid and detailed information about corrupt practices. These sources also have to be used with caution. The cases that result in enforcement actions or journalistic reports are not necessarily representative of the broader population of cases of corruption.

Monitoring the Impact of Transnational Bribery Law

In an ideal world there would be concerted efforts to study the impact of the anti-bribery regime, in other words, how it affects people's attitudes, beliefs, behavior, and welfare. Effects on the behavior of potential wrongdoers ought to be of particular interest. For instance, do those actors:

- Try to avoid the application of the regime by cutting ties with countries that enforce their laws vigorously?
- In the case of organizational actors, like multinational enterprises and state actors, invest in training and internal controls for their employees and agents?
- Do business in high-risk jurisdictions?
- Engage in bribery?

At least as important are questions about how the regime affects potential victims:

- How many victims are there?
- Who are they?
- What harm have they suffered?
- Have they been compensated?

There are also important questions to be asked about how the regime affects actors who are neither perpetrators nor victims. For instance:

- Are citizens of countries whose officials have been bribed aware of foreign enforcement actions? Do they approve of them? How prevalent do they believe corruption to be?
- How are citizens of poor countries affected when firms disinvest to avoid liability under anti-bribery law?

These questions are inherently difficult to answer.[60] To identify these kinds of causal relationships, the first step is to collect valid and reliable legal data. The next step is to compile data on outcomes. The final step is to map correlations between variations in law and variations in outcomes, and determine whether the correlations involve causal connections.

Each of these steps is a potential stumbling block. To begin with, it can be difficult to collect data about law. Statutes and regulations often are published, but decisions about enforcement are typically confidential. Data about outcomes are also difficult to collect. People are particularly reluctant to report data about illicit behavior like bribery (although social scientists have devised some clever ways to extract this information).[61]

And then there is the difficulty of establishing causation. A host of nonlegal factors can affect attitudes and behavior. For example, suppose a multinational firm ceases to do business in Nigeria. How can we tell if its decision was based on fear of liability under transnational bribery law or a change in tax law or an assessment of trends in the global economy? And even if we know that the anti-bribery regime mattered, which component was the operative factor? How do we isolate the impact of the FCPA as opposed to the U.K. Bribery Act or Nigerian law given that in some cases none or all of them may apply?

There are few formal—meaning publicly sponsored—mechanisms for monitoring the impact of transnational bribery law. As we have seen, the OECD and the UN Convention have formal mechanisms for monitoring levels of enforcement, and public actors have shown increased interest in supplementing private efforts to monitor levels of corruption. However, none of these official actors has made a significant effort to connect these two types of data to answer questions like: Has greater enforcement led to reduced corruption?

The few studies that have been conducted have been undertaken by professional academics. Studies of the impact of the FCPA prior to the adoption of the OECD Convention produced conflicting results on whether it discouraged U.S. firms from investing in relatively corrupt countries.[62] Later studies showed that countries that had signed the OECD Convention had lower levels of foreign direct investment in and exports to relatively corrupt countries.[63] As for the impact of the law on misconduct, one study using data from Ghana found that firms whose home countries were parties to the OECD Convention were generally less likely to pay or be solicited for bribes.[64] Another study, using data from Vietnam, found that foreign investors in Vietnam whose home countries were parties to the OECD Convention demonstrated lower propensity to pay bribes after the increase in enforcement that accompanied Phase 3 of the Working Groups' review process, which was initiated in 2010.[65]

Global Experimentalist Governance?

The modern anti-bribery regime is a complex, decentralized, and dynamic system. The complexity of the regime stems in part from the fact that it encompasses a vast array of legal instruments: overlapping multilateral treaties; national laws prohibiting bribery and related misconduct, together with applicable, criminal, civil, and administrative procedural rules; internal policies adopted by firms and international organizations, which have a tendency to become external as they are extended by contract to suppliers and clients; and, supplementary regulations, recommendations, and guidance documents. The sheer number of actors who participate in implementing the regime is another source of complexity, including enforcement agencies, international bodies, civil society monitoring organizations, compliance professionals, and so forth. And many of these actors behave autonomously—hence the decentralization. For instance, in some jurisdictions every individual prosecutor has to be treated as an independent actor. The ultimate source of complexity is that all of these different components of the regime have the potential to interact with one another, if only because any given corrupt transaction is likely to implicate several different laws and enforcement agencies.

The dynamism of the regime stems from the fact that several of the norms and practices it encompasses are revised regularly. Many of the most significant revisions have been prompted by the OECD Working Group. Each of its country peer review reports typically recommends multiple changes to laws and enforcement practices in order to bring the subject country into compliance with not only the OECD Convention but also the supplementary Recommendations and Guidance produced under its auspices. More often than not, the peer review recommendations are implemented. The most dramatic example was the United Kingdom, which adopted a completely new statute, the Bribery Act of 2010, after being lambasted by the OECD Working Group for closing an investigation into allegations of bribery on the part of BAE, a large British aerospace company.[66] The OECD seems determined to continue to produce new or revised supplementary instruments, and so its review process is likely to continue to induce change into the foreseeable future. It remains to be seen whether the UN Convention process or internal factors within countries will also create pressures for change.

It is inherently difficult to maintain the performance of a complex, decentralized, and dynamic system like the anti-bribery regime. Ideally, each individual component would constantly adjust its actions to reflect new information about both the environment in which it operates and other components of the system. For instance, it might be optimal for enforcement agencies in Australia, Canada, Indonesia, and Japan to coordinate their enforcement strategies to reflect the expansion of Chinese firms into high-risk jurisdictions like Papua New Guinea. In practice, however, constant adjustment is likely to be beyond the capacity of most actors, and the performance of the system as a whole is likely to be suboptimal. Analogous issues arise in the animal kingdom when animals behave collectively. For example, a migrating herd on the East African savanna will not necessarily find the shortest possible path, and in fact, the animals may occasionally stampede and trample one another or run off a cliff.

In theory, complexity, decentralization, and dynamism can be appealing features in a transnational regime, especially when actors within the system are committed to a common objective and engage in ongoing monitoring, evaluation, and revision with a view to improving their performance. A regime with these characteristics might strike an ideal balance between the kind of local control that we typically associate with legitimate governance, and the kind of informed collaborative decision-making that is key to sustained effectiveness. A regime like this is more analogous to a highly functional beehive than to a random collection of zebras and antelopes.

Viewed from a certain angle, the anti-bribery regime, or at least the part influenced by the OECD Convention, fits this description: a group of people committed to the common objective of combating transnational corruption but willing to engage in monitoring and revision of their practices. In this respect, the regime arguably qualifies as an example of "Global Experimentalist Governance."[67] Gráinne De Búrca, Robert Keohane, and Charles Sabel coined this phrase to describe an approach to solving transnational problems in which stakeholders engage in five key steps:

- "initial reflection and discussion with a broadly shared perception of a common problem" resulting in
- "articulation of a framework understanding with open-ended goals";
- implementation of broadly framed goals is left to "actors who have knowledge of local conditions and considerable discretion to adapt the framework norms to their particular contexts";
- "continuous feedback" from local contexts, with outcomes subject to peer review; and
- periodic and routine re-evaluation, and where appropriate, revision of goals and practices in light of the results of the peer review and the shared purposes.[68]

Whatever the theoretical merits of Global Experimentalist Governance, as a purely descriptive matter the current anti-bribery regime falls far short of being an ideal example of it. To begin with, it is unclear how broad a commitment there is to combating corruption. In spite of their treaty obligations, only a handful of states actively enforce laws against foreign bribery, and as we shall see, those who do may have divergent motivations. Moreover, it is not clear how much scope is allowed for adaptation to local contexts. In addition, the enforcement agencies' monitoring and review processes appear to focus entirely on enforcement, with no effort to learn about either the benefits or the costs of enforcement, such as changes in levels of corruption or foreign investment. As a result there is systematic disregard of the views and experiences of people in states whose public officials solicit or receive bribes and, most likely, too little attention paid to the costs of various enforcement strategies.

The modern anti-bribery regime is associated with a distinctive approach to transnational bribery law, both in general and in relation to specific issues such as the scope of the prohibition on bribery, the extent of organizational liability, appropriate sanctions, and allocation of enforcement jurisdiction. Many of these rules have been developed and enshrined in instruments produced by the OECD Working Group and enforcement agencies in the United States and the United Kingdom. In recognition of this pedigree, it seems appropriate to refer to the prevailing approach as "the OECD paradigm." The remainder of this book is concerned with the merits of that paradigm.

5
Criteria for Evaluation

Introduction

We move now from description to evaluation of the anti-bribery regime. The bulk of the remainder of the book will discuss four key design questions: How should bribery be defined? When should third parties be held responsible? How should the law be enforced? How should the burdens and benefits of regulation be allocated?

This chapter, however, addresses a preliminary question: What criteria should we use to evaluate the regime? To answer this question, it seems sensible to begin by looking to the regime's stated purposes as set out in its foundational documents, and in particular, the UN Convention, which contains the most extensive list. By asking whether the regime has achieved its stated purposes, we are essentially evaluating it according to the criteria that the architects of the regime have established for themselves. This kind of internal perspective is not the only way to evaluate a legal regime, but when the regime has been endorsed by the leaders of virtually every nation on earth, the internal perspective is almost by definition a reasonable one.

A careful reading of the UN Convention suggests that the transnational anti-bribery regime ought to be evaluated by reference to both the outcomes it generates and the processes that generate those outcomes. Outcomes are to be evaluated in terms of effectiveness and efficiency in addressing the problems posed by bribery. Like with many other legal regimes, addressing the problem entails some combination of condemnation, compensation, and prevention. As for the processes by which outcomes are achieved, the UN Convention suggests that they should be judged by whether they respect individuals' interests in due process.

The criteria for evaluation listed in the UN Convention are useful but not comprehensive. The regime contemplated in the Convention allocates substantial amounts of power to lawmakers and enforcement agencies around the world, including power to regulate activities they previously were not authorized to regulate. The anti-bribery regime also imposes significant burdens on some actors, most notably states responsible for conducting enforcement actions and firms that do business in highly corrupt societies, not to mention the investors and communities whose welfare is tied to those firms' activities.

Between Impunity and Imperialism. Kevin E. Davis.

The Convention neglects to mention any criteria for evaluating how the regime allocates power and resources across and within states. These kinds of evaluation are conventionally conducted in terms of legitimacy and fairness, as in, "is the exercise of power by that State in relation to that transaction legitimate"? Or, "is the resulting distribution of resources fair"? These terms are extremely open-ended and contestable, but they should nonetheless be added to the criteria used to evaluate the anti-bribery regime.

In the remainder of this chapter we examine each of these criteria in turn. We begin by cataloging the relevant provisions of the UN Convention. We then address two background questions: What are the problems to which the regime ought to respond? How do we measure progress in mitigating those problems? This sets the stage for discussion of what it means for the law to respond effectively and efficiently to those problems. We then discuss the concepts of due process, legitimacy, and fairness.

The Stated Purposes of the Anti-bribery Regime

A logical place to start in determining how to evaluate the anti-bribery regime is by identifying its stated purposes. These are set out in several portions of the Convention.

The Preamble to the UN Convention explains that corruption is a problem because it threatens stability, security, democratic institutions, democratic values, ethical values, justice, sustainable development, and the rule of law. It calls on the signatories to bear in mind "the need to safeguard integrity and to foster a culture of rejection of corruption."[1] Both the Preamble and Article 1 of the UN Convention make it clear that the key objective is to "prevent and combat corruption more effectively and efficiently," and the Preamble stresses that proceedings involving criminal sanctions or property rights must be compatible with "the fundamental principles of due process of law."[2]

Article 4 of the Convention emphasizes the importance of "the principles of sovereign equality, territorial integrity and that of non-intervention in the domestic affairs of other States."[3] However, this emphasis on sovereignty is undercut by other provisions of the UN Convention which, in various ways, require states to challenge the actions of foreign public officials and the people they deal with, even when those actions take place in the territory of the foreign state. These obligations give effect to the Preamble's assertion that "the prevention and eradication of corruption is a responsibility of all States." Fulfilling that responsibility appears to inevitably require infringements upon the sovereignty of another state. The UN Convention offers no clear way of resolving this tension.

One of the hallmarks of the UN Convention is its emphasis on ensuring that defendants are made to provide compensation to the people and states victimized by their crimes, either through confiscation of assets or orders to pay damages, even when this requires cross-border transfers of assets. Article 57 could not be clearer on this point, stating, "The return of assets pursuant to this chapter is a fundamental principle of this Convention, and States parties shall afford one another the widest measure of cooperation and assistance in this regard."

Aside from these provisions concerning the costs suffered by victims, the UN Convention makes little reference to the possibility of reallocating burdens associated with combating corruption. Those burdens include the costs incurred by states in the course of fulfilling their responsibilities and the costs that individuals, firms, and their stakeholders incur in the course of preventing corruption. One provision of the UN Convention hints that states are entitled to some sort of relief when the expenses of complying with a foreign state's request for investigative assistance are or will be "of a substantial or extraordinary nature."[4] In addition, a state which returns confiscated property to victims or another state is entitled to deduct "reasonable expenses incurred in investigations, prosecutions or judicial proceedings."[5]

The Problem of Bribery

The following chapters use four recent enforcement actions as motivating illustrations.

- Joel Esquenazi and his associates, who paid officials of Haiti Teleco to reduce debts owed by Esquenazi's company;
- Siemens, which paid bribes in multiple countries to secure government contracts;
- Marcelo Odebrecht, as well as two companies under his control, Odebrecht and Braskem, which paid bribes to government officials throughout Latin America, often in connection with large-scale infrastructure projects;
- Members of a consortium of engineering, procurement and construction firms that paid bribes to Nigerian public officials in connection with the construction of a liquefied natural gas facility on Bonny Island, just off the coast of Nigeria.

Each of these cases involves examples of paradigmatic bribes. Each demonstrates, in its own way, the reasons why bribery is considered to be a problem. Without understanding the nature and magnitude of the problem, it is impossible to determine how to craft an effective legal response.

The most obvious problem with bribery is that it undermines state policies.[6] The harm will depend on the policy being undermined. If bribes undermine policies against issuing occupancy permits to unstable buildings, then the consequences will be both direct and deadly.[7] In the *Esquenazi* case, the direct consequences were less shocking: the Haitian government merely received less money than it should have—although in that desperately poor country the ultimate consequences for people dependent on the government might have been just as deadly. Regardless of the consequences, the very idea that public officials have deliberately undermined officially adopted policies merits condemnation because it amounts to a challenge to the authority of the state. When this kind of behavior comes to light, or even is perceived to have occurred, it tends to diminish confidence in the legitimacy of the state,[8] which in turn tends, among other things, to reduce people's willingness to comply with the law.[9]

There are also several less obvious reasons to conclude that bribery is harmful. For instance, the paradigmatic form of bribery makes both the public official and the bribe payer better off than they would be in a world in which the bribe was never paid. The resulting distribution of wealth is inherently unjust—both the official and the bribe payer are better off than they ought to be. The accumulation of wealth by corrupt officials might also have the knock-on effects of inspiring undesirable envy or resentment, which might in turn lead to more corruption.[10] Bribes paid to obtain services to which the payer is entitled are likely to have similar social and political effects because they make the recipient better off than he or she ought to be, at the expense of the payer. Political unrest in the Niger Delta has been sparked in part by projects like the Bonny Island project that allowed public officials to line their pockets while the rest of the population wallowed in an impoverished, polluted landscape.[11]

Then there are the incentive effects. People have incentives to invest valuable resources in securing and retaining positions in which they can collect bribes. This can involve efforts both to expand and battle for control of powerful public offices. For example, the prospect of collecting bribes from foreign telecommunications companies gives Haitian officials incentives to maintain a state-controlled monopoly over telecommunications and gives all Haitians incentives to fight for key positions within the state-controlled monopolist. And after a bribe has been paid, both firms and officials have incentives to invest in concealing their illicit dealings—classic techniques include shell companies and sequences of wire transfers through secretive offshore financial centers.[12] All of these incentives point toward devoting valuable resources toward unproductive behavior, up to and including violent conflict.[13]

The Magnitude of the Problem of Bribery

It is reasonably straightforward to specify the types of harm generally associated with bribery, but it can be much more difficult to determine the magnitude of the harm caused in any particular case.[14] As we shall see later in this chapter, determining the magnitude of harm is an important part of the process of determining both the effectiveness and efficiency of efforts to combat bribery. It seems sensible to measure effectiveness in terms of changes in the magnitude of the harm rather than, say, the number of incidents. And efficiency should be assessed in terms of the amount of harm addressed for a given level of investment in regulation.

The ease of measurement varies depending on the type of favor the bribe is aimed at procuring. For instance, the direct consequences of favors that involve financial transfers—either a fixed amount of money, or something with a precisely ascertainable monetary value—can be relatively easy to assess. In the *Esquenazi* case, for instance, the defendants paid Haitian officials to write off very specific amounts of debt that their company owed to Haiti Teleco.[15] The direct harm to Haiti Teleco was the amount of improperly canceled debt.

Harm can be more difficult to assess when the favor involves more than a simple monetary transfer. Consider the classic kickback, in which the favor involves a percentage increase in the price paid by the government for goods or services. Think of the long history of multinational enterprises paying bribes for favorable tax treatment, including United Brands' attempt to bribe the president of Honduras to reduce an export tax on bananas from 50 cents to 25 cents per 40-pound box.[16] In these cases, calculating harm involves comparing the status quo to a counterfactual scenario in which the favor was not granted. That counterfactual can be difficult to construct. For instance, in the case of a kickback, the harm includes not only the amount of the overpayment but the value of forgone opportunities to deploy those funds productively. That value can be difficult to determine: to calculate the harm from a tax reduction we need to know not only the magnitude of the rate reduction but also how much taxable activity would have occurred under the more onerous regime. How many bananas would United Brands have exported if forced to bear the higher tax?

The value of a financial favor is even more difficult to determine precisely when it does not involve a clearly specified deviation from a price that is generally accepted as legitimate. There are many situations in which the "legitimate" terms are unknowable. For instance, where the favor involves committing the state to pay an inflated price for goods or services, the financial harm is the difference between the contract price and the fair market price. The contract price is readily observable, but the fair market price may not be. The *Odebrecht* case presents an extreme example: Odebrecht paid bribes to officials of Petrobras,

Brazil's state-owned oil company, to, among other things, ignore the fact that it colluded with several other construction companies in bidding for supply contracts.[17] As a result, the entire market was unfair; the whole point of the bid-rigging scheme was to ensure that even the lowest bid for any contract was well above the minimally profitable price one would expect to see in a truly competitive market.

In other cases, the problem is that there is no market. When a firm pays a bribe to obtain a no-bid construction contract—that is, a contract awarded without a competitive bidding process—there is, by definition, no market price to refer to. Odebrecht was awarded several no-bid contracts by governments whose officials it had bribed, including three contracts worth $219 million to update a pair of Mexican refineries.[18] The only way to determine how much the contracts would have been worth if no bribes had been paid is to go through the arduous exercise of reconstructing a hypothetical bidding process.

The harm from favors that have significant nonfinancial components can be even more challenging to measure than the harm from financial favors. Some of the most tragic examples involve distortions of laws that protect health, safety, or the environment.[19] For example, in Brazil, there are allegations that a consortium of construction companies bribed Brazilian political leaders to allow mega-dams in the Amazon to be built over objections that they would destroy environmentally sensitive ecosystems and uproot thousands of indigenous people.[20] An even more distressing case involved a U.K.-based Delaware-incorporated company named Innospec. Innospec's claim to fame was that it was the last manufacturer in the world of lead-based fuel additives. Those additives were phased out in the United States and other countries beginning in the late 1970s, and had been banned in most countries by the year 2000, because of evidence that their use in engines damaged catalytic convertors and produced toxic lead pollution. Exposure to lead is known to cause neurological damage that impairs cognition, attention, and impulse control, in ways that increase the likelihood of aggressive and antisocial acts. Early childhood exposure leads to particularly harmful and persistent effects. There is evidence that reductions in exposure to lead pollution in the United States and elsewhere have caused significant reductions in violent crime, and speculation that it has led to increases in average IQs.[21] In 2010, Innospec admitted to making payments aimed to induce regulators and state oil company officials in Iraq and Indonesia to allow them to sell a leaded fuel additive and concluded settlement agreements with authorities in the United States and the United Kingdom.[22]

Lawyers and economists tend to measure harm by calculating the amount of money required to put victims in the position they would have been in if the harmful event had not occurred; in other words, the amount required to make them whole. In each of the cases of nonfinancial harm we have discussed so far, the consequences of the bribe-influenced decision are irreversible and so there is no sense in which providing monetary compensation can make the victims whole. If that is the case, then there is no straightforward way to measure the amount of money required as compensation. How much is required to compensate 20,000 indigenous people who have lost an entire way of life? What amount will compensate for the plant and animal species that were destroyed before they were even discovered (putting aside, for the moment, the question of to whom it should be paid)? What amount of money would compensate the people who were victimized by additional violent crimes, or who lived with diminished intellectual capacities, as a result of exposure to lead pollution? Even ordinal measures of these losses are difficult to calculate. The harms caused by dams and lead pollution are very different, but which is worse?

Nonfinancial harm need not be measured in terms of the amount of money required to provide compensation after an incident has occurred. An alternative approach is to ask potential victims, presumably in advance of any misconduct, "how much would you be willing to sacrifice in order to prevent harm X?"[23] So, for example, one might ask members of an indigenous community, "How much would you pay to avoid being displaced by a new dam?" Or, a resident of Indonesia might be asked, "How much would you pay for housing options or technology that would reduce your exposure to lead pollution?" This measure of harm is arguably relevant to the selection of enforcement strategies aimed at inducing efficient prevention. It might also be used to determine the amount payable as compensation after harm has been suffered. However, when the potential victims have limited wealth, this measure seems to replace the idea of equal protection under the law, or protection according to willingness to pay, with protection according to ability to pay. In highly unequal societies, using such a philosophy to guide law enforcement will raise red flags for proponents of distributive justice.[24] Is it fair to say that an indigenous subsistence farmer in the Amazon suffers no harm from being displaced and forced into prostitution simply because she has not earned enough money to pay to save her traditional way of life? Moreover, even if she had some money, how reliable would her response to such a question be? As a practical matter, it is difficult to elicit reliable responses from people about how much they would be willing to pay for a benefit they have never before contemplated purchasing. And if it is difficult to secure reliable assessments of the value of a way of life, how much more difficult is it to value an ecosystem? A higher IQ?[25]

For all these reasons, even in theory there is no satisfying way to measure these kinds of irreparable nonfinancial harms. In fact, reasonable people might disagree about whether, on balance, some of these consequences count as harms at all. Those who assign great value to Brazil's modernization and place little value on preservation of the Amazon region in its traditional state might conclude that a bribe-induced decision to move forward with the dam created overall benefits.

These two cases also show how difficult it might be to identify victims, in other words, people who have suffered loss as a result of a particular instance of misconduct. This identification problem complicates both the delivery of compensation and, if applicable, the process of eliciting potential victims' views on levels of harm. Some of the challenges are philosophical. Who suffers when an Amazonian ecosystem is destroyed? Owners of the relevant lands? Inhabitants? All Brazilians? Everyone in the world? Identification of victims can also entail practical challenges. Imagine trying to identify all the children harmed by the additional lead pollution emitted in Iraq and Indonesia as a result of Innospec's bribes. What about the victims of the additional crimes those children will commit when they grow up?

Incidentally, the problem of identifying victims can arise even in the case of financial harms. When the victim of financial harm is an organization, even if the quantum of harm is readily ascertainable, it can be difficult to determine how the harmful effects were distributed among the organization's stakeholders. For example, it might be possible to figure out the profit that one of Innospec's competitors would have earned on contracts to supply gas additives in Indonesia if the bidding process had not been tainted by bribery. The harm to them would include not only the lost profits but also the consequences of the investments they had to forgo as a result of their reduced financial resources. In calculating the consequences of forgone investment, it will be difficult to determine how the benefits of those investments would have been distributed among the competitor's shareholders, creditors, and customers.

The discussion to this point has been limited to the harm that flows directly from misuse of power by officials who have been bribed. That is not the only channel through which bribery can harm a society.[26] The mere suspicion of bribery can have pernicious demoralizing effects. For members of the general public, perceptions of corruption can lead to loss of faith in the legitimacy of government, which might in turn make fundamentally honest people less willing to support, comply with the directions of, or participate in public institutions.[27] In other words, demoralization may diminish the integrity and effectiveness of government. Perceptions of corruption on the part of prominent members of society may also cause people to experience a sense of loss if they identify with the corrupt actors and are ashamed of their behavior. It is not far-fetched that people's sense of self-worth will be influenced by whether exemplars of their social group live up to widely accepted ideals.[28]

Can we measure demoralization effects? It seems unlikely. Social scientists have estimated the aggregate effects of corruption on legitimacy in various countries,[29] and others have produced estimates of the relationship between respect for the rule of law and political stability—which might be interpreted as products of legitimacy—and a variety of economic outcomes.[30] Can we combine and then disaggregate these calculations to determine the consequences of individual corrupt transactions? The obstacles are daunting. First, we would need to know how each transaction affects the relevant population's perceptions of the prevalence of corruption. Second, we would need to know the relationship between perceptions of corruption and the various sorts of harm associated with demoralization. Last but not least, the idea that corruption causes demoralization which in turn causes undesirable political and macroeconomic outcomes makes assumptions about the direction of causality that would have to be defended; critics will argue that corruption is a consequence rather than a cause of absence of rule of law, political instability, and economic underdevelopment.[31]

Effectiveness

The UN Convention is replete with references to the idea that anti-corruption law must be "effective." But effective in doing what? What objective or objectives must be accomplished effectively?[32] If we know the answer, we can evaluate the regime in terms of its progress toward the specified objectives.

The text of the UN Convention suggests several possible objectives, but their meanings are not entirely clear. The official text begins by stating that the purpose is to prevent and combat corruption effectively. The meaning of prevention is reasonably intuitive, but what about "combat"? What objective does legal combat help to achieve, apart from prevention? And where does the UN Convention's emphasis on asset recovery fit in with these objectives? What about the Preamble's references to "rejection of a culture of corruption"?

The overarching question here is, in response to the problem posed by corruption, what should legal intervention aim to accomplish? At least three distinct categories of accomplishments seem relevant: benefits to (1) victims, (2) wrongdoers, and (3) potential victims or wrongdoers. These correspond to a simple three-part scheme for classifying the potential objectives of legal regulation: compensation, condemnation, and prevention.[33] Compensation focuses on the victims of corruption, condemnation focuses on the wrongdoers, and prevention focuses on prospective victims and wrongdoers. When law aims for compensation, it tries to ensure that people who break the law restore their victims to the position they would have been in if the violation had never been committed.[34] When the law condemns, it aims to persuade violators of the wrongfulness of their conduct, to reaffirm the norms they have violated, and to allow their fellow citizens to express their anger and outrage.[35] When the law prevents, it aims to spare future victims from harm through deterrence, incapacitation, or dissuasion of potential wrongdoers.[36]

The UN Convention appears to embrace all three of these objectives, even though they are quite distinct. It explicitly endorses prevention and, in its provisions on asset recovery, compensation. It also implicitly supports condemnation with its reference to "rejection of a culture of corruption."

To the extent the UN Convention applies to transnational bribery law, it allows for an additional set of disagreements about its objectives. In the transnational setting it is not enough to say simply that regulation affects victims, wrongdoers, or prospective victims and wrongdoers, or, correspondingly, that it is aimed simply at compensation, condemnation, or prevention. Some forms of regulation are more helpful to victims in Brazil, while others are more helpful to victims in the United States or in Panama. Compensation for Brazilians is different from compensation for Panamanians, and preventing the Brazilian state from being harmed by overpriced infrastructure contracts is not the same thing as preventing harm to U.S. construction firms that compete for those contracts.

The fact of the matter is that the assessment of a legal regime can be very different, depending on whether we consider its effects on nationals or foreigners.[37] Consider enforcement of the FCPA by U.S. enforcement agencies. At one extreme, a "self-interested" enforcement strategy will focus on U.S. nationals. If the primary objective is to secure compensation for U.S. victims, the strategy will involve seeking restitution from bribe payers—foreign or domestic—who use corrupt means to harm firms in which U.S. nationals are stakeholders, including competitors of the bribe payer, or even state-owned enterprises victimized by bribery in which U.S. nationals have invested. By contrast, an "altruistic" regulatory strategy with compensation as its objective will focus on obtaining restitution for foreigners. This may involve targeting a different set of bribe payers and remitting funds to a different set of victims. Alternatively, an agency might take an intermediate "cosmopolitan" approach and give equal weight to compensation of U.S. nationals and foreigners. Similar contrasts can be drawn between regulatory strategies that aim at condemnation of, or prevention of harm to, nationals as opposed to foreigners.

The upshot is that the objectives of transnational bribery law can be classified along at least two distinct dimensions, one ranging across compensation, condemnation, and prevention, and the other encompassing self-interest, cosmopolitanism, and altruism. Although it still represents a significant oversimplification of reality, this way of classifying the possible objectives of regulation yields at least nine distinct possibilities: self-interested retribution, altruistic compensation, and so forth. In practice, of course, a legal official may give weight to several aims and pursue them simultaneously. This increases the number of possible aims to include combinations such as "self-interested retribution and prevention, with greater weight given to retribution." In principle then, the variety of possible regulatory objectives is almost infinite.

Reasonable people can disagree about which of these objectives to pursue. They can even disagree about the meta-question of how to go about deciding which objectives ought to be pursued. As a result, there is considerable scope for disagreement about how to evaluate the effectiveness of the anti-bribery regime. There may be a consensus that the regime is to be evaluated in terms of progress toward certain objectives, but disagreement about which objectives.

Efficiency

The term "efficiency" has several meanings.[38] In assessments of international regimes it is common to rely on the concept of productive efficiency, also known as cost-effectiveness, which entails accomplishing a given level of effectiveness while expending the smallest amount of resources.[39] This criterion is useful for evaluating legal interventions that are equally effective, but less helpful when they have different levels of effectiveness. When evaluating interventions with different levels of effectiveness, it is useful to account for differences in the benefits as well as the costs associated with the regime. We can do this by equating efficiency with the concept of welfare maximization, which means, maximizing the difference between the benefits and the costs caused by the existence of the regime.[40]

Efficiency is an important objective for transnational bribery law because its machinery is costly to put in motion, for legal institutions and citizens alike. For the legal system, imposing legal sanctions requires skilled personnel and physical resources such as cars and computers, particularly in cases of economic misconduct that involve investigations of complex cross-border transactions. As for citizens, the law sends messages about the boundaries of socially acceptable conduct, but each invocation of the law draws down citizens' limited capacity to pay attention to the messages being sent. In addition, the law often recruits private citizens, or the organizations in which they have invested, into the process of preventing, monitoring, and sanctioning transnational bribery.

Evaluating the efficiency of a legal regime is difficult and complicated because it involves comparing an existing regime to a counterfactual regime to see which generates greater costs or net benefits. First there is the challenge of identifying the outcomes associated with the alternative regimes: How many people are deterred under each regime? How many receive compensation? How many are incapacitated? As we shall see in subsequent chapters, these kinds of counterfactual analyses are fraught with uncertainty. The second challenge associated with assessing efficiency is measurement. How to measure the costs and benefits associated with the outcomes under the alternative regimes along a single scale. For example, suppose a regime that employs fewer prosecutors will deter less bribery than the current regime but will cost $5 million less to operate. To determine whether it is efficient to depart from the status quo requires measuring the benefits of greater deterrence in terms that can be traded off against the $5 million it will cost. As we have seen, these kinds of measurement exercises are fraught with difficulty.

Due Process

As used in the UN Convention, "due process" refers to an enforcement process that complies with principles set out in international human rights treaties. Those treaties grant defendants certain rights, including, as the International Covenant on Civil and Political Rights puts it, to "a fair and public hearing by a competent, independent and impartial tribunal established by law."[41] In criminal cases, due process entails additional rights, including rights to:

- be presumed innocent until proven guilty;
- be informed promptly and in detail of the charge;
- adequate time and facilities to prepare a defense and to communicate with counsel of their choosing;
- be tried without undue delay;
- examine witnesses;
- not be compelled to testify against oneself or to confess guilt;
- review of any conviction and sentence by a higher tribunal according to law; and,
- not be tried or punished again for an offense for which the person has already been finally convicted or acquitted (a principle embodied in legal doctrines variously known as *non bis in idem*, double jeopardy, and *res judicata*).[42]

Although there is more or less universal agreement about the fact that defendants enjoy these rights, their content is open to interpretation. Moreover, in the context of transnational bribery law, effectiveness and efficiency often point toward narrow interpretations of the procedural rights. As we have already discussed, evidence of violations is difficult to obtain, and it can be expensive and time-consuming to investigate and prosecute wrongdoers. This makes procedures that reduce the burden on the prosecution attractive. For example, some jurisdictions curtail the presumption of innocence by creating an offense of illicit enrichment which puts the onus on defendants to explain the origins of their wealth. In other cases, prosecutors are permitted to coerce defendants into waiving their rights, including the right to be tried within a reasonable period of time and the right not to give testimony against themselves. Negotiated agreements can also be used to negate defendants' right to judicial review of their convictions and sentences. In addition, it is common for enforcement agencies to be permitted to target defendants who have already been the subject of enforcement proceedings in respect of the same conduct on the theory that proceedings launched by a different agency do not count for the purposes of the *ne bis in idem* rule.

Legitimacy

Legitimacy is commonly defined as the extent to which a person is justified in exercising coercive power over another person in a way that creates obligations of obedience, or at least support, for the other person.[43] In the present context the concept of legitimacy captures the extent to which lawmakers and enforcement agencies are justified in putting into effect their views on how to regulate transnational bribery—that is, deciding upon the scope of prohibitions on bribery, whether third parties should be liable, and how the prohibitions ought to be enforced—as well as the extent to which other actors have obligations to comply with or support their decisions. Legitimacy typically is used as a criterion for the evaluation of the exercise of power by state officials. However, as we shall see, the concept can also be used to evaluate the conduct of private actors who wield coercive power, particularly when that power is backed by the state, as in cases where private firms use contracts to exercise power over employees, suppliers, or customers.

Legitimacy operates as an independent criterion for evaluating a legal regime, along with criteria like effectiveness, efficiency, due process, and fairness.[44] However, evaluations of legitimacy also can influence a regime's effectiveness. As we have already mentioned in passing, there is considerable evidence that peoples' willingness to comply with and support a legal regime is positively influenced by their beliefs about its legitimacy.[45] It seems plausible that people's beliefs about other people's beliefs about legitimacy also will affect their attitudes and behavior toward a regime.

There are many different views on the factors that enhance or detract from legitimacy and the weight to be given to those factors. For instance, on some accounts legitimacy depends exclusively on whether the regime in question produces beneficial consequences, suggesting that legitimacy does not operate as an independent criterion for evaluation.[46] Other views suggest that beneficial consequences such as effectiveness, fairness, and efficiency are necessary but not sufficient for legitimacy.[47] According to these accounts, the legitimacy of the anti-bribery regime depends only in part on the extent to which it is effective, fair, and respectful of due process.

Still other conceptions of legitimacy are based on factors besides the outcomes generated by the regime being evaluated. For example, there is a broad consensus that consent of the governed is an important determinant of the legitimacy of a regime, although there are disagreements about what qualifies as valid consent.[48] Another commonly cited factor is legality, meaning whether the regime is consistent with duly promulgated legal norms.[49] For the anti-bribery regime this means asking whether it conforms to the dictates of international law. However, legality generally is not regarded as a conclusive determinant of legitimacy.[50] Moreover, inquiry into legality is of little assistance when the governing legal norms are vague or ambiguous, as is often the case with international legal instruments, including the major anti-corruption treaties.

Aside from beneficial consequences, consent, and legality, commentators have developed a host of criteria for determining the legitimacy of legal institutions, including transnational regimes. There is widespread agreement that legitimate decision-making involves most or all of the following procedural characteristics: participation or consent of affected groups, transparency, reason-giving, and entitlements to recourse or review. Richard Stewart argues that these procedural criteria generally serve to ensure that "the interests of those affected by global regulatory decisions are given due consideration and sufficient weight in the final decisions made."[51] They also can be justified as means to enhance effectiveness, efficiency, due process, and fairness.[52] Unfortunately, however, procedural measures also can detract from effectiveness, efficiency, and due process, especially in the context of criminal law enforcement. Consider transparency, which at first glance might seem unambiguously desirable. A more transparent enforcement strategy can easily be a less effective one. To take an obvious case, advertising which firms or transactions or sectors will be targeted for audits might make it too easy for wrongdoers to avoid sanctions. Transparency also might be costly: it can be expensive for cash-strapped enforcement agencies to compile and publish data held in multiple systems. In addition, identifying firms or individuals under investigation might create the impression that they are guilty, which arguably would be incompatible with due process. Similar conflicts can occur between practices such as reason-giving, participation, and review on the one hand, and on the other hand, effectiveness, efficiency, and due process. These types of conflicts, or at least tensions, are especially likely in the context of punitive regulations, where it is obvious that there are limits to the extent that decision-making processes ought to have regard for the interests of wrongdoers.

Several influential philosophers, including Immanuel Kant and John Rawls, suggest that legitimacy can be assessed by reference to the concept of hypothetical consent, meaning whether the justifications for a regime are so compelling that no reasonable person should object to it.[53] This approach generally is used to justify coercive legal institutions controlled by democratic states provided they protect citizens' interests in personal security and property while respecting due process and the human rights of all concerned and without operating extraterritorially. Other legal institutions are more difficult to justify because reasonable people can easily disagree about both the value and the existence of all of the possible aspects of legitimacy that we have discussed so far. Evaluations of effectiveness, legality, the quality of consent, and the merits of decision-making procedures will inevitably depend on the values and beliefs of the observer.[54]

Fairness

Nothing in the UN Convention suggests that the benefits and burdens of law enforcement must be distributed fairly across or within countries. One possible inference to draw from this silence is that this kind of "substantive" fairness is not an independent criterion for evaluation of the regime. This might make sense to someone who believes that the only criterion for evaluation missing from the Convention is legitimacy, narrowly defined, meaning that so long as decisions that affect resource allocation are made with appropriate input from all affected actors, then the results should be considered acceptable. Or, equivalently, someone might believe that fairness is an appropriate criterion for evaluation but define it solely in procedural terms, measured according to criteria such as cosmopolitanism, impartiality, and equal opportunities for participation by affected actors.

Contrary to these views, there is widespread support for the idea that substantive fairness is an appropriate criterion for evaluation of legal institutions with transnational effects.[55] The challenge is to settle upon a definition. For present purposes it is sufficient to focus on two broad types of conceptions of fairness: egalitarian and rights-based.

Egalitarian conceptions of fairness hold that certain resources or, more commonly, opportunities to obtain certain resources or benefits, should be distributed equally across members of the relevant community.[56] There is great controversy over whether this principle ought to be applied outside the context of a community governed by a state that exercises coercive authority, but we can largely ignore this debate since transnational bribery law always involves state coercion.[57] A practical objection to egalitarianism is that it is difficult to implement at the global level because there are no institutions capable of directly accomplishing the necessary redistribution. Nonetheless, individual regimes can be evaluated according to the extent to which they contribute to or promote or undermine the quest for equality. This includes asking whether the regime in question tends to exacerbate existing inequalities by creating extraordinary burdens or benefits for certain states, groups, or individuals.

Rights-based conceptions of fairness pay special attention to the extent to which distributions of resources or opportunities allow every person to live a worthwhile life. The minimum acceptable standard of living is sometimes described as one that respects human rights,[58] but the term "human rights" carries so much baggage, in both legal and ethical discourse, that another term seems preferable. In this book, "vital interests" will be used as a substitute. Accordingly, we can say that when legal institutions are evaluated in terms of rights-based conceptions of fairness, they are evaluated according to whether they contribute to protection of vital interests.

Rights-based conceptions of fairness are less controversial than the egalitarian ones. Many philosophers who are skeptical of whether egalitarian principles apply beyond the state agree that everyone has a moral obligation to ensure that the distribution of resources, or at least opportunities, satisfies this basic standard, including by promoting and supporting legal institutions that help to achieve fairness for the populations they govern.[59]

Conclusions

The task of evaluating the anti-bribery regime is complicated by the fact that the regime is designed to achieve multiple objectives. At the very least these include: prevention, compensation, and condemnation. These are the starting points for evaluating the effectiveness of the regime. However, no legal regime can be evaluated solely in terms of how effectively it achieves its objectives. In a world of scarce resources, the costs of achieving those objectives also have to considered, both in terms of their magnitude and distribution. As a result, it also seems uncontroversial that evaluation of the anti-bribery regime has to take into account efficiency and fairness. Also relevant are the means used to achieve the various ends. This explains why due process and legitimacy are included in the list of criteria for evaluation.

These five criteria (effectiveness, efficiency, fairness, due process, and legitimacy) are easy to list, but they are not necessarily straightforward to apply. Application to any given regime involves answering a series of extraordinarily difficult questions: Who merits compensation, and has it been delivered? How much harm has been prevented? How much will be prevented? What sort of message is being sent? What are the costs of law enforcement, and who bears them? Has due process been respected throughout? Who decided on the content of the regime? Does the composition and balance of power within the regime demonstrate appropriate regard for the interests of all affected people?

It would be convenient if we could eliminate some of the criteria for evaluation. But this would be a false economy. Some things of necessity are intended to fulfill multiple objectives. Imagine building a concert hall and trying to ignore some of the design criteria. Should seating for half of the audience be eliminated for the sake of improved acoustics? What about the men's restrooms? Or the emergency exits? There is no way to avoid the fact that a successful structure will have to perform well according to multiple criteria. The same is true of a legal structure like the anti-bribery regime.

6
What Is Bribery?

Introduction

This chapter and the next are concerned with how transnational bribery law ought to define the outer bounds of prohibited behavior. This chapter focuses on a deceptively simple question: How should bribery be defined for the purposes of transnational bribery law? The answer to this question is far from simple. As we shall see, bribery can be defined along many different dimensions, and an acceptable definition can have many wrinkles.

At the core of the definition of bribery is the paradigmatic case in which a private person deliberately gives money to a government official in exchange for a favor that involves using the official's position to confer a benefit that the private person is not entitled to receive. Every legal system on earth has anti-bribery laws that cover the paradigmatic case. However, prohibitions on transnational bribery sometimes are triggered even when elements of the paradigmatic case are missing. As a result, these laws cover much more than just hard-core bribery. At the same time, there are certain respects in which transnational bribery laws exclude paradigmatic bribes. For example, the leading international legal instruments apply exclusively to bribes paid in connection with business transactions.

This chapter begins with a motivating example, a paradigmatic case of transnational bribery. After reducing the transaction to its essential elements and explaining the justifications for prohibiting similar transactions, we turn to the tremendous variety of ways in which the scope of prohibitions on transnational bribery can be expanded or narrowed by defining, or redefining, each of the elements of a paradigmatic bribe.

Esquenazi

On October 25, 2011, Joel Esquenazi, a 52-year-old Miami executive, was sentenced to fifteen years in prison for his part in a scheme to bribe officials of a Haitian telecommunications company. The U.S. Department of Justice immediately issued a press release trumpeting the sentence as the longest ever imposed in a case centered on FCPA violations.[1] Esquenazi also was ordered to forfeit $3.09 million to the U.S. government.

What did Mr. Esquenazi do to deserve this severe punishment? His crime actually was rather banal. Esquenazi was the president, chief executive officer, and majority owner of Terra Telecommunications Corp. (Terra), a Florida company that enabled customers in the United States to make telephone calls to various countries. To permit its customers to place calls to Haiti, Terra contracted with Telecommunications D'Haiti S.A.M. (Haiti Teleco). Haiti Teleco was wholly owned by Haiti's central bank and held a monopoly on landline telephone service in Haiti. Between 2001 and 2005, Esquenazi directed his employees to pay more than $890,000 to two executives of Haiti Teleco, Robert Antoine and Jean Rene Duperval. The payments were routed through a series of shell companies. In exchange, the Haitian officials arranged for Terra to gain access to Haiti Teleco's services at reduced rates. In some cases they simply billed Terra for fewer minutes of service than were actually used. As a result, Terra saved approximately $2.2 million.

The Department of Justice prosecuted virtually everyone involved in the scheme. Esquenazi was convicted of violating the FCPA and the federal money laundering statute, as well as conspiring to violate the FCPA, wire fraud, and money laundering statutes. The minority owner of Terra, who also served as its executive vice president of operations, was convicted of the same charges. He was sentenced to eighty-four months' imprisonment, in addition to being "jointly and severally" responsible with Esquenazi for the $3.09 million forfeiture order. The controller of the company was convicted on conspiracy charges and sentenced to ten months' imprisonment. Two other U.S. citizens were prosecuted for operating shell companies that funneled payments from Terra to the Haitian officials. They pleaded guilty to charges under the FCPA and money laundering statutes and received sentences of fifty-seven and six months, respectively. In addition, two of the Haitian officials, Messrs. Robert Antoine and Jean Rene Duperval, were prosecuted for money laundering and received sentences of 48 and 108 months, respectively. On top of all that, the U.S. government charged some of the same Haitian officials, together with their intermediaries, for taking bribes from a different U.S. telecommunications company. Interestingly, in that case the government charged the U.S. company whose employees paid the bribes, along with individual employees, public officials, and intermediaries.[2]

Justifications for Legal Regulation of Paradigmatic Forms of Bribery

The paradigmatic bribe involves payment of money to a public official in exchange for a favor to which the payer is not entitled. We have already discussed in chapter 5 the reasons why this is harmful to society and ought to be condemned: it undermines public policy; it leads to unjust distributions of wealth; it encourages public officials to go to great lengths to secure power; it gives all the participants in the transaction incentives to conceal their behavior; it undermines the legitimacy of governments; and so forth.[3]

It is eminently plausible that it will be both effective and efficient to respond to bribery using legal sanctions. Given the costs of resorting to law, nonlegal sanctions, such as shame, are often relatively cost-effective ways of addressing antisocial behavior. However, nonlegal sanctions may not be up to the task of condemning, preventing, and providing compensation for paradigmatic forms of bribery. These kinds of bribes are unlikely to be reported—the parties to the transaction benefit, so they have no incentive to report, while the victims often are unaware they have been harmed (because the harmful consequences are frequently indirect or diffuse). Moreover, at least one party to the transaction is in a position of power and may be relatively immune to sanctions imposed by private actors. For all these reasons, the typically extensive array of resources available to a state-sponsored legal system may be required to uncover bribery, identify wrongdoers and their victims, impose proportionate sanctions, and deliver compensation.

Both legal and nonlegal sanctions can have the undesirable effect of condemning and discouraging socially beneficial behavior. The classic examples are laws on hate speech or obscenity that discourage legitimate political commentary and artistic expression. Fear of this kind of chilling effect should not, however, be an obstacle to imposing legal sanctions on paradigmatic examples of bribery. In these cases, by hypothesis, both the payer and the recipient know that they are undermining public policy, so targeting their dealings is unlikely to affect innocents engaged in socially redeeming activities.

For all these reasons—the overall wrongfulness of bribery, the limited effectiveness of nonlegal sanctions, the low likelihood of sanctioning desirable behavior—it makes sense to devote scarce public resources to imposing legal sanctions on paradigmatic forms of bribery.

Beyond the Paradigmatic Bribe

The paradigmatic bribe can be broken down into at least five distinct elements: (1) the bribe payer transfers money; (2) the money is given to a public official, either directly or indirectly; (3) the purpose is to induce the official to provide a "favor," meaning, to act or refrain from acting in a specific way—for example, to award a contract or refrain from issuing a citation; (4) the official is induced to provide the favor by the payment; and (5) the favor involves a misuse of the official's position. When all of these elements are present, it is easy to characterize the transaction as an instance of bribery. The *Esquenazi* case provides a good illustration (again, assuming that the officials were public officials).

The essential elements of a paradigmatic bribe are easy to list, but it is not always practical for a legal system to determine whether they are present in a given transaction. Moreover, many transactions that are missing those elements raise the same concerns as paradigmatic bribes.

Transactions that display some but not all of the elements of a paradigmatic bribe create a dilemma for a legal system.[4] One horn of the dilemma is the danger of *underbreadth*. Perhaps the missing elements are present but have gone undetected; or perhaps those elements are absent but a perception that bribery has taken place will lead to the same troubling consequences as the reality. A legal system that insisted on all the elements being present would risk failing to capture all the transactions that merit sanctions, thus compromising effectiveness.[5]

The other horn of the lawmakers' dilemma is the threat of *overbreadth*. The set of transactions that are missing only a few of the elements of a paradigmatic bribe includes many transactions with considerable redeeming value, such as: political commentary, campaign finance, common courtesies, and productive business dealings on the part of public officials' friends and relatives. A legal system which expands the definition of bribery to include transactions missing key elements of paradigmatic bribes runs the danger of condemning and discouraging these and other socially beneficial transactions. That kind of legal system also will tend to dilute the message that could be sent by reserving the term "bribery" for a narrow set of paradigmatic bribes—being convicted of bribery loses some of its symbolic sting if a person who buys a cup of coffee can be convicted of the offense. And, in a world of scarce resources, breadth may come at the expense of depth. Is it really worthwhile to engage the machinery of the law to fuss over the price of a cup of coffee while murderers and rapists remain at large? In other words, overbreadth might be synonymous with inefficiency. In certain circumstances, overbreadth might also be characterized as unfair, because it concentrates a significant risk of liability on a relatively small portion of the population.

Transnational bribery law has addressed the first horn of its dilemma, the problem of underbreadth, by defining bribery expansively. The benchmark definition is set out in Article 15 of the UN Convention:

> **Article 15. Bribery of national public officials**
> Each State Party shall adopt such legislative and other measures as may be necessary to establish as criminal offences, when committed intentionally:
> (a) The promise, offering or giving, to a public official, directly or indirectly, of an undue advantage, for the official himself or herself or another person or entity, in order that the official act or refrain from acting in the exercise of his or her official duties;
> (b) The solicitation or acceptance by a public official, directly or indirectly, of an undue advantage, for the official himself or herself or another person or entity, in order that the official act or refrain from acting in the exercise of his or her official duties.

Bribery of foreign public officials and officials of public international organizations is defined in identical terms except that bribe payers—that is, the people who promise, offer, or give—can only be liable if they act:

> in order to obtain or retain business or other undue advantage in relation to the conduct of international business.[6]

This definition goes beyond paradigmatic forms of bribery to capture transactions that are only in their preliminary stages—all that is needed to trigger liability under the UN Convention is a "promise" or an "offer" or a "solicitation" made with a particular intention. Moreover, it is clear that the intended transaction need not involve all the elements of a paradigmatic bribe since it is unnecessary to show that the bribe payer intended to give a pecuniary benefit or that the benefit was to be delivered to the public official. The UN Convention also does not appear to be limited to cases in which the favor being sought involves misuse of public office, any action or inaction in the exercise of official duties appears to suffice.

There is one respect in which the UN Convention's definition of transnational bribery definitely is narrower than the paradigmatic definition. The idea that bribery must be "in relation to the conduct of international business"—the so-called "business nexus" requirement—is not an element of our paradigmatic definition but is a key feature of the offense defined by the UN Convention.

National laws that criminalize bribery of foreign public officials do not necessarily adhere to the UN Convention's definition of the offense, in part because many of those laws were enacted before the Convention was adopted.[7] For instance, the FCPA's anti-bribery provisions cover payments to political parties as well as to individual public officials.[8] On other hand, the FCPA's prohibition is limited to payments made "corruptly,"[9] and in cases involving individuals the criminal prohibition only captures violations committed "willfully."[10] The FCPA also arguably excludes payments induced by extortion, a category which might encompass a large share of all payments to foreign public officials.[11] In addition, the FCPA expressly excludes "facilitating payments,"[12] which are probably best thought of as transactions that involve de minimis harm, and provides an "affirmative defense" for conduct that is lawful under the local law of the public official's jurisdiction.[13]

In short, there are many ways for anti-bribery law to deviate from the paradigmatic definition of bribery. Most of the existing variants expand the definition to capture additional transactions. Not all of those additional transactions are necessarily suitable targets for transnational bribery law. Compared to paradigmatic bribes, they may be less wrongful, more susceptible to regulation through nonlegal sanctions, or have more redeeming characteristics. Or not. Efforts to narrow the scope of transnational bribery law to exclude transactions that fit the definition of a paradigmatic bribe can be analyzed in the same way.

The remainder of this chapter will discuss possible variations on each of the key elements of the UN Convention's definition of bribery, as well as exceptions for coercion, de minimis payments, and payments permitted under local law. For ease of reference, here is a restatement of those elements and exceptions:

- Intentional action
- Promise, offering, giving, solicitation, acceptance
- Undue advantage
- To a public official or political party, directly or indirectly
- In order that
- Official acts or refrains from acting
- In the exercise of official duties
- To obtain an undue advantage
- In relation to international business
- Absence of extortion
- Not a de minimis transaction
- Not permitted by local law

Intentionally

The crime of bribery defined in the UN Convention requires intentional action, and so does the version in the OECD Convention.[14] The FCPA does not use the term "intentionally," but, as noted previously, it does say that the acts which constitute the offense must be done "corruptly" and that an individual can only be subject to criminal liability under the FCPA if they violate its terms "willfully."[15] "Intentionally" suggests some level of awareness of the nature or consequences of the person's actions, but not awareness that the actions are unlawful. "Corruptly" and "willfully" arguably go further and entail awareness that the conduct in question is unlawful, or at least wrongful. The main anti-bribery instruments also specify that bribery involves actions "in order" to influence or "for purposes of" influencing official action, or "in order to" obtain or retain a business advantage. These are also terms which suggest that bribery involves awareness of at least some of the consequences of action.

References to mental states are common in definitions of criminal offenses. As a general rule, to be guilty of a crime a person's guilty actions must be accompanied by a guilty mind, or to use the Latin term, mens rea. This requirement serves to ensure that the defendant merits the kind of condemnation that is an inherent feature of criminal punishment—a person who ignores indications that their actions will cause harm is someone who engages in flawed moral reasoning and deserves to be condemned. Mens rea can also help to focus criminal liability on people who are likely to be deterred by legal sanctions. People who are aware of the nature and consequences of their actions are more likely to advert to and be deterred by the accompanying sanctions than people who are less aware of what they are doing. This justification for mens rea requirement is not entirely compelling, however, because punishing people who were unaware that their actions would attract criminal liability might still serve to deter people with greater foresight. Moreover, sanctions for people who lack mens rea might be useful methods of achieving compensation. In any event, the closer the connection between the definition of mens rea and knowledge that actions are unlawful, the more accurately the mens rea requirement will serve to identify people who are blameworthy and susceptible to deterrence.[16]

The mental element of bribery can be a critical determinant of guilt or innocence. It is true that a person with a guilty mind still needs to complete a certain set of actions in order to be convicted of the offense. But as we shall see in the next section of this chapter, even relatively innocuous actions can be sufficient to violate prohibitions on bribery; steps well short of a corrupt agreement generally are sufficient to trigger liability. Moreover, if other parties are involved, a person with a guilty mind who does not personally complete the offense still can be held liable for "aiding and abetting" the offense or "conspiracy" to commit the offense. In each case the actions that are played out in the defendant's mind are more important than the ones that take place in real life.

In the paradigmatic case of bribery, the guilty parties know everything—that money has been given to a public official and that it will cause the official to provide a favor that involves misuse of public office. In the paradigmatic case, the parties also know that their actions are unlawful. And not only do they know with certainty what has happened, they desire it; if events had unfolded differently, they would have been less satisfied.

Many real-world scenarios are far removed from the paradigmatic case. Business people who do business in foreign markets more often than not rely on subordinates or agents, including lawyers, accountants, or the ever-present "consultants," to help navigate the local terrain. It is not uncommon for superiors or clients to be in the dark about how their intermediaries do business—that is often the point of hiring an intermediary. This means that the superior or client will be uncertain about who the intermediary deals with, or whether there is any causal connection between their payment and any favors rendered by public officials. They may not even be clear on who is a public official in the country, since different countries draw the line between state and market in different places. In addition, the superior or client often will be indifferent as to whether the favor is obtained through bribery or some other means; they will care only about being able to get on with their business. And parties who are not expert in the law may be unaware of which interactions with public officials cross the line into illegality. On top of all that, if they are like most of us, people who act in the face of these kinds of uncertainties will have a tendency to convince themselves that they are behaving properly, even when a reasonable and impartial observer would see a substantial risk of impropriety. So while the paradigmatic case involves knowledge and desire, the common case is likely to involve uncertainty, about both facts and law, as well as indifference and self-deception.

A classic example is the case of Frederick Bourke, a U.S. businessman and investor who decided to join forces with an international man of mystery named Viktor Kozeny to invest in newly privatized companies in Azerbaijan.[17] The pair hoped to get in on the ground floor of the privatization of Azerbaijan's state-owned oil company. Kozeny oversaw the operations in Azerbaijan while Bourke provided funding and helped to recruit other U.S. investors. In order to induce the privatization, Kozeny and his associates gave various Azerbaijani officials, including the president of the country, interests in their holding companies, cash, and other benefits. Bourke denied that he knew of any bribes, but he was clearly aware of the possibility that bribes had been paid. He knew about Kozeny's past shady dealings and the allegations that earned him the nickname "The Pirate of Prague." He knew that corruption was pervasive in

Azerbaijan. Most damningly of all, he was recorded telling his attorneys that he was concerned about the FCPA and asking for advice on how to limit his liability.

Should liability for bribery extend to people like Bourke who act in the face of uncertainty, self-delusion, and indifference? The UN Convention addresses bribery through intermediaries by requiring parties to criminalize transactions that "indirectly" provide advantages to public officials, but otherwise it is silent on these questions. The OECD Convention is functionally equivalent. National laws such as the FCPA and the U.K. Bribery Act show, to varying extents, that it is possible to push the frontier of liability beyond people whose mental states fall within the bounds of the paradigmatic case.[18]

Consider cases involving factual uncertainty and self-deception. The FCPA makes it an offense to give money to an intermediary "knowing" that it will be passed on to a foreign public official and then defines the concept of "knowing" about an event to include "being aware" or having "a firm belief" that the event is "substantially certain to occur."[19] The court that presided over Bourke's case quoted this provision and then instructed the jury that Bourke had a guilty mind if he believed there was a high probability that bribes were being paid but consciously avoided confirming those suspicions. This instruction restated a legal rule known as the doctrine of conscious avoidance.[20] The doctrine is well established in U.S. law and neutralizes the potentially noxious effects of combining factual uncertainty and self-deception. Conscious avoidance only applies though when the defendant is aware of a "high probability" of misconduct, and leaves considerable room for debate over what counts as a "high probability" in any given situation. Furthermore, the doctrine of conscious avoidance does not allow a person to be held guilty for unconscious failure to confirm suspicions, even if negligent. A more aggressive response to the problems of uncertainty and self-deception would have allowed Bourke to be convicted if he failed to confirm his suspicions solely because he was too disorganized to get around to completing his due diligence.

What about people who are uncertain about the law? Bourke was presumably under no illusions about the content of U.S. law after he got off the phone with his lawyers. But what about before the telephone call? Could he have escaped liability for conduct that preceded the consultation with his lawyers on the grounds that he was unaware it was wrong? He seemed to believe that his conduct was acceptable in Azerbaijan, and in the early stages of his trial he floated the argument it was lawful under Azerbaijan law because he was a victim of extortion.[21] Bourke also may have believed that his activities as a mere investor were not covered by the FCPA.

Many legal systems preclude this kind of argument by embracing the general principle that ignorance of the law is no excuse. The U.K. Bribery Act, for instance, is drafted against the backdrop of a general presumption that ignorance of the law is no excuse, and there is little in the statute to oust that presumption (except, possibly on the issue of whether a person who pays a bribe in exchange for improper performance must know that the performance was improper).[22] The FCPA has a narrower scope along this dimension; to the extent it imposes criminal liability on individuals, it is only concerned with the legally sophisticated types of villains who feature in the paradigmatic case. Those individuals must be shown to have acted willfully, and the courts have held that in this context the term "willfully" means acting with a bad purpose to disobey or disregard the law.[23] This does not, however, mean that an individual defendant in a foreign bribery case must be familiar with all the nuances of the FCPA. In Bourke's case, the trial judge instructed the jury that they could only convict him if he was aware of the generally unlawful nature of his acts, but they did not have to find that he knew that he was breaking any particular law or any particular rule.[24]

It is also possible to design a legal regime which captures defendants who are indifferent about bribery, but it is not clear how many legal regimes achieve that result. To get at the challenges involved we need a sharper illustration than the *Bourke* case. Consider an investor who pays a law firm to help him to conclude the acquisition of a stake in a state-owned company, knowing that the firm has the option of getting the job done either by going through an arduous administrative process or by paying a bribe, and believing with a high probability that the law firm will find bribery more appealing. In other words, the investor's ultimate end is to secure a specific governmental action, but she is indifferent about whether the means to that end include bribery.[25] If the law firm pays a bribe, can it be said that the indifferent investor has intentionally paid a bribe? The language of the UN Convention, which is tracked by many national laws, does not resolve this issue because it is debatable whether the concept of acting intentionally captures the actions of someone like the indifferent investor.[26] According to one definition of the concept, a person only acts intentionally in relation to a result if achieving the result figured among the reasons for her actions. According to this definition, the indifferent investor has not intentionally paid a bribe. A more expansive definition of intention holds that a person intends the foreseeable results of her actions, regardless of whether achievement of the result played a role in her decision to act. If this is what intention means, then the indifferent investor has intentionally paid a bribe.

A reliable way to capture the indifferent investor would be to dispense with the UN Convention's requirement of intentional action and impose liability on anyone who acts knowing that there is a high probability that their actions will result in the payment of a bribe. The FCPA goes down that path,[27] but then turns around and adds that actions are only culpable if they are committed "corruptly." Corrupt intent is defined in several different ways in U.S. case law, but one of the most common definitions is, "acting with a bad purpose."[28] This evokes the narrow definition of intention and appears to exclude the indifferent investor. There is yet another twist, however. The FCPA, in contrast with the UN Convention and most national legislation, defines the physical elements of bribery to include "authorization" of an improper transaction.[29] It is plausible to argue that the indifferent investor not only knowingly but intentionally authorized the law firm to pay a bribe—her reason for handing over control of her funds was to allow them to be used for a set of purposes that included bribery. Since granting such an authorization is deemed by the statute to be a wrongful act, it seems that the indifferent investor has acted with the requisite bad purpose. So the FCPA ultimately reaches the indifferent investor by a somewhat roundabout path.

What are the arguments for and against condemning and sanctioning people like Bourke—or our hypothetical indifferent investor—when they act in the face of uncertainty, delude themselves into minimizing the likelihood that their intermediaries have overstepped, or are indifferent about the prospect of bribery? The arguments for their guilt are simple: people who think this way are more likely to cause harm than people who don't. They deserve to be condemned for failing to give adequate weight to other people's interests in avoiding harm. Moreover, condemnation might induce them to change both their thought processes and actions. Finally, sanctions might help victims of bribery to receive compensation. As between the victims and a person whose careless payment caused them harm, it is clear that the payer should bear the loss. These arguments can be bolstered by the observation that criminal laws can be designed to permit different sanctions to be imposed on people who manifest different levels of culpability. The villains of the paradigmatic case display complete disregard for other people's interests, but that does not mean that people who manifest greater but still inadequate regard should be wholly exempt from criminal liability, it only means they should receive less severe sanctions.

These arguments provide compelling reasons why civil liability, which involves lower sanctions and less moral condemnation than criminal liability, should not turn on questions of intention. In the criminal context, though, these arguments are difficult to operationalize. What does it mean to give adequate weight to the possibility that others might be harmed? How probable must corruption be to make a business person culpable for hiring a local agent? What sort of inquiry must a person undertake to determine whether a planned course of action is unlawful or wrong? Is it appropriate for a person to weigh the possible benefits of their action—for example, the jobs that will be created by an investment in a high-risk country—when deciding how much weight to give to the possibility that it will lead to corrupt behavior? What evidence can be used to resolve these issues? Faced with these challenging questions, lawmakers might reasonably take different views on whether or how to expand criminal liability beyond the set of people who act intentionally and willfully, in the narrow sense.

Promises, Offers, Gifts, Authorizations, and Acts in Furtherance Thereof

The paradigmatic bribe is an illicit bargain. The process of completing a bargain of this sort can involve a lengthy sequence of steps: information gathering and other forms of preparation; preliminary communications between the parties; one or more rounds of offers and counteroffers; agreement, which generally entails acceptance of an offer and at least one definite promise; and performance by each party. The UN Convention's bribery offenses do not require a completed transaction, or even a promise or agreement. Instead they are triggered by mere offers. The FCPA is even broader. As we have seen, its anti-bribery provisions can be triggered by not only an offer but also an "authorization" of a gift or payment. In fact, the FCPA arguably can be triggered by mere preparatory steps. Communications "in furtherance of" an offer, gift, promise, or authorization are sufficient to trigger the FCPA's anti-bribery provisions so long as they involve making use of "the mails or any means or instrumentality of interstate commerce."[30] There is no requirement that the communication qualify as an offer, or even that it be directed at the other side of the intended bargain. An aggressive prosecutor might argue that an act in furtherance of an offer which has not yet materialized is sufficient to trigger liability.

As every student of contract law knows, an offer entails a conditional commitment, specifically, a commitment to go through with the proposed bargain if the other party accepts (agrees to) the offer. Thus, to the extent that the FCPA and other laws prohibit preliminary activities that do not amount to offers, promises, gifts, or authorizations, they allow for punishment of people who have not made any sort of commitment to engage in bribery. On top of that, in some legal systems criminal offenses such as bribery are automatically extended to capture people who conspire to commit the offense.[31] It is well established that people can be found guilty of conspiracy without completing the underlying offense. All of this means that a person can become liable for a bribery-related offense—meaning a charge with bribery in its name—by taking only modest preliminary steps toward an illicit bargain.

Expanding the scope of liability for bribery to include conduct that falls short of a completed bribe has a straightforward set of pros and cons. On the pro side, the preliminary conduct is often objectionable in its own right. Whether or not an effort to pay or solicit a bribe actually affects any public official's actions, it may amount to a denial of the authority of the state and contribute to the perception that corruption is pervasive. What matters for these purposes is the nature of the transaction that was contemplated and advertised, not whether it was actually completed. And even in circumstances in which only completed transactions are objectionable, extending liability to preliminary conduct can help solve the problem of underdetection that plagues enforcement of anti-bribery law and limits its deterrent effect. Enforcement agencies will find evidence of preliminary conduct indispensable when the conduct has led or will lead to a completed transaction but the subsequent steps in the transaction cannot be observed.

On the con side, relying on evidence of preliminary conduct is not guaranteed to help with the problem of underdetection. The value of this kind of evidence depends on how frequently the preliminary conduct results in objectionable conduct, and how easy it is to observe subsequent steps in the transaction. Some transactions will be abandoned by one party or another after going through the preliminary stages—smoke does not always mean fire. And in some cases, later steps in the transaction will also be observable. Imposing liability for preliminary conduct in either of these situations is a waste of resources.

Moreover, some preliminary conduct is benign, especially if it falls short of a commitment to pursue an illicit transaction and is not widely publicized. It seems harsh to condemn people for flirting with or exploring the idea of paying or soliciting a bribe if they never make any sort of commitment to move forward. There is always a cost to placing limits on freedom of expression (even prohibitions on jokes about bombs in airports). FCPA-style prohibitions on "acts in furtherance of offers" might discourage businesspeople from even discussing the idea of paying a bribe to a foreign public official. I once set an exam in which the students were told that a low-level employee made a request to have his firm pay the travel expenses of a public official. The students were expected to realize that the mere communication of the request arguably counted as an act in furtherance of an offer, even though the request was denied! Discouraging these kinds of communication could be counterproductive. It might be helpful for members of an organization to discuss potentially problematic transactions openly in order to learn about the boundaries of acceptable conduct. In other settings, it might be helpful to raise the possibility of bribery in order to get a sense of the integrity of a business partner or employee.

Undue Advantage; Anything of Value

According to the UN Convention, a bribe necessarily involves the transfer of an "undue advantage." The FCPA speaks of the transfer of "anything of value." Legislation in other countries refers to the provision of "any gratification."[32] Some of these concepts are still susceptible to limiting interpretations. "Undue" advantage implies that some advantages are not undue. "Anything of value" is broader in some respects, but still is limited to "things." "Gratification" is potentially a broader concept. For example, Singapore's expansive definition of gratification includes any "service, favour or advantage of any description whatsoever."[33]

Money and rights to payment of money are obviously captured by these terms. Other tangible goods also are covered, which is fortunate since luxury goods such as meals, alcohol, jewelry, and purses are the currency of choice in many corrupt transactions. Services that are ordinarily provided in exchange for money are as good as money and so should also be covered. Giving the president a flight on a private jet or arranging for his security detail is as good as giving him the money it would cost to rent the plane or pay the security guards.

It is an open question whether money, goods, or services given to help defray the costs of running a political campaign qualify as either an "undue advantage" or "anything of value." Candidates who seek to enhance their political fortunes will view such expenditures as "advantages" and "of value." Even if the candidate does not receive any tangible benefit, the effect on their political power can reasonably be called a "political benefit." However, attempting to capture all transactions that create political benefits will introduce a great deal of uncertainty into the law. There are all sorts of ways of providing political benefits, many of which involve no telltale direct transfers to the beneficiary. Think of a person who purchases advertisements attacking a candidate for political office. Have they provided an "undue advantage" to the opposing candidate? What if no names are mentioned? Or how about a person who endorses a candidate? Does that kind of political benefit qualify as the subject matter of a bribe (assuming a favor is provided in return)? What if the person giving the endorsement is himself a public official? The U.S. Supreme Court has a great deal of experience with these issues. That court has repeatedly noted that expansive interpretation of anti-bribery law in this area could have a significant chilling effect on both private financing of election campaigns and political commentary.[34] Societies like the United States that place a high value on these kinds of transactions will want to tread lightly here.

Services that cannot be bought with money also test the outer bounds of undue advantage and similar concepts. Consider sexual favors.[35] If they are provided by paid professionals, then they are as good as money and clearly seem like elements of a bribe. Sexual favors provided by amateurs may be in a different category. But what of Christine Deviers-Joncour, the self-described "whore of the republic," who was employed as a lobbyist by Elf, the French oil company, during a period when she was the mistress of the French foreign minister? It is reasonably clear that she offered sex and companionship in an effort to secure official favors for her employer from the minister (who admitted the affair but denied being influenced), but she also claimed they were in love. These kinds of sexual favors almost certainly represent forms of gratification, but do they represent undue advantages or "things" of value for the officials? Or are they merely familiar perquisites of power? Courts tend to struggle with these issues.[36] Allegations of coercion, in both directions, often complicate these cases: private individuals complain that they were extorted and, after the fact, officials complain about being blackmailed.[37]

Other hard cases involve people who confer honor or status on public officials. In 2011, the London School of Economics (the LSE) was rocked by allegations that it had conferred a PhD degree on Saif al-Islam Gadaffi, son of the Libyan head of state at the time, shortly before the LSE received a lucrative training contract from the Libyan government.[38] There were allegations that Mr. Gadaffi's dissertation was not up to the institution's usual standards. It is far from clear, however, that these problems would have been evident to his examiners because the main concerns revolved around plagiarism and the possibility that he had received unacknowledged assistance from members of a consulting firm. The evidentiary difficulty of establishing that a commendation or award was unwarranted weighs strongly against treating it as a bribe. Suppose, however, for the sake of argument, that the school had deliberately lowered its standards in awarding the degree in the hope of receiving benefits from the Libyan government. Would this qualify as an unlawful "undue advantage"? It is difficult to see why not, especially since a degree from an elite academic institution has an explicit price (the amount of tuition), an ascertainable monetary cost (the operating costs of the institution), and a quantifiable monetary value (in the form of increased earnings). But what if Mr. Gadaffi had been awarded an honorary degree? What if faculty of the LSE had simply made flattering remarks about Mr. Gadaffi that had the effect of bolstering his image? Would it matter if a public relations firm had placed a monetary value on favorable publicity for Mr. Gadaffi?

It is challenging to regulate transactions with public officials that involve services that are not bought and sold and do not have any obvious pecuniary value. These transactions simultaneously present many of the dangers of bribery and the benefits of more benign transactions. Sexual relations between public officials and their constituents can clearly compromise public policy, but any restrictions limit the sex lives of both participants and might even thwart the course of true love. In the same vein, flattery of a public official can combine the best and the worst effects of bribery and legitimate political commentary. The latter is troubling to discourage in societies that value unfettered political discussion.

Public Official

Contemporary transnational bribery law usually draws a sharp distinction between bribery of public officials and bribery of other types of officials. While the UN Convention requires countries to criminalize bribery of public officials and officials of public international organizations, it only requires them to "consider" criminalization of bribery of people who represent private organizations, an offense sometimes known as "commercial bribery."[39] Depending on the jurisdiction, commercial bribery can involve anything from bid-rigging aimed at securing contracts to kickback schemes where doctors receive payment in exchange for directing patients to certain medical services or products. Some countries, like the United Kingdom, treat transnational commercial bribery in much the same way as bribery of foreign public officials.[40] In other countries, like Germany, commercial bribery is a distinct offense.[41] Either way, prohibition of commercial bribery makes it possible to sanction people without proving that the recipient or intended recipient of the bribe was a public official. This can be a great convenience when proof of public status involves obtaining evidence from overseas.

Many countries have declined to take up the invitation to regulate transnational commercial bribery. In those countries it is necessary to figure out who qualifies as a foreign public official in order to sanction foreign bribery. According to both the UN Convention and the OECD Convention, this question is to be answered by referring to a common international definition of a public official, rather than the definition used in the law of either the regulating state or the official's home state.[42] The relevant definitions from the UN Convention read as follows:

Article 2

(a) "Public official" shall mean: (i) any person holding a legislative, executive, administrative or judicial office of a State Party, whether appointed or elected, whether permanent or temporary, whether paid or unpaid, irrespective of that person's seniority; (ii) any other person who performs a public function, including for a public agency or public enterprise, or provides a public service, as defined in the domestic law of the State

Party and as applied in the pertinent area of law of that State Party; (iii) any other person defined as a "public official" in the domestic law of a State Party;

(b) "Foreign public official" shall mean any person holding a legislative, executive, administrative or judicial office of a foreign country, whether appointed or elected; and any person exercising a public function for a foreign country, including for a public agency or public enterprise;

(c) "Official of a public international organization" shall mean an international civil servant or any person who is authorized by such an organization to act on behalf of that organization."

The UN Convention's definition of a foreign public official is slightly narrower than its definition of a public official, meaning that the offense of bribing a foreign public official is somewhat narrower than its domestic counterpart. The transnational offense does not explicitly cover unpaid, temporary, or junior officials, nor does it cover people designated as public officials under idiosyncratic domestic laws despite the fact that they do not perform any public function. Examples of people in this grey area might be individuals who hold unpaid temporary or ceremonial positions, such as businesspeople who serve as members of advisory councils or honorary consuls. More importantly for present purposes, the outer limits of the definitions of both domestic and foreign public officials are unclear because the key terms, "public function" and "public service," are vague. The OECD Convention defines a "foreign public official" in virtually the same terms as the UN Convention.[43] Interestingly, neither instrument covers candidates for public office, even though their proximity to power makes them tempting targets for bribe payers.[44]

The limits of these definitions have been tested in cases involving bribes paid to representatives of state-owned enterprises. This was a central issue in the prosecution of Mr. Esquenazi; his main line of defense was that the people he bribed were not public officials for the purposes of the FCPA because Haiti Teleco was not sufficiently connected to the Haitian government. According to the UN Convention, this issue should be resolved by asking whether the person in question performs a public function or provides a public service. The OECD Convention says the same thing, but its official commentary adds an important gloss: an official of a "public enterprise"—any enterprise over which a government exercises a "dominant influence"—is deemed to perform a public function "unless the enterprise operates on a normal commercial basis in the relevant market."[45] It is unclear whether this means that an enterprise which operates on a normal commercial basis cannot be presumed to perform a public function but may be deemed to do so in certain cases, or that such an enterprise can never be deemed to perform a public function.

The corresponding definition of a "foreign official" in the FCPA says nothing about whether the intended recipient of the bribe performs a public function, but instead asks whether they are an officer or employee of "a foreign government or any department, agency, or instrumentality thereof" (emphasis added). In the *Esquenazi* case, the U.S. court said that it would interpret "instrumentality" to ensure that U.S. law conformed to the OECD Convention. Curiously, though, it went on to hold that an entity is an instrumentality of a foreign government if the government controls it and considers it to perform a public function. Applying this test, the court easily concluded that Haiti Teleco was an instrumentality of the Haitian government. Interestingly, the *Esquenazi* test ignores the normal-commercial-basis-exception in the official commentary to the OECD Convention. It also makes no mention of the fact that the OECD Convention's definition of a foreign public official includes employees who perform public functions outside of entities controlled by the government.[46]

There is a subtle but potentially important difference between the definitional approach recommended by the UN Convention and the approach set out in the commentary to the OECD Convention and in the FCPA. When a bribe is paid to an employee of a state-controlled enterprise, the UN Convention focuses on whether the individual employee performs a public function. According to the commentary to the OECD Convention and the FCPA, the key issue is whether the enterprise is public in character. The UN Convention's approach seems more demanding because it could require a separate analysis for every single job description in a state-owned enterprise. The OECD Convention and the FCPA make it possible to avoid this kind of case-by-case analysis, but at the expense of creating some anomalous interpretations. For instance, the OECD-FCPA approach would catch bribes paid to low-level agents of enterprises that perform a "public function." This might mean a gas station attendant employed by a subsidiary of a state-owned oil company.[47] Under the UN Convention, the bribe to the gas station attendant would only be covered if she performed a public function.

To treat a gas station attendant as a public official is only anomalous if it clearly serves no purpose. This brings us to the question, what is the purpose of targeting public sector bribery for a distinctive set of sanctions? Why do we draw a distinction between bribery of public and private officials? Why place a priority on sanctioning bribery of public officials?

One possibility is that public sector bribery presents a more serious problem. In most countries, the state exercises vastly more power than almost any private firm, so the adverse consequences of subverting state policy will tend to be more far-reaching and significant than the consequences of undermining the goals of a private firm.[48] In some countries, public international organizations such as the World Bank or the International Monetary Fund wield similar amounts of power. In addition, bribery of a public official, or even someone perceived as a public official, amounts to a denial of the authority of the state, with all the associated ramifications. This latter argument does not translate easily to cases involving international organizations. It is debatable how concerned we ought to be about people who deny the authority of international organizations, although one might argue that such a denial represents an indirect threat to the authority of the organizations' member states.

Public sector bribery may also be distinctive because it is relatively susceptible to influence by legal regulation. In the private sector, a firm's shareholders stand to lose the most when employees accept bribes to subvert the firm's interests. So those shareholders typically have strong incentives to deploy civil remedies and nonlegal monitoring mechanisms to discourage bribery. And speaking of monitoring, private sector firms can benchmark the performance of their officials against the performance of officials in competing firms. Self-interested shareholders have no direct analogues in the public sector or international organizations, and entities controlled by the state or international organizations often face little or no competition. This all suggests that relatively potent legal mechanisms, up to and including criminal penalties, are required to discourage bribery of public officials.

So should our gas station attendant fall on the public side of the line, assuming she is not personally responsible for implementing any public policy? If she is perceived as a public official by the local population then yes, since perceptions matter in determining the impact of bribery. The case for doing this will be even stronger if her employer is sheltered from competition and shareholder scrutiny.

Inevitably, certain forms of private sector bribery will merit as much legal regulation as public sector bribery, or perhaps even more. In some situations, officials of private organizations wield considerable amounts of power over large segments of the population—especially when states outsource important public functions to the private sector—and face little effective oversight. Take, for example, the Fédération Internationale de Football Association, generally known by its acronym, FIFA. FIFA is a private not-for-profit organization, established under Swiss law, which governs football around the world. It sets the rules of the game, regulates player transfers, organizes international competitions, and claims broad authority to regulate threats to the integrity of players, matches, competitions, players, officials, and member associations.[49] This includes deciding which country will host the World Cup and which firms get to advertise themselves as sponsors of the competition. The decisions made by FIFA officials influence the cost and quality of football competitions enjoyed by, literally, billions of people, as well as the benefits enjoyed by hosts and sponsors of competitions. So corruption on the part of FIFA has far-reaching effects. At the same time, as a not-for-profit organization whose members are themselves not-for-profit organizations, FIFA officials are subject to relatively little oversight. Finally, FIFA has a monopoly over global governance of soccer, with no prospect of competition on the horizon. For all these reasons there is a strong case for regulating corruption on the part of FIFA officials in much the same way as corruption on the part of officials of any public international organization. In a series of recent enforcement actions, the U.S. Department of Justice has done just that.[50]

Political Parties and Their Members

The FCPA is exceptional among transnational bribery laws in that it expressly regulates transfers to both officials of foreign political parties and the parties themselves. This means that giving anything of value is generally prohibited, subject, however, to a defense that applies when the defendant can show that the transfer was lawful under local law in the party's country. The UN Convention and the OECD Convention only prohibit this kind of conduct if the transfer is to a party official who exercises a public function, which the commentaries suggest might occur in the case of a one-party state.[51]

There is a historical explanation for the extension of the FCPA to party finance: the scandals that motivated the passage of the FCPA included several cases of U.S.-based multinational companies that made payments to political parties, both domestic and foreign.[52] These payments were viewed as improper by citizens of foreign nations and embarrassed the United States.[53] It may also be significant that at the time the FCPA was enacted, the United States was a global hegemon engaged in a struggle for influence with the Soviet Union. The statute's backers might have been concerned about the prospect of private corporations supporting political parties with interests opposed to those of the United States and thereby counteracting the effects of interventions by the U.S. government.

Payments to political parties are associated with some but not all the problems of a paradigmatic bribe. In many political systems, political parties wield considerable influence over elected officials, and thus state power. In those systems, payments to parties can be at least as subversive of public policy as payments to individuals, if not more. At the same time, misuse of power by political parties is subject to an important check that is largely independent of anti-bribery law, namely, elections. There are also legitimate reasons for political parties to collect funds from private actors—organization of political activity, the central purpose of a political party, is expensive.

The last two points weigh against blanket prohibitions on private contributions to political parties. Few jurisdictions come close to such broad prohibitions in their domestic law, and the United States certainly is not among them.[54] Some jurisdictions prohibit contributions to political parties in excess of a certain monetary value or anonymous donations.[55] Others prohibit or limit contributions from specific categories of donors, such as corporations, corporations doing business with the government, state-owned corporations, trade unions, or foreign interests.[56] Viewed in isolation then, the FCPA's prohibition on payments to political parties seems like a dramatic and unusual overextension of transnational bribery law. However, since the prohibition is subject to the FCPA's defense for payments that are lawful under local law, it is probably best understood as a relatively narrow and context-specific supplement to whatever prohibitions on party finance exist in local law.

Advantages and Things of Value for Other People

The UN Convention applies when an undue advantage is transferred to either a public official or a third party. Why does the prohibition extend to bribes that benefit third parties?

Some corrupt officials expect suitcases full of cash to be given to them directly. Other officials are more reluctant to dirty their hands. They prefer to have their bribes paid to some sort of intermediary. Sometimes, sadly, the intermediary is the state itself, that is, where resources given to the state are simply misappropriated by corrupt officials. The definition of bribery obviously is meant to cover transfers to intermediaries that are intended to be ultimately received by public officials. The challenge is typically to find conclusive evidence that such a transfer has taken place. To overcome this evidentiary challenge, it is useful to prohibit transfers to people such as friends, family, and business associates of public officials.

In some cases, however, the problem is not merely an evidentiary one. What if an official genuinely is content to allow friends or family members to enjoy advantages conferred by private actors without receiving anything whatsoever for himself? Take the case of Isabel Dos Santos, daughter of the president of Angola. In 2013, *Forbes* magazine estimated her net worth at $3 billion. According to *Forbes*, her wealth could be traced almost entirely to firms seeking to do business with her father's government that granted her ownership interests in the resulting telephone, oil, diamond, banking, and cement companies.[57] Or consider firms that have offered jobs to the children of high-ranking Chinese government officials, the so-called "princelings." Several prominent American banks have been investigated, and in a few cases sanctioned, for hiring princelings whose parents were in a position to direct business to them.[58] The children's jobs did not necessarily pay any more money than they would have earned elsewhere, although the prestige of working for a prominent Western firm doubtless provided a significant boost to their careers. More importantly for present purposes, even if the jobs provided material benefits for the princelings, there typically was no indication that any of those benefits flowed back to their parents. Most likely, the only benefit that flowed to the government officials was pride, or at least satisfaction, with the progress of their children's careers. Is that enough to qualify as the subject matter of a bribe?

Again, the issue here is how to balance the dangers of bribery against the dangers of discouraging socially beneficial transactions with friends, family, and associates of public officials. The danger on one side is clear: to the extent these transactions influence the decisions of public officials they raise all the dangers associated with more paradigmatic bribes. On the other side of the scales, there is no great social benefit in allowing members of an official's entourage to receive outright gifts of substantial value. But business opportunities and jobs, even lucrative ones, might be a different story. What if Isabel Dos Santos is highly sought after as a business partner because she is an extraordinarily talented businesswoman? What if the princelings are in fact the best candidates for their jobs? Overlap between friends, family, and associates of public officials on the one hand, and members of the business elite on the other hand, should not be surprising in societies in which educational and social opportunities are limited and, as a consequence, a relatively small group of people dominate both politics and business. In such societies it might be extremely damaging to use anti-bribery law to discourage business transactions with friends and family of public officials.

In the Exercise of Official Duties

The UN Convention says that to qualify as an element of a bribe, a favor must be provided "in the exercise of official duties." In practice, this tends to be a vague requirement because public officials' official duties often are not clearly specified, at least not by law. High-ranking officials may be assigned duties by particular statutes, but typically are subject to overriding general duties such as "to defend and protect the Constitution and the law" and to devote themselves to the service and well-being of the people. Elected officials typically have no specific duties other than to represent their constituents. In many cases, officials' behavior is governed by conventions, norms, or understandings that are not legally binding. For example, it may be conventional for elected officials to lobby administrative agencies on behalf of their constituents, but they have no legal duty to do so. The lack of clarity of this requirement is further exacerbated by the fact that even when the scope of official duties is clear, the phrase "in the exercise of" leaves room for doubt about what sort of relationship is required between the favor and the official duties.

Hard cases abound in this area. Particularly difficult cases are ones in which the favor consists of one official influencing the exercise of another official's duties. For example, an official might be paid to help encourage an official in another department, outside his authority, to award a contract to the payer. It is unlikely that either the recommendation or the procurement decision qualify as part of the official duties of the bribe recipient. But what if the recipient is likely to use his official powers either to reward or punish the second official? Does the recommendation then have a sufficient connection to his official duties? Or alternatively, what if the only favors provided consist of advice and introductions to the right people, but the information and connections being shared were developed in the course of official duties? Pieth et al. suggest that only the first case violates the OECD Convention's prohibition because it involves use of official powers as opposed "practical advantages" of an office.[59] The commentary to the OECD Convention suggests that in this scenario the transaction is prohibited if the first official has been paid to "use his office," albeit in a way that is outside his competence.[60] This does not resolve the question of what it means for the official to "use his office." The U.S. Supreme Court, confronted this issue in a domestic bribery case, *McDonnell v. United States*.[61] In that case the governor of Virginia (McDonnell) received approximately $172,000 in gifts in exchange for arranging meetings between a businessperson and various officials in his state's government. The Court concluded that these introductions did not count as "official acts" for the purposes of the domestic bribery statute, at least in the absence of evidence that the governor exerted pressure on the other officials.

Some foreign bribery statutes avoid these difficulties by relaxing the official duties requirement. The FCPA avoids almost all of these problems. It covers favors provided in the official's "official capacity" or "in violation of the lawful duty of such official," but also has a catch-all provision for favors that amount to "any improper advantage." The U.K. Bribery Act addresses the concern about duties specified by extralegal norms by referring to ordinary peoples' "expectations." To qualify as a bribe under the Act, the favor must involve improper performance of a "relevant function or activity." Improper performance means "in breach of a relevant expectation" (Section 4), and Section 5 says:

> . . . the test of what is expected is a test of what a reasonable person in the United Kingdom would expect in relation to the performance of the type of function or activity concerned.

What is at stake in defining the phrase "in the exercise of official duties"? Transactions outside the scope of an official's duties can still undermine public policy, so long as they affect the duties of some public official. These transactions also allow an official to earn private benefits by exploiting powers, relationships, or information that flow from their official position. This can stir resentment and create undesirable incentives to obtain official appointments. All of these considerations count in favor of either abolishing the official duties requirement or interpreting the concept of official duties expansively.[62]

On the other side of the ledger, the official duties requirement protects officials' freedom to engage in transactions that have nothing to do with their official position. Purely personal transactions, such as where an official rents out an apartment she owns, will be missing this element. Professional transactions that have nothing to do with the official's public duties, such as where a police officer is paid for moonlighting—out of uniform—as a security guard, will also lack the necessary connection to official duties, assuming that off-duty police officers are truly off-duty.

The official duties requirement also preserves officials' ability to serve constituents, which some might regard as their most important official duty. This was part of the Virginia governor's defense. He argued that he was elected on a mandate to help promote business, and that would include helping a local businessperson navigate the state bureaucracy. He and many other public officials argued that an expansive interpretation of the official duties requirement would discourage precisely the kinds of interactions demanded by the American system of representative government. The Supreme Court agreed. In a unanimous opinion, the Chief Justice pointed out how disruptive an expansive interpretation would be in settings where officials commonly (1) receive things of value such as food and entertainment or campaign contributions from their constituents, and (2) help individual constituents obtain favorable government actions.[63]

Incidentally, the Chief Justice went on to observe that in the U.S. system, states are regarded are sovereigns, and regulating the permissible scope of interactions between state officials and their constituents was an important prerogative of a sovereign state. For this reason he thought the federal government should be loath to get involved in "setting standards of good government for local and state officials."[64] The infringement on sovereignty is presumably even greater when the U.S. federal government sets standards of good government for a foreign country. We return to this issue in chapter 7.

Misuse of Official Position

A central concern about bribery is that it will induce officials to misuse their positions. If this is the only reason to be concerned, then paying an official to do his job properly should not pose a problem and should not be unlawful. This simple argument has a great deal of intuitive appeal, even though, as we will discuss in a moment, there are strong counterarguments.

To provide a concrete example, suppose that Joel Esquenazi's company, Terra, paid bribes solely to ensure fair treatment. In this hypothetical scenario Terra was in fact fully qualified to contract with Haiti Teleco, and Teleco's officials required it to pay fair market rates for access to their network. In other words, suppose that the Haitian officials accepted Terra's money but did not misuse their position in any (other) way. Should this still qualify as a form of bribery? Isn't a society entitled to condemn officials merely for profiting from their positions? Isn't condemnation appropriate, of the officials at least, if they induced the payments by making implicit threats to deny Terra the contract?

The law in this area is not always clear. We have already seen that the UN Convention's definition of bribery covers all sorts of favors. This is different from the OECD Convention, which says that the favor must be an "improper advantage." Business obtained or retained is conclusively presumed to constitute an improper advantage, regardless of whether the official was entitled to award the business to the bribe payer.[65] However, a favor that amounts to some "other improper advantage" must be "something to which the company concerned was not clearly entitled."[66] This is not quite the same thing as saying "something to which the company concerned was not entitled and that the official should not provide." The phrase "not *clearly* entitled" introduces ambiguity. What if a customs officer has unfettered discretion to waive an inspection of goods? A company that gives a customs officer a tip in exchange for a waiver may not have obtained something the official should not have provided, but has it obtained something to which it was clearly entitled?

A handful of countries, including most notably Germany[67] and Switzerland,[68] only punish bribery where the official's favor amounts to either a breach of his official duties or a discretionary act. The position under the FCPA is less clear. The FCPA, like other U.S. bribery statutes, requires proof that the defendant acted "corruptly." Some authorities suggest the word means "with intent to induce an official to misuse his or her position."[69] Other authorities reject this interpretation, suggesting that the term "corruptly" means something else, such as "with intent to obtain a quid pro quo"[70] or "with knowledge that the conduct is unlawful."[71]

So what are the competing policy considerations? Requiring proof of intent to induce an official to misuse his position raises practical obstacles to law enforcement. It invites defendants to claim that they bribed solely in order to induce the official to do his job properly. They will support their arguments with evidence that the bribe was necessary for this purpose, because the official was either lazy and unmotivated, or a greedy extortionist. Worse yet, they will try to support claims about the purity of their intentions with evidence that the bribed official did in fact use his position properly. Sifting through this kind of evidence is likely to be costly.

At the same time, transactions that are not intended to induce misuse of a government position can still be harmful. Recall the litany of pernicious ramifications of bribery that we rehearsed in chapter 5. Undermining public policy was only the first of several. There was also the problem of perceptions. An official who is paid for a ruling may well have ruled the same way without the payment, but it may be difficult to convince the general public that his judgment was untainted. As we have already seen, the perception of corruption may be as damaging as the reality. Then there is the concern about unjust distribution of wealth; independently of the merits of an official's action, the mere fact that they have benefited from their position is objectionable. Most problematic of all are the incentive effects: officials who collect benefits when they do what they are supposed to do have an incentive to avoid doing what they are supposed to do when no benefits are on offer. They also have the same incentives as other corrupt officials to engage in costly battles for positions in which they can benefit from corruption and then, most likely, to invest resources in concealing the proceeds.

There may be settings in which everyone knows and accepts that officials receive modest benefits directly from private individuals in exchange for doing their duty, and officials are sufficiently motivated to do their jobs properly—for whatever reason—that they ignore any perverse incentives. Under these conditions, bribes might be unproblematic. Outside of those settings, it is difficult to see why misuse of official position should be an element of the legal definition of bribery. Maintaining the requirement serves to increase the burden on enforcement agencies and to exclude a set of very problematic transactions from sanctions.

Quid Pro Quo

The paradigmatic bribe is a bargain, meaning that if the transaction is consummated there will be a "quid pro quo" relationship between the things given and received.[72] In U.S. law of contracts—the law of bargains—this kind of quid pro quo relationship is often described as one of "reciprocal inducement," meaning that the elements on each side of the bargain induce the provision of elements on the other side.[73] An alternative way of describing a quid pro quo relationship is to say that each side of the transaction satisfies a debt owed on account of the other side.[74] Therefore, a bribe involves a quid pro quo if its consummation entails a transfer of a thing of value that induces the provision of a favor which itself induces the transfer of the thing of value. Or perhaps more straightforwardly, some would say that a bribe involves a quid pro quo if the thing of value will be a payment for the favor and the favor will be a payment for the thing of value.

A transfer of a thing of value that is not expected to induce the provision of, or serve as payment for, any particular favor does not entail a quid pro quo. That kind of transfer fits the definition of a gift or gratuity, but not a part of a bargain. Take for example a payment to a public official—or, perhaps more plausibly, the provision of a nonpecuniary benefit like an all-expenses-paid trip to an exotic location—that is intended to produce a reservoir of goodwill but not to induce the provision of any specific favor. Even if the official eventually provides a favor, and even if that favor compromises public policy, the relationship between the transfer and the favor is relatively attenuated—perhaps so attenuated that the payer should not be considered legally or morally responsible for the favor's pernicious effects. Or so the argument would go. Similar issues arise in the case of a transfer made to an official in return for a past action if there has been no prior agreement to make the transfer. That kind of transaction is a reward or a tip, but not a quid pro quo bribe. The payer can resist condemnation on the grounds that he did not cause the provision of the favor, and the official can resist on the grounds that the favor was not provided in the hopes of personal gain.

The definitions of bribery in the UN Convention and the OECD Convention embody a quid pro quo requirement. Both instruments define a bribe as an undue advantage provided "in order that" an official provide a favor.[75] Several OECD countries, including Germany, Bulgaria, Greece, Luxembourg, Poland, and Switzerland, ignore this suggested requirement and prohibit rewards for official acts that have already been taken.[76] The FCPA is less clear on this point. Its anti-bribery provisions can be triggered by the transfer of anything of value for the purposes of "inducing" or "influencing" foreign officials to provide favors. These provisions clearly require a quid pro quo. However, other FCPA anti-bribery provisions are triggered by the transfer of anything of value to a foreign official "for the purposes of . . . securing any improper advantage." A reservoir of goodwill could be just such an improper advantage. The point is debatable because, as discussed previously, the improper advantage clause could be read to capture favors provided as part of a quid pro quo that happen to be unrelated to a public official's official duties. Further complicating matters, liability under the anti-bribery provisions always require that the payer act "corruptly," and according to some cases under the U.S. domestic bribery statute, this means that the payer must seek a quid pro quo.[77]

Quid pro quo is often difficult to prove. The challenge does not necessarily lie in uncovering the transfer of a thing of value or the provision of a favor. Parties to a bribe generally try to cover their tracks, but many of their actions, such as wire transfers or formal governmental actions, require the assistance of, and so can be recorded by, third parties. Recording facilitates detection. The problem with establishing quid pro quo is that it is not so easy to discover why people do what they do. Yet evidence of motivation—that a party was induced by the prospect of the other party's transfer or favor—is exactly what is required to establish a quid pro quo. In the face of a robust quid pro quo requirement, sophisticated actors will avoid explicit statements of their reasons for acting. All payments will ostensibly be gifts designed to cultivate goodwill. And all favors will be presented as spontaneous acts of service, unconnected to any past or future payments.

Relaxing the quid pro quo requirement will certainly help solve an underdetection problem and make it easier to sanction transactions that merit sanctions. This will also make it possible to sanction transactions that do not involve a quid pro quo but nonetheless cause problems because they are perceived to involve one.[78]

The argument against relaxing the requirement is the familiar risk of sanctioning socially beneficial transactions. Without a quid pro quo requirement, the potential for liability arises whenever a public official receives gifts from and provides favors to the same person, even if there is no connection between the two transactions. This kind of potential liability will discourage either gift-giving or the provision of favors, or both. The ramifications will depend on how expansively the law is defined along other dimensions. For example, imagine an anti-bribery regime designed to cover both campaign contributions and favors that involve no misuse of public office. Without a quid pro quo requirement, this regime will discourage elected officials from providing perfectly legitimate favors to campaign donors. This will be very disruptive in a country that expects elected officials both to finance their campaigns through private donations and to provide personalized services to their constituents—both of which are at least arguably socially beneficial practices. By contrast, imagine a regime that covers neither campaign contributions nor legal favors; it only captures direct monetary payments followed by a favor that involves misuse of public office. Elimination of the quid pro requirement will be less troubling under this alternative regime.

Business Nexus

The UN Convention draws a curious distinction between bribery of domestic, as opposed to foreign, public officials. In the case of foreign public officials it requires states to prohibit bribery only "in relation to international business." The OECD Convention has a similar limitation. The FCPA and most other statutes that supposedly implement these Conventions have a similar but slightly different structure: instead of saying that the transaction as a whole must be related to business, they require that the payer have a "business purpose."[79] For instance, the FCPA says that the offer, payment, and so forth must be made "in order to assist [the payer] in obtaining or retaining business for or with, or directing business to, any person."[80] At the same time, U.S. courts have defined this business purpose extremely broadly. In the leading case on point, the court decided that the business purpose requirement was satisfied by any payments that directly or indirectly assist in improving business opportunities. As a result, a company that paid bribes to reduce duties and taxes on imports of rice to Haiti, and thereby lowered its cost of doing business, could be held liable.[81] In practice, therefore, at least under the FCPA, the business purpose requirement operates much like a business nexus requirement (and is typically labeled as such).

Realistically speaking, most bribes paid by for-profit enterprises will have a business nexus. This does not mean that the business nexus requirement is innocuous. The requirement clearly excludes tourists who pay bribes to low-level officials, such as border agents or police officers, as well as prospective parents who bribe foreign public officials to help secure adoptions. It may also exclude refugees who have sex with employees of international aid organizations in order to obtain relief supplies.[82] Meanwhile, the status of bribes paid by not-for-profit organizations is unclear. We can be reasonably sure that an organization which pays bribes in order to reduce the cost of importing rice risks liability if it plans to sell the rice, but what if it plans to give the rice away to hungry refugees displaced by an earthquake? What if it plans to sell the rice below cost?

The underlying justification for the business nexus requirement is murky. It does not seem to have anything to do with the wrongfulness of the conduct at issue—what could be more wrong than paying a bribe to steal a child from her parents and native land, or demanding a bribe from a destitute refugee? The rationale for the business nexus requirement could have something to do with the fact that bribes with a business nexus tend to have an adverse effect on competing business entities. In most instances it will be safe to assume that some of those competitors will be located outside the jurisdiction of the official targeted for the bribe. The countries in which those competitors are based or located have a legitimate interest in implementing transnational bribery law to protect their interests. So perhaps, the business nexus requirement can be justified as a way to ensure the legitimacy of applying transnational bribery law to a transaction (as opposed to only the local law of the official's jurisdiction). This argument is not fully satisfying though; bribes paid in nonbusiness settings can have extraterritorial competitive effects as well. An example would be a bribe that allows one couple rather than another to secure a child for adoption.

The best way to understand the business nexus requirement is as a reflection of historical factors. The scandals that motivated the enactment of the FCPA all involved businesses, and in the aftermath of the FCPA, businesses subject to its provisions were the actors with the greatest interest in lobbying for the enactment of similar legislation in other countries. And when those countries adopted their own prohibitions on foreign bribery, it was, initially, at the insistence of the OECD, whose mandate is limited to regulation of business transactions.[83] To be clear, though, this historical analysis amounts to an explanation of the status quo, not a justification.

Extortion as a Defense

People accused of paying bribes often complain that they are victims rather than perpetrators of crime. From their perspective, the real perpetrators are the public officials who use the power of their office to extract bribes from innocent citizens. This argument is often met with an unsympathetic response. Enforcement officials often take the position that there is no excuse for bribery; when foreign public officials solicit bribes, businesspeople should "just say no."[84] However, a recent review found that several countries "grant immunity from prosecution to persons who engage in active bribery under threat, inducement, compulsion, coercion, duress, or intimidation by a public official."[85]

The intuition that there are cases in which bribe payers should be excused on account of "extortion" is difficult to escape. This is most evident in discussions of employees or agents of international humanitarian organizations who demand sexual favors from refugee women and girls in return for relief supplies. The entire conversation revolves around punishment of the humanitarian workers; it is taken for granted that the women or girls are victims and should be exempt from punishment.[86]

The intuition that certain forms of coercion excuse the bribe payer also appears in the context of international business transactions. Consider this rather puzzling passage from the U.S. Senate's Report on a draft of the FCPA:

> The defense that the payment was demanded on the part of a government official as a price for gaining entry into a market or to obtain a contract would not

> suffice since at some point the U.S. company would make a conscious decision whether or not to pay a bribe. That the payment may have been first proposed by the recipient rather than the U.S. company does not alter the corrupt purpose on the part of the person paying the bribe. On the other hand true extortion situations would not be covered by this provision since a payment to an official to keep an oil rig from being dynamited should not be held to be made with the requisite corrupt purposes. [emphasis added] S. Rep. 95-114, 10-11 (1977).

The thinly sketched vignette of an oil rig laced with dynamite is open to several interpretations, each of which suggests a different conception of the extortion defense. One interpretation is that the official is the person who has threatened to blow up the oil rig and the "bribe payer" is paying the official to take his finger off the switch. In this scenario the bribe payer's intention is to induce the official to do the right thing, or at least to avoid doing the wrong thing. This kind of payment seems more likely to uphold the rule of law than to corrupt or undermine it. Support for this interpretation comes from the way in which the passage contrasts the oil-rig payment with payments where the payer has a corrupt purpose. We know that many U.S. courts take the position that bribery is only possible if the defendant intends to induce a public official to misuse their official position, and they describe this intention as a "corrupt purpose." Perhaps the point of the hypothetical was to endorse and illustrate a logical implication of the corrupt-purpose-as-misuse-of-official-position requirement. However, aside from the vague reference to corrupt purposes, there is little in the Senate Report to support this reading. In fact, the report does not even state explicitly that the official controls the dynamite and that setting off the explosion will involve a misuse of his position.

Even if we treat the oil-rig hypothetical as an extreme example of a payment to induce an official to do the right thing, we should pause before exonerating the payer. Just because a payment is for a favor that involves no misuse of official position does not mean that it should be tolerated. We reviewed the arguments just a few pages ago. In this scenario there is no direct subversion of public policy, and the payer is not unjustly enriched. However, the official is unjustly enriched and so the payer's action generates incentives to seek out additional opportunities for extortion. Paying the official is like negotiating with terrorists: giving in to their demands only encourages them. It is not difficult to imagine that if we sum up the costs and benefits, the best way to minimize social harm, over the long term is to demand that people "just say no" to coercion in cases that do not involve threats of bodily harm.

The last sentence of the vignette emphasizes the fact that the situation involves extortion, and the structure of the passage contrasts the oil-rig payment with payments that involve "a conscious decision whether or not to pay a bribe." The implication is that in extortion situations, the decision to pay a bribe is not the product of an intentional decision and so does not merit condemnation. However, this argument is difficult to swallow because a victim of extortion typically does make a conscious decision whether to accede to a threat.

The Department of Justice and the SEC offer yet another interpretation of the passage from the Senate Report: they cite it in support of the proposition that a payment to remove an imminent threat to health and safety will not attract liability under the FCPA, implicitly assuming that there are people on the oil rig.[87] The U.S. enforcement agencies claim that a payment in these circumstances lacks corrupt intent and, oddly, a business purpose. They could have added that in such circumstances conventional principles of criminal law would allow the defendant to raise the defense of duress. The most accepted rationale for this defense is that it is wrong to condemn people for actions committed in the face of threats that deprive them of a fair opportunity to act lawfully.[88] Condemnation is said to be inappropriate in these cases either because the unlawful action represents the lesser of two evils or because the law should not condemn people for failing to exhibit extraordinary commitment to abiding by legal and moral principles. To the extent punishment is designed to achieve deterrence, a second rationale for the defense is sometimes advanced: punishment is pointless in these circumstances because few people will be deterred from succumbing to duress.[89]

If we reject the assumption that there are people on the oil rig, then the Senate Report is open to a more controversial interpretation: perhaps bribery is tolerable in these circumstances because dynamiting the rig would cause a loss of something of substantial value—other than life or limb—to which the payer is legally entitled. The passage from the report, read as a whole, arguably supports this view: the opening sentence mentions payments aimed at securing benefits, such as access to markets or contracts, and then contrasts them with a payment aimed at avoiding a loss. The reference to extortion suggests that the official who has made the threat is behaving improperly. The Department of Justice and the SEC, along with most U.S. federal courts, reject the idea that economic coercion can support a defense to a criminal charge of bribery.[90] This position tracks the contours of the traditional defense of duress, which has traditionally only excused conduct that is a reasonable response to an unlawful threat of death or serious bodily injury.[91] However, legislation in a few states, including New York, explicitly allows a person to escape liability for bribery if it resulted from coercion or extortion by a public official.[92]

If economic coercion is to serve as a defense to bribery, then it has to be justified on different grounds from the ones typically offered for the defense of duress. It is far from clear that paying a bribe represents the lesser of two evils as compared to suffering an economic loss, keeping in mind the potentially pernicious consequences of bribery discussed in chapter 5. And while it may be asking too much of ordinary people to expect them sacrifice life or limb for the sake of avoiding corruption, an economic sacrifice may not be too much to ask. This is especially true when the economic losses are suffered in the first instance by corporations, which can spread them across many stakeholders.[93] As for the deterrence rationale, it seems plausible that sanctions will deter a person from succumbing to a threat of economic loss, even if they would be undeterrable in the face of threats of physical harm. A person might risk a lifetime in prison to save a life, but not to save some money.

There is another rationale for excusing a person who pays a bribe in order to avoid a significant economic loss. Suppose that society as a whole will, on balance, be better off if people refuse to pay bribes in these circumstances. The distribution of costs and benefits ought to matter, not just the net sum. The costs of a "just say no" policy are borne almost entirely by the person who faces the immediate risk of coercion, the person whose oil rig will be blown up. The benefits flow to potential future victims, and everyone else in society who benefits from the marginal reduction in the prevalence of corruption attributable to diminution of corrupt incentives. Lawmakers might reasonably conclude that at some point this kind of sacrifice is too much to ask of any single victim. This argument is grounded in a distinctively egalitarian conception of fairness, which might be controversial. Moreover, the appeal of the argument in any given context will depend on the extent to which victims are risk averse and are able to spread their losses across other members of society, whether through issuing securities to large numbers of investors, or insurance, or some sort of publicly administered compensation scheme, or a lawsuit against the state that employs the official. In the context of transnational business it is eminently plausible that if a person is coerced by a public official in a foreign country, then the benefits of resistance will flow primarily to the inhabitants of the other country and will not be recaptured by the courageous victim.

Reporting as a Defense

Prior to the advent of the OECD Convention, in several countries a bribe payer who voluntarily reported the bribe to appropriate authorities automatically avoided criminal liability under the auspices of the "defense of effective regret." In some countries the defense included other elements besides voluntary reporting. For example, in the Slovak Republic the defense only applied if the official solicited the bribe and the bribe payer reported "without delay."[94]

It was not always clear whether the defense also shielded the bribe payer from noncriminal sanctions, such as confiscation of the proceeds of the bribe.[95]

The UN Convention expressly permits countries to provide immunity or mitigation of punishment to people who provide "substantial cooperation" in the investigation or prosecution of corruption offenses.[96] The defense of effective regret arguably fits within the space provided by this provision, although reporting need not amount to substantial cooperation. The OECD Convention says nothing about this topic, however, peer reviewers under the OECD Convention have repeatedly concluded that the countries which recognize the defense of effective regret are not in compliance with the OECD Convention.[97] As a result, the defense of effective regret no longer applies to foreign bribery offenses in any of the parties to the OECD Convention, although several countries allow prosecutors and/or judges to treat reporting as a basis for immunity or mitigation of punishment on a discretionary basis.[98]

The drawback of the defense of effective regret is that it exonerates people who have proven willing to violate the prohibition of bribery, conduct that clearly merits condemnation. This problem is exacerbated if the defense bars confiscation of proceeds of bribery, in which case it might also thwart the objective of compensation. These factors seemed to weigh heavily with OECD peer reviewers.[99]

The OECD peer reviewers' position assigns little weight to the potential benefit of the defense of effective regret. That benefit is straightforward: it promises to enhance detection of bribery by guaranteeing leniency to bribe payers who report misconduct; discretionary leniency provides less potent incentives to report.[100] The magnitude of this benefit depends on, first, whether reporting tends to increase the likelihood that other participants in the corrupt transaction will be sanctioned, and, second, the relative importance of sanctioning those other actors. Typically, the hope is that the report will facilitate sanctioning of public officials who solicit or accept bribes. OECD peer reviewers appear to be pessimistic about the prospect of this happening in the context of transnational bribery. As they have pointed out, although most countries are prepared to sanction their own officials for bribery, many countries are either unwilling or unable to sanction foreign public officials.[101] This means that reports of transnational bribery prompted by the defense of effective regret are only likely to be valuable if they are transmitted to an agency in another country, such as a corrupt official's home country, that is willing and able to impose sanctions.

OECD peer reviews have not cited any evidence one way or another on the likelihood that countries will follow up on reports from abroad of official corruption, and the limited publicly available evidence is mixed. For example, there are few indications that local officials follow up on allegations of corruption referred to them by the World Bank's investigators.[102] Nigeria's anemic response to the evidence of official corruption uncovered in the Bonny Island affair discussed in chapter 10 supports the pessimistic view. By contrast, in the *Siemens* and *Odebrecht* cases discussed in chapters 8 and 9, several countries followed up on allegations of official corruption that originated abroad.

De Minimis Transactions as an Exception

Some anti-bribery laws take the form of broad prohibitions followed by exceptions for specific conduct. Sometimes the exceptions are clearly motivated by the idea that though the conduct they describe is wrong, the associated harm is de minimis. The most famous exception of this sort is the FCPA's exception for "facilitating or expediting payments," also known as "grease" payments. The FCPA also contains an exception—technically, an "affirmative defense"—for payments "directly related to" promotion of products or services or performance of a government contract.[103]

The facilitating payments exception was added to the statute in 1988, although the legislative history suggests that Congress intended it to be implied in the requirements of corrupt intent and business purpose.[104] The exception is for any

> facilitating or expediting payment to a foreign official, political party, or party official the purpose of which is to expedite or to secure the performance of a routine governmental action by a foreign official, political party, or party official.[105]
>
> The accompanying definitions provide
>
> (4) (A) The term "routine governmental action" means only an action which is ordinarily and commonly performed by a foreign official in—
>
> (i) obtaining permits, licenses, or other official documents to qualify a person to do business in a foreign country;
> (ii) processing governmental papers, such as visas and work orders;
> (iii) providing police protection, mail pick-up and delivery, or scheduling inspections associated with contract performance or inspections related to transit of goods across country;
> (iv) providing phone service, power and water supply, loading and unloading cargo, or protecting perishable products or commodities from deterioration; or
> (v) actions of a similar nature.
>
> (B) The term "routine governmental action" does not include any decision by a foreign official whether, or on what terms, to award new

> business to or to continue business with a particular party, or any action taken by a foreign official involved in the decision-making process to encourage a decision to award new business to or continue business with a particular party.[106]

This exception has been interpreted narrowly by U.S. courts and enforcement agencies. The dominant view is that it only covers small payments for favors that do not involve misuse of an official's position, are performed by mid- or low-level officials, are largely nondiscretionary, and are included in the enumerated list of favors.[107]

The exception for facilitating payments is controversial. The UN Convention contains no equivalent exception. The OECD Convention initially contained a grudging endorsement of the concept—relegated to the official commentary[108]—but in a 2009 statement, the parties to the Convention signaled a retreat from even that position, recommending that member countries "review their policies and approach on small facilitation payments," citing their "corrosive effect."[109] A handful of countries have followed the lead of the United States in maintaining an explicit exception for facilitating payments.[110] In other countries, de minimis payments are not even caught by the basic prohibition on bribery, either because they are not considered to involve an undue advantage or the country only prohibits payments designed to induce misuse of an official's position.[111]

There is little doubt that facilitating payments are wrongful, especially once the incentive effects are taken into account. At the same time, it is clear that they often will be less problematic than other transactions that display more of the elements of a paradigmatic bribe. The only serious questions are whether facilitating payments are sufficiently benign to rule out legal sanctions (beyond those provided for by local law), and whether this sort of exemption from liability should be addressed by a general rule or on a case-by-case basis. The current skeptical outlook on facilitation payments recognizes that this is not the place for a blanket rule. Even if the definition of facilitating payments precisely captures payments that, on an individual basis, typically cause de minimis harm, it is far from clear that the decision to engage transnational bribery law should depend solely on the characteristics of the individual transaction; the characteristics of the parties and the relationship to other events might also matter. For instance, if a particular firm consistently pays bribes to jump the queue at customs, the resulting perception of impunity might have a sufficiently corrosive effect on either respect for the authority of the state or officials' performance incentives to merit legal intervention, even if isolated payments of the same sort could be tolerated. This example suggests that exemptions for transactions that cause de minimis harm are probably best granted through the exercise of discretion by enforcement agencies as opposed to legislated exceptions.

Even a narrower exemption, such as the FCPA's exemption for promotional expenses, presents these kinds of problems. The promotional expenses part of the exemption is apparently designed to capture cases such as where an official is reimbursed for expenses incurred in order to review a company's products or services. In some cases the transaction—payment for reviewing the company's product—involves no misuse of public office. In fact, it might qualify as a positively desirable use of the public official's time, to the extent it leads them to adopt innovative new products and service on behalf of the government. Nonetheless, even the most appealing examples of this sort of transaction raise some of the dangers associated with more classic forms of bribery: public officials should not be given incentives to review new products only when they receive private benefits. Again, it seems preferable to exempt this kind of conduct from sanctions on a discretionary basis.

Compliance with Local Law as a Defense

The upshot of this chapter is that when lawmakers decide how to define bribery for the purposes of transnational bribery law, they have to make decisions along many different dimensions. They also have to make a different set of decisions about whether, how and to what extent to align their preferred definition with the definitions chosen by other lawmakers. We will discuss the issue of who should be responsible for defining and enforcing transnational bribery law in chapter 7. For now, suffice it to say, a key issue is whether, and to what extent, to follow the lead of lawmakers with direct authority over a corrupt public official. In the case of bribery of foreign public officials, this issue translates into: Should the definition of bribery of a foreign public official be adjusted to exclude conduct that lawmakers in the public official's jurisdiction would not sanction?

The UN Convention makes no exception for conduct that is lawful under the laws of the jurisdiction represented by the public official being bribed. However, such an exception could be implicit in the fact that the UN Convention's prohibition only covers transactions in which the payer provides an "undue" advantage.[112] According to the Commentaries to the OECD Convention, which uses the identical term, bribery ought to be criminalized irrespective of "perceptions of local custom" or "the tolerance of such payments by local authorities," but not "if the advantage was permitted or required by the written law or regulation of the foreign public official's country, including case law."[113] Consistent with this language, the FCPA explicitly provides an affirmative defense if the payment "was lawful under the written laws and regulations" of the foreign official's country.[114] By contrast, the laws of Denmark and Norway track the text of the OECD Convention by prohibiting transactions that involve "unjustified" or "improper" advantages, but do not rule out the possibility of interpreting these terms by reference to unwritten local laws, customs, or practices.[115]

The scope of the local law defense depends on what counts as a local law for these purposes: which determinations, in what form, and by which lawmakers? The answers to these questions depend on how broadly courts and enforcement agencies interpret language such as "permitted or required," "lawful," and "written law." For instance, it seems clear that decisions that mitigate rather than eliminate liability will not qualify. It also seems clear that a series of decisions made in the exercise of prosecutorial or judicial discretion, without reference to any written policy, will not qualify. But how about written prosecutorial guidelines reflected in a consistent practice? Or guidelines on acceptable gifts issued by the Communist Party of China? And what does it mean to say that conduct is "lawful" or "permitted"? Can only *express permission* render conduct "lawful" or "permitted by written law" (the position of the OECD Working Group as well as U.S. enforcement authorities),[116] or is the absence of a prohibition sufficient (as suggested by the plain language of the OECD Convention)? Is the absence of a legal sanction enough to make conduct "lawful"?

On this last point, the term "lawful," as used in the FCPA, was interpreted narrowly in *U.S. v. Kozeny*.[117] The case involved allegations that bribes were paid to senior officials in the government of Azerbaijan. The defendant wanted to take advantage of the FCPA's local law defense on the grounds that he enjoyed immunity under the Azerbaijan Criminal Code. The Code protected payers of bribes in two scenarios: (1) when there was extortion, and (2) when the payer of a bribe voluntarily reported it. The U.S. court decided that neither branch of this provision triggered the FCPA's local law defense. The court framed the issue as whether local law made the payment lawful at the time it was made, the time at which FCPA liability would otherwise attach. According to the U.S. court, the Azeri law did not do that. The reporting defense obviously did not prevent a subsequently reported bribe from being lawful at the time it was made; it only seemed to operate retroactively to legalize payments that were subsequently reported. The U.S. court also refused to conclude that a bribe paid under extortion would be lawful, noting that the Azeri law referred to extorted payments as bribes. There was no direct support for the proposition that "bribe" was synonymous with "unlawful payment" under Azeri law. Earlier in its ruling, though, the court cited a damning resolution from the Supreme Court of the U.S.S.R., which it treated as an authoritative interpretation of the Azeri law. The resolution concluded: "[t]he absolution of a bribe-giver from criminal responsibility because of extortion of the bribe or the voluntary declaration of the giving of the bribe does not signify an absence in the actions of such persons of the elements of an offense. For that reason, they cannot be considered victims and are not entitled to claim restitution of the items of value given as bribes." In other words, payment of a bribe in response to extortion was not lawful under Azeri law, it was merely subject to different legal sanctions than other forms of bribery. We can only speculate what the result would have been if a court had been asked whether paying a bribe in response to extortion was "permitted" by written law in Azerbaijan.

In the end, whether or in what circumstances to defer to the decisions of local lawmakers about which conduct to sanction depends on many factors beyond the scope of the discussion in this chapter. Those factors include: what have local lawmakers in fact decided about the scope of legal sanctions; to the extent a transaction is subject to sanctions, which participants are liable to be sanctioned under the various legal regimes in play; what sanctions will be imposed; and how the relevant lawmakers compare in terms of motivations, competence, and legitimacy. The *Kozeny* case illustrates the complexity of this analysis. Whether or not it is appropriate to apply the local law defense in that case depends on the answers to questions such as: Was the U.S. court correct in concluding that Azerbaijan's lawmakers were open to legal condemnation of the bribe payers they exempted from liability? Was Azerbaijan's decision motivated by a desire to focus on prosecution of corrupt officials, as opposed to by the need to conserve scarce law enforcement resources or by the corruption of local legislators? What sorts of sanctions could and would be imposed on corrupt Azerbaijani officials, by agencies in either Azerbaijan or abroad? Are U.S. lawmakers motivated primarily by an altruistic desire to discourage high-level corruption in countries like Azerbaijan, or by more self-interested objectives such as condemning the payment of bribes by multinational firms connected to the United States? And, are U.S. lawmakers generally inclined to defer to good faith decisions made by adequately resourced local lawmakers?

Bribe Payers and Bribe Recipients

It takes two to make a bribe: a payer and a recipient. The UN Convention encourages countries to prohibit both "the promise, offering or giving" of bribes to, and "the solicitation or acceptance" of bribes by, foreign public officials. The U.K. Bribery Act follows this approach.[118] The OECD Convention and the FCPA, by contrast, only cover the conduct of bribe payers, and deliberately exclude recipients.

Money laundering laws can also be used to target bribe recipients. These laws prohibit dealings in proceeds of crime, and especially transactions designed to evade detection of the underlying misconduct. Several multilateral agreements require states to prohibit money laundering, and both the UN Convention and the OECD Convention explicitly require bribery of foreign officials to be treated as a predicate offense for money laundering.[119] In recent years U.S. authorities have used federal anti–money laundering laws (with bribery as a predicate offense) and, occasionally, state anti-bribery laws, to prosecute foreign public officials for engaging in transnational bribery. Cases in point are the prosecutions of the Haitian public officials who took bribes from Joel Esquenazi and his colleagues. In addition, authorities in several jurisdictions, and especially the United States, the United Kingdom, France, and Switzerland, have used money laundering laws to forfeit assets that represent the proceeds of bribery, including in some cases in which the officials were not prosecuted.

Should bribe payers and recipients suffer the same legal consequences? Since both payers and recipients are necessary parties to a bribe, they both "cause" any resulting harm. Their equal causal responsibility provides a prima facie reason for the law to treat payers and recipients symmetrically. Causal responsibility might not be the only determinant, however, of whether and how bribery-related misconduct ought to be sanctioned. Depending on *why* the law prohibits bribery, there may be reasons for asymmetric treatment of payers and recipients.

For instance, one category of actors may be more blameworthy than the other, which might be relevant if the law's objective is retribution. A variety of factors might determine relative blameworthiness. For example, the recipient might be a public official whose conduct violates a voluntarily sworn oath, while the payer has only fallen short of standards applicable to all private citizens. Or the payer might be a relatively poor person seeking a favor to which they are legally entitled, while the recipient is clearly not entitled to the bribe. Or the payer may be relatively wealthy, while the recipient needs the bribe in order to put bread on the table for her family.

If the aim of the law is efficient prevention, then other factors might justify asymmetric treatment. For example, granting immunity, or some other form of leniency, to one party or the other might be a step toward creating an incentive for them to report misconduct to enforcement authorities. This is the purpose behind Basu's proposal not only to grant bribe payers immunity (in cases that do not involve misuse of an official position) but also to allow them to recover the amount of the bribe from the recipient official.[120] Another possibility is that it is systematically more cost-effective to influence the behavior of payers than that of recipients, or vice versa. This kind of imbalance seems particularly likely if one category of actors generally has closer ties to the relevant legal system. For instance, it might be relatively costly to investigate and sanction foreign public officials as opposed to locally based payers. Or the relevant enforcement agency might have greater insight into strategies for dissuading or deterring local as opposed to foreign actors.

There are many other reasons why enforcement agencies might get more bang for their buck by targeting one type of wrongdoer as opposed to another. For example, if payers are more likely than recipients to be repeat offenders and there are fixed costs entailed in investigating and sanctioning each offender, then it will be relatively cost-effective to target payers. Each dollar spent discouraging a payer from bribery will prevent a larger number of bribes. The reverse is obviously true if recipients are more likely to be repeat offenders. If enforcement tends to result in incapacitation (or rehabilitation), then it also will be relatively cost-effective to target parties who are most likely to be repeat offenders.

Finally, what if compensation is the objective? Should the targets be payers or recipients? Here the answer seems straightforward. If the aim of the law is compensation, then it is difficult to justify categorical exclusion of liability for any offender who might be a source of recoveries.

Speaking of categorical exclusion, though, it is not obvious that systematic differences in blameworthiness or susceptibility to preventive measures justify categorical differences in treatment of payers and recipients. Even if the two categories of wrongdoers are different on average, there may be great variation within each category. For instance, even if most payers are more easily sanctioned than most recipients, some recipients may be readily amenable to sanctions. For example, both the Haitian officials bribed by Mr. Esquenazi appeared to have close ties to the United States—the Department of Justice described one as "of Miami and Haiti" and the other as "of Miramar, Fla."[121] This example shows that categories like payer and recipient generally shed little light on what sort of legal treatment is warranted for any given offender. For this reason it seems unwise to adopt rules that automatically treat payers and recipients differently.

If lawmakers do choose to treat bribe payers and their accomplices differently from bribe recipients and their accomplices, then they will have to confront a practical issue: some intermediaries arguably fit into both categories. For example, in the *Esquenazi* case, one of the intermediaries was a woman named Marguerite Grandison, a U.S. permanent resident who carried on her illicit business in her capacity as president of a Florida corporation called Telecom Consulting Services Corp. Grandison happened to be the sister of Jean Rene Duperval, one of the bribe-taking Haitian officials.[122] Grandison could easily be described as an agent of Esquenazi's company, Terra. But it is equally reasonable to say that she was acting on behalf of her brother, especially given that she helped several companies besides Terra to funnel bribes to him. It is artificial to say that Grandison was an agent or an accomplice of either the payer or the recipient; as an intermediary, her role was to act for both of them.

U.S. courts have held that because Congress deliberately drafted the FCPA's anti-bribery provisions to exclude foreign officials who receive bribes, those officials cannot be charged with conspiracy to violate the statute.[123] Does this mean that intermediaries who qualify as agents of foreign officials are also exempt from liability? The right answer is not obvious. The factors that weigh in favor of exempting foreign officials might also weigh in favor of exempting the intermediaries who assist them. Just like a foreign official, an intermediary may be a foreign national, based overseas, and overmatched by a wealthy and sophisticated multinational corporation. Or not. Again, this is not the place for a blanket rule.

Concealment as an Aggravating Factor

Joel Esquenazi's sentence was exceptionally harsh. Part of the reason is because he was charged with money laundering as well as violation of the FCPA. The money laundering charge was based on the efforts that he and his co-conspirators made "to conceal and disguise the nature, the location, the source, the ownership, and the control" of the proceeds of their unlawful activity.[124]

The UN Convention, as well as with several other international instruments, mandates that states criminalize concealment of proceeds of foreign bribery—along with many other offenses—as a form of money laundering.[125] Concealment of foreign bribery also can be characterized as a violation of accounting provisions. For example, under Canada's Corruption of Foreign Public Officials Act it is an offense to create false documents or misleading accounting books and records for the purpose of hiding bribery of a foreign public official.[126] In addition, efforts to conceal foreign bribery often lead to tax evasion—recipients have an incentive to refrain from declaring their illicit income, and payers who use routine expenditures as cover for illicit transactions will be inclined to flout rules against deducting bribe payments from taxable income.

It is not entirely obvious why concealment ought to lead to additional sanctions for a person who is already liable for foreign bribery,[127] especially if you take the view that concealment is an integral component of bribery. In fact, for a while several jurisdictions refused to allow a perpetrator of bribery to be convicted of laundering the resulting proceeds, on the theory that this kind of "self-laundering" is a natural consequence of the predicate offense.[128] Concealment does not seem to increase the harmfulness of bribery. If anything, concealment might make bribery less harmful; when corruption is hidden, it is unlikely to inspire emulation or delegitimize public institutions in the eyes of the public. The best argument for treating concealment as a grounds for additional sanctions presumes that the objective is deterrence. In order to deter, sanctions imposed on people caught engaging in misconduct have to be adjusted to reflect probability of detection, that is, the number of instances of misconduct that are not sanctioned—on the assumption that any given sanctions are less likely to deter if they are not certain to be imposed. If concealed transactions are less likely to be detected, then deterrence theory implies that they ought to be punished more severely.

Conclusions

Viewed from a distance, the anti-bribery regime is an astonishing display of moral and legal unity. It is built on a simple idea: hard-core Esquenazi-style transnational bribery is not only wrong but also ought to be prohibited by law. The UN Convention's provision on foreign bribery provides a template for constructing that legal prohibition, one that has won virtually global acceptance. And the template appears to be a model of simplicity: the UN Convention's provision is so compact and uses such simple vocabulary that it is difficult to imagine that it could ever be a source of complications.

As we zoom in for a closer look, the apparently simple structure reveals hidden dimensions. Virtually every word introduces another source of ambiguity. Intentionally? Public official? Undue advantage? In order that? Official duties? In relation to the conduct of international business? None of these terms is self-defining. Each one invites questions about where to draw a line between what is prohibited and what is permitted. And there are additional questions about whether and how to fill some of the silences in the Convention. Should there be exceptions for situations where the official is induced to do the right thing? What about extortion or de minimis transactions? There is no reason to believe that every legal system should or will arrive at the same answer to these questions. This raises yet another issue: If two legal systems choose different answers, should compliance with one jurisdiction's laws—say, the one where the official is based—be an excuse under the other jurisdiction's laws?

With all these potential margins for variation we should not expect the legal regimes built from the UN Convention template to be uniform. Each component requires a distinct set of judgments about the pros and cons of expanding or contracting the scope of liability. As the zone of liability expands beyond the paradigmatic case, how many more difficult-to-detect transactions will be captured? How many benign transactions will be caught? How important are they? What are the net benefits? Are the costs and benefits distributed fairly?

These judgments are about both facts and values. Ideally, laws crafted through a series of these judgments will be both effective and legitimate. To maximize the likelihood of that outcome, lawmakers will require data about the causes, consequences and prevalence of misconduct, as well as moral insight and authority.

7
Prohibitions that Extend Beyond Bribery

Introduction

As we have seen, the outer bounds of prohibitions of bribery are surprisingly difficult to demarcate. Legal officials sometimes are tempted to avoid the demarcation task altogether; instead of relying on prohibitions targeted at bribery, they rely on prohibitions that cover a broader range of conduct under the rubric of "fraud" or "improper accounting" or "illicit enrichment." This approach not only can make it easier to sanction the parties to bribes in the face of obstacles to detection, it can also capture actors who are not parties to the bribe but whose conduct increases the risk of bribery. To understand the risks this approach presents, we can conduct a thought experiment in which a prohibition on bribery is replaced with the broadest prohibition imaginable, one that simply covers "corruption." After identifying the relevant risks, we will turn to the pros and cons of resorting to prohibitions of fraud, risky accounting, or illicit enrichment instead of a prohibition of bribery.

The Risks of Broadly Worded Prohibitions

Imagine if we replaced the entire law of bribery, including all of the wrinkles surveyed in the preceding chapter, with a single law that prohibits "corruption," or perhaps, "corrupt practices."

Initially, the scope of this provision would be unclear, and so it would be left to enforcement agencies, and perhaps ultimately the courts, to give it meaning on a case-by-case basis. Would this be so bad? Most of us do not bother to refer to rules when we decide privately whether to condemn someone caught up in a scandal. Rather than relying on our lawyerly sense of whether rules have been broken, we rely on other senses: Does it "smell bad"? What are the optics? So perhaps we should take the same approach when deciding whether the legal system ought to condemn. This would be reminiscent of U.S. Supreme Court Justice Potter Stewart's refusal to define hard-core pornography in the context of a prosecution for obscenity. Justice Stewart said, "I know it when I see it." He clearly believed that his after-the-fact evaluation of conduct would be an adequate replacement for a definition provided before the fact.[1]

Between Impunity and Imperialism. Kevin E. Davis.

The "I know it when I see it" approach was problematic for obscenity law, and would be at least as problematic for anti-corruption law. Both due process and legitimacy generally weigh in favor of laws that specify prohibited conduct before the conduct occurs rather than afterward. Due process is an issue because advance specification of prohibited conduct will—so long as the specification is intelligible—make it easier for people to predict the legal consequences of their actions. Otherwise, their predictions will be based on guesswork about how legal officials will regard any given course of conduct. Legal predictability generally is considered to be an important underlying aspect of due process.

Advance as opposed to after-the-fact specification also typically allows different sets of people to participate in the process of deciding what conduct should be prohibited. When a prohibition is given content before the fact, legislators or regulators are typically involved. When a prohibition is given content after the fact, the decision is made by enforcement agencies. In most political systems, rules established by legislators and regulators are considered to be more legitimate than those set by enforcement agencies. In democratic societies this is because legislators typically are more directly accountable to the people.

Avoiding the problems inherent in case-by-case definition is only one of the challenges associated with broad prohibitions. Another challenge is to formulate a definition of prohibited conduct that captures an appropriate range of conduct, avoiding both underbreadth and overbreadth. This is more difficult than one might think. Consider, for example, the two most popular definitions of "corruption." The World Bank defines corruption as: "abuse of public office for private gain."[2] Meanwhile, Transparency International, speaks of "abuse of entrusted power for private gain."[3] Although they might at first glance seem quite broad, neither of these definitions does a good job of covering even the full range of conduct captured by the UN Convention's definition of bribery. In the first place, since they focus on the conduct of people in power—as opposed to transactions involving such people—both the World Bank and Transparency International ignore people who induce or abet abuses of entrusted power by, for instance, paying bribes.[4] In addition, since they are limited to cases involving "abuse" of power, both definitions appear to exclude cases in which there has been no misuse of an official position, such as a bribe paid for a favor to which the payer is already entitled. Therefore, a prohibition of corruption based on either the World Bank or Transparency International definition would suffer from a severe problem of underbreadth.

More broadly drafted prohibitions run the risk of overbreadth. For instance, suppose we expanded upon the World Bank and Transparency International definitions of corruption and were to prohibit involvement in "any transaction that involves use of entrusted power for private gain in a way that creates the potential for misuse." This transaction-oriented prohibition would capture all sorts of bribery, but would make no exceptions for commercial bribery, common forms of campaign finance, payments that result from extortion, or de minimis transactions. As we have seen in chapter 6, there are reasonable grounds for exempting some or all of these classes of conduct from legal sanctions.

Even if it avoids overbreadth, any prohibition that is broad enough to capture several different kinds of socially harmful behavior raises another concern: lack of precision. This kind of law will not distinguish transactions that might have very different social, economic, political, and moral ramifications and merit very different legal responses. For instance, the transaction-oriented prohibition of corruption set out above does not distinguish gains that officials receive by misappropriating money or property (embezzlement), receiving a payment from a third party (bribery), conferring a benefit upon a business in which the official has an interest (conflict of interest), or providing a nonpecuniary benefit to a friend or family member (nepotism). These may all qualify as forms of corruption, but the law should not necessarily treat them similarly. For example, conflicts of interest that are not associated with clear evidence of actual misuse of entrusted power are probably, in general, less harmful than embezzlement and bribery. It might dilute the impact of anti-corruption law to treat instances of hard-core bribery and conflicts of interest as the same offense. Or, to provide another example, embezzlement by a public official typically causes a quantifiable amount of harm to a readily identifiable victim—the state—and so might be appropriately tackled with civil liability. As we have seen, bribery often causes relatively diffuse harm and so is less amenable to regulation through civil liability.

As we shall see, these concerns about unpredictability, after-the-fact lawmaking, under- or overbreadth, and imprecision arise in connection with other sorts of broadly worded prohibitions.

Prohibition of Fraud as Opposed to Bribery

In some legal systems the offense of fraud is defined broadly enough to capture a wide range of transactions that involve misuse of entrusted power. For example, in U.S. federal law the principal fraud offenses encompass virtually any sort of "scheme or artifice" that deprives victims of money, property, or "the intangible right of honest services," and bribery is considered to be a paradigmatic example of a "scheme or artifice to deprive another of the intangible right to honest services."[5] Several of the foreign bribery cases discovered prior to the enactment of the FCPA, including the *United Brands* case, resulted in prosecutions under U.S. fraud statutes.[6]

Repurposing general fraud offenses to cover foreign bribery raises concerns about after-the-fact lawmaking and imprecision similar to the ones we have already discussed.[7] In most jurisdictions, statutes that criminalize fraud predate legislation criminalizing foreign bribery, and in many cases the anti-fraud statutes were enacted in a time when foreign bribery was entirely lawful. It seems illegitimate for enforcement agencies and judges to reinterpret criminal statutes to capture conduct that was not considered to be wrongful when the statutes were enacted.

As for imprecision, the main concern in this context is that treating foreign bribery as a variety of fraud might distort the definition of fraud used in cases that do not involve foreign public officials. For instance, in order to capture foreign bribery as a form of fraud, it might be helpful to interpret the offense of fraud to include conduct with only minimal connections to the enforcing state. This might be appropriate in cases of bribery of foreign public officials, where there is an international consensus around prohibition, but not for conduct where opinions are more divided, such as, for example, commercial bribery.[8]

Prohibition of Risky Accounting Practices

Broad prohibitions on risky accounting practices are another alternative to prohibitions on bribery. In addition to targeting bribery directly, the UN Convention and the OECD Convention encourage, but do not require, states to prohibit poor financial accounting. The relevant passage of the UN Convention, Article 12.3 states:

> In order to prevent corruption, each State Party shall take such measures as may be necessary, in accordance with its domestic laws and regulations regarding the maintenance of books and records, financial statement disclosures and accounting and auditing standards, to prohibit the following acts carried out for the purpose of committing any of the offences established in accordance with this Convention:
>
> (a) The establishment of off-the-books accounts;
> (b) The making of off-the-books or inadequately identified transactions;
> (c) The recording of non-existent expenditure;
> (d) The entry of liabilities with incorrect identification of their objects;
> (e) The use of false documents; and
> (f) The intentional destruction of bookkeeping documents earlier than foreseen by the law.[9]

The OECD Convention (Article 8) contains similar provisions, and the 2009 Recommendation offers more detailed guidance.

These provisions are designed to encourage states to adopt analogues to the FCPA's two accounting provisions.[10] Those provisions apply solely to publicly traded U.S. firms. One of the provisions imposes liability for failure to "devise and maintain" a system of "internal accounting controls" that is "sufficient to provide reasonable assurances" that transactions are authorized by management, properly recorded, and audited at reasonable intervals. The other provision imposes liability for failing to keep "books, records and accounts" which, "in reasonable detail, accurately and fairly reflect the transactions and dispositions of the assets of the [firm]." Under the books and records provision it is irrelevant what kind of accounting system the firm had in place; all that matters is whether the books, records, or accounts meet the prescribed standard. Unfortunately, it is not entirely clear what counts as a "book or record," which transactions are covered, or what standard the books, records, or accounts must meet.

The FCPA's accounting provisions were aimed at firms that create slush funds hidden from view of senior management and shareholders, inspired by the revelations from the SEC's post-Watergate inquiry into improper corporate payments. Over time, the two provisions have become the workhorses of the U.S. enforcement agencies. In fact, they are regularly used to sanction publicly traded firms for mismanagement, even in cases where no bribery is suspected. When foreign bribery is suspected, the accounting provisions allow enforcement agencies to impose liability even when they cannot prove that payments made to intermediaries are destined for foreign public officials. U.S. enforcement agencies also resort to the accounting provisions when a U.S. issuer, or even a subsidiary whose accounts are consolidated with those of the issuer, pays bribes outside of U.S. territory in a way that places the transaction outside the geographic scope of the FCPA's anti-bribery provisions.

Most OECD countries prohibit risky accounting practices, although they do not necessarily cover all possible types of legal entities or impose criminal sanctions for violations. The prohibitions can take different forms. In Germany, for example, enforcement agencies and courts have creatively interpreted the offense of breach of trust to cover situations in which an agent of an enterprise places substantial assets in "concealed funds" to be used for the purposes of bribery.[11] Some countries impose important prerequisites to criminal liability for accounting violations. For example, the relevant provision of Canada's Criminal Code only applies to accounting practices that are shown to be for the purpose of either committing or hiding bribery.[12] Since this provision is triggered only by proof of bribery, it does nothing to address the problem of underbreadth.

A good illustration of the FCPA's accounting provisions in action is the case that the U.S. SEC brought against Oracle Corporation in 2012.[13] Oracle is a California-headquartered publicly traded company. It sold software in India through an Indian subsidiary, Oracle India, and a network of local distributors. Some of the end users of the software were Indian governments. The SEC alleged that employees of Oracle India created off-the-books funds by allowing its distributors to keep unusually high portions of the difference between the price that Oracle charged to the distributor and the final price that the distributor charged to the end user. For example, after one $3.9 million sale to a government ministry, Oracle India employees told the distributor to remit $2.1 million, keep $151,000 as payment for its services, and hold $1.7 million for "marketing development purposes." The marketing and development fund was then used to pay eight fictitious vendors based on fake invoices. While there were obvious grounds for suspicion that the funds were used to pay off government officials, there was too little evidence to make a case for violation of the FCPA's anti-bribery provisions. Plus, the United States would have found it difficult to assert jurisdiction over Oracle India and its employees.

By contrast, the dealings were relatively easy to characterize as accounting violations. In this particular transaction, the balance sheet of Oracle India failed to reflect an asset, the slush fund, and the firm's income statement failed to reflect a set of expenses, namely, the payments to the fictitious vendors. The SEC also criticized Oracle for failing to install internal accounting controls that would have prevented Oracle India's employees from creating and misusing these sorts of slush funds. In its complaint, the SEC argued that Oracle should have required transparency in, or at least audited, both the prices their distributors charged to end users and third-party payments made by distributors on Oracle India's behalf. The SEC attributed all these accounting violations to Oracle India's U.S. parent, over which it clearly had jurisdiction, at least in part, because their financial statements were consolidated.

The FCPA's accounting provisions strike a delicate balance between countering some of the evidentiary and jurisdictional problems that might lead to underbreadth and avoiding the dangers of overbreadth. Strictly speaking, they offer only a partial response to underbreadth because they do not, of course, capture bribes that are properly recorded and accounted for. But those are, presumably, uncommon. At the same time, prosecutions under the accounting provisions avoid at least one of the potential drawbacks of overbreadth. They do not lump risky conduct together with hard-core bribery and so pose little risk of diluting the symbolism of anti-bribery law.

When it comes to overbreadth, the main danger of using the accounting provisions to expand the scope of anti-bribery provisions is the risk they will be used to capture relatively benign managerial lapses and thereby encourage managers to make excessive investments in monitoring, recording, and oversight. This is a live issue in the aftermath of the *Oracle* case. It is undoubtedly expensive for firms to monitor the pricing policies of their distributors, and this kind of monitoring could even help a firm like Oracle to stifle competition among its distributors, which would be costly for society as a whole. These costs have to be weighed against the benefits of reduced bribery.

Illicit Enrichment

Article 20 of the UN Convention encourages, but does not require, parties to criminalize intentional illicit enrichment, which it defines as "a significant increase in the assets of a public official that he or she cannot reasonably explain in relation to his or her lawful income."[14] By 2010, more than forty countries, almost all relatively poor, had enacted criminal prohibitions on illicit enrichment.[15] However, in several countries, critics have opposed the enactment of prohibitions on illicit enrichment, citing concerns about constitutional guarantees of the presumption of innocence and protection against self-incrimination.[16]

For bribe recipients, prohibitions on illicit enrichment are the analogues to prohibitions on improper accounting for bribe payers. Both sets of prohibitions essentially target the kinds of financial machinations that help to conceal bribery. Imposing legal sanctions for illicit enrichment is a straightforward way of addressing the difficulty of detecting corrupt transactions. With this kind of prohibition in place, the onus is no longer on enforcement agencies to prove that illicit transactions have taken place; instead the onus shifts to public officials who have accumulated large amounts of assets to prove that they were acquired through lawful means. The value of this kind of boost in law enforcement capacity depends on the prevalence of corrupt practices, as well as enforcement agencies' alternative means of addressing the problem of underdetection.

These kinds of prohibitions are burdensome for public officials, in at least two ways. First, there is the burden of sharing information about personal financial transactions. Some people might see this as an undesirable invasion of privacy. A second kind of burden is borne by public officials who do not do anything unlawful but are held liable because they are unable to "reasonably explain" the source of their wealth. The risk of this kind of "wrongful conviction" is heightened in countries with relatively corrupt or incompetent enforcement agencies.[17]

Is it appropriate to burden public officials with potential liability for illicit enrichment? Is a prohibition of illicit enrichment overbroad in the sense that it captures conduct that should not be sanctioned? Fairness to public officials is not the primary concern here. Public officials arguably consent to bearing these burdens when they take up or decide to remain in their positions. The more serious concern is efficiency: Do the benefits of prohibitions on illicit enrichment outweigh the costs? Here it is important to keep in mind that although the costs are initially borne by public officials, ultimately some of them will be borne by society as a whole—as public service becomes more burdensome, the state will have to either increase public officials' remuneration or risk losing good people.

Illicit enrichment also is problematic because it is so imprecise. A prosecution for illicit enrichment is likely to treat similarly situated officials with similar amounts of unexplained wealth in the same way. However, corrupt transactions that yield similar financial returns for the officials involved might take very different forms—for example, bribery as opposed embezzlement—have very different social ramifications, and merit different legal responses. Imagine, for example, if the Haitian officials involved in the *Esquenazi* case discussed in chapter 6 had been prosecuted solely for illicit enrichment. The prosecutors would not have had to identify any of the officials' co-perpetrators, namely, the bribe payers. There also would have been no need to determine the nature or type of harm caused by the misconduct. Consequently, there would have been little impetus to prosecute the bribe payers and to quantify the harm suffered by Haiti Teleco and its customers. In short, enforcement of a prohibition on illicit enrichment, as compared to a prohibition against bribery, might have led to a very different—and less robust—set of legal responses.

Conclusions

Transnational bribery can be tackled either with dedicated anti-bribery laws or broader laws that prohibit fraud, improper accounting, or illicit enrichment. Broader prohibitions can, if crafted with sufficient care, address the problem of underbreadth that undermines the effectiveness of prohibitions limited to bribery. However, if those laws are drafted in too open-ended a fashion, they can lead to unpredictability and illegitimate after-the-fact lawmaking. In addition, the effectiveness of broad prohibitions can be compromised by overbreadth and imprecision.

8
When Should Organizations Be Liable for Transnational Bribery?

Introduction

Who should be the targets of transnational bribery law? Transnational bribery almost invariably consists of transactions between individuals who work on behalf of relatively large organizations, often subject to multiple layers of supervision: bribe payers work for multinational corporations; bribe recipients work for states or international organizations; and money launderers work for financial institutions, law firms, and accounting firms. Which of these organizations should be targeted for sanctions?

The OECD paradigm and its associated every-little-bit-helps approach to anti-bribery law call for the net of liability to be cast widely, not only over individual perpetrators but also over the organizations they represent. It is commonplace for plaintiffs and enforcement agencies to try to pin liability—whether criminal, civil, or administrative—on entities that hire individual bribe payers. Some go further and target companies that own, merge with, or acquire those entities. There have even been moves to sanction states whose officials have solicited or accepted bribes, including by barring recovery of compensation from the bribe payer.

The modern approach to targeting is far removed from the approach taken under imperial anti-corruption law. The focus in imperial times was on making examples of high-profile individuals, even when it was clear that wrongdoing was collective. When Edmund Burke took aim at Warren Hastings, he reasoned, ". . . if you strike at him you will not have need of a great many more examples; you strike at the whole corps if you strike at the head."[1] The modern approach would be to strike at the corps through its organizational embodiment, the East India Company.

There are several plausible justifications for a more expansive approach to organizational liability, all of which are based in considerations of effectiveness and efficiency. Organizations that employ individual perpetrators, either directly or indirectly, arguably are sufficiently culpable to merit condemnation if they are in a position to prevent misconduct and fail to take reasonable steps to do so, especially when they stand to benefit. They are also capable of effectively

Between Impunity and Imperialism. Kevin E. Davis.

preventing misconduct through cost-effective self-regulation, that is, thwarting or detecting and sanctioning misconduct on the part of their employees, agents, and trading partners. In advanced economies, an entire "compliance industry" has emerged to help organizations self-regulate. Last but not least, commercial organizations may have benefited from the misconduct, and in any event they typically have deeper pockets than individual wrongdoers and so are relatively well placed to provide compensation.

At the same time, expansive organizational liability raises several important concerns. If organizations are easier to sanction than individual perpetrators, then prosecutors and plaintiffs might be distracted from pursuing the individuals. Moreover, unless the liability regime is carefully designed, it will create an incentive for its targets to cover up instances of past misconduct. Both these possible side effects of organizational liability threaten the effectiveness of the overall anti-bribery regime. In addition, imposing liability on a large organization, whether it is a multinational engineering company or a state like Argentina, runs the risk of hurting innocent stakeholders—such as employees, suppliers, customers, and citizens—which seems unfair. On top of all this, there is no guarantee that self-regulation will be efficient, meaning that organizational liability might cause overall regulatory costs to increase rather than decrease. This seems especially likely if the costs of novelty are taken into account: it typically will be relatively costly to introduce a completely novel approach to organizational liability for transnational bribery into a legal system which embraces different approaches to organizational liability in other spheres. Finally, there are concerns about whether the kinds of private regulation promoted by the OECD paradigm are legitimate.

Debates about the proper scope of organizational liability for serious misconduct—often framed as disagreements about corporate criminal liability—have long preoccupied scholars and policymakers.[2] In the domain of transnational bribery law, proponents of an expansive approach to corporate liability currently have the wind in their sails. The U.S. approach is considered exemplary. It combines expansive liability with a sophisticated set of guidelines for mitigation through the exercise of prosecutorial discretion. It is held up as a best practice by U.S. enforcement agencies, the OECD, and influential scholars, and other countries are encouraged to adopt functional equivalents (which need not be criminal). By contrast, although commentators occasionally advocate the expansion of state liability for transnational bribery, there appears to be little support among policymakers.

The anti-imperialist paradigm challenges this emerging consensus around the expansive approach to corporate liability. Rather than proposing or defending an alternative approach, it questions the very idea that there ought to be a consensus. The underlying argument is simple. Given the variety of contexts in which organizational liability is applied, and the range of competing considerations, there is unlikely to be a uniquely optimal approach.

In this chapter we begin by using the *Siemens* case to show the expansive approach in action. We will then briefly survey the legal doctrines that govern organizational liability. After setting out the traditional justifications for organizational liability, we will turn to the main concerns about taking an expansive approach and the case for rejecting a one-size-fits-all approach to the issue. Questions about what sanctions ought to be imposed are postponed until the next chapter.

Siemens

The every-little-bit-helps approach was exemplified in the *Siemens* case, a landmark in the history of transnational bribery law. The case hit the headlines in December 2008 when Siemens, a multinational enterprise based in Germany, together with some of its affiliated companies, reached settlements with the U.S. and German enforcement agencies and agreed to pay $1.6 billion in monetary sanctions.[3] At the time Siemens was one of the world's largest private firms. It had around 400,000 employees and did business in 191 countries, operating through over 1,800 legal entities. Its major product lines included equipment and systems used in mass transit, telecommunications, and the power sector. It also produced medical equipment and industrial software. Its customers were themselves invariably large organizations, including many governments.[4]

Bribery was an integral part of Siemens's business model. The company made corrupt payments around the world, in many different business units, over the course of decades. In the period between 2001 and 2007, payments identified as intended in whole or in part as corrupt payments to foreign officials totaled $805 million.[5]

Corruption on this scale required an elaborate set of supporting practices and procedures. Siemens employees routinely circumvented internal accounting systems supposedly designed to prevent, and if not prevent, to detect, corrupt payments. Payments were routed through accounts in countries with strong bank secrecy laws to a network of shadowy "business consultants" and backed up by invoices for services rendered—or not—pursuant to sham consulting or agency agreements. On many occasions, when the rules called for two authorizations, managers decided that one would do. Signatures of approval were marked on removable Post-it notes to protect the identities of guilty parties.[6]

Unsurprisingly, officials at the highest levels of the firm, up to and including the CEO, chief financial officer, and general counsel, were aware of the deficiencies in Siemens's compliance systems. When, as part of its internal investigation, the company offered amnesty to employees with information about corruption, over one hundred employees came forward.[7]

In the early 2000s, Siemens's dealings with its government clients became the subject of investigations in multiple countries, and eventually the German authorities began to investigate. Early in the morning of November 15, 2006, two hundred officers launched coordinated raids on Siemens's headquarters in Munich, as well as on the homes of several of its executives. Shortly afterward, the U.S. authorities opened their own investigation. Many of the countries whose officials were bribed also opened or continued their investigations into Siemens's conduct.

The U.S. and German enforcement agencies devoted a great deal of effort to making cases against individual Siemens employees and agents. In Germany, the Munich prosecutors pursued executives responsible for finance and accounting in the telecommunications unit. In the United States, the Department of Justice (DOJ) and the SEC targeted a set of managers and intermediaries directly involved in a scheme to bribe Argentine public officials in order to obtain a contract to produce national identity cards. The typical charges were bribery, fraud, and money laundering, or, alternatively, conspiracy to commit one of those offenses.

Cases against the public officials who received bribes from Siemens were generally pursued by enforcement agencies in their own countries—that is, if the officials were pursued at all. For example, in Israel, several senior employees of the public electric company were criminally prosecuted.[8] In China, Shi Wanzhong, a former senior executive of China Mobile, received a suspended death sentence for taking bribes from Siemens.[9] In Bangladesh, the sons of the former prime minister and one of his fellow ministers were sentenced to prison.[10] In Argentina by contrast, an investigating magistrate brought charges against several former employees and agents of Siemens but no public officials.[11]

These proceedings against individual perpetrators were not, however, what made the *Siemens* case a watershed in the history of transnational bribery law. The case was remarkable because of the way in which the net of liability stretched beyond individuals directly involved in misconduct to include the legal entities that employed them. The U.S. and German authorities sanctioned Siemens AG, the parent company of the Siemens group, as well as its telecommunications unit and subsidiaries in Argentina, Bangladesh, and Venezuela.[12] The U.S. sanctions were criminal and civil in nature.[13] German law does not provide for corporate criminal liability, and so in Germany the corporate sanctions were imposed under provisions of the Administrative Offences Act.[14]

Following the proceedings in the United States and Germany, regulators in several countries whose officials received payments, including Brazil, Israel,

Italy, and Nigeria, launched proceedings against a range of companies and individuals affiliated with Siemens. Meanwhile in the civil courts, Siemens sued or threatened to sue eleven former members of its Managing and Supervisory Board, and ultimately settled with all of them, recovering a total of €22.5 million, plus about €100 million from insurers that provided coverage for liability of directors and officers.[15] Along the way, the company won a pathbreaking ruling from a Munich court, which confirmed that one of the two board members who forced the company to sue him before settling (the former chief financial officer), had breached his supervisory duties by failing to ensure that the company had an adequate compliance system.[16]

There was no effort to sanction any of the states whose officials received payments from Siemens, even though several of them were known to be thoroughly corrupt during the period covered by the U.S. charges. Argentina was a prime example.[17] The U.S. DOJ charged that between 1997 and 2007 Siemens Argentina made over $100 million in illicit payments to obtain and retain a contract to produce national identity cards. The contract was signed during the famously corrupt administration of Carlos Menem. After a change in government, Argentina canceled the contract. This prompted Siemens to bring a claim against Argentina before an international panel of arbitrators, arguing that the cancellation violated Siemens's rights under a bilateral investment treaty. One of Argentina's defenses was that the contract was unenforceable because it was procured corruptly. This defense initially went nowhere because Argentina lacked supporting evidence, at least until Siemens's settlement with the DOJ and the accompanying admissions of guilt. Siemens withdrew its claim soon after the settlement was published, even though the arbitration proceedings to that point had gone in its favor. This decision in effect meant that Argentina escaped legal sanctions for its role in the scandal. Siemens could have tried to maintain its claim against Argentina, on the theory that the government's complicity in the corruption barred the Argentine state from raising corruption as a defense to enforcement of the contract. Siemens even could have argued that Argentina's complicity in itself amounted to a breach of the investment treaty, which included obligations to treat companies like Siemens fairly and not arbitrarily. Instead, the Argentine state emerged from the proceeding characterized as the victim of the corrupt transaction rather than a party it.

The *Siemens* case squarely raises the central issues that concern us in this chapter. First, why were so many private organizations targeted, in addition to the culpable individuals? Second, why did the list of organizational targets not include states like Argentina (or Bangladesh, etc.) whose officials solicited or accepted bribes? We have already seen that the concept of a perpetrator of bribery can cover virtually any person who knows or should know that they have taken affirmative steps toward causing harm. Is there any justification for expanding the set of potential defendants to reach organizations? And if there is a justification, does it apply to states whose officials accept bribes?

The Law of Organizational Liability

Before turning to possible justifications for organizational liability, it is important to understand how it works. In other words, under what circumstances can an organization be liable, either criminally, civilly or administratively, for foreign bribery?

The major anti-corruption treaties insist on liability for private firms. The UN Convention requires its parties to ensure that "legal persons" can be held liable for "participation in" offenses such as foreign bribery and money laundering and that legal persons are subject to "effective proportionate and dissuasive" sanctions.[18] The text of the OECD Convention is very similar, but that Convention only provides for liability for legal persons who are payers of bribes.[19] The OECD Working Group on Bribery has placed a great deal of pressure on countries to comply with this particular obligation and has emphasized the importance of extending liability to entities owned or controlled by the state.[20] These treaty provisions do not necessarily require countries to impose criminal liability on legal persons. This was deliberate because many countries historically embraced the principle *societas delinquere non potest* (a company cannot commit a crime). Nonetheless, most members of the OECD Convention have chosen to satisfy their treaty obligations by implementing corporate criminal liability, sometimes exclusively for foreign bribery.

States probably are not intended to be covered by the term "legal persons," so the treaty provisions cannot reasonably be interpreted to mean that states themselves—as opposed to entities owned or controlled by the state—should be liable for participation in foreign bribery. However, there are at least three paths through which states might be liable, or at least suffer adverse legal consequences, because their officials have participated in bribery.[21] First, the UN Convention obliges states to develop and implement "effective" measures to prevent corruption.[22] A single instance of a public official either paying or soliciting a bribe should not count as breach of such an obligation, but multiple instances might put the state in breach and, in principle, make it liable to provide compensation to states harmed by the breach. Second, if a state's public officials solicit or accept bribes, they might put the state in breach of obligations owed to foreign investors under international law. Bilateral investment treaties and customary international law typically require states to treat foreign investors fairly and equitably and not arbitrarily or unreasonably. Soliciting or accepting a bribe arguably is unfair, inequitable, arbitrary, and unreasonable, especially if the solicitation includes a threat to deny someone their legal rights. Third, many legal systems have doctrines that strip a person who is implicated in misconduct of legal rights or privileges that he, she or it would otherwise enjoy. A state which is complicit in bribery perpetrated by its officials might be barred from seeking redress from other actors, whether by bringing suit against a bribe payer for damages[23] or by seeking restitution in a criminal proceeding.[24] Similarly, as suggested above in connection with Siemens's claim against Argentina, the state might lose the right to raise corruption as a defense to its own liability.[25]

Vicarious Liability versus Direct Liability

Any form of organizational liability has to be fleshed out by legal principles that specify what kind of "participation" in the misconduct will trigger liability. Broadly speaking, there are two approaches to organizational liability: vicarious liability and direct liability. In the case of vicarious liability, one person is held liable for another person's violation. The other person's violation is a necessary, though typically not sufficient, condition for the first person to be liable. By contrast, in the case of direct liability, a person is held liable for conduct that does not necessarily involve a violation of the law by any other person.

In the *Siemens* case, for example, Siemens's subsidiaries in Bangladesh and Venezuela were held vicariously liable for their employees' offenses of conspiring to violate the FCPA's anti-bribery provisions. Meanwhile, the parent company, along with subsidiaries in Argentina, Bangladesh, and Venezuela, was held directly liable in the United States for deficient accounting practices; the charges for violating the FCPA's accounting provisions did not depend on proof that any person besides the defendant violated the law. Similarly, Siemens could have relied upon principles of vicarious liability to argue that states like Argentina were estopped from claiming corruption as a defense in arbitration under investment treaties. Siemens and other actors could also have referred to principles of direct liability to argue that Argentina was liable under the UN Convention for failing to take preventive measures against corruption—at least in principle, this sort of liability need not depend on proof that any official has solicited a bribe.

When it comes to vicarious liability for foreign bribery, legal systems use an astounding variety of rules to decide whether to attribute violations to organizations.[26] Reduced to their functional essence, these attribution rules generally condition liability on factors that relate to one of two issues: Was the organization likely to benefit from the misconduct? Was the organization in a position to prevent misconduct? In formal doctrinal terms, liability is conditioned on factors such as whether, for any given organization, the misconduct was committed:

- "through" the relevant natural persons
- with intent to benefit it
- for its actual or potential benefit or interest
- in its name or on its behalf
- within the scope of the relevant natural person's duties or authority
- with means that it provided
- as a result of a failure to supervise
- with the involvement of a person with managerial authority
- in the absence of adequate procedures to prevent it from being undertaken

So, for example, in Germany, a corporation can be held liable for bribery of foreign officials where one of its senior managers either engages in criminal conduct or breaches his or her duties to supervise other employees.[27] Under Colombian law, a corporation can be liable for bribery of foreign public officials committed "through its employees, contractors, directors or associates."[28] Similarly, under U.S. law, a corporation can be held vicariously liable for violations of the FCPA committed by employees or agents who act for the benefit of the corporation and within the scope of their duties.[29] The U.K. Bribery Act 2010 takes the same approach to vicarious liability for foreign bribery as U.S. federal law but permits an organization to escape liability for bribery if it can show that it "had in place adequate procedures designed to prevent persons associated with [the organization] from undertaking such misconduct."[30] In effect, this provision allows the absence of direct liability to negate vicarious liability. This sort of "compliance defense" is recognized in at least a dozen OECD countries, and there are ongoing debates over whether to introduce it in other countries.[31]

The Bribery Act 2010 represents a departure from the traditional English approach to corporate criminal liability. Under that approach, a corporation can only be liable for acts of a person deemed to be its "controlling mind and will."[32] This standard, sometimes known as the "identification doctrine," is often criticized for being unduly restrictive. It permits a company to escape liability so long as senior management is sufficiently isolated from the misconduct. Companies can guarantee this outcome by strategically adopting decentralized organizational structures. The OECD Working Group on Bribery has criticized countries for adhering to the directing mind and will theory.[33] The OECD parties' current position is that it is acceptable to condition corporate liability on involvement of high-level managerial personnel. However, liability must be triggered when such a person directs, authorizes, or fails to prevent a lower-level person from offering, promising, or giving a bribe.[34]

If the issue is whether a state whose officials have received a bribe is vicariously liable to another state, then the attribution process is governed by international law, specifically, the body of law known as the law of state responsibility. The general principles of the law of state responsibility resemble the broadest versions of the attribution rules used in domestic law. The general principle is that "[t]he conduct of an organ of a State or of a person or entity empowered to exercise elements of the governmental authority shall be considered an act of the State under international law if the organ, person or entity acts in that capacity, even if it exceeds its authority or contravenes instructions."[35] Actions of low-level officials and officials of subnational governments are explicitly covered.[36]

Direct liability is an important alternative to vicarious liability because it offers a way to target risky or obstructive conduct that falls short of any reasonable definition of bribery. One example of such conduct is violation of the FCPA's accounting provisions. Similarly, under France's "Sapin II" legislation, failure to adopt a corporate compliance program can trigger direct liability.[37] The rules that require financial institutions to adopt anti–money laundering compliance programs and to perform due diligence on customers also tend to provide for direct rather than vicarious liability.[38]

This approach to organizational liability is particularly valuable in cases of collective misconduct when it is hard to prove what any particular individual did, knew, or intended. For instance, it may be easy to figure out that a large multinational has maintained slush funds that create a substantial risk of corruption. It is not necessarily easy to determine whether any of the funds were actually used, or even intended to be used, for corrupt purposes. The same deficient accounting practices and internal controls that allow slush funds to exist make it impossible to trace the funds that flow through them. Even in the *Siemens* case, after one of the most exhaustive internal investigations in the history of law enforcement, prosecutors concluded that $554.5 million dollars was paid "for unknown purposes."[39] It also may be a fool's errand to try to identify any individual who knowingly or intentionally created the improper accounting system and internal controls. Direct liability for failure to adopt a compliance program, or for improper accounting and inadequate internal controls, offers a straightforward way to regulate this kind of risky or obstructive conduct while dispensing with the need to prove that any individual engaged in the kind of intentional action that is the hallmark of a traditional criminal offense.

It is worth noting that organizations are not the only actors besides the perpetrators of bribery who might be targeted for liability. In some legal systems individual members of a company have to fear vicarious liability for misconduct perpetrated by subordinates. The FCPA achieves this result by imposing vicarious liability on "control persons," or in the language of the statute, "Every person who, directly or indirectly, controls any person . . . unless the controlling person acted in good faith and did not directly or indirectly induce the act or acts constituting the violation . . ."[40] The U.K. Bribery Act uses a different but similar formula, stipulating that a "senior officer," or a person acting in that capacity, can be liable for a violation committed with their "consent or connivance."[41]

Liability of Parent Companies

In the United States at least, there are two areas in which agencies charged with enforcing transnational bribery law have tested the traditional boundaries of organizational liability. One area in which conventional limits have come under pressure is liability of parent companies for actions of employees of their subsidiaries. The UN Convention and the OECD Convention are silent on this issue, but the 2009 Recommendation under the OECD Convention advises that "a legal person cannot avoid responsibility by using intermediaries, *including related legal persons*, to offer, promise or give a bribe to a foreign public official on its behalf." (Emphasis added.)

Generally speaking, outside of the context of the FCPA it is unusual for a parent corporation to be liable under U.S. law for the wrongful actions of a subsidiary. A parent is only held liable if it exercises enough control over the affairs of the subsidiary to have effective control over the activity that triggers liability. Ownership of a controlling stake; monitoring of the subsidiary's performance; supervision of the subsidiary's finance and capital budget decisions; articulation of general policies and procedure; management of the subsidiary by officers and directors who also hold positions with the parent—all of these, even in combination, are consistent with treating the parent and the subsidiary as separate entities for the purposes of liability, according to no less an authority than the U.S. Supreme Court.[42]

It is unclear whether these rules apply to parent companies charged with foreign bribery or related offenses. The *Oracle* case discussed in chapter 7 shows that the SEC considers parent companies to be liable for violations of the FCPA's accounting provisions committed by subsidiaries under their control, regardless of whether employees of the parent were directly involved in the misconduct.[43] This seems like a fair interpretation of the FCPA when it comes to subsidiaries whose conduct leads to violations of the requirement to devise and maintain proper internal accounting controls. In the first place, the financial statements of controlled subsidiaries are required to be consolidated with those of the parent.[44] Second, the FCPA requires a parent company to make good faith efforts "to the extent reasonable under the [company's] circumstances" to implement satisfactory accounting controls in subsidiaries that it does not control.[45] The obvious implication is that a parent is liable for deficiencies in the internal accounting controls of subsidiaries that it actually controls. It is less obvious how the statute supports the SEC's practice of holding parent companies liable for violations of the FCPA's books and records provision when the books or records—which are defined to include more than just financial statements[46]—belong solely to a subsidiary and are never consolidated with those of the parent company.

As for the FCPA's anti-bribery provisions, there are at least two cases in which the U.S. SEC has held parent companies vicariously liable for bribes paid by their subsidiaries without the parent's knowledge, consent, assistance, or approval. In one case, a medical device company's Chinese subsidiary paid bribes to employees of state-owned hospitals to influence purchasing decisions. The parent company stopped the payments within two months of discovering them.[47] In the other case, a subsidiary of a defense contractor paid over $500,000 to a former general in the Egyptian Air Force for vaguely specified assistance in securing a lucrative contract with his former comrades. The CEO of the subsidiary, who approved both the entire arrangement and the individual payments, was listed as a member of the parent's management team, the consulting arrangement was approved by the parent's legal department, and an official of the parent company specifically approved a $100,000 payment.[48]

It is possible to reconcile these cases with the traditional understanding of parent liability. Perhaps the medical devices company "authorized" the bribes paid during the two months after it learned of the payments and before it stopped them. Perhaps approval of the $100,000 payment by the parent defense contractor combined with the fact that management teams of the parent and subsidiary overlapped either triggered direct liability for the parent, or amounted to sufficient control to overcome the presumption against finding an agency relationship. Or perhaps, as U.S. business interests have complained, the SEC has departed from the traditional standard for parent liability.[49]

If the standard is in fact different, then the new standard is far from clear. It appears, however, to permit liability for parents that exercise only moderate amounts of control over subsidiaries. To the extent it represents a deviation from traditional approaches to organizational liability, this revised standard could have far-reaching effects. Many firms that currently operate through wholly owned but loosely controlled subsidiaries will want to change how they do business. Some will want to assert even less control over their subsidiaries in order to minimize the risk of organizational liability, or even shift to doing business through wholly independent firms. Others will want to assert more centralized control in order to increase their chances of preventing misconduct. Siemens took this latter path. In the aftermath of its internal investigation, Siemens underwent a complete reorganization, which included the creation of a larger and more centralized compliance department and reduction in the autonomy of its country organizations.[50]

Liability of Successor Companies Following Mergers and Acquisitions

A second pressure point in the U.S. law of organizational liability is where it touches companies that acquire or merge with other companies that have paid bribes. Traditional legal principles distinguish three different ways of acquiring a business: buying its assets, buying shares of the corporation that owns the assets, or merging with that corporation. An acquirer that purchases assets rarely is subject to the liabilities of the seller.[51] If you buy a car from someone who used it as a getaway car after robbing a bank, you do not expect to find yourself in the dock facing charges of bank robbery. The situation is similar for an acquirer that purchases shares of a company which has previously broken the law. The acquired company remains liable, but its new parent should have little fear of liability.[52] As we just finished discussing, under traditional legal principles even a parent company that was on the scene during the misconduct is likely to escape liability, and so a newly arrived parent ought to be in an even stronger position. The situation is different, though, for an acquirer which merges with a firm that has violated the law. The surviving firm in a merger bears all of the liabilities of its predecessor.[53] There are exceptional cases in which courts have allowed liability to follow purchasers of assets or stock to be held liable without their consent. But those cases generally involve either de facto mergers, where ownership has not really changed, or transfers in which a seller has deliberately attempted to evade liability by putting assets beyond the reach of creditors, or, in some states, liability to people injured by defective products.[54]

The U.S. Department of Justice and the SEC read the law differently. Their official FCPA guidance document boldly asserts: "As a general legal matter, when a company merges with or acquires another company, the successor company assumes the predecessor company's liabilities."[55] No support is offered for the proposition that acquirers (as opposed to merging firms) take on pre-existing FCPA liabilities.[56] The guidance document then muddies the waters by saying on the one hand, that the U.S. enforcement agencies have not actually prosecuted any acquirers for pre-acquisition misconduct, but noting on the other hand that they have persuaded some acquirers to sign settlement agreements along with the companies they acquired.[57] The agencies ascribe their reluctance to prosecute acquirers to grace rather than legal constraint, and suggest that they will only be merciful to acquirers that investigate, remediate, and voluntarily disclose FCPA violations.

Faced with these ambiguous but ominous messages, prudent lawyers advise acquiring firms to undertake extensive investigations of prospective targets to uncover potential FCPA liabilities. And when they uncover issues, the advice is to act on the assumption that the liabilities will be borne by the acquirer as well as the target.[58] This matters when there is reason to believe that enforcement agencies will not be satisfied with going after the target firm—perhaps because it doesn't have enough money to pay a large fine, or because the acquirer has a relatively high profile and its prosecution will send a powerful message to the public.

Justifications for Organizational Liability

Now that we have a sense of the rules that govern organizational liability for foreign bribery, including some of the more controversial ones, we can turn to analyzing their merits.

The first step is to understand why liability for individual perpetrators is insufficient. The Siemens saga involved lapses on the part of many individuals who worked for Siemens, as well as many public officials. One of the first employees to be punished was Reinhard Siekaczek, the accountant who oversaw the budget for Siemens's telecommunications unit. He was chosen by his peers to oversee an annual bribery budget of $40 million to $50 million, apparently because of his personal probity and loyalty to the company.[59] Another pivotal figure was Ulrich Bock, who worked for Siemens for forty-two years, first as an employee and then as a consultant, and was at the center of the scheme to pay over $100 million in bribes to the government of Argentina in order to obtain a contract to produce national identity cards.[60] And then there was Mihalis Christoforakos, the former head of Siemens's Greek subsidiary. He ran a business that devoted between 2 and 8.5 percent of its revenue to payments to politicians and purchasing officers.[61] Greece claims that bribes paid over the course of almost two decades cost Greek taxpayers €2 billion.[62] The individual public officials who imposed those costs on their fellow citizens obviously are at least as culpable as the Siemens officials, as are their counterparts in other countries where Siemens paid bribes.

Why wasn't it sufficient to focus on the liability of these individuals and their collaborators? What purposes were served by pursuing Siemens or its senior managers? What purposes could be served by sanctioning the states whose officials received bribes? The conventional answer is that sanctioning third parties like Siemens, its managers, and the recipient states is an effective and efficient way of serving the same purposes as sanctioning perpetrators, namely: condemnation, prevention, and compensation. We will consider these in turn.

Condemnation

Organizations that fail to prevent corrupt practices are less deserving of condemnation than perpetrators who have taken affirmative steps to cause harm but they are more culpable than truly innocent bystanders, particularly when they benefit from the misconduct. Commitment to avoiding impunity demands condemnation of actors across the full spectrum of culpability rather than only the most culpable actors. In the *Siemens* case, for instance, even if every individual perpetrator were punished, if the company escaped liability, then something arguably would be left unsaid. The fact that there was something wrong with the company as a whole, including not only the policies and practices chosen by its leaders but also the values embodied in those choices, would have gone unacknowledged. The corruption of the company whole, which was greater than the sum of all the individual instances of corruption perpetrated by Siemens's employees, deserved to be condemned.

Similar arguments might support condemnation of a state. There often is an important difference, however, between a firm, like Siemens, whose agent has paid a bribe, and a state, like, say, Argentina, whose officials received the bribe. Both organizations are likely to be in a position to prevent the misconduct. Only the firm, however, is likely to have benefited from the corrupt transaction. An individual bribe payer typically secures a favor, like a government contract, that directly benefits their firm. The individual's benefits then arrive indirectly and through the firm, in the form of a bonus or a promotion or enhanced standing among their peers. By contrast, an official who receives a bribe benefits directly and the state is often harmed by the transaction, as in the case where a contract is given to an unqualified firm. Therefore, the case for condemning a bribe-receiving state seems relatively weak, at least compared to the justification for condemning a bribe-paying firm.

Prevention

Not everyone sees the value in expressing condemnation, or at least not sufficient value to justify spending scarce public resources. For those who value more tangible outcomes, liability for organizations is frequently defended in instrumental terms as a means of preventing misconduct. The premise is that the law can be used to encourage organizations to regulate misconduct. The hope is that self-regulation will be a cost-effective way to either replace or enhance the effectiveness of interventions by enforcement agencies and plaintiffs.[63]

Self-regulatory measures fall into two categories: prevention and policing.[64] Prevention includes all the measures taken before the fact, including screening out employees or agents who might be inclined to engage in corrupt practices, reducing their access to the relevant funds and payment systems, and minimizing their incentives to participate in misconduct—no bonuses for bribes! Policing includes all sorts of measures taken after misconduct has incurred, including efforts to detect and sanction misconduct, as well as to report wrongdoing to, and cooperate with, any agencies or tribunals charged with conducting investigations and imposing sanctions. A credible threat to engage in policing ought to have deterrent and persuasive effects on employees and agents. Effective policing might also serve to rehabilitate wayward employees and, if all else fails, to weed them out (a form of incapacitation).

For decades Siemens failed miserably at both preventing and policing corrupt practices. The turning point came in November 2006 when the company's offices were raided by the Munich police. From that point onward, by all accounts, the company's policing was exemplary. The audit committee of Siemens's board of directors hired a prominent New York–based law firm, Debevoise and Plimpton, to conduct an "internal investigation." Debevoise in turn hired the German branch of Deloitte and Touche, a major accounting firm, and a variety of other service providers to assist in the investigation. In the words of the U.S. Department of Justice:

> By all indications, Debevoise has been permitted to conduct its investigation in a completely independent fashion, without limitations as to scope or duration. According to Siemens's latest estimates, over 1.5 million hours of billable time by Debevoise and Deloitte professionals have been devoted to the investigation. This includes the extensive and sustained participation of approximately 100 lawyers and 100 support staff from Debevoise and 130 forensic accountants and support staff from Deloitte. The investigative work has taken place in 34 countries and has involved over 1,750 interviews and over 800 informational meetings. Over 100 million documents have been collected and preserved, many of which have been searched or reviewed for evidence relevant to the investigation. Siemens, either directly or through Debevoise, has produced to the Department over 24,000 documents, amounting to over 100,000 pages.

> To ensure that Debevoise and Deloitte had the support needed within Siemens to effectively conduct their investigation, Siemens stressed to all employees that they must fully cooperate in the investigation. In addition, Siemens established a Project Office at headquarters staffed by 16 full-time employees that facilitated interviews and document collection. To facilitate visits to regional companies by the investigation team, the Project Office communicated with regional management to explain and prepare them for the interviews and other investigative work.[65]

The Department of Justice went out of its way to explain the value of the information generated by Siemens's internal investigation:

> In certain instances, Siemens has provided forensic analyses of bank records and payments that have greatly assisted in the tracing of multi-layered financial transactions. Many of these transactions involved the movement of funds through several countries. It was only through the extensive, worldwide investigative efforts of the internal investigators that these complex criminal activities were uncovered. As a practical matter, it would have been exceedingly difficult for the Department to identify and obtain the necessary foreign financial records, review them, trace proceeds, and identify and interview potential witnesses, all between late 2006 and the present.[66]

In principle, state liability might encourage self-regulation in much the same way that corporate liability does for firms. Perhaps if the Argentine state faced the prospect of liability to Siemens (or perhaps Germany) for allowing its officials to solicit bribes, then similarly situated states would make greater efforts to prevent corruption in the first place, and failing that, to seek redress against corrupt individuals.

Arguments that organizational sanctions will induce prevention, on the part of either firms or states, rest on strong assumptions about how organizations respond to sanctions. The OECD paradigm *presumes* that sanctions deter private firms, meaning that they will expend resources to prevent liability, most likely up to the point where the value of the resources equals the anticipated liability. We will challenge this presumption in chapter 9. For now, it is sufficient to point out the difficulty with extending the presumption to states. As we pointed out in the course of discussing the differences between bribery of public and private officials (chapter 6), pressure from greedy shareholders and marketplace competition are potent influences on managers of for-profit firms that encourage them to respond to financial incentives. This includes incentives to take cost-effective steps to minimize liability under anti-bribery law. States are very different. The leaders of states do not face scrutiny from shareholders, their performance cannot easily be benchmarked against the performance of leaders of competing states, and the stakeholders who control leaders' destinies are not focused solely on their financial performance. There is no reason to presume that increased risk of liability will motivate states to regulate bribery more intensely. This is especially true when corruption extends to the very highest echelons of a state's government. In this scenario, enhanced regulation might harm the leaders personally, and the public may be so inured to official corruption that it is indifferent to new allegations.

Compensation

Besides condemnation and prevention there is one final justification for organizational liability worth mentioning: compensation. Since at least the time of Aristotle it has been considered just to strip people who benefit from legal wrongs of their profits in order to compensate victims. This can be useful when the individual perpetrator either cannot be brought to justice or has insufficient assets to provide full compensation.

Does Organizational Liability Distract Prosecutors from Prosecuting Individual Perpetrators?

Despite the compelling justifications, expansive organizational liability raises several concerns. The first is that it might be a costly distraction. To wit, if organizations are easier to sanction than individual perpetrators, then prosecutors and plaintiffs might be distracted from pursuing individual perpetrators, thereby compromising the effectiveness of the overall regime.[67]

Prosecutors have generally found it much easier to sanction firms as opposed to individual perpetrators for foreign bribery and money laundering. The seven-year-long trial of Warren Hastings foreshadowed the difficulties associated with targeting powerful individuals.

In the *Siemens* case, the U.S. and German proceedings against the Siemens corporate entities were resolved by voluntary agreement and were unambiguous successes. Consider the results: an in-depth investigation, conducted at relatively little expense to the government, which produced a detailed exposé of blatant high-level corruption, record-breaking monetary penalties, and headlines around the world, all without the burden and delay of a trial.

The proceedings against individuals yielded more mixed outcomes. In Germany, the individual proceedings met with overall success. By 2013, German enforcement agencies had sanctioned sixty-one individuals associated with Siemens's corrupt activities.[68] The proceedings against individuals moved at a very different pace in the United States. In fact, in 2010, several U.S. senators challenged the Department of Justice for failing to bring charges against any individuals in connection with the *Siemens* case.[69] It was not until December 2011 that the U.S. Department of Justice and the SEC filed cases against individual Siemens employees or agents.[70] Five years later, only one of the eight criminal cases had been resolved in the government's favor.[71] The civil cases were resolved within three years, but only five of them were successful.[72] And of course, the $1.6 billion recovered from the Siemens corporate entities dwarfed the $1.9 million that U.S. enforcement agencies recovered from individuals.[73]

The *Siemens* case is not atypical in the U.S. system. Virtually all FCPA cases against corporations are resolved through some sort of voluntary agreement, without any prior judicial hearing. In the entire history of the FCPA, only two cases involving corporate defendants have gone to trial (both companies won). By contrast, individuals are much more likely to fight; as of December 2018 at least forty-seven individuals had been tried on FCPA charges. And when individuals fight, they sometimes win—at least thirty-six of the individuals who went to trial were either acquitted or saw the charges against them dismissed.[74] In some of the cases involving individuals, judges have rejected legal arguments that the government previously relied on in settlements with organizational defendants.[75] Between 2011 and 2015, monetary recoveries from individuals totaled $20.2 million, compared to $5.3 billion from organizations.[76]

These figures are consistent with a general perception that a prosecutor who chooses to go after a firm rather than the individuals implicated in a case of transnational bribery will find it is easier to resolve the case without going to trial, will be more likely to prevail, and is likely to recover a larger sum of money. These predictions are backed by logic as well as experience.[77]

Take the prediction that individuals are more likely than corporations to go to trial. Going to trial is costly for both prosecutors and defendants, especially when witnesses and records have to be brought in from foreign countries. Given the magnitude of trial costs, prosecutors can agree to less severe sanctions than those they expect to be imposed after a trial and still be better off than going to trial. Similarly, defendants can afford to agree to significantly harsher sanctions than they expect to receive at trial and still be better off. However, for commercial enterprises, the costs of going to trial are likely to be especially high because in addition to the costs of presenting evidence and hiring lawyers to make legal arguments, they often suffer reputational harm from the associated negative publicity. In many situations, the more negative publicity, the greater the harm. In these cases it is better for the firm to settle and have one bad news day than to endure weeks or months of coverage of a protracted trial. By comparison, individuals are likely to find trial more attractive: it is unlikely to cause them additional reputational harm, and they may place a relatively high value on the opportunity to clear their name and avoid criminal sanctions.[78]

It may also be true that the government is more likely to prevail at trial against a firm as opposed to an individual. On the one hand, large firms typically have more resources to devote to their defense. On the other hand, the playing field at trial may be tilted against firms. For instance, in the case of U.S. law, the FCPA provides that the government can only hold an individual criminally liable if it proves that the person behaved "willfully," meaning, they knew that what they were doing was unlawful. Separate but neighboring provisions permit corporations to be held criminally liable without saying anything about willfulness.[79] A logical inference is that a corporation can be held liable on the basis of an agent's intentional but non-willful violation. Another example of a U.S. rule tilted against organizations is the rule against admission of hearsay evidence. That rule will often bar the out-of-court statements of one employee from being used as evidence against another employee (on the theory that the defendant ought to be able to challenge the evidence in court). In a foreign bribery case against an individual, this rule may force the prosecution to bear the burden of bringing witnesses from all over the globe to a U.S. courtroom. By contrast, in a prosecution against the corporation, the out-of-court statement would be admissible under an exception to the hearsay rule that brings in out-of-court statements by a party's agent or employee.[80]

Finally, individuals typically have more limited assets than organizations and so the tangible rewards from prosecuting organizations tend to be greater. Even the most highly paid corporate CEOs are unlikely to have access to the same amount of wealth as the corporations they serve.

For all these reasons then, the option of pursuing firms might distract prosecutors from pursuing individuals, at least in a system similar to the U.S. legal system. Similar factors encourage plaintiffs to pursue organizations rather than individuals, although for private plaintiffs, the fact that individual defendants have limited assets is likely to be a sufficient reason to focus on bribe-paying firms. In short, the enforcement game is biased in favor of organizational as opposed to individual liability.

The bias against individual liability will be even stronger if individuals can rig the game. If individual wrongdoers control a firm, they have a clear incentive to offer up the firm's assets and reputation in exchange for their own exoneration. A CEO who has paid a bribe is almost invariably better off if his firm pleads guilty than if he pleads guilty himself, and he typically would rather have the company pay an additional $10 million than spend an additional year in prison or pay an extra $10,000 in fines. So long as prosecutors are willing to exchange additional organizational sanctions for reduced individual sanctions, these types of deals are likely to allow individuals to escape liability.

Taking liability for individual perpetrators off the table is problematic for at least two reasons. First, it is inconsistent with the idea that it is important to condemn individuals in order to reaffirm society's commitment to the values that their violation has challenged. Second, diminishing the threat of individual liability undermines the deterrent and dissuasive force of law enforcement. Individuals not only might be motivated by the fear of personal liability, they might reconsider their moral values when presented with examples of corrupt actors being condemned publicly. Without the prospect of individual liability, firms and enforcement agencies have to rely primarily on self-regulation to prevent misconduct, even though liability for individuals is an important complement to self-regulation. When individual legal liability is a realistic threat, firms can deter individuals by making credible threats to report their misconduct to enforcement agencies. Removing that threat forces firms to use other potentially more costly means to achieve any given level of deterrence, for example, reducing the scale of their activities in high-risk countries. Similarly, firms will find it easier to dissuade internal misconduct when they can point to examples of individuals who have faced public condemnation.

Fortunately, distraction from prosecution of individuals is not an inevitable consequence of permitting organizational liability. Even in the United States, a modest tweak to the rules of evidence and the elimination of the willfulness requirement would make it easier for prosecutors to convict individuals. More generally, the problem of distraction can be mitigated by measures that limit prosecutors' authority to resolve cases against organizational defendants through voluntary agreements, limit the extent to which agreements with organizational defendants can make provision for leniency in relation to individuals, or give prosecutors strong incentives to pursue cases against individuals. In 2015, the leadership of the U.S. Department of Justice explicitly endorsed all of these measures.[81] Another possible solution is to encourage prosecutors to bring administrative or civil cases against individuals. These kinds of proceedings typically involve lower stakes and more favorable procedural rules. These factors should reduce defendants' incentives to fight and make it easier for prosecutors to obtain favorable results. German enforcement agencies embraced this approach in the *Siemens* case by prosecuting many individuals for commercial bribery and the administrative offense of breach of supervisory duties. The U.S. SEC, which also has the power to impose administrative and civil sanctions on individuals, could choose to follow suit.

It is worth noting that while prosecutors and plaintiffs have incentives to pursue private firms rather than individuals, they are not equally likely to be distracted by the possibility of pursuing states. Like large private firms, sovereigns have ample resources to devote to their defense. Perhaps even more importantly, states benefit from special legal doctrines such as sovereign immunity that make it difficult to hold them liable. Moreover, unlike private firms, states do not necessarily suffer reputational harm that increases with the length of a trial. Reputations arguably attach to governments rather than states. For example, a trial focused on corruption in Argentina during the Menem administration might tarnish the reputation of Menem and his fellow officials without having any appreciable negative effect on the current administration. For all these reasons, states are unlikely to be viewed as soft targets by prosecutors or plaintiffs. Consequently, the argument that states are liable for their officials' corrupt acts seems most likely to be raised by firms like Siemens as a defense to claims (or counterclaims) brought by states.

Does Organizational Liability Encourage Cover-ups?

Fear of liability ought to give organizations an incentive to adopt the kind of private regulation that prevents bribery, but unless the organizational liability regime is carefully designed, it also will create an incentive for organizations to cover up instances of past misconduct.[82] This will in turn undermine efforts to achieve any of the objectives of the broader anti-bribery regime, or in other words, limit its effectiveness.

In an ideal world, employers, parent companies, and acquirers would not only work to prevent potential perpetrators from engaging in foreign corrupt practices but also take steps to uncover, sanction, and report any past misconduct. It is easy to understand how holding organizations liable creates incentives for them to prevent misconduct. However, it is less obvious how liability encourages organizations to detect, sanction, or report, that is, to engage in policing. In fact, if anything, liability seems to discourage policing. A firm that goes out of its way to generate information about its corrupt past only increases its chances of attracting the attention of law enforcement agencies.

At Siemens, for instance, bribery of foreign public officials became entrenched in the corporate culture during a period when it was unable to compete successfully in markets in the developed world and its business was focused on emerging markets. At that time, neither U.S. nor German law prohibited foreign bribery. Once Siemens became subject to legal prohibitions on foreign bribery, its managers and directors had incentives to prevent future payments, at least in theory. And in fact, after 1999, they slowly—too slowly—began to take preventive measures. However, Siemens's managers and directors consistently avoided learning about the extent of past misconduct, much less reporting it to enforcement agencies. This reluctance may not have been entirely irrational: detection or reporting would only have served to attract liability. The unfortunate result was to aggravate a collective failure to appreciate the extent of Siemens's problems, which almost certainly hampered efforts to enhance preventive efforts.

The fundamental problem here is that liability for failure to prevent misconduct—which is what vicarious liability for bribery often amounts to—can have the perverse effect of discouraging policing. The theoretically optimal solution to the problem is to craft a liability regime that creates separate incentives for prevention, detection, sanctioning, and reporting. Even a firm or state that has failed to prevent corruption should be given incentives to detect, sanction, and report. The incentive can be either positive, in the form of reduced punishment for an organization that polices, or negative, meaning enhanced punishment for an organization that fails to police.[83] One way to accomplish this is to impose some baseline level of liability for failure to prevent, and then treat detection, reporting, or sanctioning as either mitigating or aggravating factors. Another way is to treat failure to prevent, detect, report, or sanction as distinct violations for which the firm or state can be held directly liable. In addition, a compliance defense along the lines of the one in the U.K. Bribery Act can be tailored to incentivize specific kinds of preventive and policing measures. Alternatively, a system of rewards for whistleblowers might serve as a substitute for incentives for the firm to self-report.

It is unrealistic to presume that these theoretically optimal solutions will work when transferred from the sterile world of an economist's mathematical model into the grimy reality of a working legal system. The common feature of all these complex incentive-based approaches to organizational liability is that they require enforcement agencies and courts to accurately evaluate firms' prevention and policing. It may be reasonable to expect experienced prosecutors in the United States to make these kinds of fine-grained assessments of corporations' compliance practices. The DOJ has the resources to support its prosecutors with experts in corporate governance and compliance, and the SEC has considerable experience in formulating standards for corporate governance, even for massive companies like Siemens. It is not so reasonable to expect an overworked line prosecutor in Bolivia to assess a large multinational corporation's compliance regime. An inexperienced or under-resourced prosecutor might get overwhelmed by the task, or expect either too little or too much in the way of self-regulation. For the Bolivian prosecutor, the most cost-effective regime is likely to be one that relies on a cruder analysis based on information that is relatively easy to verify, such as: Did the firm's agents make improper payments, and did it self-report?

There is another way to deal with the problem of organizational liability's perverse incentives: ignore them. Incentives are not destiny. Neither firms nor states behave solely in ways that maximize their self-interest. The people within these kinds of organizations are motivated by a variety of factors, including moral compunctions and the desire to earn and preserve the respect of their peers. Recall that in the post-Watergate pre-FCPA era, eighty-nine firms reported questionable or illegal payments under the SEC's voluntary disclosure program without any guarantee of leniency. Admittedly, the firms and executives knew that the potential legal sanctions were minimal. But they also knew that the consciences of their fellow employees, as well as their auditors, would make it hard for them all to remain silent. Of course, the feasibility of this kind of sociologically informed response to the cover-up concern depends on the institutional context, much like the feasibility of incentive-based approaches. An enforcement agency would have to be not only sophisticated but also brave and confident to base its approach to organizational liability on an assessment of prevailing corporate culture.

Collateral Consequences

Although organizational liability is generally aimed at actors who either could have prevented or who benefited from misconduct, there is a danger that it will miss its target and hit innocent bystanders. A large firm like Siemens has many innocent stakeholders, including employees, suppliers, and customers who might be adversely affected when it is sanctioned. And sanctions imposed on states are even more likely to have collateral consequences since the welfare of a state usually is deeply intertwined with the welfare of its citizens. This is incompatible with the notion that liability should be proportional to fault. Intuitively, these collateral effects also seem unfair, although in some cases it might be argued that the stakeholders have voluntarily assumed the risk of these consequences by choosing to deal with the sanctioned firm.

The collateral impact of sanctions varies depending on the type of organization and the types of sanctions at issue. For private firms, sanctions most commonly take the form of monetary sanctions. In theory these are aimed mainly at the people who have invested their money in the firm, that is, shareholders or lenders. At first glance, investors seem like legitimate targets for liability because the law says that they ultimately control the firms in which they have invested. Supposedly, fear of monetary penalties will prompt investors in firms like Siemens to demand self-regulation.

Accepting this supposition requires the sometimes heroic assumption that investors' legal control rights translate into meaningful power over firms. In fact, many investors exercise only remote control over firms in which they have invested. Investors often delegate their control rights to professional investment managers, such as managers of mutual funds or pension funds. Sometimes the ultimate investors have little power over the people who exercise control rights on their behalf. This kind of separation of ownership and control is probably most marked in state-owned enterprises, where the ultimate investors are the citizens of the state, but they typically have little meaningful control over the operations of state-owned enterprises. In other situations, managers invest in so many different firms that they have little incentive to attempt to control any individual firm. Moreover, even large investors have little direct control over the operations of a modern corporation; their control rights are mainly limited to selecting members of the board of directors. In some countries investors have found ways to overcome these obstacles and induce managers to concentrate on protecting investors' interests. Those countries tend to have well-developed markets for investment capital. In other countries, though, investor protections are weaker, and it is less reasonable to presume that threats to investors' interests will motivate changes in corporate behavior. If monetary penalties are imposed on firms with weak investor protection mechanisms, then managers may find ways to capture a disproportionate share of the benefits of corrupt practices for themselves, for example, by paying themselves large bonuses and treating themselves to corporate perquisites, while sharing the costs of any resulting penalties with investors.[84]

Innocent investors are not the only innocents who might be hurt by monetary sanctions imposed on private firms. Those sanctions may have to be paid out of funds that the firm planned to invest in its business as opposed to pay out to its investors. The firm may find it difficult to replace this kind of investment capital; only firms with assets that are exceptionally easy to value can raise external financing with little effort. If the funds are not replaced, the firm will have no choice but to curtail its operations. That means less money for employees, fewer orders for suppliers, less innovation—with all its spillover benefits for society—and fewer products for customers. There is no reason to assume that any of these people have any ability to control the firm's behavior.

Innocent stakeholders can be affected by nonmonetary sanctions in much the same way as monetary sanctions. Reputational sanctions reduce the overall profitability of a firm's operations and so have the same kind of impact on employees and suppliers as monetary penalties. Meanwhile, measures that involve ex ante restrictions on business activities or ongoing monitoring tend to be costly to firms, both in terms of the direct cost of paying the overseers and the less visible costs that come from burdening management and restricting legitimate business operations.

What about the argument that organizational sanctions deprive stakeholders of ill-gotten gains? This would be a fair point if the stakeholders hit by the sanctions were guaranteed to be the ones who gained from the misconduct. But a firm is like a living organism, whose cells regularly disappear and then are replaced. The ensemble of investors, employees, and customers affiliated with any given company is constantly changing. The shareholders and employees who collect undeserved dividends or bonuses may sell their shares or leave the firm long before any penalties are levied. Potential customers deprived of innovative new products may never even have had any connection with the firm. Imagine if Siemens's punishment delayed the introduction of a new CT scanner that could have provided a young mother with a life-saving early diagnosis of breast cancer. How likely is it that the losses that she and her children suffered were offset by benefits they received from the company's prior misconduct?

For all of these reasons it is virtually impossible to generalize about the extent to which sanctions imposed on private firms cause collateral harm. In each case the extent to which sanctions cause collateral harm is contingent on factors such as the quality of the firm's governance, the extent to which firms' profits are reinvested as opposed to distributed to investors, and the rate of turnover among stakeholders in the firm.

The only type of sanction that seems unlikely to have significant collateral effects (beyond investors) is the equity fine proposed by John Coffee.[85] The proposal is ingenious: instead of paying a monetary penalty in cash, a corporate defendant would issue equity securities with a market value equal to the desired monetary penalty. The effect will be to reduce the value of the previously outstanding equity, but there should be no other effect on the corporation's operations. Where shareholders effectively control a corporation, this can be a very effective way of encouraging them to promote compliance.

The collateral consequences of sanctioning states are even more troubling than the consequences of sanctioning private firms, especially since the countries in which official corruption is the most prevalent also tend to be relatively poor.[86] Monetary sanctions imposed on a state directly reduce the amount of resources available for providing public goods and services. In poor countries, goods and services provided by the state play a critical role in determining the welfare of the population. Diverting resources from the state is nothing to be concerned about if we assume that the resources would have been diverted to unproductive purposes anyway. This is a realistic possibility in some kleptocratic states, that is to say, states run for the benefit of their ruling officials as opposed to the general population. In all but the most kleptocratic states, however, collateral consequences provide a powerful reason to refrain from sanctioning states whose officials solicit or accept bribes.

Is Self-regulation Efficient?

One of the great virtues of organizational liability is that it encourages self-regulation. However, there is no guarantee that self-regulation will be efficient.

In other words, there is always the possibility that organizational liability will cause overall regulatory costs—the sum of the costs of public regulation and self-regulation—to increase rather than decrease, without any offsetting increase in effectiveness. This is a plausible concern because self-regulation is costly. Self-regulation also is not guaranteed to be more effective than public alternatives, especially in contexts where the applicable legal framework is hostile and private actors lack relevant expertise. Ultimately, whether or not any given form of self-regulation is efficient amounts to an empirical question, and the answers are likely to be context-specific.

Costs of Self-regulation

There is little doubt that self-regulation is expensive. Consider the costs of prevention. An organization that is serious about prevention will pull employees away from other tasks to participate in training programs; vet suppliers and agents closely; require preauthorization from multiple people for every transaction; tone down performance-based compensation schemes that boost productivity but also encourage malfeasance; retain disgruntled employees, even if they are disruptive, so as to avoid the appearance of discouraging whistleblowers; pay compliance personnel to design and implement all of these programs; and, in extreme cases, give up opportunities to do business in or with high-risk countries. All of these measures can be costly.

Detection of misconduct after the fact also requires costly efforts. It involves auditing apparently innocent past transactions to see if they are tainted by corruption as well as more in-depth investigations of suspected instances of bribery or money laundering. Corrupt actors often bury their dishonest legal, financial, and social relationships under layers of intermediaries, shell companies, and offshore accounts. It takes time and expertise to pull apart those layers of concealment, especially when they are embedded in the legitimate operations of a large-scale multinational enterprise. As a result, both auditing and investigation can be incredibly time-consuming and expensive exercises. Siemens spent over $1 billion on its internal investigation, including $100 million spent just on document collection, review, processing, and storage.[87]

Sanctions are also an important part of self-regulation, and they can be costly too. Employers can sanction employees by terminating them, demoting them, or reducing their compensation. Suppliers or customers are often vulnerable to similar measures. Following through with these kinds of sanctions might entail severing relationships that are valuable to the company. Before settling with the U.S. and German enforcement authorities, Siemens replaced about 80 percent of its top-level executives, including the chairman of its supervisory board, the chief executive officer, the general counsel, the head of internal audit, and the chief compliance officer.[88]

When tallying the costs of self-regulation, it is a mistake to attribute all of the costs to organizational liability for foreign bribery. Even without the fear of liability under anti-bribery law, organizations have incentives to screen employees and suppliers for integrity, maintain tight control over financial transactions, and investigate suspicions of bribery or money laundering. Corruption can harm a firm's reputation and trigger liability under other legal regimes, such as corporate or securities laws that require managers to maintain proper accounting controls. Measures designed to screen out or detect dishonest employees or trading partners also make sense from another perspective. Even if they don't engage in corrupt practices, those bad apples are likely to engage in other forms of misconduct that are harmful to the firm.

Organizational liability for foreign bribery is most likely to trigger additional self-regulation when it deviates from established principles for attributing other kinds of misconduct to organizations. For instance, in most legal systems employers—both individuals and organizations—generally are legally responsible for all the wrongful actions of their employees, and corporate directors are regularly held liable for wrongful actions of corporations on whose boards they sit. In addition, it is not uncommon for a firm also to be liable for the acts of its agents, meaning individuals or corporations who are not necessarily employees but who have agreed to act on the company's behalf and under its control. (All employees are agents, but not all agents are employees; employees are subject to greater control over the way in which they do their work.) Meanwhile, international law of state responsibility is used to attribute all sorts of wrongful acts to states, ranging from torture to environmental pollution. In most legal systems, the formulas for determining when people face these kinds of organizational liability, both direct and vicarious, have been worked out over centuries and are reasonably well understood. Organizational liability for foreign bribery is most likely to generate additional costs if it appears to deviate from these established principles and expands the set of actors whose conduct can trigger organizational liability. In this scenario, people are put to the trouble of learning new, and most likely underdeveloped, legal principles to figure out who can trigger liability for them. They also have to develop self-regulatory mechanisms concerned exclusively with bribery instead of relying on existing mechanisms.

Complementary Legal Institutions

Using organizational liability to encourage private regulation will be cost-effective if the additional private regulation is either more effective or less expensive than public alternatives. In general, laws that promote private regulation are most likely to be cost-effective when they are complemented by laws that place few restrictions on private actors' ability to engage in investigation and surveillance of employees, agents, and trading partners (including sellers of businesses), and allow private actors to terminate relationships with employees, agents, and trading partners for violations of privately formulated anti-corruption standards. The U.S. legal system is particularly friendly to private investigations and surveillance. Broadly defined attorney-client privileges allow firms to limit the extent to which evidence gathered in a private investigation can be used against them; employment laws allow extensive surveillance of employees' communications; and firms can use the threat of termination to induce employees and trading partners to cooperate.[89]

Not every legal system is so friendly to private regulation. Three multinational pharmaceutical companies learned this the hard way in Russia when they refused to contract with potential distributors they suspected of engaging in corrupt practices. Citing local competition law, Russia's Federal Antimonopoly Service (FAS) sanctioned the Russian affiliates of companies based in Denmark, Israel, and the United States, as well as individual employees, for their refusals to deal.[90] The companies were doing exactly what any good U.S. or U.K. lawyer would have recommended they do to comply with the FCPA and the U.K. Bribery Act. U.S. enforcement agencies have held firms liable under the FCPA for illegal payments made by foreign distributors in circumstances when they turned a blind eye to the risk of payments to foreign public officials. In order to avoid this kind of organizational liability, the DOJ and the SEC explicitly recommend that firms screen their distributors carefully and draft their distributorship agreements to allow for periodic audits of compliance with anti-corruption laws.[91] The FAS had a very different perspective. It took a dim view of pharmaceutical companies that it believed to be using their dominant position in the Russian market place to treat local distributors arbitrarily. Where the DOJ and the SEC saw efficient private regulation, the FAS saw abuse of market dominance. When the FAS eventually set out its general views on the issues raised by these cases, it made it clear that it would only tolerate refusal to deal on the grounds of corruption if the suspicions were confirmed by Russian anti-corruption authorities.[92] The message was that public not private actors ought to determine when it is appropriate to sanction firms that present a risk of corruption, a clear rejection of the concept of purely private anti-corruption regulation.

Two expatriate private investigators in China learned about hostility to another type of private regulation commonplace in the United States context, namely, private investigations. Peter Humphrey and his wife, Yu Yingzeng, British and U.S. nationals, respectively, spent two years in squalid Chinese jails after trying to conduct an investigation on behalf of GlaxoSmithKline (GSK), a multinational pharmaceutical company based in the United Kingdom. Their case was an unusual one because their investigation was aimed at uncovering the identity of a whistleblower who revealed, among other things, that their client had paid bribes to Chinese public officials.[93] They were hired after the whistleblower antagonized GSK by leaking a sex tape featuring the head of its China operations, and their investigation focused on the whistleblower rather than the alleged bribery (which the company later admitted). The treatment of Humphrey and Yingzeng made international headlines and drew attention to a host of legal pitfalls that confront private investigators in China. In particular, data privacy laws limit private actors' ability to collect information about employees without their consent. Foreign companies working in China also are wary of state secret laws that make it an offense to export state secrets—which might include almost any information about a state-owned enterprise.[94] It is important to note, however, that although Chinese law might discourage private investigations, it does encourage whistleblowing.[95] In principle, whistleblowing can serve as a substitute for private investigations and self-reporting directed by senior management. It is not that Chinese law is completely hostile to private regulation, it simply favors a different model from the one prevalent in the United States.

Complementary Expertise

Cost-effective private regulation requires other complements besides tolerant laws. In the United States at least, compliance programs and investigations are typically outsourced to a host of lawyers, accountants, trainers, compliance consultants, forensic computer specialists, and translators.[96] Some commentators refer to members of this industry pejoratively as FCPA Inc., and criticize them for exaggerating the risk of liability in order to boost demand for their services. That critique is aimed mainly at the leading lawyers—often former prosecutors—who arguably are suppliers who create their own demand, a rare and enviable feat. Below the commanding heights of the compliance industry, however, there are scores of firms competing to offer each kind of service. All of these firms know that their ultimate clients, the potential defendants, will pay a premium for services that enforcement agencies will accept as evidence that reduced sanctions are warranted. This means that service providers have strong incentives to maintain a reputation for quality among staff at the leading enforcement agencies, all while remaining competitive on price.

Although many firms that provide compliance services operate in multiple countries, and there have been efforts to formulate globally applicable compliance standards (see, for example, the guidelines developed by the International Organization for Standards, ISO 37001), it is far from clear that potential defendant companies that are answerable to enforcement agencies outside the United States will benefit from the same level of expertise and mix of competitive and reputational incentives as the companies exposed to U.S. law, or at least not in the short term. It takes time for compliance advisers to develop expertise, and expertise developed in the context of one legal and commercial culture, or even one particular industry, is not necessarily transferable to other contexts. Professionals in the compliance industry have to be familiar with not only applicable regulatory requirements but also accounting practices, systems of corporate governance, and, of course, the language in which business is conducted. The professionals best suited to advise a German industrial company like Siemens are unlikely to be the best people to advise, say, a Chinese e-commerce company like Alibaba on how to deal with Chinese enforcement agencies. Companies that have to start from scratch to develop private regulation to satisfy U.S. enforcement agencies will be at clear disadvantage to U.S. firms that can draw on years of experience.

To a certain extent, public actors and NGOs, such as enforcement agencies or international organizations, can reduce the importance of access to private compliance experts by providing guidance on self-regulation free of charge. The OECD Working Group, several national enforcement agencies (including the U.S. DOJ and the SEC), and Transparency International all provide advice on how to develop corporate compliance programs. These services might serve as substitutes for individualized professional advice, particularly for small and medium-sized firms.

Outstanding Empirical Questions about Efficiency

So how do we know whether self-regulation is likely to be cost-effective in any given context? Unfortunately, determining cost-effectiveness requires answers to difficult empirical questions such as: How much self-regulation would we see in the absence of organizational liability for corrupt practices? How much would public enforcement agencies have to spend on deterring or educating individuals to achieve the same impact as the incremental firm-level preventive efforts? Will investigations be more effective or less expensive if they are conducted by an investigating magistrate rather than internally?

Similar empirical questions have to be answered to determine whether self-regulation by states whose officials solicit or accept bribes is cost-effective. Key questions include: How much of this regulation would we see in the absence of state liability? Which states find it most costly to investigate and sanction corrupt public officials? Which states can do this most effectively? How effective are cooperative regulatory efforts?

Is Private Regulation Legitimate?

So far we have focused on questions about whether the OECD paradigm's approach to organizational liability is effective and efficient. There are also reasons to question its legitimacy. The kinds of self-regulation promoted by the OECD paradigm are particularly vulnerable on this ground. The concerns are that as private entities, firms like Siemens enjoy neither authorization from nor accountability to all the people affected by their compliance programs.[97] Those people have no say in the matter when Siemens managers decide to prohibit certain types of interactions with public officials, to dig into peoples' private lives as part of "internal" investigations, or to impose sanctions for perceived violations. Even when the affected parties are employees, suppliers, or customers bound to the firm by contract, members of the societies to which they belong arguably ought to have a say in imposing limits on freedom to contract into self-regulation. The argument for broad-based input into decision-making is particularly compelling when self-regulation affects the level of competition in markets for key goods or services. These concerns about the legitimacy of private regulation might explain why some countries are hostile to private regulation and, as in the cases of Russia and China described previously, refuse to adopt complementary legal institutions.

Conclusions

Liability for firms that employ or contract with bribe payers is now regarded as an indispensable component of transnational bribery law, to the point where many legal systems have abandoned long-entrenched hostility to the idea of corporate criminal liability. This expansion of the set of targets for anti-bribery law is a logical way of combating impunity: it recognizes the culpability of organizations that benefit from and fail to prevent bribery, it recruits a whole new set of actors into the project of regulating bribery, and it increases the pool of assets available to compensate victims. However, a regime that extends to organizations will have to be carefully designed to avoid creating more problems than it solves. The potential problems include: distracting plaintiffs and prosecutors from pursuing individual perpetrators; encouraging organizations to cover up past wrongdoing instead of helping to bring it to light; causing collateral damage to innocents; and encouraging firms to invest in self-regulation when state action would be more efficient.

The anti-imperialist paradigm challenges the presumption that there is any uniquely optimal approach to this question of institutional design. Decades of study of comparative law suggest that it is impossible to consider the impact of any component of a legal system in isolation from other components that serve as either substitutes or complements, meaning they either diminish or enhance its impact. Or to put it another way, the consequences of adopting any given legal doctrine will depend on how it fits with the surrounding legal system, defined broadly to include not only laws on the books but also the people and institutions that implement those laws.[98] The law of organizational liability for transnational bribery seems to validate this basic insight.

There clearly is no general answer to the question of whether the pros of extending liability to any given category of organizations outweigh the cons. Whether or not it will distract enforcers from pursuing individuals depends on detailed substantive and procedural rules that determine whether it is more difficult to prosecute a company or an individual. Institutional policies that shape the behavior of enforcement agencies clearly are also relevant. As for the risk of cover-ups, that can in principle be countered by an appropriate scheme of rewards and penalties for collecting and revealing information, or by more sociologically informed approaches; but in practice the level of sophistication of law enforcement agencies will determine whether those schemes can be implemented successfully. The risk of collateral harm also depends on the associated sanctions regime, together with factors such as the quality of corporate governance, rates of profit reinvestment, and rates of turnover among investors and other stakeholders. Similarly, the efficiency of self-regulation clearly depends on the broader legal context. In order to work, privatization of anti-bribery law demands not only a permissive legal regime but also capable, trustworthy private actors as well as public actors who are sufficiently sophisticated to oversee them. In addition, the transition costs associated with adopting a given approach to organizational liability in relation to transnational bribery will depend on whether that approach is novel or already has been adopted in other parts of the relevant legal system.

The case for holding states liable for bribery is also highly contingent. State liability makes the most sense when the state is in a position both to benefit from and to prevent the corrupt transaction. This is most likely to occur in the context of a truly kleptocratic state. Not only does such a state merit condemnation, it also can be punished without causing too much harm to innocent stakeholders (since its resources would have been diverted anyway). Even then, there are questions about whether sanctions actually will induce the state in question to change its ways and whether its regulatory efforts will be cost-effective. For most other states, though, the case for organizational liability is weak: they are more likely to be victims than beneficiaries of the corrupt transaction; sanctions are unlikely to have much effect on their motivations to adopt anti-corruption regulations; and they may have already reached the limits of their ability to regulate their officials cost-effectively.

Even when it makes sense to target organizations, there may not be any uniquely optimal approach to liability. It is eminently plausible that alternative approaches will yield similar results. Vicarious liability for foreign bribery might be functionally equivalent to direct liability for accounting violations. Or liability for supervisors might be equivalent to corporate liability. Again, the only general lesson to be drawn seems to be that the effectiveness and efficiency of any given approach to organizational liability for transnational bribery will depend on the context in which that approach is implemented.

9
How Should Transnational Bribery Law Be Enforced?

Introduction

So far we have considered two of the four major questions surrounding transnational bribery law: What conduct is prohibited, and who may be held liable for violations of those prohibitions? The next question is a more practical one: How is the law enforced? Enforcement makes the difference between a law that is a dead letter and a regime that strikes fear into the hearts of executives and officials and motivates firms to spend tens of millions of dollars on compliance.

Enforcement is a multistage process that encompasses monitoring risky behavior, investigating suspected wrongdoing, adjudicating whether a violation has occurred, determining the appropriate sanctions, and applying the chosen sanctions. The agencies involved include police forces, specialized anti-corruption agencies, prosecutors, investigating magistrates, judges, and correctional officers. As we discussed in the previous chapter, when they target organizations, enforcement agencies often solicit the assistance of private actors such as firms' in-house compliance personnel. The outcomes of enforcement depend on not just the formal rules that govern the process but also the people, tactics, and technology deployed, as well as, of course, the context in which enforcement takes place.

This chapter begins with a motivating case study, the enforcement actions against Marcelo Odebrecht and his family's company, Odebrecht S.A., which stemmed from a massive bribery scheme that extended beyond their native country of Brazil to eleven other countries. Then we turn to the law. We start with a summary of the legal framework that governs enforcement of transnational bribery law, including both substantive and procedural rules. There is considerable variation across jurisdictions so these sections focus on the general guidelines established by international law. The next section briefly discusses enforcement practices, with particular emphasis on the practices of the U.S. enforcement agencies, which are by far the most active enforcers of transnational bribery law. We then discuss the OECD paradigm's approach to enforcement: vigorous investigation and severe sanctions, all aimed primarily at achieving deterrence, and ultimately prevention, with compensation and

Between Impunity and Imperialism. Kevin E. Davis.

condemnation as secondary objectives. The remainder of the chapter sets out a series of increasingly potent critiques of the OECD paradigm's methods and objectives: there might be alternative ways of achieving deterrence, there might be alternatives to deterrence as a form of prevention, and prevention should not be pursued without regard to the associated costs. These objections challenge the effectiveness, efficiency, legitimacy, and fairness of the OECD paradigm's approach to enforcement.

Odebrecht

At the beginning of 2014, Marcelo Odebrecht's star was at its zenith. He was the third-generation scion of one of Brazil's most prominent families and chief executive officer of the family business. The company was the largest construction and engineering company in Brazil, with almost 170,000 employees and operations in twenty-eight countries.[1] The main company in the group, Odebrecht S.A., also held a controlling stake in Braskem, the largest petrochemical company in the Americas, and itself one of Brazil's largest companies.[2] (Braskem also happened to have securities traded on the New York Stock Exchange.) The business was founded in 1944 by Norberto Odebrecht, Marcelo's grandfather. Marcelo was named CEO of the Odebrecht Group in 2008, at a precocious forty years of age, and reportedly was known in the industry as "the Prince of the Contractors." In 2010, the Odebrecht Group was named the World's Best Family-Owned Company by Switzerland's International Institute for Management Development.[3]

During this period Brazil's economy was also on the rise, after a long history of underachievement. The inflection point was the election of the Workers Party in 2002, led by the metal worker and trade unionist turned politician named Lula. Over the next decade, the percentage of the population living in poverty plunged from 24.9 percent to 7.4 percent. Economic growth began to slow in 2014, but from 2003 through 2013 income per capita quadrupled. Brazil's emergence as an economic power was symbolized by Petrobras, the state-owned oil company, whose share issue in 2010 was the largest ever;[4] the country's selection as host of the 2014 World Cup and the 2016 Olympics; and, more controversially, the construction of massive hydroelectric dams in the Amazon to power the growing economy.[5] By 2014 Brazil appeared to have finally arrived in its proper place on the world stage, and Odebrecht was renowned for building the hydroelectric power plants, oil platforms, and stadiums that were symbols of the country's ascent.

And then came the fall. A money laundering investigation that eventually became known as *Operação Lava Jato* (Operation Car Wash) led Brazil's federal police to evidence that officials at Petrobras had been receiving illicit payments. Armed with testimony from two key participants, a money launderer and a Petrobras official, police uncovered what eventually became the largest corruption scandal in Brazil's history. The essence of the scheme was simple. Beginning in 2004, a cartel of leading construction companies colluded to overcharge Petrobras for construction and other services. The bid rigging occurred with the knowledge of key Petrobras officials who were rewarded for their participation with bribes. Those bribes were in turn shared with elected officials and their political parties. (Politicians played a significant role in Petrobras's affairs because the Brazilian government owned just over 50 percent of the company's common shares; in fact, Dilma Roussef, who became president of Brazil in 2011, was chair of the Petrobras board of directors from 2003 to 2010.) Petrobras reported that the total amount of bribes paid totaled approximately \$2 billion. One witness reported that the ruling Workers Party received up to \$200 million over the course of the scheme.[6]

The *Lava Jato* investigation upended Brazilian politics. Prosecutors quickly announced that more than fifty current or former elected officials were under investigation, and rapidly convicted several of them. Former President Lula, who enjoyed immense popularity when he stepped down in 2010, became closely linked to Marcelo Odebrecht and his company after he left power. The *Lava Jato* prosecutors concluded that his ties were illegitimately close and brought multiple charges of corruption against Lula. Lula's handpicked successor, Dilma Roussef, was not accused of personal wrongdoing, but she led Petrobras and the Workers Party while corruption swirled around her. The resulting popular disgust was undoubtedly a factor in her impeachment in 2016, ostensibly for breaking budgetary rules. Roussef's successor as president of Brazil, Michel Temer, and his political allies initially benefited from her downfall, but many of them were also implicated in *Lava Jato* and other corruption scandals. Throughout 2016 and 2017, Brazilian voters watched helplessly as Temer and other politicians used various legal and political maneuvers to avoid prosecution and to undermine *Lava Jato* and related investigations.[7]

The *Lava Jato* prosecutors also targeted bribe payers, focusing on the Odebrecht Group and nine other major Brazilian construction companies. On June 19, 2015, Marcelo Odebrecht was arrested by Brazilian authorities, and nine months later he was sentenced to nineteen years in prison for his involvement in the scheme. In December 2016, his sentence was reduced to two and one-half years in prison and five years of house arrest after he signed an agreement to cooperate with Brazilian authorities and provide evidence against others. His father, Emílio Odebrecht, who served as chairman of Odebrecht S.A.'s board of directors while his son was CEO, was sentenced to four years of house arrest. That same month, Odebrecht S.A. and Braskem signed separate agreements with authorities in the United States, Switzerland, and Brazil resolving foreign bribery and money laundering charges. Each of the enforcement agencies issued press releases describing the agreements, and the U.S. authorities, following their usual practice, published the full text of the agreements and judicial filings, which included detailed factual admissions.[8] Another seventy-six Odebrecht employees or shareholders also entered into agreements to cooperate with the investigation.

These agreements represented a controversial innovation in the Brazilian criminal justice system. Like many countries with a civil law heritage, until recently Brazil had no tradition of using negotiated agreements to resolve criminal proceedings.[9] In 2000, Brazil's competition agency was given the power to resolve administrative and criminal proceedings through "leniency agreements."[10] Laws enacted in 2013 extended the practice to criminal proceedings involving organized crime, as well as civil or administrative proceedings brought against corporations accused of corruption.[11] Federal prosecutors and Brazil's competition agency relied heavily on agreements negotiated pursuant to these laws to resolve cases against both individual and corporate *Lava Jato* defendants. However, a pair of 2017 judicial decisions generated uncertainty about the extent to which judges would approve terms negotiated by prosecutors and whether other enforcement agencies would be bound by the agreements.[12]

The information disclosed in the various settlement agreements revealed misdeeds that went far beyond the Petrobras bid-rigging and bribery scheme. The Odebrecht Group's much-vaunted business model was revealed to be built on corruption. Odebrecht admitted to paying bribes of approximately $788 million in connection with more than one hundred projects in twelve countries (Angola, Argentina, Brazil, Colombia, Dominican Republic, Ecuador, Guatemala, Mexico, Mozambique, Panama, Peru, and Venezuela). The bribery was so extensive that Odebrecht had an entire "Structured Operations" division dedicated to managing bribe payments for the group.[13] For its part, Braskem admitted to using Odebrecht's Structured Operations division not only to obtain favorable terms in dealings with Petrobras but also favorable tax treatment from federal and state governments.[14]

Odebrecht initially agreed with the U.S. authorities that the appropriate criminal fine for its violations of U.S. law would be $4.5 billion, 1.8 times the firm's ill-gotten benefits, less a 25 percent discount for cooperation (but not self-reporting) and remedial efforts. The fine was scheduled to be paid, with interest, over twenty-three years.[15] Even at the time of the initial agreement, however, Odebrecht claimed to be unable to pay more than $2.6 billion. Accordingly, the parties agreed that the final amount of the penalty would be determined after an analysis of the company's financial situation. After completing that analysis, the U.S. Department of Justice agreed to reduce the total penalty to $2.6 billion and to require only $93 million of that amount to be paid to the U.S. Treasury.[16] Braskem agreed to pay a total criminal penalty of $632 million and to settle a civil complaint brought by the SEC by disgorging $325 million in profits.

In addition to the monetary penalties, both Odebrecht and Braskem agreed to continue to cooperate with enforcement agencies around the world, to adopt enhanced compliance procedures, and to retain independent compliance monitors for three years.[17] By April 2017, fifty-one of the seventy-seven employees who admitted to misconduct had been terminated and the others were disciplined in various ways. Odebrecht also reportedly created a compliance staff of sixty people and increased their budget from R$11.3 million to R$64.8 million.[18] The new compliance staff included an attorney from the United States hired as the chief compliance officer of Odebrecht's engineering and construction unit.[19] In December 2017, Emílio Odebrecht stepped down as chairman of the board of directors and announced that "by a decision of the controlling shareholder, no member of the Odebrecht family may henceforth be the CEO of Odebrecht S.A."[20]

The *Lava Jato* investigation extended well beyond Odebrecht. By the end of 2017, the investigation encompassed crimes that allegedly involved around R$6.4 billion (approximately US$2 billion) worth of bribes and was seeking to recover a total of R$38.1 billion (approximately US$11.9 billion). At that point the *Lava Jato* Task Force had brought criminal charges against 289 people and obtained 113 convictions. It also had accused fifty individuals, sixteen firms, and one political party of administrative impropriety.[21] As a result of the investigation, Brazil's national development bank, commonly known by its acronym, BNDES, suspended disbursements on export credits it had granted to Odebrecht and several other construction companies.[22] In addition, several of the firms implicated in *Lava Jato* signed leniency agreements to which Brazil's competition agency was a party and which required the firms to reveal anti-competitive conduct unrelated to the *Lava Jato* affair. Those revelations led to further investigations by the competition authority.[23]

The Odebrecht enforcement action was a truly multinational effort. Most prior efforts of this sort were led by the U.S. enforcement agencies, but in this case Brazilian agencies took the lead. This division of labor was reflected in the division of the monetary penalties. The United States was only slated to receive 10 percent of the monetary penalty imposed on Odebrecht, and that proportion eventually fell to less than 4 percent. (Technically, the U.S. Department of Justice agreed to give Odebrecht credit for paying the remainder of the penalty to the Brazilian and Swiss governments.)[24] The Swiss government accepted CHF 117 million (about US$113.75 million) in settlement of bribery and money laundering charges.[25] The Brazilian government agreed to accept the balance of the agreed amount, relying on a recently adopted procedure for entering into leniency agreements with companies that would otherwise face administrative and civil liability for corruption. Brazil claimed that most of the money it received would be used to compensate victims. As for Braskem, the United States agreed to keep only 15 percent of the criminal penalty ($94.8 million) and 20 percent of the amount disgorged ($65 million).[26] Switzerland accepted CHF 94.5 million (about US$91.87 million) from Braskem.[27]

The United States, Brazil, and Switzerland were the first countries to conclude enforcement actions with Odebrecht and Braskem, but they were not destined to be the last. Odebrecht admitted paying bribes in eleven countries besides Brazil, and the detailed disclosure appended to its agreement with the U.S. Department of Justice provided a road map for enforcement agencies in those countries interested in making their own cases against Odebrecht. The sanctions imposed by those countries could include not only monetary penalties but also avoidance of existing contracts and debarment from future contracts. Within days of the publication of the U.S. plea agreement, Panama announced that it would cancel a $1 billion contract awarded to Odebrecht in 2014 for a hydroelectric project and ban the company from bidding on future public projects.[28] Odebrecht also feared that multilateral development banks would seek to bar it from bidding on projects they financed, a potentially crippling blow for a company that generates substantial amounts of revenue from infrastructure projects in emerging markets. In addition, since Braskem's shares were traded in the United States, it faced the risk of civil litigation under famously liberal U.S. securities laws.

The OECD paradigm generally favors the approach to enforcement adopted in the Odebrecht case: harsh sanctions, of various types, tempered only by grants of leniency to firms and individuals who provide information that advances the investigation. The most frequently cited justification for this approach is the need to achieve deterrence. Most commentators agree that although existing sanctions might seem harsh, in many countries they are not sufficiently severe to achieve deterrence in light of the benefits from paying bribes, the length of time required to complete investigations, and the low probability of detection.[29]

Substantive Rules Governing Enforcement

It is far from clear how the Brazilian, U.S., and Swiss enforcement authorities arrived at the sanctions they imposed in the *Odebrecht* case. Why nineteen years in prison for Marcelo Odebrecht (before he agreed to cooperate)? Was this appropriate in light of the sentences given to the officials he bribed? What about the sanctions imposed on his company? What role did factors such as the magnitude of the loss, the magnitude of the gain, the sanctions imposed on the controlling shareholder, efforts at concealment or cooperation, play in the determination of the sanctions imposed on the corporate actors? How much more credit should Marcelo Odebrecht and the Odebrecht Group have received if, hypothetically, they had voluntarily reported their misconduct before the *Lava Jato* investigation got underway? Why the reluctance to impose a fine that would put the company out of business? Was the appropriate amount dedicated to compensation of victims, and if so, how should the compensation be delivered? Why did the authorities require that Odebrecht and Braskem submit to ongoing oversight instead of assuming that the threat of further monetary sanctions would induce compliance? Are Panama and other countries justified in stripping the Odebrecht Group of rights under existing contracts tainted by bribery? Should it be barred from entering into future contracts, and if so, which types of contracts and for how long?

Some of these questions hint at further complications. Authorities in Switzerland and the United States might reasonably believe that the sanctions for a company like Braskem should remain proportional to the sanctions imposed on defendants in cases like Esquenazi and Siemens. In other words, in determining the sanction for any given defendant, they may wish to take into account the sanctions imposed on defendants in other cases. This approach to setting sanctions implies that it is wrong to isolate the decision about what sanction to impose in any individual case from other enforcement decisions. It suggests that the appropriate way for an enforcement agency to proceed is to set an entire enforcement strategy, consisting of decisions about how to allocate investigative resources, which processes to employ, and which sanctions to impose, for a broad set of cases. In other words, the question is not simply what sanction ought to be imposed in any given case of transnational corruption, but what enforcement strategy should be adopted for the entire universe of cases?

The OECD Convention, and to a lesser extent the UN Convention, provide surprisingly large amounts of guidance on enforcement strategy. With regard to the type of sanction, the OECD Convention stipulates that the sanctions for individuals must include "deprivation of liberty sufficient to enable effective mutual legal assistance and extradition."[30] This effectively means that the sanction must include imprisonment for a term of at least one year.[31] The Convention also requires that the sanctions for foreign bribery must include confiscation of the proceeds. The UN Convention does not go quite so far—it says nothing about whether the sanctions for foreign bribery must include imprisonment, but it does require that confiscation be an option. The UN Convention also is notable for its emphasis on ensuring that both private parties and states have means of obtaining compensation.

With respect to the severity of sanctions, both the OECD Convention and the UN Convention demand that the sanctions imposed on legal persons for foreign bribery be "effective, proportionate and dissuasive," a phrase borrowed from the jurisprudence of the European Court of Justice.[32] However, the OECD Convention extends this requirement to sanctions imposed on natural persons and includes an overarching requirement that the sanctions for foreign bribery be comparable to those imposed for bribery of domestic public officials. The UN Convention merely says that sanctions must "take into account the gravity of the offence."[33] The UN Convention also permits, but does not require, states to take steps to encourage people to cooperate in the investigation or prosecution of offenses established under the Convention, including through offers of immunity from prosecution or mitigation of sanctions.[34]

The OECD regime also has a great deal to say about how much effort states ought to exert to enforce prohibitions on foreign bribery and associated misconduct. This reflects the fact that an important purpose of the OECD Convention was to "level the playing field" in international business by inducing states to take equivalent measures to combat foreign bribery. That purpose would be thwarted by self-interested under-enforcement, either across the board or in the form of selective exemptions for local firms. Consequently, in a carefully worded provision, the OECD Convention attempts simultaneously to prevent countries from considering their national economic or diplomatic interests in the course of making enforcement decisions and to respect their authority to select their own enforcement strategy. That provision, reads as follows:

> **Article 5**
> Investigation and prosecution of the bribery of a foreign public official shall be subject to the applicable rules and principles of each Party. They shall not be influenced by considerations of national economic interest, the potential effect upon relations with another State or the identity of the natural or legal persons involved.

The reference here to "national" economic interest is probably best understood as a call for impartial—as opposed to self-interested—enforcement, rather than an absolute bar on consideration of economic factors in setting enforcement strategy.

The supplementary materials to the OECD Convention, including the 2009 Recommendation, go further. They state that complaints of foreign bribery should be "seriously investigated," and that "adequate resources should be provided to permit effective prosecution."[35] Since 2010, the OECD's peer-driven monitoring system has included in-depth assessments of whether parties to the Convention have complied with these obligations. By contrast, the UN

Convention merely says that prosecutorial discretion must be exercised "to maximize the effectiveness of law enforcement measures" and "with due regard to the need to deter."[36]

National laws and the internal policies of international organizations also establish standards for enforcement of prohibitions on transnational bribery. Those laws and policies permit a wide variety of sanctions for transnational bribery. The main types are:

- Deprivations of liberty, including imprisonment and home confinement
- Confiscation of proceeds
- Monetary fines or penalties, including those designed to achieve disgorgement of benefits
- Obligations to compensate victims
- Obligations to take measures designed to prevent future wrongdoing
- Loss of benefits or privileges, including eligibility for public contracts
- Loss of ability to enforce contracts tainted by bribery—that is, contracts procured through bribery or whose performance entails payment of a bribe—or other legal rights

Countries vary considerably in terms of the permissible types and severity of sanctions. For example, when it comes to fines, some countries impose fixed maximums, others set maximum fines at a multiple of the amount of the bribe or the benefit obtained.[37] In 2016, OECD researchers produced a study showing that the financial returns for an organizational defendant caught participating in a simulated bribery scheme could, depending on which member state's (maximum) sanctions were imposed, vary by $1.7 billion.[38] The researchers identified several variations in the ways that countries calculate monetary penalties. For instance, in some countries, monetary sanctions and confiscation are mutually exclusive.[39] Moreover, many, but not all, countries set maximums for fines and penalties. Occasionally those maximums are a fixed amount of money, with the highest legislated maximum in the world being almost twenty times higher than the lowest. More commonly, maximum monetary penalties are based on a formula that takes into account the amount of the bribe, the benefit or loss received, or the economic size of the wrongdoer.[40] For example, the maximum fine for an organization which violates the U.S. FCPA is the greater of twice the pecuniary gain or twice the pecuniary loss resulting from the offense.[41] Under the corporate liability law that Brazil enacted in 2013, penalties can range up to 20 percent of a company's gross revenue from the previous year (or, if less, three times the value of the advantage sought). The Brazilian regime also establishes a minimum penalty of 0.1 percent of gross revenue.[42]

Even superficially similar laws may differ in important ways. For instance, there are important variations in how countries define assets eligible for confiscation, including: whether indirect proceeds are included, whether assets equivalent in value to the proceeds can be confiscated when the actual proceeds cannot be found, and whether gross or net proceeds are eligible.[43]

National laws do not generally commit any particular amount of resources to enforcement of foreign bribery laws. As a result, the allocation of resources to enforcement of transnational bribery law generally is left to the discretion of individual enforcement agencies, subject to oversight from their superiors as well as monitoring by NGOs and international organizations such as the OECD Working Group.

Procedural Rules Governing Enforcement

In practice, the range of enforcement strategies that a country can pursue is constrained by not only substantive laws that specify the range of permissible sanctions but also the procedural laws that govern enforcement actions. The UN Convention and the OECD Convention demand that foreign bribery be treated as a criminal offense, which implies that some sort of criminal process must be available. The rules of criminal procedure vary from one jurisdiction to another, but some elements of a criminal process are fairly standard. The process is controlled by either a judge or prosecutor; when it concludes, a judge is entitled to impose punitive rather than only compensatory sanctions; and a finding of guilt is associated with a relatively large amount of stigma for the defendant. In many jurisdictions, foreign bribery also can be sanctioned through publicly initiated proceedings that are "civil" or "administrative" in nature. These generally involve less severe sanctions and less stigma. These civil or administrative proceedings are sometimes initiated by the staff of administrative agencies, and in some cases are adjudicated by the agency itself. Most of this range of procedural options is illustrated by the U.S. approach to enforcement of the FCPA. FCPA violations may be the subject of a criminal prosecution controlled by the U.S. Department of Justice, a civil proceeding initiated by the Department of Justice, a civil suit initiated by the staff of the U.S Securities and Exchange Commission, or an administrative proceeding before the U.S. Securities and Exchange Commission.

In an increasing number of jurisdictions, the agency entitled to bring an enforcement action can bypass a trial and impose sanctions pursuant to an agreement negotiated with the defendant. The practice of relying on negotiated agreements to determine sanctions in foreign bribery cases originated in the United States and has subsequently spread to other jurisdictions, including, as illustrated by the *Odebrecht* case, Brazil and Switzerland. Different jurisdictions provide for varying levels of transparency and judicial oversight of these agreements. In the United States there are several procedural routes to a negotiated resolution and some of them give judges very little authority to review the terms of the agreement. At the same time, the U.S. agreements, including agreed statements of the underlying facts, are routinely published in their entirety on the websites of the relevant enforcement agencies. However, agreements to limit the scope of an investigation or the range of misconduct alleged generally are not disclosed. Moreover, U.S. prosecutors generally refrain from disclosing the names of individuals and firms who have been implicated in misconduct but not charged, including bribe recipients and co-conspirators.[44] Most jurisdictions which have adopted the practice of negotiated resolutions in foreign bribery cases have explicitly tried to draw lessons from the U.S. experience.[45] Legislation in those countries, which include Brazil, typically requires more judicial oversight of negotiated resolutions than in the United States.[46]

An additional procedural wrinkle is that it is sometimes possible for an enforcement action in one jurisdiction to rely on evidence or legal conclusions generated as part of an enforcement action in another jurisdiction. The UN Convention explicitly requires parties to assist in enforcing confiscation orders issued by foreign authorities.[47] The Convention also requires parties to impose sanctions for money laundering predicated on corrupt acts committed outside their jurisdiction, which might well have been established in the course of foreign proceedings.[48] As for loss of privileges, under European Union law, "a conviction by final judgment" for corruption involving a member state of the European Union is grounds for mandatory debarment (which, as of 2014, can be avoided by providing evidence of reliability).[49] Similarly, the World Bank and other major multilateral development banks have agreed to enforce one another's debarment decisions.[50]

Enforcement Practices

The enforcement strategies that countries actually pursue are only partly determined by the laws that specify permissible sanctions and the procedural steps to be followed. Within those legal boundaries, enforcement agencies have considerable room to decide which targets to pursue, how many resources to allocate to them, which sanctions within the permissible range to seek, and how to disseminate information about their actions.

It is difficult to generalize about the choices enforcement agencies have made to date. Many countries fail to collect or publish detailed enforcement data on foreign bribery.[51] In other countries it has been difficult to discern the patterns in enforcement practices. Sometimes this is because there have been too few enforcement actions to establish a pattern—in the first round of peer reviews under the OECD Convention, roughly two-thirds of countries were criticized for failing to devote adequate resources to investigating and prosecuting foreign bribery.[52] To the extent patterns are discernible, there appears to be a fair amount of variation in enforcement practices both across and within countries.

Consider sanctions aimed at individuals. Between 1999 and the end of 2016, OECD Convention countries imposed criminal sanctions on 443 individuals for foreign bribery.[53] The OECD Working Group reports that "at least 125" were sentenced to terms of imprisonment (the reason there could be more is because many states do a poor job of collecting statistics of this sort).[54] Most of the prison terms ranged between one and five years, but as we have seen, some offenders, like Joel Esquenazi (fifteen years), have received much longer sentences. There is considerable variation across countries in this area: twenty countries which had applicable laws in force during the period did not sanction any individuals whatsoever in criminal foreign bribery cases, while 326 of the 443 individuals sanctioned were targeted by either the United States (82) or Germany (244).[55] There is also variation within countries. For example, in the United States, sentences for FCPA violations—thus excluding bribe recipients prosecuted for money laundering—for the five years ending in 2016 ranged from zero to sixty months in prison, with a median sentence of nineteen months. It also is difficult to discern the pattern in these sentences, which is not entirely surprising given that they were handed down by different judges, sitting in different parts of a large and diverse country.

It is difficult to compare sanctions imposed on organizations across countries because there are relatively few cases, many of them involve joint enforcement actions, and there is limited information about the circumstances surrounding the firms' misconduct. One interesting dimension along which legal systems have varied is in terms of their willingness to order corporate wrongdoers to take preventive measures. U.S. prosecutors frequently mandate that firms like Odebrecht and Braskem institute regular training programs, enhance the authority of compliance professionals, and appoint outside monitors, at their own expense, to evaluate and report on their progress.[56] Other countries have begun to follow the lead of the United States in this respect, but the practice is controversial. For instance, in the course of sentencing a company named Innospec, which was also being sanctioned by U.S. authorities, a U.K. judge complained about the cost of implementing these sorts of requirements. He mused that if the risk of future misconduct is so high that extraordinary monitoring is appropriate, then it might make sense to impose a fine that puts the company out of business, and otherwise it might be more cost-effective to rely on a company's auditors to detect future misconduct.[57]

As far as enforcement procedures are concerned, in the United States, negotiated agreements are virtually the exclusive process used to resolve foreign bribery actions against corporations, and they are used frequently against individuals as well. Enforcement agencies in other members of the OECD Convention, including Brazil, France, Italy, Norway, and the United Kingdom, are permitted to rely on negotiated resolutions and appear to be increasingly keen on using them.[58] This trend has not been welcomed in all quarters. Critics in the United States have focused primarily on the absence of judicial review of negotiated resolutions, claiming that it is inconsistent with traditional conceptions of due process or the rule of law.[59] In a similar vein, a Brazilian judge, asked to approve a negotiated agreement between the *Ministério Público Federal* and an individual *Lava Jato* defendant, expressed reservations about the way in which the process of negotiated resolution departed from the traditional civil law conception of the judicial role and curtailed judges' ability to ascertain facts and determine sanctions.[60] More generally, the use of negotiated resolutions has also been criticized in terms of effectiveness and lack of transparency.[61] In 2016, a group of NGOs issued a letter urging the OECD to join other international bodies in developing global standards for the use of negotiated resolutions in foreign bribery cases against corporate defendants. Among other things they complained that the outcomes of these negotiations were too lenient on companies that had failed to self-report or were recidivists, shielded companies from debarment and adverse reputational consequences, left individuals unpunished, and ignored the goal of providing compensation to victim countries. They also complained about lack of judicial oversight and transparency.[62]

The OECD Paradigm

Proponents of the OECD paradigm value certainty and severity in the imposition of sanctions. This comes through loud and clear in peer reviews conducted under the auspices of the OECD Convention. Countries are most frequently taken to task for failing to impose sanctions on legal persons that are sufficiently "effective, proportionate, dissuasive" and for failing to devote sufficient resources to investigating and prosecuting foreign bribery. Both the OECD and observers like Transparency International also lament the fact that while a handful of countries, like the United States, have vigorously enforced laws against foreign bribery, many countries have engaged in little or no enforcement.[63]

The theory that underpins these complaints about countries' enforcement strategies generally is not articulated explicitly, but it is consistent with a common-sense idea of how to achieve prevention through deterrence in an efficient manner.[64]

Deterrence theory presumes that potential wrongdoers decide whether to comply with the law and to cooperate with enforcement efforts based on a rational analysis of which course of action will yield the consequences they prefer the most. In this model of human behavior, people compare the consequences of compliance and cooperation with the consequences of alternative courses of action, and choose the path with the highest returns.[65]

According to the theory, in order to induce compliance, the anticipated adverse consequences of noncompliance must be sufficiently unattractive to outweigh the net benefits of noncompliance. The adverse consequences include legal sanctions as well as a variety of nonlegal factors that we can lump together under the term "shame." The net benefits of noncompliance reflect both the net gains from wrongdoing—in the case of bribery, the value of officials' illicit favors less the cost of the bribe—and the "benefit" of avoiding expensive prevention and monitoring of employees or agents. So, for example, suppose that a firm would have to incur $1 million in compliance costs to prevent its employees from paying bribes that will yield net gains of $9 million. Noncompliance will put the firm $9 million ahead, while compliance will leave it $1 million behind. A legal sanction of at least $10 million will be required to induce the requisite compliance effort. This logic can be extended to support sanctions regimes that provide separate incentives for different kinds of behavior, such as, for example, prevention, monitoring, and reporting.

Careful readers will notice that, in theory, the same incentives can be created by paying firms a reward of $10 million to comply. Rewards and sanctions are not perfectly interchangeable, however.[66] If compliance is commonplace, then rewards will be relatively costly to implement—not only must funds be raised to finance the reward, the administrative costs of paying the reward will have to be incurred relatively frequently, more frequently than the administrative costs associated with the corresponding sanction. However, rewards have their advantages. For one, rewards ease the problem of detection. People willingly come forward to claim rewards while they hide from sanctions. Rewards also automatically provide compensation to people who incur the cost of compliance, which might seem only fair when costs of compliance are high and are concentrated on a small number of people. Consequently, rewards are attractive when they are aimed at inducing a relatively small number of individuals or firms to report wrongdoing at significant personal cost. In these situations the reward can be funded out of monetary sanctions imposed on the wrongdoer, the administrative costs are low because the targeted group is very small, and the result is to ensure that no single individual or firm bears an unusually large portion of the burden associated with behavior that benefits society as a whole.

Calculations of the deterrent effects of sanctions have to be adjusted to account for uncertainty: the costs of hiring compliance personnel are not stable over time; bribed officials may or may not deliver what they have promised; enforcement agencies may or may not detect misconduct; and enforcement agencies may or may not impose any given type of sanction. It is conventional to assume that people assign value to sets of uncertain outcomes by multiplying the probability of each outcome's occurrence by the value of the outcome. So, for example, a choice that exposes a person to a 10 percent chance of receiving a $100 million fine will be treated as equivalent to a choice to be subjected with certainty to a $10 million fine.

This classical version of deterrence theory has a straightforward implication for enforcement strategy: to enhance compliance, it will be necessary to increase either the severity or the certainty of sanctions, or both. Which kind of reform to undertake depends on the applicable constraints. The ability to increase severity might be limited if: sanctions are already approaching inherent limits, such as insolvency in the case of monetary sanctions; it is important to maintain proportionality between sanctions for various offenses; or, new legislation is required. Meanwhile, the ability to increase the certainty of being sanctioned might be limited if enforcement agencies lack expertise or have trouble finding additional resources to allocate to regulation of foreign bribery.

The OECD paradigm's general preference for using severe sanctions as a means of deterrence is qualified by the need to preserve incentives for cooperation. For the reasons given previously, it might make sense to mitigate sanctions, or even provide rewards, to whistleblowers, firms that self-report misconduct, or similar actors. Mitigation might involve reducing sanctions or even taking some of them off the table entirely. For instance, by declining to insist upon a resolution that involves a criminal conviction, or by limiting disclosure of the details of misconduct that has led to a conviction, enforcement agencies can reduce defendants' exposure to other forms of liability such as reputational sanctions, civil liability, and debarment. The value of offering leniency in exchange for cooperation is accepted by many enforcement agencies, including the U.S., Brazilian, and Swiss agencies that took the lead in the Odebrecht enforcement action. However, acceptance of the idea is not universal. For instance, the leading cases on whether international arbitral tribunals ought to permit firms implicated in bribery to enforce tainted contracts make no reference to whether the firm has cooperated in subsequent enforcement efforts.[67]

Negotiated resolutions are compatible with the idea of efficient prevention because they allow enforcement agencies and defendants to achieve a mutually acceptable resolution while avoiding significant expense. For enforcement agencies, the money that would have been devoted to trying a single defendant can be directed toward other enforcement efforts.

Even if it is motivated by deterrence and efficiency the OECD paradigm's approach to enforcement might be compatible with other theories of enforcement. Some of the sanctions favored under the current paradigm are consistent with the idea of prevention through incapacitation. The practice of debarment, that is, deeming firms which have engaged in misconduct to be ineligible for contracts, is the most obvious example of a strategy aimed at incapacitation. Sentences which encourage or require organizations to dismiss specific individuals also seem like a form of incapacitation. As for condemnation and compensation, imposing severe penalties is a straightforward way to express condemnation, and if those penalties are monetary, they can be used to fund compensatory payments. Meanwhile, on the procedural side, negotiated resolutions at first glance seem to compromise entitlements such as the right to be tried by an impartial adjudicator and to appeal a criminal conviction. However, proponents of negotiated resolutions argue that this problem is illusory because defendants are entitled to waive their due process entitlements.

Alternative Approaches to Deterrence?

A key aspect of the anti-imperialist critique is that reasonable people can disagree about the design of transnational bribery law, particularly when the people in question are considering laws that will apply in different contexts. This insight provides the basis for challenging both the effectiveness and the legitimacy of universalistic prescriptions associated with the OECD paradigm. To the extent that the OECD paradigm creates pressure to harmonize enforcement strategies, it opens itself up to this kind of criticism.

Even if the basic precepts of deterrence theory are valid, at least three factors ensure that the relationships between law enforcement strategies and outcomes will be complex and context-dependent: variations in compliance costs, the variable and complex impact of nonlegal consequences of noncompliance, and uncertainty about how to manipulate people's perceptions of enforcement strategies. Adjusting enforcement strategy to account for these factors is likely to entail difficult judgment calls because they tend to vary across individuals, sectors, and countries, as well as over time.

Compliance Costs

Compliance costs play a critical role in determining the deterrent impact of legal sanctions. All other things being equal, the greater the costs of compliance, the greater the sanctions required to induce compliance. For example, the illustration used in the preceding section showed that a penalty of $10 million would be sufficient to induce a firm to incur $1 million in compliance costs to prevent its employees from paying bribes that will yield net gains of $9 million. That penalty would not be sufficient to deter the firm if its compliance costs were $2 million. In that scenario, deterrence would require a penalty of $11 million.

Compliance costs are most relevant in organizational settings where achieving compliance requires substantial investments in prevention and monitoring. As Odebrecht eventually acknowledged, an effective compliance program is likely to entail more than instructing employees to "just say no" to bribery.

The cost of achieving any given level of compliance within an organization will depend on the costs of monitoring and how employees respond to supervision. These will in turn depend on the nature of the business and employees' propensities to engage in wrongdoing. One way to gain insight into those propensities is to examine reported attitudes toward bribery. All indications are that those attitudes are highly variable. For example, surveys suggest that women tend to be more opposed to bribery than men, people in Ethiopia are more opposed to bribe taking than people in Ghana, and that opposition to bribery declined in the United States between 1995 and 2006.[68]

All of this suggests that compliance costs might vary significantly from one firm to another. It also suggests that it might be difficult to measure the costs faced by any given firm. For example, to assess the compliance costs for a firm like Odebrecht we would have to answer questions such as: Did employees have qualms about bribery that were overcome only by the magnitude of the potential gains, or did they view it as a morally acceptable way of doing business? Were employees' attitudes toward bribery uniform, or did they vary across the firm, or across units? How would all those attitudes change in the aftermath of *Lava Jato*? In a closely held company like Odebrecht—and many other Latin American corporations—is the only way to induce compliance to invest in costly monitoring and controls, or is it sufficient to replace or deter the controlling shareholders?

The Impact of Shame

The deterrent effect of legal sanctions will depend on the extent to which noncompliance also leads to other adverse nonlegal consequences.[69] Those consequences include pangs of conscience as well as nonlegal sanctions imposed by private actors, ranging from sideways glances, to insults, to exclusion from social networks and business opportunities. For the sake of convenience, we can use the term "shame" to refer to this entire category of consequences. Individuals value self-esteem, social interactions, and emotional validation, and we should assume that they will try to avoid behaving in ways that lead to being reviled and shunned, just as they will try to avoid imprisonment. Even if Marcelo Odebrecht never expected to spend a day in prison, he undoubtedly would have tried to avoid the experience of seeing his reputation destroyed. Organizations are also susceptible to shame, not only because individual employees within the organization might be affected by or concerned about their employer's shame but also because there are real financial consequences associated with being shunned by customers and suppliers.[70]

The potential impact of shame varies depending on factors such as the moral attitudes that prevail among people who would have to impose the sanctions, and the extent to which the target is dependent on the affected relationships. A person who does business and socializes in a closely knit community in which most people disapprove of bribery is much more vulnerable to nonlegal sanctions than someone who lives in a more tolerant community or has more fluid social and business relationships. Notice the implication that compliance costs and susceptibility to shame are likely to be correlated with one another—it will be relatively easy for an organization to induce compliance when its employees are morally committed to integrity and have nonlegal reasons to comply with anti-bribery laws. And people who are morally committed to integrity are more likely to impose nonlegal sanctions.

Even if it is possible to measure the deterrent effects of shame, it can be difficult to figure out how to adjust legal sanctions so that the cumulative impact of the legal and nonlegal consequences of noncompliance achieves optimal deterrence. Where shame is powerful, relatively weak legal sanctions might be enough to deter; where shame is less powerful, more potent legal sanctions are required to deter, all other things being equal. A complicating factor, however, is that sometimes shame is triggered by legal sanctions, or at least by the initiation of legal processes. Without legal intervention, people may be reluctant to condemn misconduct they have not directly observed—and direct observation is unlikely in the case of transnational bribery. When shame requires at least modest legal sanctions as a trigger, deterrence cannot be achieved without legal sanctions. In these settings, the deterrent effects of introducing modest legal sanctions will be large, but the impact of further enhancements in those sanctions will be relatively small (since they will not trigger further nonlegal consequences). To further complicate matters, the amount of shame associated with violating the law will depend on factors such as how harshly the law condemns the relevant misconduct, and what proportion of wrongdoers are detected.[71] Marcelo Odebrecht's prosecution should lead to great shame if it signals a gross deviation from the behavior of the average Brazilian businessperson, but less shame if it shows only that he was one of many equally corrupt businesspeople.

Officials who try to assess the implications of shame for deterrence necessarily engage in acts of judgment rather than purely scientific analyses. The underlying parameters are both highly variable and largely unobservable, especially in the context of unprecedented enforcement strategies. Consider the problem of how to sanction the *Lava Jato* defendants. There was no precedent for imprisoning a Brazilian corporate leader of the stature of Marcelo Odebrecht. Would the shame of being incarcerated for any period of time be enough to deter similarly situated executives, or were people of that kind truly shameless?

Enforcement Agencies' Abilities to Manipulate Incentives Effectively

According to deterrence theory, prevention depends critically on how potential wrongdoers *perceive* the consequences of their actions. In order to implement effective deterrence-oriented enforcement strategies, an enforcement agency must be able to figure out how to manipulate those perceptions, and especially perceptions of the likelihood of being sanctioned.[72]

The most obvious approach to this task is the direct one: enforcement agencies could calculate the likelihoods of being sanctioned for all the relevant types of foreign bribery under various enforcement strategies, select and implement their preferred strategy, and then publicize information about the likelihood of being sanctioned along with information about typical sanctions. Each step in this process is fraught with difficulty.

First, the calculations required to estimate the probability of detection associated with alternative enforcement strategies are daunting. The variables in play begin with the quantity and quality of the personnel charged with investigating and sanctioning transnational bribery. Then, since even the most insightful investigators require clues, their rates of success will depend on the kinds of records that are kept of corrupt transactions. Also relevant is the extent to which private actors are willing and able to report suspicions of wrongdoing to enforcement authorities, which will in turn depend on their moral attitudes and incentives to cooperate with the state. Another critical variable is the volume of corrupt activity over which investigative resources are distributed—for instance, when bribery is pervasive, wrongdoers might reasonably expect to benefit from safety in numbers. And these data will have to be collected separately for many different types of misconduct; there is no reason to expect the probability of detection to be the same for bribes involving, say, high-level officials in Brazil and low-level customs officials in Nigeria.

In principle it ought to be possible to find an algorithm that uses these data as inputs to calculate the likelihood of sanctions being imposed. Identifying this kind of enforcement algorithm will inevitably require a certain amount of data on the relationship between the various inputs and historical outcomes. But that requires agencies to draw on historical data on the overall volume of foreign bribery. These are data they generally don't have: as a paradigmatic example of a victimless crime, bribery often goes unreported and undetected. This problem can be circumvented to some extent through surveys that ask people to self-report misconduct anonymously. As we discussed in chapter 4, efforts to collect these kinds of data are in their infancy. For the time being, however, enforcement agencies know the resources they have historically allocated to enforcement, the enforcement actions they have taken, and the number of instances they have detected, but they typically do not have historical data on baseline levels of wrongdoing.[73]

The next step in the process of manipulating perceptions is to select and commit to a particular enforcement strategy. Commitment generally is a problem for enforcement agencies.[74] The problem begins with the fact that investigation of bribery and other economic crimes is generally reactive. The likelihood that a bribe paid today will be sanctioned in the future depends on whether enforcement agencies decide to investigate and prosecute before the applicable time limits expire. For example, in the United States, federal criminal law generally allows a defendant to be prosecuted so long as they have been indicted within five years after the commission of an offense (28 U.S.C. § 2462). And this five-year limitation period can be extended by agreement or in cases in which the government requires evidence from a foreign country (18 U.S. Code § 3292). These lengthy limitation periods provide ample time for enforcement strategy to change after a wrongdoer has engaged in misconduct, including as a result of changes in the availability of resources. Moreover, the combination of short budget cycles and broad prosecutorial discretion makes it implausible for U.S. enforcement agencies to commit themselves to any particular enforcement policy through the end of the applicable limitation period. FCPA enforcement is a case in point. The United States ramped up enforcement beginning sometime around 2006, but the cases resolved in 2007 generally involved misconduct that began at least five years earlier. In 2002, no one in the U.S. government could have made a credible commitment about the level of enforcement that eventually would be brought to bear on bribes paid in that year.

Similarly, in the aftermath of *Lava Jato*, what could any enforcement agency credibly say about the likelihood of being sanctioned for transnational bribery in Brazil? The investigations yielded shocking information about the prevalence of corruption in certain sectors of the Brazilian economy. Why should enforcement agencies be confident that they know how much misconduct is taking place in other sectors? And given the country's political turmoil, who can predict the resources that will be devoted to anti-bribery law over the next few months, much less years?

The final step in an effective campaign to manipulate perceptions of enforcement is communication with potential wrongdoers. In a world characterized by information overload lawmakers cannot take the attention of their intended audiences for granted, and they have to make conscious efforts to make sure that information about enforcement reaches its intended audiences.[75]

The communication process is not wholly independent of the process of selecting other aspects of an enforcement strategy: some enforcement strategies are easier to communicate than others. The best way to break into the newsfeeds of corporate decision makers and public officials is to do things that are newsworthy, such as imposing surprisingly harsh penalties or targeting high-profile figures. For all but the most careful analysts, perceptions of transnational bribery law have been influenced more strongly by well-publicized cases such as *Esquenazi, Siemens*, and *Lava Jato*, than by less-publicized but more typical cases. In principle, enforcement agencies can use high-profile cases to shape perceptions in ways that compensate for other constraints on their enforcement capabilities. For instance, a few aggressive enforcement actions can leave the impression that sanctions are more certain and severe than in reality. This cuts both ways, though—a few high-profile botched prosecutions can create a misleading perception of impunity. Moreover, as a practical matter, it is likely to be difficult for an agency to anticipate accurately how potential wrongdoers will extrapolate from well-publicized cases to their own situations—after hearing about Marcelo Odebrecht's case, will a typical Brazilian executive expect to be treated more or less favorably if caught paying a bribe?

For any given set of enforcement actions communication entails, at a minimum, making the relevant information available to the public, if only by posting it on a government website. Even this minimal level of effort may be beyond many enforcement agencies—Phase 3 peer reviews under the OECD Convention suggest that many member states (seventeen out of thirty-seven) have struggled to publish adequate statistics about enforcement of laws against foreign bribery and that almost all can do more to raise awareness of laws against foreign bribery.[76] However, given the challenge of information overload, settling for a minimalist communication strategy is risky. A more robust communication strategy is likely to include press releases salted with titillating details, dramatic press conferences, glossy publications summarizing enforcement statistics, regular speeches and interviews by enforcement officials, and well-organized websites archiving all sorts of information and publications. The

U.S. Department of Justice and Brazil's *Ministério Público Federal* are advanced practitioners of these kinds of tactics.

Given all the challenges and strategic options, enforcement agencies can reasonably disagree about how to manipulate incentives to engage in foreign bribery. This, combined with the possibility that different kinds of manipulations will be required in different contexts, opens the door to reasonable disagreements about how to achieve deterrence.

Alternatives to Deterrence as Means of Prevention?

Even if we focus on the objective of prevention, deterrence is not the only channel through which legal sanctions influence behavior. Other theories of decision-making emphasize factors such as persuasion and rehabilitation—roughly speaking, consent rather than coercion—and they point to different enforcement strategies as approaches to prevention.

As we have seen, deterrence theory can accommodate the idea that moral constraints are significant influences on behavior. However, in deterrence theory, moral constraints are simply taken as given, exogenously specified, and presumed to be immutable. That presumption is highly suspect. It is perfectly reasonable to believe that moral attitudes are not only mutable but might be influenced by the actions of enforcement agencies. Enforcement strategies that wish to capitalize on this possibility can draw on a substantial body of research which suggests that people comply with rules, including both rules established by generally applicable laws and rules established by employers, at least in part because they think it is right thing to do, not because they fear sanctions for noncompliance. The literature points to several potential sources of this kind of obligation to comply with the law.[77]

One possible source is people's well-documented drive to conform to the behavior of their peers, independently of whether anyone will sanction them for deviance. The set of peers used to evaluate what counts as deviance is known as the "reference group." If bribery is the norm in their reference group, then people will be willing to pay bribes. If bribery is the exception, then they will refrain.[78]

Another reason why someone might comply with the law is because it conforms to their moral values.[79] In the case of anti-bribery law, this obvious answer may be the most important one. Many people refrain from paying or demanding bribes simply because they believe bribery is wrong, independently of what the law dictates.

People might also feel an obligation to comply with rules that represent justifiable assertions of power, in other words, rules they perceive to be legitimate.

In other words, some people feel obligated to obey the law simply because it is *the law*, regardless of whether they agree with its content and whether they expect to be the targets of enforcement.[80] Several factors might drive perceptions of legitimacy.[81] Some people might focus on whether law enforcement agencies demonstrate effectiveness in fighting crime. Or, they might focus on whether the law is enforced fairly and in accordance with due process. As we suggested in chapter 5, fairness is a function of how the benefits and burdens of the law are distributed across individuals or groups or societies. For instance, people may be reluctant to comply with rules that an enforcement agency uses selectively against foreign bribe payers, to the exclusion of both domestic bribe payers and foreign public officials. Meanwhile, perceptions of due process are based on the quality of decision-making processes, taking into account whether decisions are made transparently, by impartial decision makers, who behave consistently, and who provide opportunities for people to present their side of the dispute and seek review of decisions with which they disagree. Perceptions of due process also might reflect perceptions of the quality of treatment, such as whether suspected wrongdoers are treated with respect, dignity, and courtesy.[82]

Like deterrence, persuasion operates by influencing people's perceptions of the law. Both approaches to prevention suggest that what enforcement agencies say about transnational bribery law may be more important than what they do. However, persuasion and deterrence may point to very different communication strategies. For instance, an agency that plays on tendencies to conform may soft-pedal a crackdown on an industry-wide bid-rigging scheme in order to maintain perceptions that integrity is the norm in public procurement. By contrast, an agency focused on deterrence might brag about its high success rate.

Persuasion and deterrence also may entail communicating different types of information. For instance, persuasion might require presenting compliance as a moral rather than a purely legal obligation.[83] Establishing the legality of an obligation involves proving that it emanates from a legally authoritative source. Establishing that an obligation is morally binding might involve the analogous exercise of showing that the purported obligation is derived from an accepted moral principle, but that is not necessarily the most effective approach to moral education. While some people learn from moral commandments, many others learn from parables—stories of relatable characters who earn praise when they do the right thing and condemnation when they do wrong. U.S. enforcement agencies frequently produce these kinds of moralistic narratives when they announce the resolution of FCPA enforcement actions. Their press releases include detailed descriptions of the misconduct characterized in morally loaded terms. For example, in announcing its actions against Odebrecht, a prosecutor from the Department of Justice said, "Such brazen wrongdoing calls for a strong response from law enforcement," and an FBI official said, "The FBI will not stand by idly while corrupt individuals threaten a fair and competitive economic system or fuel criminal enterprises."[84]

Thinking more broadly, the communications strategy of an agency focused on persuasion probably should treat transparency as an overarching goal, as a way of promoting legitimacy. This might include publicizing how officials are chosen, the criteria used to select cases for investigation or prosecution, the outcomes of individual enforcement actions, and indicators of overall effectiveness. This kind of transparency can be in tension with the dictates of deterrence since there are circumstances in which uncertainty about the probability of enforcement enhances deterrence.

There are other ways in which an enforcement strategy aimed at persuasion might be at odds with one aimed at deterrence. If the probability of detection is low, deterrence favors harsh sanctions combined with the promise of leniency for those who provide information to enforcement agencies. This points to long terms of imprisonment, arrests, and trials designed to do maximal damage to the reputations of offenders, and large monetary sanctions. If, however, the aim is to persuade people that the law is fair, and therefore ought to be complied with, then enforcers should strive to ensure that sanctions are proportional to the harm, or risk of harm, posed by misconduct. In fact, disproportionate sanctions might do more harm than good if they undermine the law's moral force. Managers might view obviously disproportionate sanctions as a cost of doing business rather than the products of considered moral judgments. The result may be that rational cost-benefit analysis crowds out decision-making based on moral considerations. Similarly, humiliating senior executives might deter, but it might also encourage resentment and defiance.

Persuasion and deterrence might even point to different enforcement processes. Settlements that avoid costly trials might be a good way to enhance deterrence by conserving enforcement resources and maximizing the number of people who can be investigated and sanctioned. But settlements that deny defendants any opportunity to challenge their sanctions before an impartial decision maker might undermine legitimacy.

Sometimes it will be necessary to choose between enforcement strategies based on deterrence and persuasion, or to adopt some sort of hybrid approach.[85] The philosophy of enforcement—deterrence, persuasion, hybrid, and so forth—can be chosen for an entire legal system, or at a more granular level, such as for a particular sector. In some cases it might even make sense to tailor the enforcement philosophy to fit an individual defendant. For example, it might become clear in the course of an enforcement action that the defendant, whether a firm like Odebrecht S.A. or an individual like Marcelo Odebrecht, is immune to ordinary forms of deterrence or persuasion and that special measures will be required to prevent reoffending. Perhaps the gains from offending are so high, or the probability of detection is so low, that the only sanctions large enough to serve as a deterrent would impose unacceptably large costs on the firm's stakeholders. Or perhaps it is apparent that the managers of the firm have escaped the control of investors and that selfish short-term considerations will lead them to ignore investors' interests and court even ruinous liability. Or perhaps a culture of corruption is so unusually entrenched that social pressures to persist in misconduct will override forms of deterrence and persuasion that are likely to succeed in other firms. Yet another possibility is that the managers are genuinely ignorant about how to reduce the risk of future misconduct.

Prevention of future misconduct by defendants who display some or all of these characteristics will require extraordinary measures. One option is indefinite incapacitation, whether through debarment or a crippling monetary penalty, but the collateral costs might be excessive (more on this later). Alternative measures that might be more cost-effective include enhanced monitoring, prohibitions on risky behavior, mandatory training programs, and, in the case of organizations, reforming internal compliance processes.[86] Enhanced monitoring combined with prohibitions on risky behavior and stronger internal compliance processes all tend to facilitate deterrence by increasing the probability of detection. Training represents a commitment to persuasion, possibly a deeper commitment than might be appropriate for the typical organization. Finally, specifying the compliance measures that organizations ought to take can be a way of overcoming ignorance by sharing best practices. Determining whether any of these extraordinary measures are warranted obviously entails difficult judgment calls.

The Costs of Enforcement: Implications for Efficiency and Fairness

So far we have focused on concerns about whether the enforcement strategies associated with the OECD paradigm maximize the benefits of enforcement, in terms of harm prevented, compensated, or condemned. Another line of attack sets its sights on the costs associated with those enforcement strategies. Those costs stem from both enforcement and anticipated enforcement. They fall directly on enforcing states and wrongdoers and less directly upon suspected wrongdoers and potential wrongdoers, as well as innocent stakeholders. It is inherent in the nature of transnational bribery law that costs—as well as benefits—of enforcement frequently land on people outside the countries that design or implement enforcement strategies. Depending upon the magnitude and distribution of these enforcement costs they might compromise the efficiency or fairness of an enforcement strategy, and perhaps even the entire regime.

The direct costs incurred by enforcement agencies are difficult to estimate. The costs of prosecuting Odebrecht and Braskem were almost certainly at the high end of the range. Brazil's *Lava Jato* Task Force (which was responsible for far more than just prosecuting Odebrecht and Braskem) included at its peak, almost sixty federal police officers and another twenty-nine prosecutors.[87] Meanwhile, the U.S. DOJ and the SEC listed eleven prosecutors as part of the team responsible for the cases against Braskem and Odebrecht, and acknowledged support from a dedicated anti-corruption unit at the U.S. Federal Bureau of Investigation.[88]

The costs of the enforcement action also include the costs incurred by wrongdoers and suspected wrongdoers. Marcelo Odebrecht, together with the executives and public officials who were convicted by the *Lava Jato* prosecutors, obviously suffered, and will continue to suffer. Meanwhile Odebrecht S.A. was hurt not only by the fines and penalties assessed but also by having contracts canceled and being shut out of bidding for new public contracts. Odebrecht's head count shrank from a high of 168,000 in 2014 to just under 80,000 in December 2016, although it is impossible to disentangle the impact of legal sanctions from the effects of the overall decline in the Brazilian economy (admittedly caused in part by Odebrecht's misconduct) and normal fluctuations in the scale of the firm's operations.[89] As for the rest of the construction sector, one study estimated that Brazil's leading construction companies would cut investment by 30 percent in 2015 as a result of *Lava Jato*.[90] Some of those losses were suffered even before the full cost of the sanctions was known—the risk of crippling sanctions was enough to frighten potential investors and clients who were worried about whether the companies would survive to repay their investments or perform their contracts.

The sanctions (or anticipated sanctions) that hit Brazilian construction companies and their executives had severe knock-on effects on their employees, suppliers, and customers, in the form of lost jobs and delayed infrastructure projects.[91] These effects were exacerbated by the fact that many of the companies implicated in *Lava Jato* performed services that were difficult to replace, at least in the short term. This made it difficult to simply shuffle projects, and their associated networks of employees and suppliers, away from compromised firms to new entrants. The companies implicated in *Lava Jato* worked on large projects characterized by complex contractual arrangements. Consequently, for projects already underway there inevitably would be delays in renegotiating agreements to replace one firm with another. Meanwhile, it was difficult to allocate new projects to new entrants because all the leading Brazilian firms were implicated in the scandal, and in some sectors, Brazil's complex regulatory environment and regime for public procurement discouraged entry by foreign firms.[92]

The effects of *Lava Jato* were felt not just in Brazil but throughout Latin America, where Odebrecht was a dominant player in infrastructure construction. In Peru, for example, the governor of the Central Bank estimated that *Lava Jato*-related delays in two major infrastructure projects would reduce GDP growth by between 0.5 and 0.6 of a percentage point.[93]

At the same time that Brazilian firms were grappling with the prospect of liability for past misconduct, the fear of being sanctioned for future misconduct led to a boom in expenditures on compliance by all companies doing business in Brazil. One multinational accounting firm reported that in the two years preceding 2017 it had doubled the size of its compliance department in Brazil to four hundred people, "and planned to increase it by 50–100% by the end of 2017." The leader of the group fretted that he would be forced to bring in professionals from outside the country in order to satisfy demand—and all of this in the midst of an unprecedented economic crisis.[94]

An increase in compliance expenditures might signal an increase in the overall cost of doing business. But then again it might not. The increase in compliance expenditures might coincide with a reduced need to pay bribes in order to obtain favors from public officials, which might mean an overall reduction in the cost of doing business. In other words, firms might prefer to spend money on compliance officers rather than on bribes. The reverse is also possible, however. The shifts in Brazil's anti-corruption enforcement strategy might well have increased the overall cost of doing business in the country and discouraged both foreign and domestic investment.

An enforcement strategy as costly as *Lava Jato* is vulnerable to two sorts of cost-related objections. First, the strategy's costs might outweigh its benefits, which would make it inefficient.[95] Recall our discussion from chapter 5 of reasons to question the magnitude of the harm associated with bribery. In the case of *Lava Jato*, there is a reasonable argument that the bribes were paid to facilitate the approval of worthwhile infrastructure projects that would otherwise have been strangled in their infancy by Brazil's forbidding combination of red tape and judicial activism. Even the bid rigging might be defended as a way to avoid litigation by losing bidders, who might otherwise seek injunctions to delay construction. In the context of a poor country, unemployment and delayed infrastructure lead to massive amounts of human suffering. The strongest version of these arguments suggests that the benefits of *Lava Jato* are outweighed by the costs it has imposed on Brazil and other Latin American countries.

Building on this concern about the human costs of law enforcement, a second kind of objection to an enforcement action like *Lava Jato* is that it is unfair because the costs fall on people who do not share in the associated benefits. Defenders of the OECD paradigm tend to assume either that the costs and benefits of vigorous enforcement of transnational bribery law are diffused broadly and proportionately, or that enforcement disproportionately benefits the poor.[96] This might be true. It is possible that Brazilians who bear the costs of an economic slowdown caused by a crackdown on corruption in the construction sector will earn offsetting benefits in the economic upturn that eventually results as the overall business environment improves and trust in government is restored. More generally, there is evidence that the poor are disproportionately harmed by bribery because they are more likely to depend on public services controlled by corrupt officials.[97]

At the same time, there are several ways in which enforcement of transnational bribery law might generate costs skewed against certain groups, including those whose members are poor or underprivileged. To begin with, vigorous enforcement of anti-bribery laws will tend to benefit firms that operate best in environments in which public-private actions are governed by formal legal rules, as opposed to firms that have developed expertise in building personal relationships with corrupt officials and negotiating corrupt bargains and whose employees and agents have few compunctions about paying bribes.[98] So for instance, a crackdown on corruption in Brazil might generate disproportionate benefits for foreign firms accustomed to being subject to the FCPA while hurting homegrown firms and other firms based in other relatively corrupt countries. As a result, the effect of enforcing anti-bribery law might be to transfer significant amounts of wealth from domestic to foreign firms.

An alternative possibility is that high-powered enforcement strategies will entail disproportionate costs, rather than benefits, for foreigners. Take the case of a firm that has a dominant position in a foreign market, but not at home. An enforcement action that puts a firm like that out of business will have a disproportionate negative impact on foreigners. Odebrecht, for instance, was only the largest of several large construction companies in Brazil, but it played a dominant role in Venezuela. Reuters reports that between 2003 and 2017 Odebrecht won thirty-two contracts for large projects in Venezuela, while its three leading Brazilian rivals won a total of eight.[99] As of mid-2017, twenty-three of the projects were stalled, leaving 200,000 people out of work. It is not clear that the stoppages had anything to do with the enforcement actions against Odebrecht since the Venezuelan government was experiencing severe financial problems at the time. It is also unclear whether Venezuela's citizens would have been well served by completion of the projects at the full contract price; many of the contracts were procured through bribery and appear to have been overpriced. Nonetheless, the situation highlights Venezuelans' dependency on Odebrecht and their disproportionate exposure, compared to Brazilians, to collateral damage from sanctions aimed at the company.

In addition to creating cross-border disparities, enforcement can be biased against certain types of political regimes. Most notably, an otherwise neutral enforcement strategy might impose disproportionate costs on governments that espouse relatively interventionist policies and the citizens who benefit from those policies. More government intervention creates more opportunities for officials to solicit bribes and so, all other things being equal, ought to lead to more exposure to liability under anti-bribery law. Leftists in Latin America are particularly attuned to this concern because *Lava Jato* has disproportionately affected public officials associated with left-wing governments in the region, including, most notably, Lula, who ruled Brazil from 2003 to 2016 and was regarded as one of the most successful progressive leaders in world history when he left office. Lula and his successor, Dilma Roussef, have characterized *Lava Jato* as an abuse of the legal system designed to advance a right-wing political agenda. This specific charge is difficult to substantiate because at least some of Lula's and Dilma's political opponents have been successfully prosecuted as part of the *Lava Jato* investigation. Nonetheless, the more general argument that enforcement of anti-bribery law might be biased against governments most interested in undertaking direct action against poverty has an air of plausibility.[100]

Prevention Is Not the Only Objective

The OECD paradigm's approach to enforcement is typically justified in terms of the objective of achieving a resolutely cosmopolitan kind of prevention. In chapter 5 we saw that there are several other intuitively appealing objectives that transnational bribery law might pursue. In principle, the prevention-oriented enforcement strategies favored by the OECD paradigm might preclude strategies that promote other more legitimate objectives. For example, a focus on efficient prevention might dictate incurring relatively high costs to prosecute and imprison individual bribe payers, while giving priority to compensation might lead to greater emphasis on extracting monetary settlements from a few relatively deep-pocketed firms and using the proceeds for the purposes of restitution. Similarly, a focus on condemnation would lead to greater emphasis on imprisoning individual bribe recipients whose breaches of the public trust lead to substantial symbolic and material harm, such as officials who agree to overlook environmental offenses, regardless of whether those officials are in a position to make restitution. In addition, a focus on compensation or condemnation generally will point toward penalties calculated based on harm caused by a defendant, as opposed to benefits received.

The OECD paradigm also is evolving toward widescale acceptance of negotiated agreements as a means for resolving foreign bribery cases, presumably in the name of efficiency. These procedural innovations can threaten effectiveness, due process, fairness, and legitimacy. Negotiated resolutions streamline the enforcement process by limiting the roles of judges, other enforcement agencies, other potential defendants, and victims in directing the investigation assessing the evidence, and setting sanctions. The most stripped-down examples of negotiated resolutions, U.S. nonprosecution agreements, involve agreements negotiated between a single enforcement agency and a single defendant and no judicial oversight. Problems arise to the extent that the parties involved in the negotiation are incapable of representing the interests of the parties left out of the process. For example, U.S. prosecutors may not have the interests of foreign enforcement agencies and victims at heart and so may fail to seek compensation. Or they may fail to disclose, or compel defendants to disclose, evidence of wrongdoing that can be used to prosecute other wrongdoers. Or they may ignore the costs that their preferred sanctions will impose on foreigners. Moreover, regardless of the outcomes associated with negotiated resolutions, they compromise due process to the extent they exclude judges from the enforcement process and defendants are incapable of giving valid consent to abrogation of their rights. Finally, as we will discuss in the next chapter, failure to include foreign enforcement agencies generally compromises legitimacy. The logical cure for these problems with negotiated resolutions is to include a broader range of actors in the process, but this solution brings its own complications, especially if the other actors are numerous or have limited expertise or cannot be trusted to act in good faith.

The *Odebrecht* case illustrates some of the reasons why these seemingly fundamental objections to the OECD paradigm do not necessarily have practical bite. To begin with, notice that *Lava Jato* targeted a wide range of individuals and firms, including both payers and recipients of bribes. This is a reminder that a prevention-oriented strategy is compatible with targeting a broad range of offenders, if only because an enforcement agency that predictably ignored certain categories of offenders would effectively give up on the possibility of deterring them. The case against Odebrecht S.A. demonstrates that it is possible for monetary penalties simultaneously to deter, condemn, and compensate, particularly when those penalties are augmented by other sanctions. Deterrence and compensation coincide when monetary penalties are remitted to a state like Brazil that can plausibly claim to represent the principal victims of the harm. In theory, a monetary penalty calculated based on benefits received might be insufficient to compensate for the harm caused by an offense. However, the likelihood of this scenario is reduced if penalties are set at a multiple of benefits received, as they were in the *Odebrecht* case, which is appropriate if the penalty is to serve as an effective deterrent in settings where the likelihood of detection is low. This still leaves a concern that a penalty that achieves optimal deterrence will be disproportionately large in relation to the harm associated with the offense and so will be inconsistent with an enforcement strategy designed to abide by the principle that severity of punishment should be strictly proportional to relative harm.[101]

The *Odebrecht* case should also allay some, but not all, of the concerns about the legitimacy of negotiated settlements since Brazilian prosecutors by all accounts played a leading a role in the negotiation process, alongside their U.S. and Swiss counterparts. There remain, however, outstanding questions about whether these kinds of negotiations allow for sufficient judicial oversight and transparency.

Conclusions

The OECD paradigm stresses deterrence, harsh sanctions, and intense enforcement. Countries are regularly scolded if they set sanctions for foreign bribery too low, allocate few resources to enforcement, or generally fail to portray their portion of the anti-bribery regime as a potent and dynamic. These concerns are especially pronounced where prohibitions on bribery are drafted narrowly (for example, there is no liability for poor accounting) and only a few actors (for example, individual bribe payers as opposed to organizations with which they are affiliated) are potentially liable.

The OECD approach to enforcement does not necessarily represent the most effective response to the problem of transnational bribery. It may not even be the most effective in terms of achieving prevention through deterrence. This uncertainty is not unique to the strategies associated with the OECD paradigm. The deterrent effects of any enforcement strategy are both highly context-specific and extraordinarily difficult to calculate. This is in part because the incentive effects of legal sanctions are augmented by moral constraints and nonlegal sanctions. Those incentive effects also ultimately depend on people's predictions about future enforcement practices in a world in which enforcement agencies rarely are capable of committing themselves to any particular strategy. The impact of prosecuting Odebrecht and its leaders will depend considerably on whether it leaves the defendants shamed, scorned, and scared or makes them into symbols of persecution who eventually become objects of sympathy and solidarity. The impact of these kinds of enforcement actions also will depend on whether potential wrongdoers believe that enforcement agencies in countries like the United States and Brazil have been exhausted or emboldened by their efforts.

Even if we accept the basic idea that the purpose of enforcement is to prevent future misconduct, the most effective strategy might be one designed to persuade rather than to deter. This might involve less emphasis on getting tough on crime and more emphasis on using enforcement actions as opportunities for moral instruction. The story of Marcelo Odebrecht's fall from grace, along with the other members of his team, is likely to change more aspects of corporate decision-making than just calculations of the costs and benefits of compliance and cooperation. It is also likely to change attitudes toward what is right and wrong and reasonable to expect in corporate boardrooms.

Another concern is that the goal of efficient prevention might be pursued at the expense of objectives such as compensation, as well as respect for fairness, due process, and legitimacy. A chronic problem with enforcement of transnational bribery law is that its undeniable benefits will come at the expense of not only defendants but also a wide range of innocent stakeholders who depend on defendants and potential wrongdoers for employment, goods, services, and investments. The *Lava Jato* operation has wreaked havoc on the economies of Brazil and the other countries in which Odebrecht and its co-conspirators conducted business. It is plausible but by no means certain that the benefits outweigh the costs and that the costs of the enforcement action have been distributed fairly.

These kinds of concerns about the outcomes of enforcement cannot be separated from concerns about the enforcement process itself. Only two of the twenty-eight countries in which Odebrecht did business were represented in the negotiations around resolution of its enforcement action. Perhaps if representatives of those other countries had been involved, or there had been more judicial oversight of the agreement, their interests would have been better protected and the process would have had a stronger claim to legitimacy. Realistically, though, adding an array of Latin American enforcement agencies and judges to the negotiating process, some of which are reputed to be corrupt and/or incompetent, would undoubtedly have delayed matters and eliminated the efficiency gains that make negotiated resolutions so attractive.

This leads to a more general objection to the OECD paradigm, namely, that it places too much emphasis on protecting potential victims from future harm as opposed to securing compensation for victims of past misconduct or ensuring that perpetrators receive their just deserts. In theory, enforcement strategies focused on compensation or condemnation might target different defendants or impose different types of sanctions, but the *Lava Jato* case shows that there can be considerable overlap between strategies designed to achieve different objectives.

Perhaps the most important point to take away from the discussion in this chapter is that the optimal enforcement strategy for any given society will be contingent on the results of a set of complex context-specific judgments. Selecting an appropriate strategy requires empirical judgments about the extent of the problem to be addressed, value judgments about the objectives of enforcement, assessments of the capabilities of the relevant enforcement agencies, and predictions about the impact of alternative strategies. This implies that the strategy chosen is likely to vary depending on who is responsible for selecting and implementing it. In the next chapter we turn to the question of who ought to make those judgments.

10

How Should Responsibility for Regulation Be Allocated?

Introduction

By definition, every instance of transnational bribery touches at least two countries, and many cases affect far more. Sometimes a single firm pays bribes in many countries. Siemens paid, or is alleged to have paid, bribes in 26 of the 190 countries in which it did business, leading to investigations by agencies in 23 countries and by 4 international organizations. In other cases—like the Bonny Island cases we examine in greater detail later—firms from several different countries have gotten together to pay bribes in a single foreign country. In still other cases, public officials have transferred corruptly procured assets to multiple foreign destinations. Efforts to recover the billions of dollars stolen by Sani Abacha, a former leader of Nigeria, prompted at least thirteen separate proceedings in eight different countries. Perhaps just as importantly, the adverse effects of corrupt transactions frequently are felt across borders: foreign competitors can be prejudiced when officials allocate favors to bribe payers; officials who invest proceeds of bribery overseas can seize control of foreign enterprises and drive up the prices of foreign assets; and, to the extent that bribery creates economic or political instability in a country, the resulting social, economic, and political problems can spill over to neighboring countries in the region, or even the entire world.

Bribery with geographically complex facts inevitably raises the question: Who should regulate? Or to be more precise, which countries' agencies are either permitted or required, not just legally, but morally, to regulate corrupt practices? It seems intuitive that every country should try to regulate bribery of its own officials, but why should any country be permitted or required to regulate bribery of foreign public officials? And if they do regulate, are there any constraints on their decisions about which conduct or actors to target or what sanctions to impose?

As we have seen in earlier chapters, the OECD paradigm takes an expansive approach to virtually every aspect of transnational bribery law. This includes questions concerning jurisdiction, meaning, the scope of application of each state's laws. In recent years, enforcement agencies in the United States and

Between Impunity and Imperialism. Kevin E. Davis.

elsewhere have aggressively applied their anti-bribery laws to transactions with only minimal connections to their people or territory. For legal support they rely on both domestic laws and treaties like the UN Convention and the OECD Convention. When an international regime that promotes an expansive approach to jurisdiction encounters cases with geographically complex facts, the resulting enforcement actions tend to involve agencies in multiple countries. Sometimes these cases involve multiple relatively independent proceedings. It is becoming increasingly common, however, to see cases that involve significant amounts of cross-border coordination, including agreements to share monetary penalties and forfeited assets, as exemplified by the enforcement actions against Odebrecht and Braskem, discussed in chapter 9.

The OECD paradigm's expansive approach to jurisdiction is typically defended in terms of effectiveness and legitimacy. The orthodox view is that when enforcement agencies respond to bribery of foreign public officials, they bring valuable resources to bear in the service of universally cherished objectives. The resources are considered to be valuable because they supplement the resources available to local agencies and help to fill an "enforcement gap." This in turn serves several purposes, including: regulating the conduct of the state's citizens and people who act while in its territory; protecting the state's citizens and residents from harmful effects of corruption that spill across borders; protecting inhabitants of countries governed by corrupt officials; and respecting the wishes of states which have signed the UN Convention and thereby consented to assertions of jurisdiction that would otherwise infringe on their sovereignty. At first glance these all seem like legitimate grounds for assertions of regulatory power.

Any regime that invites multiple enforcement agencies to intervene in individual cases necessarily creates space for disagreement, conflict, and redundancy. The anti-imperialist critique homes in on this aspect of the OECD approach to jurisdiction. Regulation of transnational bribery requires difficult decisions about matters such as which conduct or actors to target and what sanctions to impose. Reasonable people can disagree about these issues. When hard cases arise, it is difficult to justify a situation in which one country imposes its views about how to regulate on the people who will be most greatly affected by the decision, namely, the inhabitants of the country governed by corrupt officials. This sort of imperialistic approach to anti-corruption law was difficult to justify when Edmund Burke attempted to impeach Warren Hastings for corruption in India without calling a single witness from the subcontinent; it is even more difficult to justify in an age in which equality has become the guiding rule. The fact that many affected countries have signed the UN Convention does not dramatically alter this conclusion. A close examination of what was agreed upon in the UN Convention suggests that it does not provide as much cover as proponents of the OECD paradigm believe. Furthermore, with so much room for disagreement, there is a significant risk that collective action problems will compromise the effectiveness or efficiency of transnational bribery law. Some of these dangers can, or could, be avoided by assigning enforcement authority to an international organization such as a multilateral development bank, or even a new international anti-corruption agency, but the problems of legitimacy are likely to remain.

The remainder of this chapter describes the international and domestic laws that define jurisdiction in cases of transnational bribery; explains the various arguments used to justify the current regime, in terms of both effectiveness and legitimacy; outlines a two-pronged anti-imperialist critique; and considers whether reliance on international organizations to regulate transnational bribery avoids the force of that critique. We begin, however, with a motivating example, a famous set of cases that stem from a massive bribery scheme involving Nigerian public officials and a corrupt ring of multinational companies.

The Bonny Island Affair

The rules that determine whether any given country can regulate a particular transaction typically refer to factors such as the country's ties to the actors involved and where the relevant conduct takes place. Those rules frequently permit multiple countries to regulate. To illustrate, we can use the legal responses to the Bonny Island affair, a paradigmatic example of a bribery scheme with geographically complex facts.

Bonny Island is an island in the Niger Delta region of Nigeria, the main source of oil and gas in the country. It is the location of, among other things, a large facility for piping natural gas from wellheads and converting it into liquefied natural gas (LNG) so that it can be delivered to ocean-going tankers. The facility allows oil companies to sell gas associated with oil production that they would otherwise simply burn off, a wasteful and environmentally damaging practice. Bonny Island became infamous when U.S. enforcement agencies laid charges alleging that a consortium of multinational enterprises paid over $180 million in bribes to Nigerian public officials in order to obtain and retain contracts to build the LNG facility. The contracts were worth over $6 billion dollars. The losing bidder for the initial contract was a consortium led by Bechtel, a prominent U.S. firm, joined by firms from Japan, the United Arab Emirates, and Italy.

The winning bidder, TSKJ, was a joint venture between four companies with expertise in engineering, procurement, and construction (EPC):

- Technip S.A., incorporated in France and headquartered in Paris;
- Snamprogetti Netherlands B.V. (Snamprogetti), a Dutch corporation headquartered in Amsterdam that was a subsidiary of ENI, an Italian company headquartered in Milan;
- Kellogg Brown and Root, Inc. (KBR), incorporated in Delaware and headquartered in Houston, Texas, and a subsidiary of Halliburton Company, a multinational oil field services company that was also incorporated in Delaware and headquartered in Houston; and,
- JGC Corporation (JGC), a Japanese company headquartered in Yokohama.

Technip had securities traded on the New York Stock Exchange, as did the parent companies of Snamprogetti (ENI) and KBR (Halliburton).

TSKJ operated through three special purpose companies registered in Madeira, each of which was jointly owned by the four joint venturers. TSKJ hired two agents to administer payments to the Nigerian officials: Jeffrey Tesler, a London-based lawyer and U.K. citizen, who operated through a Gibraltar corporation named Tri-Star; and Marubeni, a Japanese corporation. Tesler was responsible for payments to high-level Nigerian officials and a Nigerian political party, while Marubeni was responsible for dealings with lower level officials. Between 1994 and 2004, TSKJ paid over $130 million to Tri-Star, and $51 million to Marubeni.

The critical events in the implementation of the bribery scheme apparently consisted of meetings in London and Nigeria, as well as payments from TSKJ accounts in Amsterdam to accounts controlled by Tesler and Marubeni in Switzerland, Monaco, and Japan, respectively. U.S. prosecutors documented only a handful of instances in which the misconduct touched the United States: the payments to Tesler were transferred from the Netherlands to Switzerland and Monaco by way of correspondent bank accounts in New York; a couple of vaguely incriminating faxes were sent to Houston by Tesler and Marubeni; and a more incriminating email from KBR to Tesler was sent through Houston.[1]

There is little conclusive publicly available information about who received the payments from Tesler and Marubeni or what they did with the funds. Media reports suggest that the recipients included three successive heads of state; a vice president; and a Minister of Petroleum, as well as various executives in the state-owned oil company.[2]

The Bonny Island affair came to light in 2003 when a French investigation into unrelated misconduct by another French company, Elf Acquitaine, revealed that Technip had paid bribes in several countries, including Nigeria.[3] The information was turned over to the U.S. enforcement agencies, which pursued the case vigorously. Between 2009 and 2012, all of the companies that participated in the joint venture, as well as Marubeni, were sanctioned under the FCPA in proceedings initiated by both the U.S. Department of Justice and the Securities and Exchange Commission.[4] Jack Stanley, CEO of KBR and a U.S. national, was sentenced to thirty months in prison. Jeffrey Tesler and Wojciech Chodan, an executive in KBR's U.K. subsidiary (who was also a U.K. national), were extradited from the United Kingdom to the United States and subsequently pled guilty before a U.S. court. Tesler forfeited $148,964,568 and received a sentence of twenty-one months in prison as well as a $25,000 fine. Chodan forfeited about $725,000 and received a fine of $20,000 plus one year's probation. In total, the corporate and individual defendants were ordered to pay more than $1.7 billion to the U.S. Treasury.[5]

Other enforcement agencies followed the lead of the U.S. agencies. Late in 2010, Nigeria's Economic and Financial Crimes Commission (EFCC) arrested several employees of the joint venture companies and reportedly laid charges against the current and former CEOs of KBR and its parent company Halliburton, including former U.S. Vice President Dick Cheney (the former CEO of Halliburton). Shortly afterward, the joint venture companies reached a confidential settlement with the EFCC. In 2011, a U.K. subsidiary of KBR was ordered to pay roughly $11 million to the U.K. government.[6] In 2013, an Italian court ordered Saipem to forfeit €24.5 million and to pay a fine of €0.6 million.[7] That same year, a Paris court ordered two Technip executives to pay fines of €5,000 and €10,000, respectively.[8] In 2014, the joint venture companies paid penalties totaling $22.7 million to the African Development Bank.[9] Meanwhile, as late as 2018 French prosecutors continued to pursue criminal charges against Jeffery Tesler for much the same actions that led to his guilty plea in the United States and succeeded in persuading France's highest court to reject Tesler's argument that the proceedings would be unfair.[10]

No individual Nigerian officials have been charged in connection with the Bonny Island affair, either in Nigeria or elsewhere. Since the scandal was uncovered, however, senior officials connected to the oil industry, including two former Ministers of Petroleum and two former governors of states in the Niger Delta, have faced unrelated money laundering charges in Nigeria, the United Kingdom, the United States, and France.[11]

The Scope of Transnational Bribery Law: International Law

Why did the U.S. legal system play the leading role in regulating a transaction that had so little connection to the United States? Why did U.S. law even apply? Did other laws apply besides those of the countries and international organizations that launched enforcement actions? The answers to these questions lie in the complex set of laws and practices that determine which laws apply to the regulation of transnational bribery.

Every legal system has its own methods—sometimes only tacitly understood—for determining which transactions it governs. The conventional view is that national legal systems are bound to abide by overarching principles of international law—known technically as the law of "prescriptive jurisdiction"—in defining the scope of their laws. In other words, international law purports to set outer bounds on the potential scope of any given state's laws. The applicable principles of international law can be established by treaties, but in the absence of an applicable treaty they are determined by reference to custom.

In the case of anti-bribery law, or at least its criminal aspects, most states are now bound by jurisdictional principles found in the UN Convention against Corruption. The vast majority of countries in the world have ratified the UN Convention and thereby endorsed its remarkably expansive—but still nonexclusive—set of jurisdictional principles.[12] The Convention came into force in 2005, after the initial French investigation into the Bonny Island affair was already under way and well after the misconduct took place. Nonetheless, we can use the Bonny Island cases to illustrate how the legal principles set out in the UN Convention would apply to other similar multijurisdictional cases. We will also consider the jurisdictional rules set out in the OECD Convention, which came into force in 1999, part of the way through the period of wrongdoing and prior to the investigation.

The foremost of the jurisdictional principles set out in the UN Convention is territoriality: the Convention requires parties to assert jurisdiction over corruption offenses, including corruption relating to foreign public officials, on the basis of territoriality.[13] In other words, states must regulate corrupt practices that occur in their territory. The UN Convention does not specify what sorts of territorial connections suffice, but the OECD Convention, which has a similar territoriality provision, says that "the territorial basis for jurisdiction should be interpreted broadly so that an extensive physical connection to the bribery act is not required."[14]

The UN Convention also permits, but does not require, parties to assert jurisdiction on the basis of several other principles, namely, nationality, protective, and passive personality. Nationality permits a state to regulate conduct of its nationals, regardless of where the conduct takes place. The protective principle permits a state to regulate conduct that threatens its "fundamental national interests."[15] Passive personality permits a state to regulate offenses committed "against" its nationals.[16] As if these principles weren't sufficient, in the case of money laundering the Convention permits states to assert jurisdiction over anyone who is complicit in misconduct that takes place in their territory, even when the person acts outside the state's territory.[17] Another section of the Convention permits states to assert jurisdiction over people present in their territory whom they fail to extradite, and requires them to assert jurisdiction in such cases when the person is one of their nationals.[18]

The UN Convention does not go quite as far as it could have in permitting the exercise of jurisdiction. For instance, it does not endorse the effects doctrine, which says that it is acceptable for a state to assert jurisdiction over any conduct that has effects within its territory. This controversial extension of the territoriality principle is sometimes used in antitrust law.[19] The UN Convention also does not endorse the universality principle, which permits states to exercise jurisdiction over conduct with which it has no particular connection "in the interests of the international community" if the offense is of "universal concern."[20]

The UN Convention expressly acknowledges the need to limit expansive assertions of jurisdiction. Under the heading "Protection of Sovereignty," Article 4.1 says:

> States Parties shall carry out their obligations under this Convention in a manner consistent with the principles of sovereign equality and territorial integrity of States and that of non-intervention in the domestic affairs of other States.

To those versed in the argot of international law, Article 4.1's references to sovereign equality and non-interference point to the conclusion that ultimate power in relation to many aspects of transnational bribery law ought to reside primarily with states whose public officials are implicated in misconduct. For instance, one component of the principle of sovereign equality traditionally has been the proposition that a state cannot be bound without its consent by norms imposed by any other state.[21] The principle of non-interference points in a similar direction. Among other things it prevents states from interfering with other states' choices about how to govern themselves.[22] It would not be unreasonable to assume that the zone of non-interference includes choices about how to regulate interactions between private actors and public officials.[23] Consistent with this view, in *McDonnell v. United States* the Supreme Court of the United States explained its reluctance to use a vague federal law to sanction the practices of a state governor in the following terms: "A State defines itself as a sovereign through the structure of its government, and the character of those who exercise government authority . . . That includes the prerogative to regulate the permissible scope of interactions between state officials and their constituents."[24]

The principles of sovereign equality and non-interference traditionally have been regarded as the bases of the doctrine of state immunity, which bars one state from using its law to hold another state liable. These principles are also the bases for doctrines that grant individual public officials immunity from liability.[25] For instance, foreign heads of state and foreign ministers enjoy immunity simply by virtue of their status. Other state officials enjoy immunity for acts they have undertaken on behalf of the state they represent. Unlike status-based immunity, conduct-based official immunity persists beyond the individual official's term in office. The better view of the law seems to be that Article 4.1's references to sovereign equality and non-interference impliedly incorporate all of these legal immunities into the UN Convention.

Article 4.1 stands in an ambiguous relationship to the Convention's express provisions concerning jurisdiction. The express provisions encourage states to define their jurisdiction over bribery and related offenses quite expansively. Their entire thrust is to give states power to judge and influence the performance of other states and their officials. States are supposed to give foreign actors the power to hold them accountable for failing to prevent corruption, to prosecute their officials for falling short of broadly defined standards of integrity, and to regulate private actors' dealings with those officials. The logic is clear: traditional principles of respect for state sovereignty have to be abandoned in order to address effectively the problems that arise when public officials fail in their basic function of representing their people with integrity. These ideas are in tension with both general conceptions of sovereign equality and non-interference and specific doctrinal corollaries such as the doctrines of state immunity and official immunity. For example, an individual who solicits or receives a bribe for their own personal benefit seems unlikely to qualify for immunity because the culpable action is not undertaken on behalf of the state,[26] however, an official who either pays a bribe or facilitates the payment of a bribe to another person might conceivably have a basis for claiming conduct-based immunity. If a case like this is ever brought, someone will have to determine whether the UN Convention overrides or incorporates traditional principles of state and official immunity, thus bringing to a head the tensions within the Convention.

Leaving aside the Article 4.1 caveat, contemporary international law, as embodied in the UN Convention, would permit a large number of countries to apply their anti-bribery laws to some or all aspects of the Bonny Island scheme. That list of countries would certainly include Nigeria, not only because Nigeria's national interests were threatened but also because it would be entitled to target Nigerian nationals (such as its public officials) or firms that paid bribes in Nigerian territory. The passive personality principle would add several more countries to the list of countries entitled to apply their laws, specifically, every country whose national firms were placed at a competitive disadvantage by the bribery scheme. At the top of this list would be the home countries of the members of the consortium that lost out to TSKJ in bidding for the initial EPC contract, namely, the United States, the United Kingdom, Japan, Italy, and the United Arab Emirates. On the passive personality theory, each of those countries would be within its rights to apply its laws to the entire Bonny Island affair. Meanwhile, other principles endorsed by the UN Convention would permit additional countries to regulate specific components of the scheme. The nationality principle would allow each defendant to be regulated by its country of incorporation or citizenship. This would open the door for France, the United States, the Netherlands, Japan, Portugal, and Gibraltar to regulate the conduct of Technip, Snamprogetti, KBR, JGC, Marubeni, the TSKJ entities, and Tri-Star, respectively. The territoriality principle would permit each country in which misconduct took place to regulate the actors involved. Finally, in the case of money laundering, the territorial states would be entitled to apply their laws to everyone complicit in the transaction. So, for instance, on this last basis, Switzerland and Monaco could apply their money laundering laws to virtually everyone involved in the scheme on the grounds that they all conspired with Tesler to launder money in those two countries. However, the law of sovereign immunity would prevent the Nigerian state from being held liable anywhere other than in Nigeria. Meanwhile, assuming it is not overridden by the UN Convention, the law of official immunity would have protected any Nigerian head of state (or diplomat) from being held liable under foreign law while in office.

The Scope of Transnational Bribery Law: National Laws

In practice, countries do not apply their anti-bribery and anti–money laundering laws quite as broadly as permitted by international law. Most countries purport to rely only on territoriality and nationality. However, some countries, and in particular the United States and the United Kingdom, have pushed the limits of those principles. In fact, one set of commentators describe the jurisdictional principles used in U.S. anti-bribery law as "potentially quasi-universal."[27]

As far as bribery of foreign public officials is concerned, the key U.S. anti-bribery provisions are found in the FCPA. One of those provisions permits the United States to assert jurisdiction over foreign individuals and firms who act in furtherance of a bribe of a foreign public official while in U.S. territory.[28] The concept of an act in furtherance is defined broadly to include "use of the mails or any means or instrumentality of interstate commerce." Consequently, an act as innocuous as mailing a letter or transferring funds through the U.S. payment system will qualify. Still, this part of the FCPA is basically consistent with the traditional principle of territorial jurisdiction since there is a strong argument to be made that it applies only to people who engage in misconduct while they are physically present in U.S. territory.[29] This provision was not at issue in the Bonny Island affair because the foreign participants in the scheme appear to have avoided traveling to the United States.

The FCPA has two other anti-bribery provisions, and they both stretch the bounds of the territoriality principle. One of those provisions applies to "issuers" that are subject to certain reporting requirements under U.S. securities laws—basically, firms with securities traded on U.S. exchanges.[30] The other anti-bribery provision applies to "domestic concerns," defined as nationals or permanent residents of the United States, as well as organizations that either have their principal place of business in the United States or are organized under U.S. law (national or subnational).[31] The FCPA's issuer and domestic concern provisions are both triggered only when an act in furtherance of a bribe "make[s] use of the mails or instrumentalities of interstate commerce." Unlike the provision based on territoriality, these provisions do not require the perpetrator to be present in U.S. territory. Nor does the perpetrator necessarily have to be aware of the connection to U.S. territory.[32] Consequently, the U.S. government takes the position that these provisions extend to any person who pays a bribe by transferring money through a U.S. payment system, or who sends an email offering to pay a bribe through a U.S. server, regardless of where the person otherwise would be considered to be located.[33] This is significant because most transfers denominated in U.S. dollars are made through a clearinghouse based in New York and many email communications are routed through U.S. servers.

There is more. Each of the anti-bribery provisions also explicitly extends to a set of related individuals, specifically, any "officer, director, agent, employee or stockholder acting on behalf of" the person who acts in U.S. territory, issuer, or domestic concern, as the case may be. In addition, in U.S. law anyone who conspires to commit, or aids or abets the commission of, an offense—that is, an accomplice—ordinarily is liable in the same way as the person who actually commits or attempts to commit the offense. This suggests that the net of liability under the FCPA can be stretched to capture anyone who qualifies as an accomplice of an issuer, domestic concern, or a related individual, although there is debate over whether a nonresident foreign national can be caught in this way.[34]

The Bonny Island affair involved all these categories of defendants: Technip was an issuer, and KBR and its CEO were domestic concerns. Marubeni and Tesler were clearly both agents and accomplices of Technip and KBR, though the U.S. government charged Marubeni only as an accomplice.[35] In addition, according to the U.S. Securities and Exchange Commission (but not the Department of Justice), Snamprogretti also acted as an agent of an issuer, namely, its parent company, ENI. Finally, Snamprogetti and JGC signed agreements accepting the Department of Justice's argument that they could be liable under the FCPA as accomplices of KBR and the other defendants.[36]

Some of the applications of the FCPA to conduct with tenuous territorial connections to the United States can be justified under international law by pointing to the nationality principle, since many issuers, domestic concerns, and related individuals qualify as U.S. nationals. In fact, the FCPA explicitly permits regulators to dispense with territorial links as the basis for jurisdiction over U.S. nationals (including both individual U.S. nationals and enterprises organized under U.S. law). The statute prohibits these "United States persons"—a subset of all issuers and domestic concerns—from acting in furtherance of a bribe outside the United States, whether or not they make use of the means or instrumentalities of interstate commerce.[37] This still leaves many cases in which the nationality principle is unavailing as a basis for jurisdiction, and the territorial fig leaf of "use of the means or instrumentalities of interstate commerce" seems critical. The most prominent examples are firms like Technip that are subject to U.S. securities laws and therefore qualify as issuers, but are neither organized under U.S. law nor based in the United States. As Messrs. Tesler and Chodan discovered, foreign nationals who are officers, directors, employees, agents, or shareholders of issuers or domestic concerns can also be caught by the FCPA based on their use of instrumentalities. The same issue arises, though admittedly in a less troubling way, in relation to "domestic concerns" that are not U.S. nationals, a category which includes foreign nationals who are permanent residents of the United States and firms organized under foreign law whose principal place of business is in the United States. And then of course there are the cases in which U.S. law dispenses with the territorial fig leaf altogether, and tries to capture accomplices like Snamprogetti and JGC who do nothing whatsoever in U.S. territory.

Although it didn't come up in the Bonny Island cases, U.S. anti-money laundering law also relies on the territoriality and nationality principles; the relevant statutes only apply to extraterritorial conduct if it either occurs at least in part in the United States or is by U.S. nationals.[38] Even limited in this way, the territorial scope of these laws is extremely broad. Recall that money laundering involves two distinct acts: a "predicate offense" and some sort of financial transaction or transfer designed to promote or conceal that offense. Under U.S. law, the predicate offense can be a violation of foreign rather than U.S. laws. This means that a corrupt transaction that takes place wholly outside the United States and involves no U.S. nationals may still be caught by U.S. law. All that is required is for some of the money involved in the scheme to pass through the United States. So, for example, in principle, a Nigerian official who transferred the proceeds of a bribe from an account in Switzerland to a bank in Nigeria via a correspondent bank account in New York could be caught by U.S. money laundering law.

U.K. law also was in play in the Bonny Island cases. The misconduct occurred before the comprehensive revision of the United Kingdom's law embodied in the Bribery Act of 2010. Nonetheless, for the purposes of the present discussion, it is most useful to consider how the Bonny Island defendants would have been dealt with under current law.

The core provisions of the U.K. Bribery Act of 2010 apply when any part of an offense takes place in the United Kingdom or is done by a U.K. national or resident—straightforward applications of the territoriality and nationality principles.[39] The extraordinary feature of the Bribery Act is the famous Section 7, which makes it an offense for a corporation or partnership to fail to prevent bribery by people who provide services for it or on its behalf (including subsidiaries, as well as employees or agents). That provision applies even if no part of the violation takes place in the United Kingdom, so long as the organization carries on business, or part of a business, in the United Kingdom.[40] This goes well beyond the principles of either nationality or territoriality.

Many legal systems include doctrines that serve to limit overly expansive assertions of jurisdiction. Sometimes those limitations are set out expressly in legislation. For instance, some countries' anti-bribery laws carve out exceptions for conduct that is legal under local law or require double criminality. The FCPA and the U.K. Bribery Act contain local law exceptions, and Belgium's anti-bribery law only applies to extraterritorial conduct on the part of Belgian nationals that is criminal where it takes place.[41] In addition, in some countries the international law doctrine of state immunity is codified in domestic legislation and can be used to shield foreign states from liability for foreign bribery.[42]

Other jurisdictional limitations have been created by the courts, particularly in the United States. In the U.S. federal courts, the presumption against extraterritoriality holds that in the absence of explicit statutory language, U.S. statutes do not apply to extraterritorial conduct, meaning conduct with only tenuous connections to U.S. territory. So, for example, the presumption limits the extent to which general purpose fraud statutes can be applied to foreign corrupt practices.[43] In 2010, the U.S. Supreme Court handed down a landmark decision invoking the presumption against extraterritoriality to limit the scope of U.S. securities legislation, and since that time the presumption has been applied with renewed vigor.[44] For instance, it appears that the presumption prevents private actors from bringing a civil claim under the RICO statute—for example, because the defendant's bribery caused competitive harm or their money laundering facilitated embezzlement—if the injury was suffered outside of the United States.[45] The express provisions of the FCPA, such as the ones that make U.S. persons liable for bribery anywhere in the world, are sufficiently clear to rebut the presumption against extraterritoriality. The presumption can, however, be used to resist efforts to apply the FCPA to nonresident foreign nationals who act as accomplices of people or firms named expressly in the statute.[46]

The U.S. Constitution commands that no person be deprived of life, liberty, or property "without due process of law."[47] U.S. courts interpret this requirement to mean that in most cases brought before them, two conditions have to be satisfied: (1) the defendant must have sufficient contacts with the United States (or the relevant U.S. state), and (2) it is reasonable for the court to hear the case. This test gives the courts broad scope to consider factors such as whether the defendant expressly aimed to harm residents of the United States and thus had fair notice that they would be subject to U.S. law, the burden that the hearing will impose on the defendant or witnesses, the interests of the United States and other states, and whether those interests can be served by proceedings in other jurisdictions.[48] Like the presumption against extraterritoriality, the due process requirement can be used to limit the application of U.S. anti-bribery law, especially to nonresident foreign nationals.[49] Unlike the presumption, the constitutional due process requirement overrides express statutory language.

Enforcement Gaps and the Effectiveness of the OECD Paradigm

Expansive definition of jurisdiction over bribery of foreign officials is a hallmark of the modern approach to transnational bribery law. It may also be the most controversial feature of the regime.[50] What gives a country like the United States the right—not legally, but morally—to regulate conduct that has little connection to its territory? Why does the United States have a say in what an English solicitor and a Nigerian public official do in Nigeria? How is it any of the business of the United States? And what makes U.S. officials think they will be any better at regulating this conduct than officials in the Nigeria? Or in more technical terms, how are these kinds of assertion of jurisdiction effective and legitimate?

The arguments that support the current approach are diverse. Rather than being rooted in a single broad principle, the OECD paradigm seems to rely on several ideas, each of which supports some but not all the branches of the current regime. Perhaps the most important of these intellectual supports is the idea that transnational bribery law compensates for the inability of local institutions to enforce anti-bribery law effectively or efficiently because foreign legal institutions are able and willing to provide valuable resources that local institutions are unable or unwilling to match. In other words, foreign institutions help to fill "enforcement gaps." Analogous arguments can be used to justify external interventions by organizations like the International Criminal Court.[51] In each case, the argument is that without the resources and commitment that foreign actors can provide, powerful actors will enjoy impunity.

The most obvious example of a resource that foreign actors are uniquely able to provide is the ability to deploy coercive force in their territory. Foreign courts, law enforcement agencies, and other branches of the state typically regulate the use of force within their territory quite closely and so may be indispensable in efforts to arrest individuals or seize assets located overseas. The Bonny Island cases provide at least some evidence in support of this hypothesis. The United States clearly had a great deal of leverage over the TSKJ defendants, and almost certainly had more leverage than Nigeria. Nigeria was not entirely powerless, however. It not only tried but was successful in asserting jurisdiction over members of the TSKJ consortium, as well as the Halliburton group and its executives. Not only did the defendants have property and personnel located in the jurisdiction, they also presumably valued the ability to do business in Nigeria's large market in the future. In addition, they might have feared the embarrassment of a criminal prosecution.

Foreign actors may also have access to superior information. This is particularly plausible in cases of transnational bribery. Information about corporate misconduct generally flows to enforcement agencies from other agencies, employees, competitors, or financiers. Those sources often will be located both inside and outside the jurisdiction of the corrupt official, and enforcement agencies in that jurisdiction are likely to be at a disadvantage in tapping foreign sources. In the Bonny Island cases, it seems reasonably clear that Nigeria required foreign assistance to access evidence about all the meetings, communications, and financial transactions that took place outside the country.

Foreign actors may also be better able to process whatever information is available about a corruption case. In other words, they may have superior expertise, either across the board, or in relation to specific aspects of the investigation or prosecution, or to specific forms of misconduct. For instance, foreign prosecutors may possess special expertise in forensic accounting, asset tracing, or money laundering techniques; or, they may have special insight into the tactics that will induce whistleblowers in their jurisdiction to come forward. In general, enforcement agencies based in wealthier, less-corrupt countries probably have more expertise. At the same time, wealth is not always a substitute for experience, so it may be unwise to presume that foreign agencies from rich OECD countries have superior expertise. To settle the matter would require an international sleuthing competition between, say, the U.S. Department of Justice/FBI/SEC and Nigeria's EFCC.

Foreign actors may be particularly effective because they are not impeded by local political obstacles. If corruption has compromised local legal institutions, then foreign intervention may be the only viable response. Foreign enforcement agencies may be inherently less corruptible than local institutions, whether because they have been selected more carefully or because they are subject to more effective schemes of monitoring, rewards, and punishments. Perhaps more plausibly, even if they are not inherently less corruptible than local institutions, foreign agencies are less likely to have been corrupted in a way that impairs their ability to deal with the local problem. Local actors will find it relatively difficult to establish illicit relationships with foreign agencies that allow them to subvert the course of justice. The fact that Nigeria's enforcement agencies failed to prosecute any Nigerian officials in connection with the Bonny Island affairs provides strong circumstantial support for these generalizations.

Contributions from foreign legal systems can have positive effects on both local anti-corruption institutions and the broader societies in which they operate. Those effects may be felt well beyond the specific cases in which foreign agencies intervene. For instance, in the course of an investigation, foreign agencies might share information about investigative techniques that local institutions can use in subsequent cases. There may also be demonstration effects. Foreign enforcement actions that hold corrupt firms or officials accountable can publicize the nature and extent of corruption in a society and, if successful, undermine perceptions of impunity. The result can be new awareness among local actors—including not only anti-corruption officials but also members of business, civil society, and the public sector—of what can or should be done to combat bribery. This claim is borne out by the Bonny Island cases to the extent that foreign intervention prompted the EFCC to act against the bribe payers.

Of course, the potential benefits of foreign intervention will only be realized if foreign institutions actually choose to deploy their resources in support of local institutions. The OECD paradigm is premised on the assumption that they are willing to do this. As we saw in chapter 5, enforcement agencies can have a range of motivations for regulating activity that does not affect their own nationals. At the altruistic end of the spectrum are agencies motivated by concern about the welfare of foreign nationals whose officials have been corrupted. At the other extreme are self-interested agencies, which decide whether to regulate corruption based entirely on whether it affects their nationals, either directly or through its effect on firms in which their nationals are stakeholders (shareholders, creditors, employees, suppliers, and customers, and so forth). Finally, there are cosmopolitan regulators which take an intermediate approach and give equal weight to the interests of their own nationals and foreigners. The OECD paradigm seems to presume that when foreign public officials are corrupted, the effects transcend national borders, so that even self-interested and cosmopolitan regulators will be motivated to act. It helps that truly self-interested regulators ought to be keen to sanction foreign firms that compete with their nationals. Allowing multiple regulators to assert jurisdiction increases the likelihood that at least one will be willing to act.[52] In the Bonny Island cases, the U.S. regulators were the ones who stepped forward.

Overall, therefore, the Bonny Island enforcement actions provide a great deal of support for the claim that foreign anti-corruption institutions can complement local ones. Without foreign intervention, a group of multinational engineering and procurement companies would have been able to pay bribes in Nigeria with impunity. At the same time, the Bonny Island affair shows that external regulation of official bribery is unlikely to ever be sufficient. The United States and the United Kingdom were unable to prosecute the Nigerian officials implicated in the Bonny Island affair. More ominously, they would have struggled to assert jurisdiction over a group of bribe-paying firms that took greater care to avoid ties to OECD member countries. Foreign enforcement agencies can extend the reach of local agencies, but their reach is limited.

Consent, Nationality, and Territoriality as Bases for Legitimacy

The idea that foreign institutions can fill an enforcement gap provides a basis for believing that foreign interventions in cases of transnational bribery will be effective and efficient. However, those are not the only relevant criteria. Transnational bribery law involves state-sponsored coercion. It also involves a distinctive form of moral condemnation, coupled with an implicit claim that the state's moral judgment is authoritative.[53] As we saw in chapter 5, this kind of exercise of power demands justification, or in other words, an inquiry into its legitimacy. This means that in addition to asking "can that enforcement agency do X?" we ought to ask "should it do X?" And if it tries to do X, who is obligated to support it?[54] The most widely accepted sources of legitimacy are consent, nationality, and territoriality. Together these principles justify many, but not all, aspects of the OECD paradigm's approach to jurisdiction.

Consent is the most widely accepted source of legitimacy: a state is clearly justified in regulating people who have given express consent to the application of its laws.[55] In business settings, express consent to the application of a particular body of law is commonplace. Commercial agreements routinely include clauses specifying which body of law should be used to resolve any disputes. This kind of clause often can be interpreted reasonably as a manifestation of consent to using the specified state's laws to determine the legal implications of corruption, at least as between private parties. So, for instance, if any of the agreements used by TSKJ or its members were governed by U.S. law, it would be reasonable to refer to U.S. law to determine whether those agreements remained in force after evidence of the Bonny Island affair came to light. In principle, a person could go further and try to consent to application of the criminal laws of the United States (or some other state). Express consent to the application of criminal law, as opposed to laws concerning private parties' rights, would be novel, but in theory it should be sufficient to establish legitimacy.

In principle, tacit consent may also justify legal coercion. The most plausible situation in which this might happen is when a foreigner deliberately enters the territory of a state. The idea that states regulate conduct in their territory is a well-established convention—we do not need the wisdom of St. Augustine to know what to do when in Rome.[56] It is usually reasonable to assume that a foreigner who travels to the United States understands the territoriality convention and tacitly consents to application of U.S. laws.[57] Moreover, a person present in a state's territory likely enjoys many of the benefits afforded to citizens.[58] These arguments had little bearing on the U.S. enforcement actions in the Bonny Island cases because the participants did not enter the United States, although a weak argument can be made that Chodan agreed to be bound by U.S. law when he agreed to serve as an employee of KBR's British subsidiary. Tacit consent did, however, make a cameo appearance in the Bonny Island affair. It is fair to conclude that KBR consented to the application of U.S. anti-bribery law by choosing to incorporate in the United States, and that Technip consented to the application of U.S. anti-bribery law by choosing to issue securities governed by U.S. law (and not just because the FCPA technically forms part of a securities statute).

A more controversial basis of legitimacy is the idea of hypothetical consent, which means essentially that coercion is permissible when the affected parties have good reasons to consent to it. It is widely accepted that there are good reasons why a state is justified in legal coercion of its own citizens, even in the absence of express consent, although there is no consensus about what those reasons are.[59] Some scholars believe that justified coercion is inherent in the relationship between a state and its citizens.[60] Others suggest it is rational for citizens to accept the burdens of a legal system in exchange for the benefits it affords to them.[61] More cautious views hold that acceptance is rational provided the legal system displays certain characteristics, such as promotion of "basic human rights" and allowing people subject to coercion to participate in democratic lawmaking processes.[62] Others suggest that nationality jurisdiction serves to ensure due process and effectiveness when neither can be guaranteed by the state in whose territory the misconduct occurred.[63] Each of these arguments supports legal coercion of citizens in order to promote interests of other citizens. This conclusion leaves little doubt that the United States was justified in applying coercive sanctions to a citizen like Jack Stanley, CEO of KBR.

In short, based on widely accepted ideas about when consent and hypothetical consent generate legitimacy, a state is typically justified in applying its anti-bribery laws to people who expressly agree to be subject to its laws, who act while physically present in its territory, or who are its nationals. As a result, many of the participants in the Bonny Island affair were legitimate targets of U.S. law.

The hard cases then are the ones involving nonresident noncitizens who have not entered the relevant state's territory. Some of these might still qualify as easy cases because they do not involve much coercion. Less coercive forms of regulation do not require the same kind of justification as highly coercive forms such as fines and imprisonment. So, for example, it might be legitimate to deny a corrupt foreign official a visa, even if it would not be legitimate to arrest and imprison her. Similarly, sanctioning of foreign corporations like JGC and Marubeni, which has only indirect impact on individuals, arguably requires less justification than direct regulation of the firms' individual stakeholders. The point is arguable because compelling investors and stakeholders in two corporations to pay over $270 million in penalties seems to cross into the realm of coercion that demands justification.

In the Bonny Island affair, the hard case, meaning the most difficult enforcement action to justify, is the prosecution of Jeffrey Tesler. It is unlikely that Tesler consented expressly to be bound by U.S. law, even in the course of agreeing to act as TSKJ's agent. Tesler also was never physically present in U.S. territory, so there is no basis for arguing that he consented to anything by entering the country. A prosecutor might argue that his use of emails and wire transfers through the United States amounted to tacit consent to the application of U.S. law. This would be an update for the electronic age of John Locke's argument that anyone who enjoys any of the benefits of a government, "whether it be barely travelling freely on the Highway," is obliged to abide by that government's laws.[64] However, the modern version of Locke's argument is significantly less persuasive than the original. Use of electronic services with ties to the United States should only count as consent to application of U.S. law if the potential defendant is aware of the service's ties to the United States and that its use can be construed as consent to U.S. jurisdiction. Even then, a purist might argue that use of the service only qualifies as valid consent if the person has access to alternative service providers. Without these kinds of limitations it is conceivable that virtually every country in the world would be able to claim jurisdiction over a transfer of an asset such as bitcoin that exists solely as an entry in a ledger that is hosted on multiple computers simultaneously. Finally, none of the standard arguments that justify coercion of citizens are available to justify coercion of a noncitizen like Tesler: there is nothing inherent in the nature of the relationship between the United States and a noncitizen that justifies coercion; nonresident noncitizens generally do not share in the benefits of U.S. law, and noncitizens have no rights to participate in the U.S. lawmaking process.

Enforcement actions against foreign public officials can also become hard cases for a consent-based theory of legitimate jurisdiction. Suppose Tesler transferred funds to a Nigerian official's Swiss bank account, and some of the funds were routed through the U.S. financial system in the course of being transferred to accounts in the United Kingdom and Nigeria. Let's assume that the official never left Nigeria. The "location" of an account is typically spelled out in an agreement between a client and a financial institution; otherwise, it can be inferred from the physical location of the branch with which the client has dealt. Either way, the client has ample reason to believe that the laws of the designated jurisdiction will govern transactions concerning the account. This means that holding proceeds of bribery in a country generally should be treated as a form of consent which justifies that country's regulation of corrupt transactions involving the account. So, in our hypothetical case, Switzerland, the United Kingdom, and Nigeria would be justified in asserting jurisdiction over the official's actions. The United Kingdom would have an even stronger interest if the corruptly procured funds were used to buy a townhouse in Central London, since we generally presume that physical assets are subject to the laws of the place where they are located. The United States would not, however, be justified in prosecuting our hypothetical Nigerian official. Emails or wire transfers through a country's financial system seem like too flimsy a basis for concluding that a person has consented to its jurisdiction.[65]

Vital Interests of Citizens as Bases for Legitimacy

Consent, territoriality, and nationality are not the only ways to justify the assertion of jurisdiction. There is a compelling argument that a state is justified in asserting jurisdiction in order to achieve protection of its citizens' and residents' truly vital interests—meaning interests so vital that any rational person would accept the need for them to be protected through law. The argument is based on two premises: that hypothetical consent can serve as a source of legitimacy and that any reasonable person would agree that assertion of jurisdiction is appropriate when regulation is necessary to achieve a minimal standard of substantive fairness, which we defined in chapter 5 as protection of vital interests. A good example might be regulation required to protect citizens' interests in freedom from physical harm while they are in their home state's territory—surely a state is permitted to punish someone who murders its citizens in their homes by shooting them across the border.

Is application of anti-bribery law to nonresident noncitizens ever necessary to serve the vital interests of a states' citizens? Since Cicero's speech against Verres, echoed in Burke's speeches against Hastings, it has been clear that corrupt practices in distant lands can threaten the interests of inhabitants of even the most powerful states.[66] This is even more true in modern times, when people are connected across borders through international markets and social networks, and can exploit those connections through ever-more sophisticated communication technologies. Under these conditions it should not be surprising if economic activities in one country, including but not limited to bribery of public officials, have effects on the material well-being, personal freedoms, and collective identity of people in other countries. In an interconnected and interdependent world, it is eminently plausible that a state serves the interests of the people it represents when it prevents, condemns, or secures compensation for bribery of foreign public officials.[67]

Take the Bonny Island cases. There are several ways in which the interests of people outside of Nigeria, for example, in the United States or France, might be affected by the corrupt behavior documented there. For starters, people outside of Nigeria are likely to have economic interests in firms that lose out to bribe payers in the competition for government contracts. They also are likely to have economic interests in firms that may be asked to pay bribes in the future. Many firms consider bribery to be an expensive way of doing business with the government—in part because agreements with corrupt officials are unreliable and unenforceable—and appreciate preventive regulation that gives them an excuse to "just say no" to requests for bribes. In addition, foreigners collectively might prefer to avoid gaining a reputation among Nigerians for being willing to engage pay bribes, since that kind of reputation can lead to ill will or even retaliation. Meanwhile, with respect to money laundering, citizens who aspire to live in New York or London or Paris may not appreciate being priced out of real estate markets by foreign officials who use the proceeds of corruption to bid up the prices of properties. More generally, virtually every state in the world has an interest in discouraging firms or individuals from facilitating criminal activity by holding themselves out indiscriminately as money launderers.

And then there are the noneconomic interests at stake. Left unregulated, bribery of foreign public officials may pose a threat to values that are important to a society. The history of the FCPA suggests that, at least during the period following Watergate, it was important to Americans' sense of national identity to have laws in place that expressed a firm commitment to integrity in both business and government. As we saw in chapter 3, the FCPA was designed in part to make a moral statement about who Americans were and what values they stood for. When it enacted the FCPA, the U.S. House of Representatives went out of its way to describe foreign bribery as "counter to the moral expectations and values of the American public."[68] It also justified the statute on the grounds that bribery "erodes public confidence in the integrity of the free market system" and "puts pressure on ethical enterprises to lower their standards or risk losing business," evoking fears of moral contagion.[69] The FCPA clearly was intended to quell fears raised by the post-Watergate revelation that many large U.S. companies had made illicit payments in both foreign and domestic markets, disclosures that raised the specter of firms learning to pay bribes overseas and then bringing their corrupt practices back home.[70]

In an ideal world ethical businesspeople would not be susceptible to moral contagion,[71] but in the real world it is a plausible concern. Take the Bonny Island affair. The bribery scheme was apparently masterminded by KBR, its Houston-based American-born CEO was personally involved, and both KBR and its parent, the Halliburton Company, did a lot of business with and had close ties to the U.S. government. Remember, Halliburton's CEO during the relevant period was Dick Cheney, former secretary of defense and future vice president of the United States! If a culture of corruption took root at KBR, it could easily lead to corruption of U.S. officials, a development that would clearly affect the interests of U.S. citizens. U.S. lawmakers could reasonably look for inspiration to Edmund Burke's efforts to prevent "the breakers of law in India from becoming the makers of law for England."[72] Corrupt foreign officials who acquire control of domestic firms present a similar risk of moral contagion.

Does any of this justify the U.S. government's treatment of Jeffrey Tesler, or prosecution of our hypothetical corrupt official? If the question is whether those actions would be necessary to protect vital interests, then the answer is not obvious. The interests at stake for U.S. citizens do not seem as vital as, say, the interest in not being shot in their homes. In fact, they do not seem to qualify as vital at all. The impact of transnational bribery on the economic and noneconomic interests of U.S. citizens may be significant but does not seem certain to compromise their ability to lead a meaningful and worthwhile life. A person in Tesler's position could reasonably say, "I disagree with your conclusion that my conduct threatens the ability of any U.S. citizen to live a life characterized by dignity and worthy of respect, or treats them as means rather than ends."

Vital Interests of Noncitizens as Bases of Legitimacy

The OECD paradigm can point to yet another source of legitimacy for expansive jurisdiction. A comprehensive assessment of the legitimate scope of transnational bribery law has to account for more than just the interests of citizens of the regulating state and potential defendants. There are others whose interests might be affected by transnational bribery law, both positively and negatively. First and foremost in this group are noncitizens governed by foreign corrupt officials.

When the United States first enacted the FCPA, its lawmakers appeared to be motivated primarily by self-interest. Over time, as the U.S. government and anti-corruption advocates pressed other countries to adopt their own laws regulating foreign corrupt practices, the stated rationales shifted to include appeals to concern about the plight of foreigners, especially the inhabitants of developing countries.[73] The new rhetoric captures the powerful moral intuition tapped into by Burke, namely, that the inhabitants of countries governed by corrupt officials are the primary victims of corruption. The Bonny Island affair qualifies as a moral outrage mainly because it left millions of Nigerians trapped in poverty while an insatiably corrupt political class gorged itself on profits from their nation's resources, not because of its impact on the shareholders of Bechtel, or any other U.S. citizens. With this intuition in mind, perhaps the U.S. legal response is best understood as an effort to promote the interests of Nigerians, as opposed to those of people in the United States. Is this an adequate justification?

As we discussed in chapter 5, it is not difficult to make the case that bribery tends to prejudice citizens of the country whose officials are bribed. Nigeria provides as good an illustration as any country. Since independence, the Nigerian government has been renowned for pervasive corruption, and in particular, for the breathtaking sums of money diverted by high-level officials. The Bonny Island affair is not an outlier. The oil and gas sector, which recently has accounted for as much as 95 percent of Nigeria's export earnings, historically has suffered from lax oversight that makes it especially prone to corruption. In 2013, the central bank governor at the time reported that the state-owned oil company had failed to account for between $10.8 billion and $20 billion in oil revenue over a nineteen-month period. He was soon replaced.[74] *The Economist* summarized the impact of corruption on Nigeria in graphic terms:

> The cost of all this graft vastly exceeds the actual amounts stolen. Investors are reluctant to put money into a country if they cannot be sure that contracts will be honoured. Local businesses deliberately stay small, hoping to stay beneath officialdom's radar. Citizens are generally loth to pay taxes because they assume the money will be stolen. Billions of dollars in state spending are wasted on useless projects. On the outskirts of Sokoto in the far north of Nigeria a brand new power plant is going up, years behind schedule and over budget. The delay may be a mercy, for once it is switched on it will instantly start racking up big losses . . . Graft has also been one of the factors behind an

insurgency in Nigeria's north which its army, hollowed out by corrupt generals, has struggled to contain.[75]

In a poor country like Nigeria, corruption causes more than just inconvenience: it gravely impairs ordinary peoples' abilities to lead satisfying and worthwhile lives. In rural parts of the country, nearly half the population lived in poverty in 2012, and poor public services were part of the reason why.[76] In 2016, an economist estimated that 25 million Nigerians would have escaped poverty but for the country's "excess corruption."[77] The methods used to generate this estimate were dubious, but the claim that there was a causal relationship between corruption in Nigeria and the impoverishment of millions of Nigerians was not.

On these facts there is little doubt that many inhabitants of Nigeria have vital interests in preventing, condemning, and securing compensation for corruption of their public officials. In the absence of preventive intervention or compensation, millions will go without the minimum resources they need to live satisfying and worthwhile lives. If the question is whether expansive application of transnational bribery law is morally justified, the answer is, at least in the case of Nigeria, compellingly, yes. Every state in the world is justified in resorting to coercive sanctions, when reasonably necessary, to protect such vital interests.

When truly vital interests are at stake, regulatory intervention might be more than just morally acceptable, it might be morally required. As we saw in chapter 5, many philosophers agree that the basic obligation for all human beings to respect human dignity and autonomy entails an affirmative obligation to protect the vital interests of foreigners.[78] This implies that we all have an affirmative obligation to combat corruption when it compromises foreign governmental institutions in ways that threaten other people's vital interests.[79] In political philosopher John Rawls's distinctive formulation, "well-ordered peoples have a duty to assist burdened societies."[80] As Thomas Pogge has pointed out, this proposition implies that states have an affirmative duty to protect the interests of people whose ability to enjoy the benefits of just institutions is threatened by corruption, whether through coercive sanctions or other measures.[81] On this view, KBR and its co-conspirators violated a moral obligation not to interfere with institutions necessary to protect the vital interests of people in Nigeria, and the United States and other countries have an obligation to intervene in support of efforts to respond to and prevent this kind of violation. The latter obligation only appears to exist, however, when intervention is reasonably necessary to protect vital interests, not when corruption threatens institutional integrity but does not immediately imperil people's vital interests. So for instance, the United States might be justified in taking an expansive approach to regulation of corrupt practices affecting the government of Nigeria, but not practices affecting the government of a country like New Zealand, where foreign intervention in corruption poses less of a threat to the population's well-being, and even if it does, local institutions are likely to be capable of addressing the problem.[82]

To be clear, the issue is whether an expansive enforcement strategy is necessary to protect vital interests, not whether any specific enforcement action is reasonably necessary. It is nearly impossible to trace the connection between a particular corrupt transaction and the deplorable living conditions of people in the Niger Delta or anywhere else, even when the amounts at stake are as substantial as those in the Bonny Island affair. It also is impossible to say that an effective enforcement strategy aimed at combating corruption in Nigeria would necessarily have to target the Bonny Island affair; it is always possible that another high-profile prosecution would make a similar statement and have similar effects. At the same time, the fact that protection of vital interests can be achieved using either of two enforcement strategies cannot be a reasonable objection to pursuing either strategy. That would lead to the absurd conclusion that neither strategy is justifiable. No reasonable person should accept this outcome. Therefore, so long as a given enforcement strategy is a reasonable means of achieving the objective of protecting vital interests, any actions pursuant to that strategy should be acceptable.

International Agreements as Bases for Legitimacy

How robust is this defense of the OECD paradigm's approach to jurisdiction? Suppose we confront a situation in which foreign enforcement agencies are likely to be effective in combating a particular form of corruption, even though it involves noncitizens acting outside the foreign agencies' territory, but no one's vital interests are at stake. The arguments we have canvassed to this point suggest that only local actors can regulate legitimately in this scenario. We are left then with a mismatch between effectiveness and legitimacy.

This problem appears to have a straightforward solution. If it is legitimate for a state to regulate a particular corrupt transaction, then it should be legitimate for it to call on other states for assistance, including states that are either more willing or able to regulate, in much the same way that the Sicilians called on Cicero to prosecute Verres. Or, to return to our more contemporary example, even if Nigeria and the United Kingdom were the only countries that could legitimately regulate Jeffrey Tesler's activities in relation to Bonny Island, and Nigeria's interests should have been given priority, it might have been legitimate for the United States to regulate his conduct at Nigeria's invitation.

Can a state legitimately delegate regulatory actions to another state? Delegation in and of itself should not be a concern since a state can only act through agents and so must delegate in order to accomplish anything. The question is whether delegation of regulation to agents of another state, whose loyalties are necessarily divided, somehow compromises legitimacy. The most plausible reason why this kind of regulatory outsourcing might be illegitimate is because it unduly diminishes the accountability mechanisms that ordinarily make it legitimate for a state to coerce its own citizens. Ultimately, the extent to which the foreign state is accountable will be an empirical question, since an invitation to regulate can include both formal and informal accountability mechanisms, up to and including the possibility of revoking the invitation. Therefore, it seems reasonable to admit the possibility that one state's invitation can make it legitimate for another state to regulate corrupt practices that it would not otherwise be able to regulate legitimately.

An international invitation to regulate corruption can be offered and accepted either through a formal treaty or an ad hoc international agreement. The UN Convention incorporates an invitation of this sort since it binds its signatories to permit one another to assert jurisdiction expansively. The OECD Convention has the same effect to the extent its parties agree to permit broad assertions of territorial jurisdiction. To be clear though, neither of these treaties operated as an invitation from Nigeria to prosecute Jeffrey Tesler. The UN Convention only came into force in December 2005, after Tesler's corrupt practices had ended. The OECD Convention came into force part of the way through the affair, but although the United States and the United Kingdom were both parties (as was Japan), Nigeria was not.

Extradition and mutual legal assistance treaties, as well as memoranda of understanding concluded among agencies without criminal enforcement authority, cure other mismatches between legitimacy and effectiveness. An extradition treaty ordinarily permits a state that has effective control over an individual to transfer control to the state that can legitimately prosecute or impose sanctions. Mutual legal assistance treaties and memoranda of understanding among securities regulators operate similarly but govern transfer of evidence or information rather than people. In the case of Jeffrey Tesler, the U.K.-U.S. Extradition Treaty worked in a slightly different way. The United Kingdom not only had control over Tesler, it also could have legitimately prosecuted him since he was a U.K. national who engaged in egregious misconduct on English soil (assuming that U.K. law prohibited foreign bribery). Instead, pursuant to the treaty, the United Kingdom transferred Tesler to a country whose prosecutors had a doubtful claim to legitimacy. Whether or not the principle of territoriality supported the U.S. assertion of jurisdiction was the central issue in the extradition hearings, because U.K. law only permitted extradition if the offense was committed "in the territory" of the requesting state. The U.K. courts concluded that there was a sufficient territorial connection to the United States and blessed the extradition.[83] In legal terms the decision simply confirmed that the United States would be permitted to prosecute, but in moral terms it seems more appropriate to say that the U.K. courts conferred permission to prosecute and lent legitimacy to the U.S. proceedings.

At first glance, therefore, modern anti-corruption treaties seem to cure the legitimacy deficit that would otherwise haunt states that try to sanction transnational bribery without regard to traditional principles of territoriality or nationality. The UN Convention is particularly important here because it permits regulation on a quasi-universal basis and has been signed by many countries that suffer from high levels of corruption. This means that most of the states in which bribery is likely to pose a threat to peoples' vital interests have explicitly authorized intervention by virtually every foreign state likely to be interested in intervening.

At the same time, the UN Convention provides at least two safeguards against the possibility of foreign actors intervening in ways that ignore the interests of locals. First, recall that parties' obligations under the Convention are expressly subject to an obligation to respect one another's sovereignty. This vaguely worded qualification presumably does not require parties to condone regulatory approaches that are clearly contrary to the purpose of the Convention. However, the qualification can and should be interpreted to require the parties to defer to states' reasonably held views on how to regulate the bribery of their own officials. As suggested previously, if sovereignty means anything, it should mean the ability to regulate official bribery without interference.

The UN Convention protects countries governed by corrupt officials in a second way: it grants them rights to share in the benefits of enforcement undertaken by other countries. Those rights are set out in the Convention's pathbreaking chapter on "Asset Recovery" and are widely understood to be the key reasons why developing countries supported the adoption of the UN Convention. Chapter V of the UN Convention is titled "Asset Recovery" and its very first provision states:

> The return of assets pursuant to this chapter is a fundamental principle of this Convention, and States Parties shall afford one another the widest measure of cooperation and assistance in this regard.[84]

Taken literally, the term "asset recovery" covers only return of misappropriated assets to their prior owners. In fact, Chapter V covers not only stolen assets but also proceeds of crime and amounts owed as compensation for the harm caused by corruption. The Convention virtually mandates return of stolen assets. Notably, it also says that once a state party to the Convention has received an appropriate request from another state party, return of proceeds of corruption and payment of compensation should be given "priority consideration."[85]

This dimension of the Convention has been neglected, at least until recently. Several developed countries have made efforts to return proceeds of corruption seized from corrupt officials, but they have been less inclined to return proceeds of bribery taken from bribe payers. Remarkably, for the period between 1999 and 2012, only 3 percent of monetary sanctions imposed by states for bribery of foreign officials (that is, not their own officials) was shared with other countries.[86] This occurred despite the fact that a large portion of those monetary sanctions represented confiscation of proceeds of crime. For example, in the Bonny Island affair, of the $1.7 billion paid to the U.S. Treasury, $400 million represented disgorgement by the TSKJ firms, and Tesler's forfeiture accounted for another $149 million. The United States also arguably violated the spirit of the UN Convention by imposing monetary penalties in the form of fines, which it was not obligated to share, rather than confiscations. To be fair, however, it is unclear how frequently sharing has been requested. It remains to be seen whether the kind of sharing of recoveries witnessed in the enforcement actions against Odebrecht and Braskem signals a change in practice on the part of the United States and other states active in enforcing their laws against foreign bribery.

States cannot point to the UN Convention as a source of legitimacy for enforcement actions that fail to comply with its provisions on asset recovery. If they wish to take advantage of the expansive rights conferred by the UN Convention, they must also abide by the corresponding duties.

The Potential for Disagreement

There is little doubt that countries like the United States and the United Kingdom are willing and able to provide valuable anti-corruption resources that countries like Nigeria need, and that in some cases the need is vital. It is also clear that by signing on to the UN Convention, Nigeria and most other countries in the world have formally agreed to accept this kind of foreign assistance. Consequently, although the OECD approach to jurisdiction is expansive, its claims to legitimacy and effectiveness seem to rest on secure footing. What could be the problem?

The anti-imperialist critique does not deny that foreign actors are willing and able to intervene decisively in local affairs, the question is whether there will be a consensus that they have intervened wisely. In many situations, legal interventions will raise difficult questions, both factual and moral, especially once we push beyond general statements such as "there ought to be strict laws against bribery" and look closely at specific prohibitions and enforcement strategies.[87]

With any given set of allegations, the challenges begin with the process of figuring out what actually happened—who did what, when, and with whom—and evaluating its impact. In most cases, bribery is difficult to detect and so enforcement agencies are forced to draw inferences from inconclusive evidence. In many cases, agencies bring enforcement actions without direct evidence showing whether anything of value found its way to a public official and what, if anything, the official provided in exchange. Meanwhile, in many money laundering cases it is easy to show that an official's wealth exceeds anything that could have been earned from legitimate sources but extraordinarily difficult to prove that the assets were derived from any specific corrupt act.

As we have seen in chapter 6, most legal systems respond to these factual uncertainties by allowing liability to be imposed even in the absence of definitive proof that bribery, at least in an obvious form, has taken place. The discussion in chapter 6 also showed that this way of circumventing factual obstacles quickly leads to challenging moral issues. Outside of the paradigmatic forms of bribery it is difficult to decide which conduct deserves condemnation. In many instances the overarching question becomes, does the proven conduct pose an undue risk of harm? Deciding what level of risk is undue is ultimately a question of values, informed by empirical judgments about what is likely to have happened given what is known to have happened. For example, suppose the issue is whether to condemn the payments Tesler made to the unnamed Nigerian political party. That decision requires weighing the value of private financing of election campaigns against the risk of improper influence, taking into account any constraints on party power imposed by electoral politics. Or consider the payments that Marubeni made to "lower-level" Nigerian officials on behalf of TSKJ. Suppose, hypothetically speaking, that the consortium members claimed these payments were the products of extortion, meaning that they were made to secure services to which TSKJ was legally entitled—perhaps, work visas for its employees—and were only made because the public officials threatened to shut down the project, which would cause ruinous losses for TSKJ (and others). Reasonable people can disagree about whether to condemn these payments as bribes or to excuse them on the grounds of extortion.[88]

There may also be divergent views about how to investigate and adjudicate misconduct, often stemming from differences of opinion about what due process entails. The most profound differences are generally between the adversarial model exemplified by the U.S. systems of both civil and criminal procedure, and the inquisitorial model generally favored in continental Europe and

Latin America. As we have seen in chapter 9, these philosophical differences can lead to sharp disagreements about whether practices such as negotiated settlements, privately conducted investigations (in the case of the United States), and compelled testimony (in the case of more inquisitorial systems) comport with the requirements of due process.

The factual and moral challenges continue when an enforcement agency evaluates possible sanctions. To begin, there may be disagreements about the objectives the sanctions ought to achieve. For example, in the Bonny Island cases, U.S. enforcement agencies may have been motivated by self-interested retribution while the Nigerian agencies may have been primarily concerned with self-interested compensation. In fact, disagreement about objectives necessarily exists whenever self-interested agencies are loyal to different communities since each agency's principal objective is to further interests of its own nationals. As we have seen in chapter 9, Article 5 of the OECD Convention attempts to regulate manifestations of this kind of disagreement by barring self-interested in enforcement, but it is unlikely to be perfectly effective.

Disagreement about sanctions may exist even in the context of agreement about their objectives. Suppose, for instance, that an enforcement agency is focused on imposing sanctions that will prevent future misconduct, keeping in mind the downside risks of setting penalties so high that they discourage people from entering politics or discourage firms from doing business in "high-risk" countries like Nigeria. As we saw in chapter 9, crafting sanctions that will deter or persuade people likely to be involved in economic crime is more of an art than a science. Was $1.7 billion worth of fines and forfeitures too much, just enough, or insufficient? Should there have been more individual prosecutions or longer terms of imprisonment? To predict the impact of any given enforcement strategy requires a certain amount of psychological insight, some of which is likely to be culturally specific. The culprits in the Bonny Island affair comprised a remarkably diverse cast of characters, including Nigerian politicians, Texan oilmen, employees of Japanese trading companies, and an English solicitor. No court or enforcement agency can predict with confidence how its sanctions will influence people from all these different backgrounds, especially when they operate in organizational settings.

Even if the behavioral consequences of an enforcement strategy can be predicted, value judgments are required to decide whether the benefits of prevention outweigh the costs of discouraging foreign investment and scaring people out of politics. It is important for die-hard corruption fighters to recognize that these value judgments will not always come out in favor of corruption control. For instance, in the aftermath of the Haitian earthquake of 2010, there were suggestions that it would be appropriate to suspend enforcement of the FCPA in relation to Haiti in order to encourage foreign investment.[89] Haiti has long been the most impoverished nation in the Western hemisphere and in desperate need of foreign investment. The idea of suspending the FCPA went nowhere, but it was based on a provocative hypothesis, namely, that foreign investors were indispensable to the recovery effort but would find it impossible to operate without paying bribes. If this hypothesis had been valid, it would have been fair to say that protection of the vital interests of Haitians demanded that the United States and other countries tolerate bribery, even if committed by their nationals or within their territory. Threats to the vital interests of noncitizens can stand alongside threats to the liberty interests of defendants as reasons to refrain from regulation of bribery.

Local and foreign actors might disagree about whether the costs of preventing bribery outweigh the benefits. In Brazil there is a well-known saying, *rouba mas faz*. It means, "he (or she) steals but gets things done." There is some evidence that Brazilian voters take this aphorism to heart and, at least in mayoral elections, are willing to vote for politicians known to be corrupt if they are sufficiently effective.[90] How can a foreign prosecutor say that those voters are making the wrong decision? Non-Brazilians who are inclined to support foreign intervention should test their intuitions by asking how they would feel if their own institutions were being second-guessed. For instance, Americans might ask how they would feel if Russia decided to prosecute Hillary Clinton for bribery in connection with the dealings of the Clinton Foundation, or France decided to prosecute Donald Trump in connection with the operation of his hotel in Washington, D.C.

The task of determining an appropriate enforcement strategy is no easier if the goal is to impose sanctions that appropriately condemn, as opposed to prevent, bribery. Societies differ dramatically in the meanings they attach to different sanctions and so they frequently have different views on appropriate sanctions. The €5,000 fine imposed on Etienne Gory, Technip's ex-commercial manager for Africa, might have expressed appropriate condemnation according to French standards, and seemed to be in line with the $20,000 fine imposed in Texas on KBR's Chodan. More recently though, U.S. courts have seemed inclined to impose tougher sentences, including terms of imprisonment. Again, potentially contestable value judgments are inevitable.

Using the legal system to provide compensation for bribery can be even more challenging. The first step is to calculate who lost what, a difficult task when there is limited information about exactly how officials have been corrupted, and what would have happened if they had behaved properly. Who is to say what would have happened if TSKJ had not paid bribes. Would the LNG facility have been completed? If yes, at what cost? To the same specifications and in the same time frame? How much profit would the competing bidders have earned? How would the local community have been affected? And so forth. The next step is to ask whether any victims should be denied compensation because they contributed in some way to the misconduct. U.S. courts have sometimes accepted this argument as a reason to deny compensation to governments whose high-level officials have been corrupted.[91] If any government ever was culpable in that sense, it was the government of Nigeria during the planning and construction of the Bonny Island project. Finally, there is the thorny issue of how to deliver compensation to Nigerians. Should it be paid to the federal government, state governments, or nongovernmental organizations that provide public services in the region? Leaving aside questions of legitimacy, there is the very real risk that officials of those bodies will misappropriate funds designated for compensation. It seems pointless to give stolen money back to the same people who stole it.

In short, except in the clearest of cases involving hard-core forms of bribery or money laundering, there may be reasonable doubts about whether any given legal prohibition or enforcement strategy is the most effective way to protect the various interests served by anti-bribery law. This is true even in cases like the Bonny Island affair, where truly vital interests were at stake and many aspects of the case were clear-cut. This disagreement has implications for both the effectiveness and the legitimacy of a regime that permits expansive assertions of jurisdiction.

Effectiveness in the Face of Disagreement and Collective Action Problems

Contrary to the assumptions of the enforcement gap theory, allowing enforcement agencies from a wide range of countries to regulate transnational bribery does not automatically enhance effectiveness. Giving multiple agencies overlapping jurisdiction creates the possibility of conflicting or redundant enforcement strategies.[92] The risk of these sorts of problems seems especially high in a context in which there is ample room for even reasonable enforcement officials to disagree about strategy.

Conflict arises when agencies have either divergent objectives or divergent views about how to achieve a common objective. For example, the Bonny Island cases arguably resulted in U.S. enforcement agencies motivated by self-interested retribution collecting fines that frustrated the objectives of Nigerian agencies primarily interested in compensation. Self-interested agencies can also come into conflict when they impose sanctions on one another's local firms. Of course, this kind of conflict may not be objectionable to independent observers.

Another type of conflict that might arise from disagreement is where an agency focused on deterrence offers leniency to actors who self-report. This is now the official policy of the U.S. Department of Justice and the SEC. Agencies in other jurisdictions can and have undermined this strategy by refusing to guarantee leniency to those who step forward. This may reflect inattention on the part of the non-U.S. agencies, but it may also reflect a greater level of concern about retribution or compensation. Alternatively, it might reflect disagreements about an empirical matter, such as the relative importance of deterring the firms likely to benefit from leniency as opposed to the other firms or individuals likely to be revealed by self-reports.

Agencies might pursue conflicting strategies even when they have the same objectives, at least in the absence of mechanisms that mitigate collective action problems. At least two broad categories of conflict are possible in these circumstances. First is overenforcement, a situation in which agencies' combined strategies result in more investigations or prosecutions, or greater sanctions, than are required to achieve the common objective. This might occur because agencies free-ride unduly on one another's efforts; for example, Nigeria might take advantage of the information uncovered by the United States to prosecute the members of the TSKJ consortium. This kind of "piling on" can undermine both retribution and deterrence. If the objective is retribution, overenforcement might entail sanctions that are disproportionately large in relation to the defendant's culpability. Alternatively, regardless of the outcome, subjecting a defendant to the burden of being investigated or prosecuted multiple times might itself be viewed as a disproportionate sanction. Similarly, if the common objective is deterrence, the fear is that multiplicity of proceedings will result in overdeterrence—the prospect of an unending sequence of enforcement actions resulting from the same offence might be enough to dissuade firms from investing in high-risk jurisdictions like Nigeria. To date there is no clear evidence of these forms of overenforcement, but it is impossible to rule out the possibility that they will emerge as problems in the future.

Overenforcement might be troubling even when the common objective is achieved, simply because it is wasteful. Redundancy in law enforcement has some benefits: it provides a way to detect errors, and it may be a necessary feature of interagency or interjurisdictional competition, which in turn creates incentives to innovate and maximize productivity. Nonetheless, it often will be inefficient for multiple agencies and courts to interview the same witnesses, review the same documents, and assess the consequences of the same transaction.

Agencies with common objectives are prone to a second type of conflict, namely, underenforcement, the opposite of overenforcement. It can occur if agencies limit their enforcement to the point where enforcement is suboptimal from a collective perspective. In other words, rather than piling on, agencies hold back. How can increasing the number of potential enforcers ever have this effect? The most plausible scenario is where agencies delay enforcement in the hopes of free-riding on the actions of other agencies. That obviously did not happen in the Bonny Island cases, where the United States ended up taking the initiative, but there might well be other incidents of misconduct that have failed to result in any sort of enforcement action because other countries waited in vain for the United States to take the lead. Since these kinds of under-enforcement generally involve inaction as opposed to action they are inherently difficult to observe.

Under-enforcement might also arise when agencies have common objectives but their strateges undermine one another. For instance, the first-mover in an investigation might tip off the targets, thereby giving them opportunities to destroy evidence.

It is worth emphasizing that both overenforcement and underenforcement sometimes can be avoided through coordination. Coordination in this context simply means working together to achieve common objectives. In practice this entails: acknowledgment of common goals; sharing of information required to pursue the common goals; provision of information about the effects of actions (feedback); adjustment of actions or objectives in response to feedback; and adoption of rules or processes for assigning activities among various actors. There is increasing evidence of successful coordination among enforcement agencies in cases involving transnational bribery. Notable examples include the *Siemens* case discussed in chapter 8 and the *Odebrecht/Braskem* case discussed in chapter 9.

Coordination is facilitated by the existence of *coordination mechanisms*. These include organizations or social networks that establish channels for information flows and opportunities for face-to-face interaction, as well as protocols for making decisions or formulating rules. Those organizations, networks, or protocols can be established through hierarchical commands or adopted by explicit or implicit agreements, all of which may or may not be legally binding. Some of these networks and protocols tend to strengthen with use; the more communication there is among members of a network, the more effective it becomes.

An important example of a legally binding coordination mechanism is the principle of *ne bis in idem*, also known as the prohibition on double jeopardy. In national legal systems this rule generally prevents a person from being prosecuted more than once for the same offense. It serves to coordinate by assigning priority among prosecuting authorities to the first in time. The members of the European Union have embraced the principle of *ne bis in idem* in cases involving prosecutions by different EU member states.[93] In France, the principle is applied to bar French prosecution on the basis of extraterritorial jurisdiction when there has been a prior judgment overseas.[94]

There are other important coordination mechanisms. Members of the European Union have agreed to guidelines on how to assign jurisdiction among multiple agencies[95] and conduct joint investigations.[96] In addition, the OECD Convention and the UN Convention require their parties to consult one another in cases of overlapping jurisdiction.[97] The UN Convention also makes extensive provision for various forms of international cooperation, including mutual legal assistance, extradition, and sharing of confiscated assets.[98] Finally, there are informal social networks between enforcement agencies, particularly those located in OECD countries that regularly find themselves working on the same matters. Among the members of the OECD Convention these networks are supported by the regular meetings of prosecutors that occur alongside the meetings of the OECD Working Group.[99]

Despite the existence of these mechanisms there remain formidable obstacles to international coordination. There are no global counterparts to either the rule of *ne bis in idem* or the European Union's guidelines on how to allocate jurisdiction or conduct joint investigations.[100] There are also legal obstacles to coordination, such as rules that make it difficult to use evidence that has been influenced by overseas investigative practices. This issue arose in the Tesler case. The Paris Court of Appeal refused to permit Jeffrey Tesler to be tried in France because it was concerned that his agreement with the U.S. prosecutors limited his right to defend himself at trial by contesting the facts set out in the plea agreement. This decision was overturned by the France's highest court, the Cour de Cassation, which held that the plea agreement did not govern Tesler's conduct in the French proceedings.[101] Meanwhile on the other side of the Atlantic, a U.S. court in another case refused to admit evidence obtained in the United Kingdom through the use of compelled testimony, even though this is a standard investigative tactic for U.K. regulatory agencies.[102]

Maximal coordination may not be optimal. Coordination is costly, and some forms of coordination might stamp out healthy debate and competition. The same is true for cooperation, which occurs when agencies work together without necessarily sharing objectives. For instance, self-interested enforcement agencies might cooperate by entering into implicit mutual non-aggression pacts in which they each agree to turn a blind eye to misconduct by firms from other states. Or error-prone agencies might coordinate in a way that eliminates opportunities to catch oversights. Forgoing cooperation or coordination in favor of competition and redundancy can expose and overcome the limitations of self-interested or ineffectual agencies. As mechanisms for cooperation and coordination among enforcement agencies in transnational bribery cases continue to evolve, the effectiveness of the regime will depend on the balance between these considerations.

Due Process at a Distance

As a practical matter, officials who are geographically distant from where defendants reside and do business will struggle to guarantee due process. Due process requires, among other things, that a person have had fair notice of the norms they are charged with violating, have a fair opportunity to contest the charges against them, not be subject to cruel and unusual punishment, and not be prosecuted more than once for the same misconduct. These entitlements are difficult to guarantee when a person is prosecuted and sanctioned in one or more places with which they have relatively weak ties, especially places where they have not given any kind of consent to jurisdiction. These concerns generally support limiting jurisdiction to nationality and territoriality, especially in jurisdictions whose trial procedures rely heavily on live testimony and adjudication by a jury of the defendant's peers.[103] Jeffrey Tesler could reasonably have complained that his due process rights were threatened if the United States had prosecuted him solely for violating one of the more idiosyncratic aspects of the FCPA, like its prohibition on payments to foreign political parties. He could also reasonably complain that it would be much more difficult for him to mount a defense in a Texas courtroom than closer to home, in say, London. Moreover, it was presumably more arduous for him to be imprisoned in the United States, far from family and friends, than closer to home. In fact, during his sentencing hearing, Tesler pleaded to be allowed to be reunited with his wife, daughters, and grandchildren. It was also troubling that after being convicted in the United States, Tesler was prosecuted in France for virtually the same conduct.

At the same time, concerns about due process often can be addressed on a case-by-case basis through mechanisms such as publicly sponsored legal assistance for defendants, international agreements that permit prisoners to serve sentences in their home countries, and extension of protection against double jeopardy to the international context.

Legitimate Regulation in the Face of Potential Disagreement

The potential for disagreement about how to regulate transnational bribery has important implications for the question of who should regulate it. Recall our conclusion about when a state can legitimately coerce a nonresident person who acts extraterritorially: only when any rational person would agree that coercion is necessary to protect vital interests. This standard is less likely to be met if a rational person would have doubts about the need for a particular set of coercive sanctions. So where does this leave us? Is it legitimate for states to regulate transnational bribery when they cannot rely on traditional principles of territoriality or nationality? The answer seems to be that coercive regulation is only justifiable in clear-cut cases where vital interests are at stake. This means that in difficult cases, that is, cases in which there is factual or moral uncertainty, a relatively small number of states can legitimately exercise coercion.

In some of these difficult cases, vital interests are at stake and deserve to be given priority. In a country like Nigeria—and perhaps to an even greater extent in a poorer country like Haiti—decisions about what conduct to prohibit, who to target, what penalties to impose, and how to distribute any benefits from enforcement actions can literally make the difference between life and death. Ideally, those decisions would be made by actors who have the motivation and ability to protect the interests of the people affected, taking into account the risks of both expansive and restrained approaches to regulation. Concretely, this means that anti-bribery laws should be drafted by legislators sworn to protect the people's interests, and implemented by judges, prosecutors, and police officers subject to the same duty. Those officials should be informed about the needs and values of the people whose interests they are obliged to protect and should be accountable to them, either directly, through elections, or indirectly, through accountability mechanisms recognized by a constitution that enjoys widespread support. In many cases it will not strictly be necessary to formalize these obligations, information channels, and accountability mechanisms because the officials will be drawn from the affected community. Officials who pay taxes to corrupt governments only to feel shortchanged every time they try to drive to work, who are called out in local media for their failure to respond to the latest scandal, and who have to listen to complaints about corruption from friends and family, are likely to be motivated, informed, and responsive even in the absence of legal mechanisms.

For all these reasons, it is difficult to escape the conclusion that anti-bribery law generally ought to be designed and enforced by institutions located in countries governed by corrupt officials. If legal institutions from other states attempt to impose their views through coercion, they are likely to make mistakes about where the affected people's interests lie. Putting these decisions in the hands of foreign officials will violate the affected people's interests in being able to choose, at least collectively, how to govern their own affairs.[104] Moreover, without appropriate safeguards, expansive assertions of jurisdiction also risk violating due process.

This line of reasoning implies that states should refrain not only from legal coercion but also from legal condemnation in relation to transactions that are condoned by the people most affected, keeping in mind that in highly corrupt societies the views of public officials cannot be treated as dispositive on this point. This is not to say that all condemnation is problematic in these cases, only the paradigmatically legal kind of condemnation. There is nothing wrong with a foreigner expressing views about moral issues at odds with the views of the people most directly affected. Foreigners should be entitled to call a bribe a bribe; if Canadians want to call U.S. campaign finance a form of legalized bribery, they should feel free. There is nothing wrong with passing moral judgments of this kind. It is, however, objectionable to claim that those judgments ought to be binding on people who are better placed to make them. In other words, states should refrain from making claims to authority when confronted with difficult questions about how to respond to allegations that foreign officials have been bribed. Advice and comment are acceptable, coercion and legal condemnation are not.

In legal terms, this means that states inclined to regulate transnational bribery should generally defer to good faith determinations made by local legal institutions about how to proceed in particular cases. This is not necessarily incompatible with expansive assertions of jurisdiction. Again, expansive assertions of jurisdiction may be necessary to protect the vital interests of people ruled by corrupt officials. However, states that define their jurisdiction expansively should give themselves the option of deference to more legitimate decision makers by building in and giving effect to limitations such as double criminality conditions, local law defenses, the presumption against extraterritoriality, due process requirements, and the doctrines of state and official immunity.

This conclusion hearkens back to Hastings' defense to the charges laid against him by Edmund Burke. Hastings argued that his actions should be judged by the "Manners, Customs, Principles and Laws, peculiar to the Countries in which such Measures were adopted."[105] Burke rejected this "geographical morality" with his famous declaration that "the laws of morality are the same every where" and that bribery and peculation were just as actionable "in Europe, Asia, Africa and all the world over."[106] Burke was not entirely right. It is reasonable to expect only a partial moral consensus about how to respond to allegations of corruption. In the absence of such a consensus, legal regulation and the associated moral judgments are best left to local actors.

A Note on Regulation by International Organizations

States are not the only bodies involved in regulating transnational bribery. Working alongside states, the major multilateral development banks and development agencies have developed elaborate regimes for investigating and sanctioning firms that engage in corrupt practices in connection with projects they fund. In the Bonny Island affair, the African Development Bank imposed more substantial penalties on the members of the TSKJ consortium than the

U.K. government! It is far from obvious though why an organization styled as a "bank" should act as an anti-corruption agency, and observers in developing countries sometimes question the appropriateness of development banks playing this role.

At first glance, regulation by development finance institutions involves lower stakes than regulation by states. These institutions have no armies or police forces to enforce their rules and so they cannot directly coerce anyone. Development finance institutions do, however, have other sources of leverage. They can transmit information about corrupt practices to national enforcement agencies, which do have the power to arrest and imprison individuals—both bribe payers and recipients. Alternatively, they can release information to the public that shames firms or individuals or governments. Most important of all, the development finance institutions control access to capital, arguably the ultimate source of power. Some firms, and particularly EPC firms like the members of the TSKJ consortium, earn large proportions of their revenue from projects funded, at least in part, by multilateral development banks. For those firms, exclusion from bank-funded projects would be a death sentence, especially if several banks acted collectively. As a result, the development banks can use the threat of suspension or debarment to induce firms to pay financial penalties, adopt compliance programs, or even fund anti-corruption programs. In a similar vein, the development banks, together with organizations like the UN Development Program and the International Monetary Fund, can condition countries' access to funding on compliance with anti-corruption norms. Importantly, though, this only provides leverage over countries without access to alternative sources of funding.

For all these reasons, the resources and capabilities that international organizations can provide seem likely to complement the resources of other anti-corruption agencies. In principle international organizations could also help to coordinate the activities or national enforcement agencies, although to date there is little evidence they have played this kind of role. Still, there are many reasons why getting international organizations involved in enforcement is likely to enhance the effectiveness of transnational bribery law

The outstanding question, then, is whether intervention by international organizations in individual cases is legitimate. Basically, when they get into the business of regulating transnational bribery international organizations face the same challenges to their legitimacy as states.

It is generally legitimate for international organizations to protect the interests of their member states by sanctioning bribery. For instance, the members of the African Development Bank might reasonably believe that bribery is an avoidable expense and object to their funds being used to line the pockets of Nigerian officials. They might also wish to avoid being morally implicated in a project tainted by corruption. At the same time, development finance institutions and their member states share in an overriding moral obligation—typically made express in the legal mandates of the development finance institutions—to protect inhabitants of badly misgoverned countries whose abilities to lead meaningful lives might be threatened by both bribery and regulatory interventions designed to address it.

It is not always easy, however, to determine how to fulfill these potentially competing obligations. For instance, if there are only a handful of firms operating in a particular sector, debarment of one firm might reduce competition for contracts to complete future projects, leading to higher costs or reduced quality. Reducing loans to a country may or may not prompt reform and could easily delay projects that would meaningfully improve standards of living. Sanctions that involve financial penalties are also difficult to evaluate because there is so much room for debate about what is required to achieve deterrence, retribution, or compensation. The African Development Bank promised that the $22.7 million in penalties collected from the TSKJ companies would "flow to projects preventing and combating corruption in the Bank's Member Countries on the African continent."[107] It is far from obvious how the figure of $22.7 million was arrived at and why the funds collected were not remitted to or used exclusively for the benefit of Nigeria, or even just the Niger Delta.

In recent years there have been intermittent calls for the establishment of an international body responsible for investigating and sanctioning corrupt practices, comparable to the International Criminal Court.[108] A suitable international agreement could make it legitimate for a body of this sort to impose coercive sanctions on people who are citizens of, or act while in the territory of, the parties to the agreement. Such a body would still face all the same challenges as a foreign state or a development finance institution in determining how best to protect the vital interests of people governed by corrupt officials.

Conclusions

The OECD paradigm encourages states to push traditional principles of territoriality and nationality to their limits, or perhaps beyond, and to regulate on what has been aptly called a quasi-universal basis. The most palatable justification for the more aggressive interventions is that they represent necessary responses to grave threats to the vital interests of people governed by corrupt officials. Those interventions may be necessary because states governed by corrupt officials cannot always be counted on to protect their citizens' interests against threats from within the state itself. Nigeria is a case in point: the fact that Nigerian enforcement officials never quite got around to prosecuting any

Nigerian public officials in connection with the Bonny Island affair is telling but not surprising given indications that the corruption allegedly extended up to and included successive heads of state. The relatively half-hearted responses by France, Japan, and even the United Kingdom illustrate a point we noted in chapter 4—historically, relatively few states have been inclined to invest heavily in sanctioning transnational bribery, even when the bribes are paid by their nationals or in their territory. The response of the United States shows that sometimes the only state willing to intervene might have little meaningful connection to the misconduct (although this situation may be changing; some recent enforcement actions have involved a wider range of enforcement agencies and even raised the specter of overenforcement).

This argument legitimates an anti-bribery regime that permits interventions by a wide range of both foreign states and international organizations. The challenge is to determine when any given intervention is truly necessary, and who should make that determination. If the focus is on the interests of the people most at risk, then the right thing to do typically will be to defer to the views of their local institutions—at least so long as those institutions are operating in good faith and not simply trying to defend the indefensible. Foreign actors who ignore those local interests court the danger of being labeled neo-imperialists. Ideally, local agencies will also play a coordinating role, as there appears to be a growing need for coordination mechanisms that avoid conflicting or redundant enforcement strategies. This prescription is consistent with the UN Convention, taking into account its overarching statement that parties ought to respect one another's sovereignty. In any event, the UN Convention provides little support for enforcement actions that fail to comply with both the letter and the spirit of its provisions on asset recovery.

These recommendations will not necessarily lead to ideal outcomes. Given the competing considerations, in terms of effectiveness, efficiency, legitimacy, due process, and fairness, the ideal may be impossible to achieve. It always will be a challenge to ensure that scruples about legitimacy, due process, and fairness, or calls for coordination, do not become excuses for impunity.

11
Concluding Thoughts

Introduction

Transnational bribery law has emerged as one of the most important sources of regulation of cross-border business activity. Scores of major firms and prominent officials have become ensnared in enforcement proceedings, and tens of thousands of people in law enforcement agencies, law firms, accounting firms, and the compliance departments of multinational enterprises are preoccupied with either enforcing or complying with anti-bribery law.

The anti-bribery regime is a formidable edifice, but it is also a work in progress. The question is: What work remains to be done? Proponents of the OECD paradigm want to see more prohibitions that cover a broad range of conduct, target a wide range of actors, and empower as many agencies as possible to enforce harsh sanctions while balancing the benefits of coordination and competition. The anti-imperialist critique challenges all of these prescriptions. It is powered by multiple concerns. First, there are doubts about whether the elements of the OECD paradigm are necessarily effective. Second, there is concern that the disadvantages of the OECD approach, which include the risk of sanctioning benign or even beneficial conduct, outweigh the advantages. Third, it is worrisome that regardless of the magnitude of the benefits, implementation of the OECD paradigm threatens to impose substantial costs on innocent stakeholders, like the inhabitants of countries governed by officials who solicit or accept bribes. Fourth, some of the enforcement procedures associated with the OECD paradigm compromise due process. Finally, it is troubling that the power to decide on the shape of the regime is concentrated in a handful of enforcement agencies located in wealthy OECD countries. In other words, there are concerns about effectiveness, efficiency, fairness, due process, and legitimacy. At first glance these seem like distinct complaints, but in fact, they are inevitably intertwined. Ineffective institutions are likely to be inefficient since their modest benefits are likely to be outweighed by their costs. Ineffective, inefficient, and unfair institutions tend to be illegitimate, and illegitimate institutions tend to be ineffective and inefficient.

The tensions between the OECD paradigm and the anti-imperialist critique have been detailed in the preceding chapters of this book. This chapter proposes a path to reconciliation. The premises are that: (1) transnational bribery is a significant problem, but (2) reasonable people can and will disagree about the appropriate legal responses. Left unresolved, those disagreements threaten to compromise effectiveness, efficiency, fairness, legitimacy, and due process. This implies that architects of transnational bribery law ought to develop mechanisms that reduce the scope for disagreement about appropriate legal interventions, identify reasonable disagreements that ought to be tolerated, and offer a legitimate process for determining how to overcome disagreements that stem from unreasonable objections.

Transnational Bribery Is a Problem

There is no doubt that transnational bribery is a problem. Critics who attack transnational bribery law by trying to downplay the extent of the harm caused by bribery are profoundly misguided. This should be obvious from the cases we have discussed so far.

Consider the case of Joel Esquenazi, introduced in chapter 4. At first glance it looks minor relative to the other cases. Esquenazi and his accomplices extracted millions of dollars from Haiti Teleco, but that is far less than the hundreds of millions, or billions, of dollars in losses caused by Siemens, Odebrecht, and the TSKJ consortium. Esquenazi also caused nothing comparable to the heartbreaking but incalculable losses that Innospec inflicted when it paid to be allowed to poison Iraqis and Indonesians with lead additives. By stealing from Teleco, Esquenazi effectively stole from its owner, the government, and/or its customers. Either way, the victims were ordinary Haitians. It would have been hard to find a more vulnerable group. Their vulnerability magnifies the relatively small monetary value of their losses. At the time of the offense the per capita income in Haiti was less than $500 per year. Haitians depended on international telephone connections to maintain ties with friends and family in the diaspora, who, among other things, provided remittances worth over 20 percent of the country's GDP.[1] Esquenazi's crime also did nothing to enhance Haitians' faith in their public officials, in a country where popular support for the rule of law was desperately needed. At the time, Haiti's government was struggling with an armed insurgency, U.S. political interference, and, in 2004, a hurricane that killed more than 1,900 people.

Transnational bribery may not be the most serious problem facing Haiti, or any other country for that matter, but there is little doubt that it is a significant problem. The question is what sort of legal response is appropriate.

Reasonable People Can and Will Disagree about Transnational Bribery Law

If there is one thing this book should have demonstrated so far, it is that legal regulation of transnational bribery is complicated. The central questions of institutional design are easy to identify: What should be prohibited? Which actors should be targeted? What sanctions ought to be imposed? Who ought to make and implement these decisions? Although these questions are easy to pose, they are difficult to answer. As we saw in chapter 10, there is room for disagreement on every one.

The potential disagreements revolve around three types of issues: facts, counterfactuals, and values. The first of these categories includes disagreements about topics such as: Who is paying bribes? How much are they paying? To whom? In exchange for what sorts of favors? What sort of liability was imposed? How many enforcement actions have been brought? How reliable are our beliefs about the answers to these questions?

The second kind of disagreement concerns counterfactuals, states of the world that never occurred and will never occur. Disputes about the consequences of bribery fall into this category. Did Joel Esquenazi really harm ordinary Haitians or would the money he stole have been misappropriated in any event by officials of Haiti Teleco? Would Haitians have had any more faith in public officials if he had not paid any bribes? How much would Odebrecht have earned from its contracts with Petrobras if it had not paid bribes? How much more pride would Brazilians have had in their country in the absence of the Odebrecht scandal? Would they have still allowed their politicians to impeach the president? Would crime rates and cognitive performance in Indonesia have been any different if Innospec had not paid bribes?

Controversies about the impact of legal interventions also turn on ideas about counterfactuals. For instance, what would happen if the FCPA were restricted to cases involving favors provided in the exercise of official duties? Would this lead to an explosion of payments for unofficial favors, like introductions and unofficial encouragement? Would it eliminate a source of uncertainty that discourages people from seeking public office? Similarly, what if economic coercion were recognized as a defense to liability? There are also alternative attribution rules and penalties. What if firms were consistently held liable for the actions of their foreign subsidiaries? Or suppose firms and individuals who self-reported were consistently exempted from all liability? What if monetary penalties for foreign bribery were tripled? What about the impact of some combination of all these changes? What if different enforcement agencies were to implement different changes? How would any of these interventions affect patterns of desirable and undesirable conduct? What about the distribution of benefits and burdens within or across societies?

Beliefs about counterfactuals are inherently unverifiable and so are based on theories of how the world works. Generally speaking, divergent beliefs are most likely when people disagree about broad theoretical propositions, such as whether potential wrongdoers are motivated primarily by material incentives or moral intuitions. Sometimes theoretical disagreements can be resolved by referring to evidence. For instance, given enough data on variations in peoples' behavior and corresponding variations or changes in past legal regimes, we can test and rule out certain hypotheses about what motivates potential wrongdoers. Those data are not always available, either when the theory is being developed or when it is being applied. Perhaps as a result, many social scientific theories produce only noisy probabilistic predictions, such as: employees of large firms generally respond to financial incentives in deciding whether to pay bribes, but firm culture and tone at the top are also relevant. As a result, there is no guarantee that people who work with a common theoretical toolkit will construct identical, or even similar, pictures of how events will unfold in the aftermath of a bribe or a legal intervention.

The third kind of disagreement is about values. Even if it were possible to arrive at a consensus about the consequences of all the relevant legal interventions, there would remain ample room for disagreement about how to choose among them. Suppose we knew exactly what the world would look like under every possible legal regime. How do we know whether the world associated with any given regime is better than the status quo, or the world associated with some other regime? The answer will depend on the objectives of the person conducting the evaluation. Deciding on those objectives requires answering many fundamental questions. To what extent should anti-bribery law be aimed at retribution, prevention, or compensation? How should the interests of local as opposed to foreign actors be weighted? What price should be paid to achieve these objectives, whether in terms of material resources or respect for due process? Is a cost-effective intervention acceptable if some people bear a disproportionate portion of the costs? Since there are many possible combinations of answers to these questions, an enormous number of reasonable positions can be taken. The differences between these positions reflect disagreements about values, and there is no obvious path to reconciliation.

All of this goes to show that reasonable people can have profoundly different understandings of the facts and values that provide the underpinnings for anti-bribery law. Legal regimes built on foundations with such different orientations are unlikely to be completely convergent.

Disagreement is especially likely given that the anti-bribery regime is complex, decentralized, dynamic, and global in scope, and has multiple open-ended objectives. The fact that the regime is global and decentralized means that a large number of people are likely to be both interested and involved in evaluating it. Transnational bribery law attracts attention from not only enforcement agencies around the world but also all sorts of firms engaged in international business, not to mention a host of NGOs concerned with good governance. Since the regime is dynamic and global, in the sense that it operates in a vast number of different and constantly changing environments, these observers and participants will tend to have access to different and incomplete information about both the regime and the problems it faces. No one has complete information about levels of bribery or the enforcement strategies of enforcement agencies around the world, updated on an ongoing basis. Like blind men touching different parts of an elephant, people arrive at different conclusions about what they are confronting. For example, U.S. and U.K. prosecutors working with oil and gas firms doing business in Nigeria might witness an increase in firms' compliance efforts and infer that transnational bribery in that sector is declining in response to implementation of the OECD approach. At the same time, officials with the Nigerian anti-corruption agency, working with a different set of firms, might reasonably plot a trend line pointing in the opposite direction and question the effectiveness of the OECD approach.

Meanwhile, the fact that the anti-bribery regime is not only global but complex, in the sense that outcomes are influenced by many different actions, means that there are many possible connections between actions and outcomes. For instance, the impact of FCPA enforcement strategy are felt around the world. However, the impact in any given country, say Nigeria, also is determined by the actions of enforcement agencies in the United Kingdom, Switzerland, Japan, and so forth, as well as, of course, Nigeria itself. This leaves considerable room for disagreement about counterfactuals such as, for example, the consequences of changing the U.S. approach to credit for self-reporting. Finally, the fact that the regime has multiple open-ended objectives creates considerable space for disagreements about how to interpret and balance the various objectives, in other words, disagreements about values.

Under the circumstances, it should not be surprising that there are many significant disagreements about the design of transnational bribery law. These differences of opinion are apparent even among members of the OECD. The United States tolerates facilitation payments, while most of the other members of the OECD Convention do not. Several European countries favored the defense of effective regret, at least initially, but were overruled by officials from other countries who were more skeptical of its impact. The United Kingdom and almost a dozen other OECD members treat the existence of a compliance program as a defense to corporate liability, but the others do not. Sanctions also vary widely across OECD members, in terms of the magnitude of monetary penalties they are willing to impose as well as the types of nonmonetary sanctions. The United States and the United Kingdom are more aggressive in asserting extraterritorial jurisdiction than other OECD countries. Last but not least, there are profound disagreements between members of the OECD Convention and other countries about the extent to which monetary recoveries from enforcement actions ought to be shared with states whose officials have been bribed.

Disagreement is dangerous in the context of a vigorously enforced transnational legal regime with an expansive approach to jurisdiction, in which a large and diverse set of lawmakers and enforcement agencies will make decisions that have powerful cross-border effects. The greater the likelihood of disagreement, the greater the likelihood of challenges to the authority of foreign decision makers and consequent international tensions. A greater likelihood of disagreement also increases the likelihood that different enforcement agencies will adopt strategies that either conflict with one another or involve wasteful redundancy. In short, disagreements about potent transnational legal regimes can be very divisive. As we saw in chapter 10, this is all true of the anti-bribery regime, where disagreements about a variety of issues threaten its effectiveness, efficiency, and legitimacy.

At the same time, we should not overstate the level of disagreement. There appears to be general agreement about how transnational bribery law ought to respond to hard-core bribery. In particular, there seems to be a consensus around the following principles: transactions that involve payments in exchange for favors that involve misuse of official power, the paradigmatic bribes, should be prohibited. The law should target not only the individuals who pay and receive those bribes but also private firms that control and benefit from bribe payers' misconduct. The sanctions should include penalties that deprive wrongdoers of the benefits of their misconduct, although even those might be offset by rewards for self-reporting or cooperation. A state's enforcement agencies are entitled to assert jurisdiction over its nationals and other actors who have at least tacitly agreed to be bound by its laws, as well as anyone who engages in significant misconduct while in its territory or who threatens its vital interests.

Reducing the Extent of Disagreement

Even if a certain amount of disagreement is inevitable in transnational bribery law, there are still steps that can be taken to minimize the likelihood of disagreement. This is especially true when the root of the problem is the distribution of information.

The parable of the blind men and the elephant often is used to demonstrate how disagreement can originate in differences of perspective, but the story also points to ways of resolving disagreement. In some versions of the parable the blind men disagree so violently about the characteristics of an elephant that they come to blows, and in every version the disagreement is clearly a heated one. In at least one of the Jain versions, however, the conflict ends when a wise man points out to the blind men that they are looking at different parts of the same creature and that they will achieve a better understanding of the whole if they all stitch together their different observations.[2]

The moral of this story is that acknowledging uncertainty and then collecting and sharing relevant information can both help to resolve disagreements and improve understanding. This point can be generalized to transnational bribery law. Collecting and sharing information of the "who did what when" kind obviously helps to resolve factual disagreements. It also contributes to the process of testing competing theories against evidence and so indirectly helps to resolve theoretical disagreements about issues like "why they did it" and "what will they do next." It is also possible that the process of exchanging information about moral values will tend to produce convergent beliefs. For example, U.S. prosecutors focused on deterrence might become more sympathetic to the idea of using U.S. law to pursue compensation if exposed to the arguments of lawyers from the asset recovery unit of a poor developing country. The prediction that exposure to competing moral arguments will lead to convergence in values is, however, based largely on conjecture. It may well have the opposite effect. In line with the idea that familiarity breeds contempt, exposure to alternative moral viewpoints might sharpen and entrench disagreements.

As we have seen, the empirical foundations of the anti-bribery regime are surprisingly shallow. Only limited data on enforcement strategies are available, especially from agencies outside of the OECD. And there is a pressing need for data on the prevalence and the consequences of misconduct as well as the direct and indirect consequences of enforcement. Collecting and sharing this information might go some distance toward resolving some of the disagreements that currently characterize the regime.

Tolerating Disagreement

Disagreements about the design of transnational bribery law that cannot be avoided should sometimes be tolerated. There are at least two compelling arguments for toleration.

First, sometimes several points of view are valid. The blind man who feels an elephant's tail and concludes that the animal is most like a rope is not wrong. But nor is his colleague who feels one of the tusks and says it resembles a spear. Each one's perspective is valid, given where they stand. The same is true of lawmakers who observe the anti-bribery regime operating in different environments and evaluate it according to different values. In the Slovak Republic, an automatic exemption from liability for people who report foreign bribery might in fact be an effective way of prompting proceedings against foreign public officials. It might also serve as a proxy for a defense of coercion and avoid concentrating the costs of the fight against corruption on a handful of businesses in a way that Slovak society considers unfair. The experience in Turkey with the defense of effective regret and Turkish conceptions of fairness might be different. There is no basis for a drawing a blanket conclusion about the effectiveness or fairness of the defense.

Second, tolerating diversity can be a way to learn about the impact of alternative legal interventions. Diversity is a necessary feature of an experimentalist regime; an experiment by definition involves the comparison of at least two interventions. When the effects of a particular feature of a legal regime are uncertain, the best way to resolve the uncertainty might be to gather comparative data, that is to say, to compare outcomes associated with the legal intervention of interest and some other intervention. For example, if the impact of the defense of effective regret in foreign bribery cases is uncertain, the best way to learn about its impact might be to allow a few countries to leave it in place, or even introduce it for the first time, and then examine the outcomes.

Overcoming Disagreement

Our conclusion so far is that disagreements about the design of transnational bribery law ought to be tolerated when they reflect uncertainty about whether any given approach is universally valid, even as steps are taken to gather information that will help to resolve the uncertainty. These are good faith disagreements about how best to promote the objectives of the anti-bribery regime. Not all disagreements fall into this category. Inevitably, some will stem from objections designed to undermine the regime and perpetuate impunity.

If the anti-bribery regime is to be successful, it will have to allow these unhelpful objections to be overridden. The sad truth is that local legal institutions are not always capable of combating corruption of local public officials. The fight against impunity for corruption sometimes demands intervention by legal institutions that operate at a distance from the corrupted officials. The Romans recognized this when they established the *quaestio de pecuniis repetundis* (the tribunal that heard the case against Verres) to address corruption in the provinces. The modern anti-bribery regime is built on a similar premise, namely, that interventions by multiple legal institutions, including foreign ones, might be necessary to avoid impunity. Disagreement among as well as between foreign and local institutions seems like a feature, not a defect, of this kind of regime. In other words, a successful regime will have to retain some elements of imperialism.

Efforts to promote the objectives of the anti-bribery regime in the face of objections that appear to be unhelpful are defensible so long as they meet the most basic measure of legitimacy: displaying adequate regard for the interests of all affected parties. This includes reasonable efforts to become informed about those parties' interests and to include them in decision-making. A process for resolving disagreements which is both inclusive and informed will not only be more legitimate, it is also likely to lead to better outcomes since it will tend to identify instances in which disagreements can be reduced or tolerated. A process that has the hallmarks of legitimacy may also minimize tension and resentment.

Hallmarks of a Successful Regime

How does current transnational bribery law fare when evaluated using the principles set out in this chapter? There are two ways to answer this question. One involves detailed evaluation of the actual or potential impact of the anti-bribery regime, focusing on whether alterations would have or will contribute to or detract from achievement of its objectives. This will necessarily involve trying to determine whether the regime has adopted the best possible answers to the four key design questions: Which conduct, which actors, which enforcement strategy, which agencies? The conclusions that flow from this kind of evaluation inevitably will be strongly influenced by the evaluator's perspective, meaning his or her knowledge base, theoretical commitments, and values. An academic monograph is not an ideal vehicle for this kind of evaluation: the author's knowledge is likely to be relatively limited—as compared, for instance, to an agency centrally involved in the regime—and many of the conclusions are likely to be out of date almost before the book is published.

The second mode of evaluation steps back from the details of the anti-bribery regime and examines its structural features, focusing on those which determine the likelihood that the regime will achieve its objectives. In other words, is it the type of regime that is likely to generate and adopt good answers to key design questions? This type of analysis does not require detailed knowledge of either the regime or the environment in which it operates. Nor does it require commitment to a particular set of theories or values. This kind of structural evaluation is specifically intended to determine how well the regime will fare if it is evaluated from a range of perspectives.

For the reasons given previously, a regime like the anti-bribery regime is likely to be successful if it collects and distributes information about both problems and solutions, tolerates diversity in contexts where there is uncertainty about appropriate interventions, and resolves disagreements using processes that are both informed and inclusive. These hallmarks of an effective regime track the ones associated with global experimentalist governance, which emphasizes ongoing information gathering and tolerance of diversity.

Judged by these standards, the current anti-bribery regime falls short in some important respects. Generally speaking, insufficient effort has been made to gather information about the interests of affected parties, especially people in countries governed by corrupt officials. Moreover, to date, the most important elements of the regime have been designed by members of the OECD, a group of wealthy countries, which is in turn dominated by the largest and wealthiest countries of all, most notably the United States. Other actors are systematically excluded from key decision-making processes, including decisions in individual enforcement actions, decisions about overall enforcement strategy, and decisions about the overall legal framework of the anti-bribery regime.[3] Within the OECD these problems are exacerbated by a tendency to insist on uniform approaches to regulation, even in situations where the merits of alternative approaches are uncertain and many affected parties have been excluded from the decision-making process.

These features of the regime are not particularly difficult to reform, many of the necessary legal instruments, enforcement agencies, and supranational bodies are already in existence. It would not be difficult for the secretariats charged with implementing the OECD Convention and the UN Convention to push member states to take the requisite steps. Here is a summary of what would be entailed on the part of lawmakers and enforcement agencies, both individually and collectively:

- expand data-collection efforts to include regular standardized surveys on the prevalence of transnational bribery;
- sponsor in-depth studies of the harm associated with specific types of bribery;
- tolerate diversity in approaches to defining prohibited conduct, third-party liability, sanctions, and jurisdiction where good faith disagreement is reasonable;
- sponsor regular evaluations of the impact of alternative approaches to regulation;

- ensure that the interests of all affected parties are represented, or at least considered, when key decisions are made, including decisions about sanctions.

If implemented, these reforms would continue the process of eliminating the most imperialistic features of the anti-bribery regime. The modern regime reflects a remarkable evolution of not just norms, institutions and practices, but also of ideas about transnational bribery law. It is now rooted in a deep commitment to combating impunity and faith in the power of vigorous law enforcement. While many features of this regime are laudable, its one-size-fits-all approach to a phenomenon that is essentially global in scope inhibits its prospects for success, in part because it inhibits experimentation and innovation. Many of the reforms sketched in this chapter hold out the hope of enhancing effectiveness at the same time as they promote efficiency, due process, fairness, and legitimacy. To that extent they demonstrate that it is not always necessary to choose between impunity and imperialism.

Notes

Chapter 1

1. Transcript of Proceedings, Apr. 17, 2015, United States v. Vassiliev, 14-cr-341 (N.D. Cal. filed June 26, 2014), p. 7.
2. The written order granting the defendants' motion to dismiss is reported as: United States v. Sidorenko, 102 F. Supp. 3d 1124 (N.D. Cal. 2015).
3. Transcript, p. 11.
4. *See* the *Siemens* case discussed in chapter 8.
5. *See* the case against *Marubeni* discussed in chapter 10.
6. United States v. Lazarenko, 564 F.3d 1026 (9th Cir. 2009). For further information about the case, *see* United States v. Pavel Ivanovich Lazarenko, UNODC No.: USAx004, in United Nations Office on Drugs and Crime SHERLOC Case Law Database, available online at https://sherloc.unodc.org/cld/case-law-doc/moneylaunderingcrimetype/usa/united_states_v._pavel_ivanovich_lazarenko.html.
7. The minister in question is Teodoro Nguema Obiang Mangue, who served as Minister of Agriculture and Forestry and then vice president in the government of his father. The story of the legal proceedings against him is recounted in Sharman, *Despot's Guide to Wealth Management*, pp. 71–78.
8. Foreign Corrupt Practices Act of 1977, Pub. L. No. 95-213, 91 Stat. 1494 (1977) (codified as amended at 15 U.S.C. §§ 78dd-1, 78dd-2, 78dd-3, 78ff, 78m(b), (d)(1), (g)–(h) (2012)), amended by Foreign Corrupt Practices Act Amendment of 1988, Pub. L. No. 100-418, 102 Stat. 1107, 1415 (1988) (codified at §§ 78dd-1 to 78dd-3, 78ff (2006)) and International Anti-Bribery and Fair Competition Act of 1998, Pub. L. No. 105-366, 112 Stat. 3302 (1998) (codified at §§ 78dd-1 to 78dd-3, 78ff (2012)).
9. Transcript, p. 11.
10. Obama, "Remarks by the President at the Millennium Development Goals Summit in New York."
11. This nomenclature follows Jessup's definition of transnational law as "all law which regulates actions or events which transcend national frontiers . . ." As Jessup explains, the sources of transnational law include public international law (law whose subjects are states) and private international law (which concerns private actors or states acting in their private capacity) as well as purely domestic laws that affect actions or events with a transnational character. *See generally* Jessup, *Transnational Law*, p. 2. *See also* Boister, " 'Transnational Criminal Law'?"; Vagts, Koh, Dodge, and Buxbaum, *Transnational Business Problems*, ch. 2. For a pair of case studies that illustrate the multiplicity of sources of transnational law, *see* K. Davis, Jorge, and Machado, "Transnational Anticorruption Law in Action: Cases from Argentina and Brazil."

Between Impunity and Imperialism. Kevin E. Davis.

12. Nov. 21, 1997, 37 I.L.M.
13. G.A. Res. 4, U.N. GAOR, 58th Sess., Agenda Item 108, U.N. Doc. A/RES/58/4 (Oct. 31, 2003).
14. The use of the term "regime" here is idiosyncratic. International relations scholars use the concept of an international regime to refer to an ensemble of international rules and processes focused on a single issue. A sufficiently large set of overlapping regimes is called a regime complex. *See generally* Alter and Raustiala, "The Rise of International Regime Complexity." To the extent the anti-bribery regime is grounded in international agreements it qualifies as an international regime or regime complex. However, as defined here, the anti-bribery regime also includes norms that emanate from and bind private actors as opposed to only states and interstate organizations. Accordingly, the anti-bribery regime is probably better understood as an example of what Abbot called a "transnational" regime or regime complex, or what Halliday and Shaffer call a "transnational legal order." *See* Abbott, "The Transnational Regime Complex for Climate Change"; Halliday and Shaffer, "Transnational Legal Orders," pp. 7–21.
15. The every-little-bit-helps approach is most evident in the OECD's *Recommendation of the Council* (with amendments adopted by Council 18 February 2010 to reflect the inclusion of Annex II, *Good Practice Guidance on Internal Controls, Ethics and Compliance*). The OECD Working Group uses this Recommendation to guide its oversight efforts.
16. *See, e.g.*, Dell and McDevitt, *Exporting Corruption*; Heimann and Pieth, *Confronting Corruption*, p. 245 ("At the risk of demanding 'more of the same,' the next steps on the anticorruption agenda need to bring the existing tools to life."); Blanco, "Remarks at Foreign Corrupt Practices Act/Organization for Economic Cooperation and Development Anniversary Conference at the NYU School of Law" (describing OECD Convention as "unique" and "effective").
17. Most of these arguments are set out in Søreide, *Corruption and Criminal Justice*.
18. Huntington, *Political Order in Changing Societies*; Leff, "Economic development through bureaucratic corruption"; Leys, "What Is the Problem about Corruption?."
19. For reviews of the literature, *see* Rose-Ackerman and Palifka, *Corruption and Government*; Søreide, *Corruption and Criminal Justice*, ch. 2; Olken and Pande, "Corruption in Developing Countries." For examples of recent studies that challenge the conclusion that corruption is problematic, *see* Méon and Weill, "Is Corruption an Efficient Grease?"; Dreher and Gassebner, "Greasing the Wheels? The Impact of Regulations and Corruption on Firm Entry."
20. Attributed to Lord Chancellor Edward Thurlow. *See* Clinard, *Corporate Corruption*, pp. 170–171.
21. *See generally* Huntington, *Political Order in Changing Societies*; Leff, "Economic Development through Bureaucratic Corruption"; Leys, "What Is the Problem about Corruption?"
22. *See generally* Rose-Ackerman and Palifka, *Corruption and Government*, pp. 83–92.

23. Salbu, "The Foreign Corrupt Practices Act as a Threat to Global Harmony"; Salbu, "Extraterritorial Restriction of Bribery: A Premature Evocation of the Normative Global Village."
24. K. Davis, "Does the Globalization of Anti-Corruption Law Help Developing Countries?," p. 302; Nichols, Siedel, and Kasdin, "Corruption as a Pan-Cultural Phenomenon: An Empirical Study in Countries at Opposite Ends of the Former Soviet Empire."
25. Individual elements of this critique appear in works such as: Gutterman, "Banning Bribes Abroad: US Enforcement of the Foreign Corrupt Practices Act"; Spalding, "Unwitting Sanctions: Understanding Anti-Bribery Legislation as Economic Sanctions Against Emerging Markets"; Boister, "Transnational Criminal Law?" *See generally* K. Davis, "Does the Globalization of Anti-Corruption Law Help Developing Countries?" The general point that transnational law has to account for the possibility of reasonable disagreement about appropriate institutional design even when there is substantial agreement about general principles parallels arguments that have been made about international criminal law. *See* Müller, "Universal Jurisdiction, Pirates and Vigilantes."
26. This language is taken from the accounting provisions of the FCPA; *see* 15 U.S.C. § 78m.
27. Henning, "The Mounting Costs of Internal Investigations."
28. CNBC Squawkbox, May 15, 2012.
29. The total number of corporate enforcement actions in 2017 was significantly lower than in 2016 but in line with historical averages. The large number of enforcement actions in 2016 appears to have been due to a rush to resolve cases prior to the change in administrations. *See* Debevoise and Plimpton, "Anti-Corruption Enforcement in 2017: A Return to Normalcy."
30. De Búrca, Keohane, and Sabel, "Global Experimentalist Governance."
31. Buttonwood, "What Is the OECD?."
32. The World Bank reports that as of 2016 the World's population was 7.355 billion and the population of OECD member countries was 1.29 billion. World Bank, "Population, total."

Chapter 2

1. Exodus 23:8.
2. Cicero, *Verrine Orations*, 2.3 (embezzlement), 2.4 (plunder), 2.5.158–170 (crucifixion of Publius Gavius).
3. Morrell, *Pompey, Cato, and the Governance of the Roman Empire*, pp. 129–152. *See also* Greenwood, "Introduction," p. ix; Long, "Repetundae."
4. The trials are reported in Alexander, *Trials in the Late Roman Republic*.
5. Morrell, *Pompey, Cato, and the Governance of the Roman Empire*.
6. Ibid., pp. 98–100.
7. Morrell, *Pompey, Cato, and the Governance of the Roman Empire*, p. 48.
8. Cicero, *On Obligations*, 2.75–2.77; Cicero, *The Republic*, 3.41.

9. Greenwood, "Introduction," p. xi.
10. Cicero, *Verrine Orations*, 1.5.
11. Ibid., 2.2.79.
12. Ibid., 2.1.82, 2.2.160.
13. Ibid., 2.3.207, 2.4.68, 2.5.125.
14. Ibid., 1.1.49; 2.3.224; 2.5.178.
15. Ibid., 2.2.68–2.2.81.
16. Ibid., 2.2.78.
17. Ibid.
18. The following account of the Hastings trial draws heavily on the speeches of Edmund Burke as reproduced in *Writings and Speeches VI* and *Writings and Speeches VII*.
19. Burke, "Speech in Reply, 3 June 1794," *Writings and Speeches VII*, pp. 335–342.
20. Burke, "Opening of Impeachment," *Writings and Speeches VI*, p. 406 (Rajah of Dinagepore).
21. Burke, "Articles of Impeachment 14, 21, 28, May 1787," *Writings and Speeches VI*, pp. 182–188.
22. Burke, "Speech on Sixth Article: Presents, 21 April 1789," *Writings and Speeches VII*, p. 35. *See also* Burke, "Speech on the Sixth Article of Charge: Fourth Day: Thursday, May 7, 1789," pp. 396–439, 447–449.
23. Burke, "Speech in Reply, 3 June 1794," *Writings and Speeches VII*, p. 340.
24. Burke, "Opening of Impeachment," *Writings and Speeches VI*, pp. 415–422.
25. Dirks, *The Scandal of Empire*, pp. 40–85.
26. Carp, *Defiance of the Patriots*, pp. 7–24.
27. Dirks, *The Scandal of Empire*, p. 64.
28. The East India Company Act, 1772, 13 Geo. 3 ch. 63, §§ XXII–XXXII.
29. Pavarala, "Cultures of Corruption and the Corruption of Culture: The East India Company and the Hastings Impeachment," p. 300.
30. House of Commons of Great Britain, *First Report from the Select Committee*.
31. The East India Company Act, 1784, 24 Geo. 3 Sess. 2 ch. 25.
32. Marshall, "Introduction," *Writings and Speeches VI*, p. 30.
33. Ibid.
34. "In these [Verrine] Orations you will find almost every instance of rapacity and peculation which we charge upon Mr. Hastings." Ibid., p. 29.
35. Burke, "Opening of Impeachment," *Writings and Speeches VI*, p. 277.
36. Ibid., p. 459.
37. Sir Blackstone, *Commentaries on the Laws of England*, p. 105, quoted in Noonan, *Bribes*, p. 399.
38. *Journal of the House of Lords* 23 (1727–1731): p. 56, quoted in Burke, "Opening of Impeachment," *Writings and Speeches VI*, p. 346.
39. Burke, "Opening of Impeachment," *Writings and Speeches VI*, p. 346.
40. Noonan, *Bribes*, pp. 398–401.
41. Burke, "Opening of Impeachment," *Writings and Speeches VI*, p. 365.
42. Ibid., p. 366.

43. Burke, "Motion Relative to the Speech from the Throne, 14 June 1784," pp. 264–265, quoted in Marshall, "Introduction," *Writings and Speeches VI*, p. 2.
44. Marshall, "Introduction," *Writings and Speeches VI*, p. 2.
45. The timeline is summarized in Marshall, "Introduction," *Writings and Speeches VI*, pp. 1–15, and Marshall, "Introduction," *Writings and Speeches VII*, pp. 1–11.
46. Marshall suggests that in 1786 and 1787, when Burke launched his impeachment, many members of the House of Commons saw a strong affinity between the movement to reform British policy in India and the movement to regulate or abolish slavery. "For William Wilberforce in particular the affinities were very clear: both were issues of national morality. Neither in ruling India nor in providing the labour-force for the Caribbean colonies could national 'expediency' be allowed to displace principles of 'morality.'" Marshall, "Introduction," *Writings and Speeches VI*, pp. 5, 12.
47. Marshall, "Introduction," *Writings and Speeches VII*, p. 12.
48. Burke, "Opening of Impeachment," *Writings and Speeches VI*, pp. 289–291.
49. Ibid., p. 275.
50. Ibid., p. 276.
51. Hastings, "Address of Warren Hastings, Esq. in his Defence Upon the Several Articles of the Charge, 2d June 1791," pp. 483–485.
52. Ibid., p. 487.
53. Ibid., p. 486.
54. Ibid., p. 488.
55. Ibid.
56. Ibid., pp. 491–499.
57. Ibid., p. 503. For discussion of the infirmities in the evidence that Hastings turned these sums over to the Company, *see* Noonan, *Bribes*, pp. 404–412.
58. Hastings, "Address of Warren Hastings, Esq. in his Defence Upon the Several Articles of the Charge, 2d June 1791," p. 500.
59. Ibid.
60. Marshall, "Introduction," *Writings and Speeches VII*, p. 19.
61. For a similar effort to trace aspects of the modern anti-corruption regime back to Burke's rejection of geographical morality, *see* Ala'i, "The Legacy of Geographical Morality and Colonialism: A Historical Assessment of the Current Crusade Against Corruption."
62. The statement is attributed to Ralph Waldo Emerson in Holmes, Ralph Waldo Emerson, p. 71. A more modern version is "Come at the king, you best not miss." *The Wire*.
63. Noonan pithily observed, "At the most obvious level, the prosecution failed because it had the wrong jury." Noonan, *Bribes*, p. 412.
64. This political background is described in detail in Marshall, *The Impeachment of Warren Hastings*, pp. 1–38.
65. *See generally* Lintott, *Cicero as Evidence*, pp. 83–86, 93.
66. As Pavarala points out, "All through the trial of Warren Hastings, Indian voices were heard only through their British interlocutors." Pavarala, "Cultures of Corruption," p. 321.

67. Ibid.
68. "... the East India Company did not seem to be merely a Company formed for the extension of the British commerce, but in reality a delegation of the whole power and sovereignty of this kingdom sent into the East. In that light, the Company began undoubtedly to be considered, and ought to be considered, as a subordinate sovereign power; that is, sovereign with regard to the objects which it touched, subordinate with regard to the power from whence this great trust was derived." Burke, "Opening of Impeachment," *Writings and Speeches VI*, p. 283.
69. *See generally* Bowen, "A Question of Sovereignty? The Bengal Land Revenue Issue, 1765–67."
70. Burke, "Opening of Impeachment," *Writings and Speeches VI*, p. 45.
71. Manion, *Corruption by Design*, pp. 35–36.
72. Ibid., p. 40.
73. Ibid., p. 72.
74. Gilby, *Deception in High Places*, pp. 10–117.
75. Ibid.
76. Financial Services Authority, *Banks' Management of High Money-Laundering Risk Situations*; Financial Services Authority, "FSA publishes results of money-laundering investigation." *See generally* Sharman, *Despot's Guide to Wealth Management*, pp. 118–138.
77. Before the enactment of the Bribery Act 2010, the United Kingdom relied on the Prevention of Corruption Act 1906 and the common law offense of bribing a public officer. Consent of the Attorney or Solicitor General was necessary to prosecute a person under the 1906 Act. This requirement was supposed to prevent "improperly motivated prosecutions." The U.K. laws did not clearly cover bribing foreign officials, and in 1999 the U.K. Home Secretary reported that "there have been no prosecutions under the common law offence or the corruption statutes in relation to the bribery of foreign Ministers, members of Parliament or Judges." OECD, United Kingdom Review of Implementation, p. 3.
78. The Swedish prohibition, like the FCPA, was initially enacted in 1977. The original version prohibited both payment and receipt of bribes by foreign public employees. It only applied to conduct that occurred at least in part in Sweden or conduct committed wholly abroad, which also was punishable under the law of the foreign place. It was understood that Sweden would only prosecute bribery of foreign public officials if prosecution either was requested by the foreign state or required by Swedish public interests. Bogdan, "International Trade and the New Swedish Provisions on Corruption."
79. Henley, "Gigantic Sleaze Scandal Winds Up as Former Elf Oil Chiefs Are Jailed."
80. Henley, "Dumas Spreads Elf Blame to Ministers."

Chapter 3

1. Articles of Confederation, art. VI, cl. 1. Virtually identical language was carried over to Constitution of the United States, art. I, § 9, cl. 8, but that clause permits Congress to consent to the acceptance of an otherwise prohibited gift. Also relevant is art. II,

§ 4, of the US Constitution, which permits members of the executive to be removed from office on impeachment for and conviction of bribery (among other offences). For discussion, *see* District of Columbia v. Trump, 315 F. Supp. 3d 875 (D. Md. 2018); Sills, "The Foreign Emoluments Clause: Protecting Our National Security Interests," and Teachout, *Corruption in America*, pp. 18–28.

2. Oscanyan v. Arms Co., 103 U.S. 261 (1880).
3. Ibid., p. 277.
4. Noonan, *Bribes*, pp. 564–578.
5. "It is made clear . . . that . . . payments in order to meet competition or to respond to extortionate threats by public officials are within the prohibition." Model Penal Code § 240.1 and Explanatory Note for §§ 240.1–240.7 American Law Institute, 1962.
6. Ibid., § 240.1.
7. Ibid., § 240.7.
8. 18 U.S.C. 201(c) (2016).
9. 18 U.S.C. §§ 1341, 1343 (2008).
10. The Hobbs Act of 1946, 18 U.S.C. §§ 1951 (1946).
11. Evans v. United States, 504 U.S. 255 (1992).
12. 18 U.S.C. § 1952 (2014).
13. 18 U.S.C. §§ 1961–1968 (2016).
14. 18 U.S.C. § 1962 (2016).
15. 18 U.S.C. § 1964 (2016).
16. United Nations Convention against Illicit Traffic in Narcotic Drugs and Psychotropic Substances, art. 3.1(b) and (c), UN Doc. E/CONF.82/15, United Nations, *Treaty Series*, vol. 1582, No. 27627; United Nations Convention against Corruption, art. 23, *opened for signature* Dec. 9, 2003, 41 U.N.T.S. 2349 (entered into force Dec. 14, 2005) [hereinafter, UN Convention].
17. United Nations Convention against Transnational Organized Crime, 2000, art. 7, United Nations, *Treaty Series*, vol. 2225, p. 209; UN Convention, art. 14.
18. Naylor, "Wash-Out: A Critique of Follow-the-Money Methods in Crime Control Policy."
19. Noonan, *Bribes*, pp. 652–680; Sporkin, "The Worldwide Banning of Schmiergeld: A Look at the Foreign Corrupt Practices Act on Its Twentieth Birthday."
20. The payments are detailed in US Congress, Senate, *Final Report of the Select Committee*, pp. 445–492.
21. SEC, *Report of the Securities and Exchange Commission on Questionable and Illegal Corporate Payments and Practices*, p. 3.
22. Sporkin, "The Worldwide Banning of Schmiergeld: A Look at the Foreign Corrupt Practices Act on Its Twentieth Birthday," p. 269.
23. SEC, SEC Report, p. 13.
24. Ibid., pp. 14–15.
25. Ibid., p. 4.
26. Newcomb, *Digests of Cases*, pp. 75–76 https://stg.justice.gov/sites/default/files/criminal-fraud/legacy/2012/12/03/response2-appx-a.pdf; "United Brands Pleads Guilty to Plotting Honduran Bribe; $15,000 Fine Ends Case," p. 4.

27. *See* US Congress, Senate, "Prohibiting Bribes to Foreign Officials: Hearing on S. 3133, S. 3379 and S. 3418 Before the S. Comm. on Banking, Hous. & Urban Affairs" [Richardson Letter] (letter from Elliot Richardson, Secretary of Commerce and Chairman of Task Force on Questionable Corporate Payments Abroad, to Senator William Proxmire); US Congress, House, "The Activities of American Multinational Corporations Abroad: Hearings Before the Subcomm. on Int'l Econ. Policy of the H. Comm. on Int'l Relations"; US Congress, Senate, "Multinational Corporations and United States Foreign Policy: Hearings Before the Subcomm. on Multinational Corps. of the S. Comm. on Foreign Relations," Part 12 [Church Hearings]; US Congress, Senate, "Lockheed Bribery: Hearings Before the S. Comm. on Banking, Hous. & Urban Affairs" [Lockheed Bribery Hearings]. President Ford established the Task Force on Questionable Corporate Payments Abroad on March 31, 1976. *See* H.R. Doc. No. 94-572, p. 1 (1976). The Task Force's findings were set out in the Richardson Letter.
28. Lockheed, "Report of the Special Review Committee of the Board of Directors of Lockheed Aircraft Corporation" [Lockheed Report], pp. 18–19.
29. Church Hearings, p. 131.
30. Ibid., pp. 351–392; Lockheed Bribery Hearings; SEC Report, B-23; "Lockheed Executive Dies."
31. Kihss, "44-Story Plunge Kills Head of United Brands"; "Buying Favor: United Brands Paid Bribe of $l.25 Million to Honduran Official Cut in Banana-Tax Rate Was Goal; SEC Probes Affair; Other Payoffs Conceded Suicide Sparked the Inquiry," p. 1; "SEC Files Charges on United Brands"; US Securities and Exchange Commission v. United Brands Co., Litigation Release No. 6827 (D.C. Cir. 1975).
32. The SEC does not appear to have promised leniency. For example, Commissioner Irving Pollack was quoted as saying that although nobody could give a company "an absolute immunity" from SEC enforcement action, coming in voluntarily "is a gold star." *See* Bacon, "Amnesty Gap," p. 1.
33. SEC Report, p. 8; Wolff, "Voluntary Disclosure Programs," pp. 1059–1060. Two companies that participated in the SEC's program, Westinghouse and United Brands, subsequently were criminally prosecuted for foreign bribery. Newcomb, *Digests of Cases*, p. 75.
34. "Peru Expropriates Gulf Oil Subsidiary."
35. Church Hearings, p. 7; Gulf Oil Corporation, "Report of the Special Review Committee of the Board of Directors of Gulf Oil Corporation."
36. "Honduras Plans to Buy Operating Facilities of U.S. Banana Firms," p. 6.
37. Noonan, *Bribes*, pp. 654–680.
38. As a Washington Post editorial put it:

    > It would have been unfortunate enough to have any American corporation involved in this kind of transaction. But Lockheed is not considered, in other countries, to be just another American company. It is the largest U.S. defense contractor, and it owes its existence to federally guaranteed loans. It is seen abroad as almost an arm of the U.S. government. Its misdeeds, thus, have done proportionately great damage to this country and its reputation.

"Mr. Tanaka and Lockheed," A10, quoted in Koehler, "The Story of the Foreign Corrupt Practices Act," p. 935.

39. Lockheed Report, pp. 29–33.
40. Lockheed Report, pp. 34–35 ("we believe the publication of this material by us would be irresponsible"); Noonan, *Bribes*, pp. 658–663.
41. "Italian Court Believes Politician Got Bribe from Lockheed Corp."; "Payments Ordered in Italy."
42. Lohr, "Tanaka Is Guilty in Bribery Trial."
43. Weinraub, "Dutch Prince Quits Posts as Inquiry Board Assails His Links with Lockheed."
44. 15 U.S.C. §§ 78 dd-1 to 78dd-3.
45. 15 U.S.C. §§ 78m(b)((2)(A).
46. 15 U.S.C. § 78m(b)(2)(B).
47. 15 U.S.C. § 78dd-2.
48. FCPA, §§ 78dd-1, 78m(b)(2).
49. FCPA, § 78dd-3.
50. 15 U.S.C. § 78dd-1.
51. Criminal Division of the US Department of Justice and the Enforcement Division of the US Securities and Exchange Commission, *Resource Guide*, p. 11 ("placing a telephone call or sending an e-mail, text message, or fax from, to, or through the United States involves interstate commerce—as does sending a wire transfer from or to a U.S. bank or otherwise using the U.S. banking system") [hereinafter, *Resource Guide*]; Information, United States v. ABB Vetco Gray, Inc., 04-cr-279 paras. 39, 41 (S.D. Tex. filed June 22, 2004) (In a settled case, asserting that foreign non-issuer violated FCPA while in US territory by causing agents to wire funds to a US bank account while outside the United States and by receiving an email sent from the United States to Scotland).
52. Windsor and Getz, "Multilateral Cooperation to Combat Corruption: Normative Regimes Despite Mixed Motives and Diverse Values" p. 743. *See* Abbott and Snidal, "Values and Interests: International Legalization in the Fight Against Corruption," p. S161; Surrey, "The Foreign Corrupt Practices Act: Let the Punishment Fit the Crime," p. 293 (characterizing the background to the FCPA as the development of a new sense of morality and claiming that "[n]o one was really concerned with overseas bribery of foreign officials until the post-Watergate revelations of questionable corporate conduct. . . .").
53. H.R. REP. NO. 95-640, pp. 4–5 (1977).
54. *See* Spalding, "Unwitting Sanctions: Understanding Anti-Bribery Legislation as Economic Sanctions Against Emerging Markets," pp. 359–360 ("[T]he [FCPA] was in fact widely understood as an instrument of foreign policy, intended to impact relations between the United States and other nations, and not merely a component of a domestic ethics crisis.").
55. Saigon fell to Communist troops from North Vietnam on April 30, 1975. Esper, "Communists Take Over Saigon; U.S. Rescue Fleet Is Picking Up Vietnamese Who Fled in Boats." A leftist government backed by the Soviet Union and Cuba

took power in Angola on November 11, 1975. "Angola Due to Move Toward Marxist Rule."

56. H.R. REP. NO. 95-640, p. 5. In a similar vein, *see* S. REP. NO. 95-114, p. 3 (1977) ("Foreign governments friendly to the United States in Japan, Italy, and the Netherlands have come under intense pressure from their own people. The image of American democracy abroad has been tarnished."), and Richardson Letter, p. 42 (discussing "[t]he problem of adverse effect on foreign relations").
57. *Compare* H.R. REP. NO. 95-640, p. 6 ("After carefully considering all the testimony adduced, the committee concluded that [foreign bribery] should be outlawed rather than legalized through disclosure."), with Richardson Letter, pp. 61–65 (proposing a disclosure-based regime and rejecting criminalization). *See* SEC Report, pp. 57–66 (proposing a disclosure-based regime).
58. Richardson Letter, p. 63 ("[T]he President has decided to oppose, as essentially unenforceable, legislation which would seek broad criminal proscription of improper payments made in foreign jurisdictions.").
59. Ibid., p. 61 ("[Legislation criminalizing foreign bribery] would represent the most forceful possible rhetorical assertion by the President and the Congress of our abhorrence of such conduct.").
60. *See* H.R. REP. NO. 95-640, p. 5.
61. SEC Report, pp. 42–43.
62. For example, the chief executive of Gulf Oil denied that legislation against foreign bribery would place his firm at a competitive advantage, noting that competition among major oil companies was limited to seven companies, five of which were based in the United States. *See* testimony of Robert Dorsey, Gulf Oil, in Church Hearings, p. 20.
63. H.R. REP. NO. 95-640, p. 5 (testimony of former SEC Chairman Hills, partially quoting former Secretary of Commerce Richardson).
64. SEC Report, pp. 57–59 (describing the proposed action's primary aim as restoring integrity of corporate disclosure and accountability systems). For criticism of the SEC's approach to the problem, *see* Richardson Letter, pp. 53–56 (concluding that "[SEC disclosure] is, arguably, not an appropriate mechanism to deal with the full array of national concerns caused by the problem of questionable payments.").
65. SEC Report, pp. 18–20.
66. *See* H.R. REP. NO. 100-576, p. 916 (1988) (Conf. Rep.) (citing "unnecessary concern among exporters about the scope of the Act" and "unnecessary and costly paperwork burdens imposed on issuers of securities by unclear and excessive accounting standards").
67. Omnibus Trade and Competitiveness Act of 1988, Pub. L. No. 100-418, 102 Stat. 1107 (codified as amended at 19 U.S.C. § 2901, pt. 3 (2006)), §§ 5001–5003.
68. Ibid., § 5002 (codified as amended at 15 U.S.C. § 78m(b)).
69. Ibid., § 5003 (codified as amended at 15 U.S.C. §§ 78dd-1 to 78dd-2).
70. Ibid., § 5003I(4) (codified as amended at 15 U.S.C. §§ 78dd-1(e), 78dd-2(e)–(f)).
71. *Compare* 15 U.S.C. § 78dd-1(e) (providing for DOJ advisory opinions to issuers upon request), and § 78dd-2(f) (providing for DOJ advisory opinions to domestic concerns upon request), *with* § 78dd-3 (silent with respect to whether the DOJ will

make advisory opinions for persons and business entities other than issuers or domestic concerns). *See* Foreign Corrupt Practices Act Opinion Procedure.

72. Sarbanes-Oxley Act of 2002.
73. Ibid., § 404.

Chapter 4

1. As explained in the notes to chapter 1, the anti-bribery regime qualifies as an example of what some scholars would call either a transnational regime or a transnational regime complex or a transnational legal order.
2. Because of this overlap, international relations scholars might say that the anti-bribery regime represents part of a larger anti-corruption regime complex. On the concept of a regime complex, *see* Alter and Raustiala, "The Rise of International Regime Complexity." For an example of an analysis of international anti-corruption law that encompasses several regimes in addition to the anti-bribery regime, *see* Rose, *International Anti-Corruption Norms*.
3. Ibid., pp. 56–57 (summarizing US efforts to encourage regulation of questionable payments through the OECD, the General Agreement on Tariffs and Trade, and the United Nations).
4. *See, e.g.*, Richardson Letter, p. 22.
5. *See* 1988 Amendments at § 5003(d)(2)(A)(ii) (requiring the president to report to Congress on actions that might be taken in the event that negotiations failed to "eliminate any competitive disadvantage of United States businesses").
6. 1988 Amendments, § 5003(d) (codified as amended at 15 U.S.C. § 78dd-1).
7. Abbot and Snidal, "Values and Interests: International Legalization in the Fight Against Corruption."
8. Ibid., pp. S162-163.
9. Heimann and Pieth, *Confronting Corruption*, p. 42. Theobald makes the related point that with the end of the Cold War Western countries became more willing to voice criticisms that had previously been suppressed for strategic reasons. Theobald, "So What Really Is the Problem About Corruption?," p. 498.
10. Abbott and Snidal, "Values and Interests: International Legalization in the Fight Against Corruption," pp. S158–160. *See* Tarullo, "The Limits of Institutional Design: Implementing the OECD Anti-Bribery Convention," pp. 675–676. For an important contemporary survey of the scholarly literature, *see* Rose-Ackerman, *Corruption and Government*.
11. On the history of Transparency International, *see* Heimann and Pieth, *Confronting Corruption*, pp. 49–67.
12. For histories of the movement, *see Governments, NGOs and Anti-corruption*; Heimann and Pieth, *Confronting Corruption*; Abbot and Snidal, "Values and Interests: International Legalization in the Fight Against Corruption."
13. Abbot and Snidal, "Values and Interests: International Legalization in the Fight Against Corruption," pp. S162–165.

14. Wolfensohn, "People and Development. Annual Meetings Address." World Bank, discussed in Heimann and Pieth, *Confronting Corruption*, pp. 21, 59.
15. Leroy and Fariello, *World Bank Group Sanctions Process*, p. 10.
16. OECD, Convention on Combating Bribery of Foreign Public Officials in International Business Transactions.
17. OECD Working Group on Bribery, "Annual Report 2006," p. 13; Heimann and Pieth, *Confronting Corruption*, pp. 84–86.
18. African Union, *African Union Convention on Preventing and Combatting Corruption*; Council of Europe, *Civil Law Convention on Corruption*, Nov. 4, 1999, Eur. T.S. No. 174; Council of Europe, *Criminal Law Convention on Corruption*, Jan. 27, 1999, Eur. T.S. No. 173.
19. G.A. Res. 71/313 (July 6, 2017).
20. UN Convention, art. 16(2).
21. Ibid. The UN Convention also goes beyond the other conventions by extending to corruption of private actors, a topic that is beyond the focus of this chapter. *See* UN Convention, arts. 12, 21, and 22.
22. Ibid., arts. 54-59.
23. Individual members of FATF began to express concern about laundering of the proceeds of corruption somewhat earlier. *See, e.g.*, Financial Action Task Force on Money Laundering, "Annual Report," para. 43: "Written submissions from some of the members also mentioned an increase in the number of cases in which laundering was related to official corruption or the funding of international terrorism."
24. FATF, *International Standards*, Recommendation 36.
25. *See generally* Leroy and Fariello, *World Bank Group Sanctions Process*, and Boissonde Chazournes and Fromageau, "Balancing the Scales: The World Bank Sanctions Process and Access to Remedies."
26. Agreement on Mutual Enforcement of Debarment Decisions.
27. World Duty Free Co. v. Republic of Kenya, ICSID Case No. Arb/00/7, Award, paras. 138–157, 172 (Sept. 25, 2006).
28. Metal-Tech Ltd. v. The Republic of Uzbekistan, ICSID Case No. ARB/10/3, Award (Oct. 4, 2013).
29. *See, e.g.*, Spalding, "Deconstructing Duty Free: Investor-State Arbitration as Private Anti-Bribery Enforcement"; Reeder, "Estop That! Defeating a Corrupt State's Corruption Defense to ICSID BIT Arbitration"; Klaw, "State Responsibility for Bribe Solicitation and Extortion." Countervailing arguments are set out in K. Davis, "Contracts Procured Through Bribery of Public Officials: Zero Tolerance versus Proportional Liability," and Yackee, "Investment Treaties and Investor Corruption: An Emerging Defense for Host States?."
30. *See* Brewster, "Enforcing the FCPA: International Resonance and Domestic Strategy"; Brewster and Buell, "The Market for Global Anticorruption Enforcement"; Turk, "A Political Economy Approach to Reforming the Foreign Corrupt Practices Act," pp. 345–347.
31. Dell and McDevitt, *Exporting Corruption*. For previous discussions of enforcement patterns, *see* Heimann, Földes, and Coles, *Exporting Corruption*; Gilbert and

Sharman, "Turning a Blind Eye to Bribery: Explaining Failures to Comply with the International Anti-corruption Regime."

32. OECD Working Group on Bribery, "2015 Data on Enforcement of the Anti-Bribery Convention."
33. Newcomb, *Digests of Cases*, p. 75.
34. Ibid.
35. Department of Justice, "Odebrecht and Braskem Plead Guilty and Agree to Pay at Least $3.5 Billion in Global Penalties to Resolve Largest Foreign Bribery Case in History."
36. The average monetary sanctions in some years are significantly lower if outliers are excluded. For example, if the sanctions imposed on Societe Generale ($568 million) and Petrobras ($1.1 billion and $170 million) are excluded, the average of monetary sanctions in 2018 becomes $36.4 million. The average monetary sanctions are calculated based on data from the Foreign Corrupt Practices Act Clearinghouse database. Stanford Law School. fcpa.stanford.edu (accessed Feb. 5, 2018). All monetary sanctions are represented, including fines, penalties, forfeitures, and disgorgement. Dismissals are not included. As in Figure 4.1, sanctions imposed on related entities by the same enforcement agency *and* arising from the same misconduct are aggregated under a single enforcement action.
37. OECD, "Is Foreign Bribery an Attractive Investment in Some Countries?"
38. In the United States, creative prosecutors have characterized foreign bribery as a violation of state anti-bribery laws ostensibly aimed at private actors, capitalizing on the fact that in some states, including New York and California, those statutes apply to any "employee, agent or fiduciary" who receives a bribe. This argument in turn permits prosecutors to allege a violation of a federal statute known as the Travel Act, 18 U.S.C. § 1952, which covers violations of state bribery or extortion laws that have an international dimension. A foreign official's role in a transnational bribery scheme might also be characterized as a species of fraud or extortion. *See, e.g.*, United States v. Gonzalez, 13-cr-901 (S.D.N.Y. Jan. 19, 2016) (Venezuelan official charged with violation of the Travel Act and money laundering); United States v. Lazarenko, 564 F.3d 1026 (9th Cir. 2009) (Ukrainian official charged with laundering proceeds of extortion and fraud).
39. *See generally* Sharman, *Despot's Guide to Wealth Management.*
40. Ibid.
41. http://www.oecd.org/daf/anti-bribery/ (accessed Mar. 2, 2018).
42. OECD Working Group on Bribery, "2016 Data on Enforcement of the Anti-Bribery Convention: Special Focus on International Co-Operation" (OECD: 2017).
43. UN Office of Drugs and Crime, "Country Profiles."
44. *See, e.g.*, World Bank, *Group Sanctions System Annual Report FY18*, pp. 63–64.
45. Dell and McDevitt, *Exporting Corruption.*
46. Transparency International, *Civil Society Participation*. On the history of private actors' attempts to participate in proceedings under the UN Convention, *see* Rose, *International Anti-Corruption Norms*, pp. 50–53.
47. World Bank, "CPIA Criteria 2017," p. 43.

48. *Transformation Index of the Bertelsmann Stiftung 2018*, pp. 21, 40 (describing questions 3.3 and 15.3); World Justice Project, *Rule of Law Index*, pp. 12, 14 (describing factor 2).
49. For a survey of the sources of data on the incidence of corruption, *see* Søreide, *Corruption and Criminal Justice*, pp. 64–73.
50. G.A. Res. 71/313 (July 6, 2017).
51. *See, e.g.*, UN Office on Drugs and Crime, *Corruption in Nigeria*.
52. World Bank, *World Bank Enterprise Survey*, Question J.6.
53. *See, e.g.*, UN Office on Drugs and Crime, *Corruption in Nigeria*.
54. Transparency International, "Global Corruption Barometer: Overview," and "Bribe Payers Index: Overview."
55. Ibid.
56. *See, e.g.*, Malesky et al., *The Vietnam Provincial Competitiveness Index*; Jensen and Malesky, "Nonstate Actors and Compliance with International Agreements: An Empirical Analysis of the OECD Anti-Bribery Convention."
57. Transparency International, "Corruption Perceptions Index 2016: Short Methodology Note."
58. World Bank, "Control of Corruption."
59. Porto, "The Media and Political Accountability."
60. K. Davis, "The Limits of Evidence-Based Regulation: The Case of Anti-Bribery Law."
61. *See, e.g.*, Gingerich et al., "When to Protect? Using the Crosswise Model to Integrate Protected and Direct Responses in Surveys of Sensitive Behavior"; Kraay and Murrell, "Misunderestimating Corruption"; *New Advances in Experimental Research on Corruption*.
62. *Compare* James R. Hines, Jr., "Forbidden Payment: Foreign Bribery and American Business After 1977" (for US firms, corruption is associated with lower rate of growth in foreign direct investment, joint ventures and aircraft exports) *and* Wei, "How Taxing Is Corruption on International Investors" (across twelve source countries corruption is associated with a lower stock of foreign direct investment, but the effect is not especially significant for US firms).
63. Cuervo-Cazurra, "Who Cares About Corruption?"; D'Souza, "The OECD Anti-Bribery Convention: Changing the Currents of Trade."
64. Spencer and Gomez, "MNEs and Host Country Corruption." Spencer and Gomez also examined whether firms that invested in Eastern Europe were less likely to report a need to engage in bribery if their home country was a party to the OECD Convention. They found no evidence to support this hypothesis.
65. Jensen and Malesky, "Nonstate Actors and Compliance with International Agreements: An Empirical Analysis of the OECD Anti-Bribery Convention," pp. 1–37.
66. Noon, "OECD Concerned by U.K. Move on BAE."
67. The OECD Convention is characterized this way in Jensen and Malesky, "Nonstate Actors and Compliance with International Agreements." The US regime was described this way in Hess and Ford, "Corporate Corruption and Reform

Undertakings." For skepticism about whether this is an appropriate characterization of U.S. federal law see Baer, "Governing Corporate Compliance."

68. de Burca, Keohane, and Sabel, "Global Experimentalist Governance."

Chapter 5

1. UN Convention, Preamble.
2. UN Convention, Preamble and art. 1.
3. UN Convention, art. 4.
4. UN Convention, art. 46.28.
5. UN Convention, art. 57.4.
6. Rose-Ackerman and Palifka, *Corruption and Government*, pp. 27–36, 51–125. For examples of studies documenting connections between bribery and specific adverse policy-induced outcomes, *see* Bertrand, Djankov, Hanna, and Mullainathan, "Obtaining a Driver's License in India: An Experimental Approach to Studying Corruption" (licensing of unqualified drivers); Olken and Barron, "The Simple Economics of Extortion: Evidence from Trucking in Aceh" (allowing overweight trucks on the road).
7. Ambraseys and Bilham, "Corruption Kills," pp. 153–155.
8. *See, e.g.*, Seligson, "The Impact of Corruption in Regime Legitimacy: A Comparative Study of Four Latin American Countries"; Anderson and Tverdova, "Corruption, Political Allegiances, and Attitudes toward Government in Contemporary Democracies"; Canache and Allison. "Perceptions of Political Corruption in Latin American Democracies."
9. The connection between beliefs about legitimacy and compliance has long been a theme of the work of Tom Tyler and his collaborators. For a recent contribution, with references to the literature, *see* Jackson, Bradford, Hough, Myhill, Quinton, and Tyler, "Why Do People Comply with the Law?: Legitimacy and the Influence of Legal Institutions."
10. For a discussion of economic models in which corruption becomes a self-reinforcing phenomenon, in the sense that people are more likely to engage in corrupt behavior when they perceive the level of corruption to be high, *see* Bardhan, "Corruption and Development: A Review of Issues." For a forceful argument that corruption leads to political unrest, *see* Chayes, *Thieves of State*.
11. Idemudia and Ite, "Demystifying the Niger Delta Conflict: Towards an Integrated Explanation.."
12. Rose-Ackerman and Palifka, *Corruption and Government*, p. 58.
13. For an early analysis of this dynamic and the associated welfare implications (in the context of tariffs), *see* Krueger, "The Political Economy of the Rent-seeking Society."
14. For a similar assessment, *see* Søreide, *Corruption and Criminal Justice*, ch. 2. For a more optimistic assessment and a proposal to allow judges to calculate social damages arising from corruption, *see* Costa Rica, *Corrupción y daño social*.
15. Indictment, United States. v. Esquenazi, 09-CR-21010 (S.D. Fla. filed Dec. 4, 2009).

16. "Buying Favor: United Brands Paid Bribe of $l.25 Million to Honduran Official Cut in Banana-Tax Rate Was Goal; SEC Probes Affair; Other Payoffs Conceded Suicide Sparked the Inquiry," p. 1.
17. Segal, "Petrobras Oil Scandal Leaves Brazilians Lamenting a Lost Dream."
18. Dube, "Odebrecht Bribery Scandal Shakes Up Latin America."
19. The examples which follow involve transnational bribery. Bribes typically paid by domestic actors also are likely to generate these kinds of harm. For instance, one study found statistical evidence that most earthquake deaths over the past three decades have occurred in countries like Haiti and Iran, reputed to be relatively corrupt, even taking into account their levels of per capita income. The authors suggest that those countries have more shoddily constructed buildings because developers have paid bribes to subvert processes for licensing and inspecting buildings. *See* Ambraseys and Bilham, "Corruption Kills," pp. 153–155.
20. Watts, "Brazil: Insider Claims Rousseff Coalition Took Funds from Belo Monte Mega-dam."
21. Reyes, "Lead Exposure and Behavior: Effects on Antisocial and Risky Behavior among Children and Adolescents."
22. R. v. Innospec Ltd., Sentencing Remarks of Lord Justice Thomas, [2010] 3 WLUK 784, [2010] Crim. L.R. 665 (In the Crown Court at Southwark).
23. *See generally* Viscusi, "The Value of Risks to Life and Health."
24. For a thorough discussion of the distributional implications of allocating legal entitlements to those most willing to pay for them, *see* Liscow, "Is Efficiency Biased?"
25. Analyses of the economic impact of lead exposure are frequently conducted for the purpose of justifying environmental regulations. As far as I can tell, those analyses are devoted exclusively to estimates of the earnings lost by people exposed to lead as a result of reductions in their cognitive ability. This ignores lost earnings resulting from noncognitive behaviors. There is also no reason to believe that lost earnings are a good measure of the amount a person would be willing to pay to avoid exposure to lead. *See* United States Environmental Protection Agency, *Regulatory Impact Analysis*, p. 48; Grosse, "How Much Does IQ Raise Earnings." These measures also ignore the costs incurred by victims of antisocial behavior induced by lead exposure.
26. For a seminal discussion of the political effects of corruption, *see* Nye, "Corruption and Political Development: A Cost-Benefit Analysis."
27. *See, e.g.*, Seligson, "The Impact of Corruption on Regime Legitimacy: A Comparative Study of Four Latin American Countries"; Anderson and Tverdova, "Corruption, Political Allegiances, and Attitudes toward Government in Contemporary Democracies"; Canache and Allison, "Perceptions of Political Corruption in Latin American Democracies."
28. For a formal economic model that accounts for these kinds of attitudes, *see* Akerlof and Kranton, "Economics and Identity."
29. Seligson, "The Impact of Corruption on Regime Legitimacy"; Anderson and Tverdova, "Corruption, Political Allegiances, and Attitudes toward Government in Contemporary Democracies"; Canache and Allison, "Perceptions of Political Corruption in Latin American Democracies."

30. *See, e.g.*, Feng, "Democracy, Political Stability and Economic Growth."
31. The difficulties of determining whether corruption causes or is a consequence of adverse political and macroeconomic outcomes are discussed in Treisman, "What Have We Learned About the Causes of Corruption from Ten Years of Cross-National Empirical Research?"
32. The definition of "effectiveness" used here follows Oran Young's suggestion that the effectiveness of an international regime means "the extent to which regimes contribute to solving or mitigating the problems that motivate those people who create the regimes." Young, "Effectiveness of International Environmental Regimes: Existing Knowledge, cutting-edge themes, and Research Strategies"; Young, *Governance in World Affairs*. Young describes more and less ambitious versions of this definition. The definition used in the text is one of the less ambitious ones since it focuses on whether the regime achieves "outcomes or changes in the behavior of actors relevant to the problem at hand." *See* Raustiala, "Compliance & Effectiveness in International Regulatory Cooperation," p. 394. A more ambitious definition would measure a regime's success in solving or mitigating problem along multiple dimensions, including ones such as efficiency. The more ambitious definition seems inappropriate in the present context because art. 1 of the UN Convention requires pursuit of both efficiency and effectiveness, suggesting that the drafters did not regard efficiency as a component of effectiveness.
33. Different bodies of literature use different terms for these concepts. The literature on punishment often uses the terms "restitution" and "crime reduction" instead of "compensation" and "prevention." That literature also draws a distinction between "retribution" and "condemnation," which I have ignored by employing only "condemnation." *See generally* A. Duff and Hoskins, "Legal Punishment."
34. The term "compensation" is intended to include "restitution" as well as the concept of "restoration," as that term is used by advocates of restorative justice. Some scholars view compensation as a particularly important objective of private law, meaning the legal norms applied in the course of litigation between private individuals. *See* Weinrib, *Idea of Private Law*. However, there is no reason why compensation cannot also be an objective of proceedings initiated by the state. *See* Barnett, "Restitution: A New Paradigm of Criminal Justice," and Braithwaite, "Restorative Justice: Assessing Optimistic and Pessimistic Accounts."
35. *See, e.g.*, R.A. Duff, *Punishment, Communication, and Community*.
36. *See* Andenaes, "The General Preventive Effects of Punishment" (distinguishing deterrence, moral education, reformation, and incapacitation).
37. The discussion in the following paragraphs draws on ideas initially set out in K. Davis, "Multijurisdictional Enforcement Games: The Case of Anti-Bribery Law." For a related discussion of whether and how cost-benefit analysis ought to account for the interests of foreigners, *see* Alemanno, "Is There a Role for Cost-Benefit Analysis Beyond the Nation-State? Lessons from International Regulatory Cooperation."
38. Coleman, *Markets, Morals, and the Law*, ch. 4.
39. *See, e.g.*, Young, *Governance in World Affairs*, p. 12. On the definition of productive efficiency, *see* Kornhauser, "A Guide to the Perplexed Claims of Efficiency in the Law."

On the application of the concept of efficiency to anti-corruption law, *see* Søreide, *Corruption and Criminal Justice*, pp. 31–33, 167–205.

40. Welfare maximization is commonly used in economic analysis of law. *See* Shavell, *Foundations of Economic Analysis of Law*, pp. 2–4, 595–598.
41. *International Covenant on Civil and Political Rights*, G.A. res. 2200A (XXI), 21 U.N. GAOR Supp. (No. 16), p. 52, U.N. Doc. A/6316 (1966), 999 U.N.T.S. 171, *entered into force* Mar. 23, 1976, art. 14. For present purposes the concept of due process includes a process that complies with safeguards against deprivation of property contained in certain regional human rights treaties. For an in-depth discussion of how proprietary sanctions under transnational anti-corruption law might violate rights to property, *see* Ivory, *Corruption, Asset Recovery, and the Protection of Property in Public International Law*.
42. Ibid.
43. For surveys of the relevant literature, *see* Bottoms and Tankebe, "Beyond Procedural Justice: A Dialogic Approach to Legitimacy in Criminal Justice"; Peter, "Political Legitimacy."
44. The concept of legitimacy presented in the text is clearly a normative concept, meaning that it is accompanied by a sense that legitimacy is commendable and ought to be pursued, as opposed to being merely a morally neutral fact. This not meant to imply, however, that there is any uniquely valid "objective" conception of legitimacy. *See* Hinsch, "Legitimacy and Justice: A Conceptual and Functional Clarification."
45. *See* Jackson et al., "Why Do People Obey the Law"; Bottoms and Tankebe, "Beyond Procedural Justice." Bottoms and Tankebe distinguish beliefs about legitimacy held by "power-holders" from those held by the "audiences" over whom power is exercised. This sharp dichotomy is difficult to maintain when the audience also wields power within the regime, as is the case in a regime like the anti-bribery regime which involves significant amounts of private regulation. *See also* Beetham, *Legitimation of Power*, pp. 136–137 (describing reciprocal relationship between effectiveness and legitimacy).
46. Peter, "Political Legitimacy," section 3.2, citing the views of Hume, Bentham, Mill, Raz, and Wellman. For discussions of the extent to which people adopt this conception of legitimacy, *see* Chen, "The Dilemma of Eudaemonic Legitimacy In Post-Mao China"; Tankebe, "In Search of Moral Recognition? Policing and Eudaemonic Legitimacy in Ghana."
47. An example of this kind of conception of legitimacy is offered by Buchanan and Keohane. Their conception of legitimacy includes minimum moral acceptability, comparative benefit and institutional integrity along with democratic accountability and transparency. *See* Buchanan and Keohane, "The Legitimacy of Global Governance Institutions."
48. Bottoms and Tankebe, "Beyond Procedural Justice," pp. 134–137 (citing Beetham, Coicaud, and Raz); Peter, "Political Legitimacy," section 3.1, citing the views of Grotius, Locke, Nozick, Raz, Simmons, and Rousseau. Consent also plays a central

role in David Beetham's social scientific conception of legitimacy. *See Legitimation of Power*, p. xiv.

49. Bottoms and Tankebe, "Beyond Procedural Justice" (citing Beetham, Coicaud, and Dixon). For a theory of global governance which places particular emphasis on legality as a basis for presumptive legitimacy, *see* Von Bogdandy, Goldmann, and Venzke, "From Public International to International Public Law: Translating World Public Opinion into International Public Authority." *See also* Beetham, *Legitimation of Power*, p. xii.
50. Bottoms and Tankebe, "Beyond Procedural Justice," pp. 138–141 (citing empirical studies). Von Bogdandy et al., "From Public International to International Public Law," p. 125 ("Instead, acts that are legal are presumed to be legitimate—a presumption that can, and has often been, rebutted.").
51. Stewart, "Remedying Disregard in Global Regulatory Governance: Accountability, Participation and Responsiveness," p. 227. Other scholars have described "equal regard" as ideal. *See, e.g.*, Grant and Keohane, "The Legitimacy of Global Governance Institutions," pp. 433–434.
52. Buchanan and Keohane, "Legitimacy of Global Governance Institutions," pp. 425–433 (discussing epistemic conditions for satisfaction of their standard for legitimacy).
53. On Kant's justification for the use of coercive political power, *see* Ripstein, "Authority and Coercion" (the claim that people "must agree" to state coercion appears at p. 33). For Rawls' view, *see Justice as Fairness*, p. 41.
54. This is consistent with Beetham's claim that legitimacy depends on whether the rules that govern the exercise of power can be justified in terms of beliefs shared by both dominant and subordinate. *See*, Beetham, *The Legitimation of Power. See also* Bottoms and Tankebe, "Beyond Procedural Justice," pp. 141–147.
55. For a leading example of an argument that international law and institutions should be evaluated in terms of both procedural and substantive fairness, *see* Franck, *Fairness in International Law and Institutions*.
56. For a leading argument in favor of global egalitarianism, *see* Caney, "Cosmopolitan Justice and Equalizing Opportunities," and Caney, *Justice Beyond Borders*, ch. 4.
57. *Compare* Blake, "Distributive Justice, State Coercion, and Autonomy," and Nagel, "The Problem of Global Justice" (egalitarian justice does not apply beyond members of community over whom a state claims authority and in whose name it claims to act), *with* Cohen and Sabel, "Extram Republicam Nulla Justitia?"
58. A notable example of a scholar who advocates evaluation of institutions concerned with transnational corruption in terms of respect for human rights is Thomas Pogge. *See World Poverty and Human Rights*. Buchanan and Keohane outline some of the reasons why it is appropriate to use a relatively limited set of human rights for the purposes of evaluating global institutions. *See* Buchanan and Keohane, "The Legitimacy of Global Governance Institutions," pp. 419–420.
59. Rawls, *Law of Peoples*, p. 31; Nagel, "Problem of Global Justice," pp. 118, 130–132; Blake, "Distributive Justice, State Coercion, and Autonomy," pp. 271, 294.

Chapter 6

1. US Department of Justice, "Executive Sentenced to 15 Years in Prison for Scheme to Bribe Officials at State-Owned Telecommunications Company in Haiti."
2. US Department of Justice, "Florida Telecommunications Company, Two Executives, an Intermediary and Two Former Haitian Government Officials Indicted for Their Alleged Participation in Foreign Bribery Scheme."
3. *See* chapter 5, under the heading, "The Problem of Bribery."
4. The dilemma described here is a familiar one to scholars of criminal law. *See, e.g.*, Buell, "The Upside of Overbreadth."
5. In a similar vein, Tina Søreide complains about "corruption-like circumstances," which are activities that fall into gray areas not covered by bribery laws. Søreide, *Corruption and Criminal Justice*, pp. 87–88.
6. UN Convention, art. 16.
7. For a survey, *see* United Nations Office on Drugs and Crime, *State of Implementation of the United Nations Convention against Corruption*, pp. 29–38.
8. FCPA, §§ 78 dd-1(a)(2), 78 dd-2(a)(2), and 78 dd-3(a)(2).
9. FCPA, §§ 78 dd-1(a), 78 dd-2(a), 78 dd-3(a). Similarly, under Singapore's law a person is held liable for bribery if they "corruptly solicit or receive for himself . . ." or "corruptly give, promise or offer to any person . . . any gratification. . . ." Prevention of Corruption Act (Cap. 241, 1993 Rev. Ed.), ch. 241, pt. III, § 5.
10. FCPA, §§ 78 dd-2(g)(2)(A), 78 dd-3(e)(2)(A).
11. *See* section below, "Extortion as a Defense."
12. FCPA, §§ 78 dd-1(b), 78 dd-2(b), dd-3(b).
13. FCPA, §§ 78 dd-1(c)(1), dd-2(c)(1), dd-3(c)(1).
14. OECD Convention, art. 1.1.
15. FCPA, §§ 78 dd-1(a), 78 dd-2(a), 78 dd-2(g)(2)(A), 78 dd-3(a), 78 dd-3(e)(2)(A).
16. Buell, "Culpability and Modern Crime," pp. 590–595.
17. United States v. Kozeny, 664 F. Supp. 2d 369 (S.D.N.Y. 2009), aff'd, 667 F.3d 122 (2d Cir. 2011).
18. For a brief survey of the laws of selected parties to the OECD Convention, *see* Pieth, Bonucci, and Low eds., *Commentary*, pp. 193–198 (art. 1, III).
19. FCPA, §§ 78dd-1(a)(3),(f)(2); 788dd-2(a)(3), h(3); 78dd-3(a)((3), (f)(3).
20. United States v. Kozeny, 664 F. Supp. 2d 369, p. 385 (S.D.N.Y. 2009), aff'd, 667 F.3d 122 (2d Cir. 2011).
21. United States v. Kozeny, 582 F. Supp. 2d 535 (S.D.N.Y. 2008).
22. Section 2(7) says that if a person is charged with receiving a bribe in exchange for improper performance "it does not matter" if the recipient knows or believes that their performance was improper. This could be read to imply that such knowledge or belief is relevant in other cases. Alternatively, this provision could be read as confirmation of the ordinary rule, i.e., for greater certainty. *See* Sullivan, "Reformulating Bribery: A Legal Critique of the Bribery Act 2010," pp. 22-23.
23. United States v. Kay, 513 F.3d 432, pp. 447–451 (5th Cir. 2007).

24. United States v. Kozeny, 664 F Supp. 2d 369 (S.D.N.Y. 2009), aff'd, 667 F.3d 122, p. 135 (2d. Cir. 2011). *See also* United States v. Kay, 513 F.3d 432, pp. 447–451 (5th Cir. 2007).
25. For a historical example, consider the following exchange before a Senate subcommittee from the testimony of a representative of the Northrop Corporation (Millar), who appeared together with an attorney (Willens):

    SENATOR CLARK: Is it fair to say, Mr. Millar, that the Northrop Corp. and Mr. Khashoggi knowingly violated the Saudi Arabian law in passing this money on?

    MR. WILLENS: I do not think it would be fair Mr. Millar to respond because of our absence of knowledge as to what Mr. Khashoggi, in fact, did with the money. And so if you assume that the money was passed on to generals we would agree that would be a violation of the law.

    SENATOR CLARK: Was it the intention of the Northrop Corp. to bribe the generals?

    MR. WILLENS: Whether an intention implemented by the overt action of the kind that had been identified and can be proved even amounts to a crime under Saudi law, I do not know. Those facts may be illegal under U.S. law given comparable facts, but I do not know what the Saudi law is on that precise issue.

    Multinational Corporations and United States Foreign Policy: Hearings Before the Subcomm. on Multinational Corps., p. 132. Testimony of Richard W. Millar Chairman of the Executive Committee of Northrop Corporation Board of Directors and Howard P. Willens, attorney.
26. For helpful discussions, *see* Hornsby, "On What's Intentionally Done"; Williams, "Oblique Intention."
27. FCPA, §§ 78dd-1(f)(2); 78dd-2 (h)(3); 78dd-3 (f)(3).
28. *See, e.g.*, United States v. Kay, 513 F.3d 432, pp. 446–451 (5th Cir. 2007) (approving jury instructions on the "corruptly" element of an FCPA offense where instructions define a "'corrupt act' as one that is 'done voluntarily and intentionally, and *with a bad purpose*. . . .") (emphasis added); Stichting Ter Behartiging v. Schreiber, 327 F.3d 173, p. 182 (2d Cir. 2003) (concluding that "'corruptly' in federal bribery statutes" . . . "denot[es] an evil motive or purpose. . . ."); *but see* United States v. Hanson, 2 F.3d 942, pp. 964–947 (9th Cir. 1993) (concluding that "corruptly" requires, not only "an improper motive or bad or evil purpose," but also "an intention to secure an unlawful benefit for oneself or another. . . .").
29. FCPA, § 78dd-1(a).
30. Foreign Corrupt Practices Act of 1977 (FCPA), 15 U.S.C. §§ 78dd-1, 78dd-2, 78dd-3.
31. Pieth et al. point out that this is most common in common law jurisdictions. Pieth et al., *Commentary*, pp. 206–208 (art. 1, IV.4).
32. *See, e.g.*, Prevention of Corruption Act (Cap. 241, 1993 Rev. Ed.), § 5.
33. Prevention of Corruption Act (Cap. 241, 1993 Rev. Ed.), § 2.
34. McCormick v. United States, 500 U.S. 257 (1991).

35. Under the UN Convention, "advantage" apparently is intended to cover sexual favors. UNODC, *State of Implementation*, p. 19.
36. Ran, "Sexual Favours Are Not Considered Corruption in China."
37. Gitlin, "Beyond Sextortion: How Corruption Uniquely Affects Women https://globalanticorruptionblog.com/2015/01/02/beyond-sextortion-how-corruption-uniquely-affects-women/."
38. There was also a significant donation from a foundation run by Mr. Gaddafi.
39. UN Convention, art. 21. Many states have resisted adoption of this offense. *See* UNODC, *State of Implementation*, pp. 60–64.
40. Bribery Act 2010, §§ 1, 7.
41. Strafgesetzbuch, § 299.
42. As Pieth et al. put it, these treaties contemplate an "autonomous definition" of corruption. Pieth et al., *Commentary*, p. 74 (art. 1, II.2.1).
43. The OECD Convention does not mention a person holding "executive" office of a foreign country. *See* OECD Convention, art. 1.4(a).
44. Belgian law extends to candidates for public office. Code Pénal, art. 246(3). The FCPA prohibits bribery of "any candidate for foreign political office." 15 U.S.C. §§ 78dd-1(a)(2), 78dd2-(a)(2), 78dd-3(a)(2).
45. OECD Committee on International Investment and Multinational Enterprises, *Commentaries on the Convention*, para. 15.
46. OECD, *Commentaries on the Convention*, para. 16. *See also* Pieth et al., *Commentary*, pp. 86–89 (art. 1, II.2.3.4).
47. *See* United States v. Carson, 09-cr-77, 2011 WL 5101701, p. 10 (C.D. Cal. May 18, 2011).
48. Stuart Green makes the related but somewhat different argument that public and private sector bribery ought to be distinguished because they involve distinct types of harm. S. Green, "Official and Commercial Bribery: Should They Be Distinguished?"
49. Fédération Internationale de Football Association, *FIFA Statutes*, arts. 2–6.
50. Viswanatha, Robinson, Morse, and Matthews, "FIFA Rocked as U.S. Charges 14 in Corruption Investigation"; Viswanatha, Robinson, and Revill, "U.S. Indicts 16 New Suspects in FIFA Corruption Case."
51. OECD, *Commentaries on the Convention*, para. 16.
52. SEC, *Report on Questionable and Illegal Corporate Payments and Practices*; H.R. Rep. No. 95–640, p. 5 (1977).
53. H.R. Rep. No. 95-640, p. 5.
54. Countries that both prohibit corporate contributions to political parties and impose a ceiling for donations to political parties by natural persons for amounts exceeding USD5,000 per year include Bhutan (BTN100,000 or approximately USD4,800 limit for natural persons), Estonia (EUR1,200 or approximately USD1,370 limit for natural persons), Israel (NIS1,000 or approximately USD267.50 limit for natural persons), Jordan (IQD50,000 or approximately USD1,192 limit for natural persons), and Peru (PEN120 or approximately USD35.47 limit for natural persons). "Political Finance Database."

55. At least one hundred countries prohibit anonymous donations to political parties, including the United States, the United Kingdom, Russia, Mexico, Haiti, Iran, Iraq, Nigeria, and the Philippines. "Political Finance Database." Approximately eighty-eight countries prohibit contributions to political parties in excess of a certain monetary value, including the United States, the United Kingdom, Japan, Mexico, Russia, Haiti, Kenya, and the Republic of Korea. "Political Finance Database."
56. "Political Finance Database"; *see* Norris, Abel van Es, and Fennis, *Checkbook Elections*, p. 59.
57. Dolan and de Morais, "How an African 'Princess' Banked $3 Billion in a Country Living on $2 a Day."
58. Security and Exchange Commission (SEC), "SEC Charges BNY Mellon with FCPA Violations"; Protess and Silver-Greenberg, "On Defensive, JP Morgan Hired China's Elite."
59. Pieth et al., *Commentary*, p. 168 (art. 1, II.7.1).
60. OECD, *Commentaries*, para. 19.
61. McDonnell v. United States, 136 S. Ct. 2355 (2016).
62. UNODC takes this position, arguing in favor of criminalization of "investive corruption practices" that "involve the offer or acceptance of benefits given by virtue of the public official's position, without a direct link to a concrete act or omission in the unlawful exercise of the recipient's official duties." UNODC, *State of Implementation*, p. 26.
63. Ibid., p. 2372.
64. Ibid., p. 2373 (quoting McNally v. United States, 483 U.S. 350, p. 360 (1987)).
65. OECD, *Commentaries*, para. 4.
66. OECD Convention, art. 1.
67. German Criminal Code, §§ 334(1) and (3) and Gesetz zu dem Übereinkommen vom 17. Dezember 1997 über die Bestechung ausländischer Amsträger im internationalen Geschäftsverkehr—IntBestG, September 10, 1998, BGB1, II, at 2327, Annex 1.
68. Schweizerisches Strafgesetbuch, Code pénal suisse, Codice penale svizzero, art. 322septies.
69. Stichting Ter Behartiging v. Schreiber, 327 F.3d 173, p. 182 (2d Cir. 2003); United States v. Liebo, 923 F.2d 1308, p. 1312 (8th Cir. 1991); S. Rep. No. 95-114, p. 10 (1977).
70. United States v. Strand, 574 F.2d 993, p. 995 (9th Cir. 1978); United States v. Muldoon, 931 F.2d 282, p. 287 (4th Cir. 1991); United States v. Jennings, 160 F.3d 1006, p. 1015 n.4 (4th Cir. 1998).
71. United States v. Kay, 513 F.3d 432, p. 451 (5th Cir. 2007).
72. For example, the US Supreme Court has concluded that a quid pro quo refers to a "payment made in return for an explicit promise or undertaking by the official to perform or not to perform an official act." McCormick v. United States, 500 U.S. 257 (1991). The Court has affirmed that the quid pro quo requirement can be satisfied without evidence of an agreement between both parties. Evans v. United States, 504 U.S. 255, p. 1884 (1992).
73. *Restatement (Second) of the Law of Contracts*, § 71.

74. This is a paraphrase of a formulation proposed and defended in Lewinsohn. "Paid on Both Sides: *Quid Pro Quo* Exchange and the Doctrine of Consideration."
75. UNODC, *State of Implementation*, pp. 23–24 (UN Convention does not require prohibition of ex post facto payments).
76. Pieth et al., *Commentary*, p. 143 (art. 1, II.5.4.2).
77. United States v. Alfisi, 308 F.3d 144, p. 149 (2d Cir. 2002).
78. *See generally* Teachout, *Corruption in America* (arguing that a strict quid pro quo requirement has diminished the effectiveness of US anti-corruption law).
79. Exceptions are listed in Pieth et al., *Commentary*, p. 188 (art. 1, II.8.3.1).
80. *See also* UK Bribery Act, § 6(2); Corruption of Foreign Public Officials Act, S.C. 1998, ch. 34, § 3(1).
81. United States v. Kay, 359 F.3d 738 (5th Cir. 2004); *see also* US Securities and Exchange Commission v. Mattson, 01-cv-3106 (S.D. Tex. Sept. 9, 2002); US Securities and Exchange Commission, "SEC Charges Texas-Based Layne Christensen Company with FCPA Violations"; US Department of Justice, "Oil Services Companies and a Freight Forwarding Company Agree to Resolve Foreign Bribery Investigations and to Pay More Than $156 Million in Criminal Penalties."
82. The business nexus requirement of the UN Convention is intended to apply to the provision of international aid. United Nations Office on Drugs and Crime, *Travaux Préparatoires of the Negotiations*, p. 176, para. 1(c).
83. Pieth et al., *Commentary*, pp. 66–67 (art. 1, I.1).
84. Pieth et al. suggest that the OECD Convention is incompatible with any version of an extortion defense that applies exclusively to bribe payers, but does not preclude defenses, such as physical duress, that apply to all offenses. *Commentary*, pp. 139–140, 146–148 (art. 1, II.5.2 and 5.4.4). An expert review of the UN Convention cautioned against an extortion defense defined so expansively as to be triggered by mere request or solicitation by a public official. UNODC, *State of Implementation*, pp. 27–28.
85. UNODC, *State of Implementation*, p. 27. Countries that offer an extortion defense include Armenia, Azerbaijan, Bangladesh, Bulgaria, Kazakhstan, Kyrgyzstan, Latvia, Moldova, Montenegro, Pakistan, Romania, Russia, Serbia, and Ukraine. UNODC, *Country Review Report of Armenia*, p. 89; UNODC, *Country Review Report of Bulgaria*, p. 80; UNODC, *Country Review Report of Latvia*, p. 102; UNODC, *Country Review Report of Ukraine*, pp. 101–103; *see also* OECD Anti-Corruption Network for Eastern Europe and Central Asia, *Foreign Bribery Offence*, pp. 22–23; ADB/OECD Anti-Corruption Initiative for Asia and the Pacific, *Criminalisation of Bribery*, pp. 32–33.
86. Gitlin, "Beyond Sextortion," https://globalanticorruptionblog.com/2015/01/02/beyond-sextortion-how-corruption-uniquely-affects-women/; Naik, "Protecting Children from the Protectors: Lessons from West Africa," pp. 16–19, https://www.fmreview.org/sites/fmr/files/FMRdownloads/en/displaced-children-and-adolescents/naik.pdf.
87. *Resource Guide*, p. 27.
88. Dressler, "Duress."

89. Ibid. The lesser of two evils explanation is also used to explain the defense of necessity, which is sometimes defined to cover crimes committed in response to threats. For example, the necessity defense codified in the American Law Institute's Model Penal Code § 3.02 is expressly limited to situations in which the actor has engaged in otherwise unlawful conduct in order to avoid a greater harm or evil.
90. *See Resource Guide*, p. 27 ("Mere *economic* coercion, however, does not amount to extortion."); United States v. West, 746 F. Supp. 2d 932 (N.D. Ill. 2010) and cases discussed therein.
91. *See, e.g.*, United States v. Liu, 960 F.2d 449 (5th Cir. 1992).
92. New York Penal Law § 200.05, 11 Delaware Code § 1202, and Oregon Revised Statutes § 162.035.
93. John Coffee turns this argument on its head to suggest that corporations ought to be allowed to pay bribes to avoid injury to a broad constituency of employees, creditors, suppliers, and customers. His motivating example involves a bribe paid to a union official, which arguably causes less harm than bribery of a government official. *See* Coffee, Jr., "Beyond the Shut-Eyed Sentry: Toward a Theoretical View of Corporate Misconduct and an Effective Legal Response," pp. 1208–1213.
94. OECD Working Group, *Phase 3 Report on the Slovak Republic*, para. 30.
95. OECD Working Group, *Slovak Republic: Phase 2 Report*, paras. 155–156.
96. UN Convention, art. 37.
97. *See* OECD Working Group *Phase 3 Reports* on the *Czech Republic* (paras. 28–32); *Portugal* (para. 41); *Slovak Republic* (paras. 30–31, 70); *Slovenia* (paras. 27–30); and *Spain* (para. 39). *See also Phase 1 Report of the Russian Federation* (para. 27) and *Phase 2 Reports* on *Greece* (paras. 134–136); *Czech Republic* (paras. 153–163); *Slovak Republic* (paras. 150–161); *Slovenia* (paras. 171–178); *Spain* (paras. 123–125), and *Poland* (paras. 138–141).
98. *See Phase 4 Report: Czech Republic* (para. 95) (describing abandonment of proposal to reintroduce the defense of effective regret for corruption offenses), as well as *Follow-ups to Phase 3 Reports* for *Portugal* (pp. 10–11), (describing amendment removing automatic defense), *Spain* (p. 12) (describing repeal of exemption for foreign bribery), *Slovak Republic* (p. 7) (describing removal of defense from amendment to Criminal Code and draft legislation on liability of legal persons), and *Slovenia* (pp. 9–10) (explaining steps Slovenia has taken to clarify application of defense of effective regret).
99. Pieth et al. defend the OECD's position on a more formal ground. They argue that the Convention bars signatories from treating effective regret as a defense exclusively in bribery cases, but permits it be recognized as a defense if it applied to all offenses. Pieth et al., *Commentary*, p. 148 (art. 1, II.5.4.4).
100. UNODC, *State of Implementation*, p. 37.
101. *But see* discussion later in this chapter under the heading "Bribe Payers and Bribe Recipients" regarding prosecutions of recipient officials under money laundering statutes.
102. World Bank, *Fiscal Year 2017 Annual Update Integrity Vice-Presidency* (World Bank Group, 2017), pp. 44–47.

103. FCPA, §§ 78dd-1(c)(2), 78dd-2(c)(2), 78dd-3(c)(2).
104. The original version of the FCPA did not contain an explicit grease payment exception, although at that time the definition of foreign public official excluded "any employee . . . whose duties are essentially ministerial or clerical." *See* §§ 30A(b) and 104(d), added by P.L. 95-213. The House of Representatives suggested that the corrupt intent requirement would exclude payments which "merely move a particular matter toward an eventual act or decision or which do not involve any discretionary action." Comm. on Interstate and Foreign Commerce, H.R. Rep. No. 95-640, p. 8 (1977). Meanwhile, according to the Senate Committee that considered the Senate's version of the bill, payments to obtain or retain business would not include "payments for expediting shipments through customs or placing a transatlantic telephone call, securing required permits, or obtaining adequate police protection, transactions which may involve even the proper performance of duties." Comm. on Banking, Housing, and Urban Affairs, S. Rep. No. 95-114, p. 10 (1977).
105. FCPA, §§ 78dd-1(b), 78dd-2(b), 78dd-3(b).
106. FCPA, §§ 78dd-1(f)(3), 78dd-2(h)(4), 78dd-3(f)(4).
107. United States v. Kay, 359 F.3d 738, pp. 750–751 (5th Cir. 2004); US Securities and Exchange Commission v. Jackson, 908 F. Supp. 2d 834, pp. 857–858 (S.D. Tex. 2012).
108. The comment, which relates to art, 1, para. 1, defining the offence of bribery of foreign public officials, reads:

> Small "facilitation" payments do not constitute payments made "to obtain or retain business or other improper advantage" within the meaning of paragraph 1 and, accordingly, are also not an offence. Such payments, which, in some countries, are made to induce public officials to perform their functions, such as issuing licenses or permits, are generally illegal in the foreign country concerned. Other countries can and should address this corrosive phenomenon by such means as support for programmes of good governance. However, criminalisation by other countries does not seem a practical or effective complementary action.

OECD Committee on International Investment and Multinational Enterprises, *Commentaries on the Convention*.
109. OECD, *Recommendation of the Council*, para. VI.
110. Pieth et al., *Commentary*, pp. 178–183 (discussing laws of Australia, New Zealand, and South Korea).
111. Pieth et al., *Commentary*, pp. 178–183 (art. 1, 7.3.3) (discussing Denmark, Germany, Iceland, Sweden, and Switzerland).
112. Local law can also be relevant to determining whether the favor provided by an official involves misuse of an official's position. For instance, the U.K. Bribery Act only covers transactions that contemplate "improper performance" of "a relevant function or activity," and the standard for determining whether performance is improper is, what would expected by "a reasonable person in the United Kingdom." In deciding what such a person would expect, the adjudicator may have regard to "any local custom or practice" that is "permitted or required by the written law applicable to the country or territory concerned." This language suggests that the U.K. statute

has two distinctive features: the local law defense is discretionary rather than mandatory and it can be triggered by local customs or practices so long as they are not prohibited (i.e., are permitted) by written laws. U.K. Bribery Act, § 5.

113. OECD, *Commentaries on the Convention*, paras. 7, 8. The interpretive notes to the UN Convention seem to reject the idea that national law is relevant in this setting. The commentary to art. 16, para. 1, states:

> A statute that defined the offence in terms of payments "to induce a breach of the official's duty" could meet the standard set forth in each of these paragraphs,
> provided that it was understood that every public official had a duty to exercise
> judgement or discretion impartially and that this was an "autonomous" definition not requiring proof of the law or regulations of the particular official's country or international organization.

United Nations Office on Drugs and Crime, *Travaux Préparatoires of the Negotiations*, part one, chap. III, art. 16, § C, para. 1 *(b)* (p. 176).

114. FCPA, §§ 78dd-1(c)(1), 78dd-2(c)(1), 78dd-3(c)(1).
115. OECD Working Group, *Phase 3 Report on Denmark*, para. 40; OECD Working Group, *Phase 3 Report on Norway*, para. 22.
116. OECD Working Group, *Australia: Phase 2 Report* , para. 140; *Resource Guide*, p. 23 (Congress sought "to make clear that the absence of written laws in a foreign official's country would not by itself be sufficient to satisfy this defense."), citing H.R. Rep. no. 100-576, p. 922. *See also* Pieth et al., *Commentary*, art. 1, II.4.2.2.
117. United States v. Kozeny, 582 F. Supp. 2d 535 (S.D.N.Y. 2008).
118. U.K. Bribery Act, § 2.
119. UN Convention, arts. 23, 24; OECD Convention, art. 7. *See also* United Nations Convention against Illicit Traffic in Narcotic Drugs and Psychotropic Substances; the United Nations Convention against Transnational Organized Crime; and, FATF (2012–2017) International Standards on Combating Money Laundering and the Financing of Terrorism and Proliferation, Recommendation 3.
120. Basu, "Why, for a Class of Bribes, the Act of *Giving* a Bribe Should Be Treated as Legal ."
121. US Department of Justice, "Former Haitian Government Official Sentenced to Prison for His Role in Money Laundering Conspiracy Related to Foreign Bribery Scheme," and "Former Haitian Government Official Sentenced to Nine Years in Prison for Role in Scheme to Launder Bribes."
122. United States v. Vasconez Cruz, Second Superseding Indictment, 09-cr-21010 (S.D. Fla. filed Jan. 19, 2012).
123. United States v. Castle, 925 F.2d 831 (5th Cir. 1991).
124. United States v. Vasconez Cruz, Second Superseding Indictment, 09-cr-21010 (S.D. Fla. filed Jan. 19, 2012), pp. 27–28.
125. UN Convention, art. 23; United Nations Convention Against Transnational Organized Crime, in force 29 September 2003, art. 6.
126. Corruption of Foreign Public Officials Act, S.C. 1998, ch. 34, as amended.

127. Cuéllar, "The Tenuous Relationship between the Fight against Money Laundering and the Disruption of Criminal Finance," pp. 404–425; Levi and Reuter, "Money Laundering."
128. Financial Action Task Force, *Mutual Evaluation Report*, paras. 147–153; Pieth et al., *Commentary*, pp. 439–440 (art. 7, V.2.5).

Chapter 7

1. Jacobellis v. Ohio, 378 U.S. 184, p. 197 (1964) (Stewart, J., concurring).
2. The World Bank, *Helping Countries Combat Corruption.*
3. "Our Organisation—FAQs on Corruption," Transparency International.
4. Andrew Spalding offers a similar criticism of a definition found in Black's Law Dictionary, which defines corruption as "a fiduciary's or official's use of a station or office to procure some benefit either personally or for someone else, contrary to the rights of others." *See* Spalding, "Corruption, Corporations, and the New Human Right," pp. 1390–1391.
5. 18 U.S.C. §§ 1341, 1343, 1346; Skilling v. United States, 561 U.S. 358, pp. 407–409 (2010) (bribes and kickbacks constitute the core of honest services fraud).
6. Shearman and Sterling, *FCPA Case Digest* 2002, pp. 75–76 https://stg.justice.gov/sites/default/files/criminal-fraud/legacy/2012/12/03/response2-appx-a.pdf; "United Brands Pleads Guilty to Plotting Honduran Bribe; $15,000 Fine Ends Case," p. 4.
7. In United States v. Giffen, 326 F. Supp. 2d 497 (S.D.N.Y. 2004), a US court rejected the idea that bribery of foreign public officials qualified as a scheme or artifice to deprive the citizens of a foreign country of the honest services of their government. The reasons given, namely, concerns about legislative intent and international comity, echo the concerns listed in the text.
8. US courts have split on the question of whether the federal mail and wire fraud offences apply extraterritorially. *See generally* United States v. All Assets Held at Bank Julius, 251 F. Supp. 3d 82, pp. 101–103 (D.D.C. 2017).
9. *See also* OECD Convention, art. 8, and OECD Working Group on Bribery in International Business Transactions, *Recommendation of the Council*, para. X.
10. FCPA, § 78m(b)(2).
11. Federal Constitutional Court, Second Senate, June 23, 2010, Doc. Nos. 2 BvR 2559/08, 2 BvR 105/09, 2 BvR 491/09, cited in OECD Working Group, *Phase 3 Report on Implementing the OECD Anti-Bribery Convention in Germany*, p. 18.
12. Corruption of Foreign Public Officials Act, S.C. 1998, ch. 34, as amended, § 4.
13. US Securities and Exchange Commission v. Oracle Corporation, Complaint, 3:12-cv-4310 (N.D. Cal. Aug. 13, 2012).
14. UN Convention, art. 20.
15. Muzila et al., *On The Take*, pp. 8, 89–90.
16. Ibid., pp. 27–39.
17. Ibid.

Chapter 8

1. "Speech on Opening of Impeachment, 15 February 1788," *Writings and Speeches VI*, p. 275.
2. To get a flavor of the debate, *see* Laufer, "The Missing Account of Progressive Corporate Criminal Law"; Beale, "A Response to the Critics of Corporate Criminal Liability"; Alschuler, "Two Ways to Think About the Punishment of Corporations"; Weigend, "Societas delinquere non potest?: A German Perspective"; Arlen and Kraakman, "Controlling Corporate Misconduct: An Analysis of Corporate Liability Regimes"; Fisse and Braithwaite, *Corporations, Crime and* Accountability; Fisse, "Reconstructing Corporate Criminal Law: Deterrence, Retribution, Fault, and Sanctions"; Coffee, Jr., "Beyond the Shut-Eyed Sentry: Toward a Theoretical View of Corporate Misconduct and an Effective Legal Response," pp. 1208–1213.
3. US Department of Justice, "Siemens AG and Three Subsidiaries Plead Guilty to Foreign Corrupt Practices Act Violations and Agree to Pay $450 Million in Combined Criminal Fines."
4. Siemens made corrupt payments to "government officials in Asia, Africa, Europe, the Middle East and the Americas." Ibid. These dealings spanned bid-rigging and kickbacks, including the awarding of forty-two contracts from the Ministries of Electricity and Oil of the Republic of Iraq and payments to government officials in Argentina, Venezuela, and Bangladesh, for the purpose of receiving favorable business treatment in connection with national identity card, mass transportation, and cellphone service projects. Ibid.
5. Law enforcement was unable to identify the sources of some of the payments captured in Siemens's corporate books. Ibid. The total amount of bribe payments to foreign officials exceeds $1.4 billion. Ibid.
6. Department's Sentencing Memorandum, p. 4, United States v. Siemens Aktiengesellschaft, 08-cr-367 (D.D.C. filed Dec. 12, 2008) [hereinafter, Sentencing Memorandum].
7. Schubert and Miller, "At Siemens, Bribery Was Just a Line Item"; Sentencing Memorandum, p. 20.
8. *See, e.g.*, Kamisher, "Five Senior Israel Electric Company Employees Sentenced in Massive Siemens Bribery Case."
9. "China Mobile Executive Gets Death in Bribery Case."
10. "Ananya Sengupta, Khaleda Son Sentenced to 6 Years in Jail for Graft."
11. K. Davis, Jorge, and Machado, "Transnational Anticorruption Law in Action: Cases from Argentina and Brazil."
12. US Department of Justice, "Siemens AG and Three Subsidiaries Plead Guilty to Foreign Corrupt Practices Act Violations and Agree to Pay $450 Million in Combined Criminal Fines."
13. Ibid.
14. OECD Working Group, *Phase 3 Report on Implementing the OECD Convention in Germany*, p. 22.
15. *Siemens Annual Report 2009*, p. 182; *Siemens Annual Report 2015*, p. 88.

16. LG Munchen, I, 10 December 2013 (5 HK O 1387/10).
17. This discussion of Siemens' misconduct in Argentina and the subsequent legal proceedings draws on K. Davis, Jorge, and Machado, "Transnational Anticorruption Law in Action: Cases from Argentina and Brazil."
18. UN Convention, art. 26.
19. OECD Convention, art. 2.
20. *See* recommendations made in the Phase 3 reports on Iceland, Portugal, South Africa, Spain, and Turkey. Working Group on Bribery in International Business Transaction, *Compilation of Recommendations.*
21. Klaw, "State Responsibility for Bribe Solicitation and Extortion: Obligations, Obstacles, and Opportunities."
22. *See* UN Convention, ch. II, especially art. 5.
23. *See, e.g.*, Republic of Iraq v. ABB AG, 768 F.3d pp. 145, pp. 160–169 (2d Cir. 2015), cert. denied, 135 S. Ct. 2836 (2015).
24. *See generally* Frick, "'Ice' Capades: Restitution Orders and the FCPA."
25. *See generally* Reeder, "Estop That! Defeating a Corrupt State's Corruption Defense to ICSID BIT Arbitration."
26. For a survey of the law of selected jurisdictions, *see* Pieth and Ivory eds., *Corporate Criminal Liability*.
27. OECD Working Group on Bribery, *Phase 3 Report on Implementing of the OECD Convention in Germany*, pp. 23–24.
28. L. 1778/2016, febrero 2, 2016, D.O. art. 2.
29. *Resource Guide*, p. 27.
30. U.K. Bribery Act, § 7(2).
31. OECD Working Group on Bribery, *Stocktaking Report*, p. 22.
32. Tesco Supermarkets Ltd. v. Nattrass, [1972] A.C. 153 HL; Meridian Global Funds Management Asia Ltd. v. Securities Commission, [1995] 2 A.C. 500.
33. OECD, *Stocktaking Report. See, e.g.*, United Kingdom Phase 3 report, para. 32 ("Since 2005, the Working Group has repeatedly criticised the use of the identification theory for imposing liability against legal persons for foreign bribery. . . ."); Ireland Phase 3 report, paras. 56–61. *But see also* Australia Phase 3 report, para. 18, and Canada Phase 3 report, paras. 40 and 41 (demonstrating that some countries are moving away from "identification doctrine").
34. OECD, *Recommendation of the Council*, Annex I: Good Practice Guidance on Implementing Specific Articles of the Convention on Combating Bribery of Foreign Public Officials in International Business Transactions, Part B.
35. United Nations International Law Commission, *Draft Articles*, art. 7.
36. Ibid., art. 4 (conduct of a state organ is considered an act of the state "whatever position it holds in the organization of the State, and whatever its character as an organ of the central Government or of a territorial unit of the State"), especially comments 7–10.
37. Loi 2016-1691 du 9 décembre 2016 relative à la transparence, à la lute contre la corruption et à la modernization de la vie économique, J.O., Dec. 10, 2016, art. 17.

38. *See, e.g.*, Bank Secrecy Act, 12 U.S.C. §§ 1730(d), 1829b, 1951–1959 (1970); 31 U.S.C. §§ 1051–1122 (1970); Customer Due Diligence Requirements for Financial Institutions, 31 C.F.R. §§ 1010, 1020, 1023, 1024, 1026 (May 11, 2016) (amending regulations under the Bank Secrecy Act to require financial institutions to identify and verify beneficial owners of legal entity customers).
39. US Department of Justice, "Press Release Siemens AG and Three Subsidiaries Plead Guilty to Foreign Corrupt Practices Act Violations and Agree to Pay $450 Million in Combined Criminal Fines."
40. Exchange Act § 20(a) (codified at 15 U.S.C. § 78t).
41. U.K. Bribery Act, ch. 23, § 14(2).
42. United States v. Bestfoods, 524 U.S. 51 (1998) (determining whether a parent qualified as an "operator" of a facility so as to be liable for environmental cleanup costs and citing "norms of corporate behavior" in support of conclusion).
43. US Securities and Exchange Commission v. Oracle Corp., Complaint, 3:12-cv-4310 (N.D. Cal. Aug. 16, 2012).
44. Financial Accounting Standards Board, "Topic 810, Consolidation"; International Accounting Standards Board, "IFRS 10: Consolidated Financial Statements," and "IFRS 12: Disclosure of Interests in Other Entities."
45. FCPA, § 78m(b)(6).
46. This is suggested by the fact that the provision refers to "books, records, and accounts." Both the SEC and US courts have interpreted this language broadly. *See, e.g.*, US Securities and Exchange Commission v. World-Wide Coin Investments, 567 F. Supp. 724, pp. 748–749 (N.D. Ga. 1983) ("Congress' use of the term 'records' suggests that virtually any tangible embodiment of information made or kept by an issuer is within the scope of section 13(b)(2)(A) of the FCPA, such as tape recordings, computer print-outs, and similar representations."); United States v. Jensen, 532 F. Supp. 2d 1187, pp. 1197–1199 (N.D. Cal. 2008) (rejecting defendant's argument that provision is limited to records necessary for the preparation of financial statements or records with a nexus to public securities filings).
47. In the Matter of Diagnostics Products Corp., Admin. Proc., File No. 51724, 2005 WL 1211548 (May 20, 2005), available at http://www.sec.gov/litigation/admin/34-51724.pdf.
48. In re United Industrial Corp., Exchange Act Release No. 60005, 2009 WL 1507586 (May 29, 2009), available at http://www.sec.gov/litigation/admin/2009/34-60005.pdf SEC Litig. Rel. No. 21063, 2009 WL 1507590 (May 29, 2009), available at http://www.sec.gov/litigation/litreleases/2009/lr21063.htm.
49. Weissmann and Smith, *Restoring Balance*, pp. 23–24.
50. Sentencing Memorandum, p. 22; Löscher, "The CEO of Siemens on Using a Scandal to Drive Change."
51. Fletcher et al., *Fletcher Cyclopedia*, § 7122.
52. Ibid.
53. Ibid.
54. *See, e.g.*, R.C.M. Executive Gallery Corp. v. Rols Capital Co. 901 F. Supp. 630 (S.D.N.Y. 1995) (federal law); Fehl v. S. W. C. Corp., 433 F. Supp. 939 (D. Del. 1977) (Delaware

law); Ray v. Alad Corp., 560 P.2d 3 (1977) (creating exception to general rule for product liability claims).

55. *Resource Guide*, p. 28.
56. In the cases cited, liability was imposed on firms that either had been dissolved, as in Melrose Distillers v. United States, 79 S. Ct. 763 (1959), or had survived mergers. *See* United States v. Alamo Bank of Texas, 880 F.2d 828, p. 830 (5th Cir. 1989); United States v. Polizzi, 500 F.2d 856, p. 907 (9th Cir. 1974); and United States v. Shields Rubber Corp., 732 F. Supp. 569, pp. 571–572 (W.D. Pa. 1989).
57. *Resource Guide*, p. 30. One of the cases cited could be described as a merger. The firm that committed the violations was acquired by and then merged into another firm controlled by its parent company. The SEC alleged that the parent company, which was a US issuer, failed to institute adequate internal controls. Both the acquirer and the parent were liable under the settlement agreement, but only the predecessor company was charged criminally. *See* Complaint, US Securities and Exchange Commission v. ENI, S.p.A., 4:10-cv-2414 (S.D. Tex. filed July 7, 2010); Deferred Prosecution Agreement, United States v. Snamprogetti Netherlands B.V., 10-cr-460 (S.D. Tex. filed July 7, 2010); Criminal Information, United States v. Snamprogetti Netherlands B.V., 10-cr-460 (S.D. Tex. filed July 7, 2010).
58. *See* Phillips, "The Federal Common Law of Successor Liability and the Corrupt Practices Act" ("silence by enforcers may lead overly conservative acquirers to abandon transactions out of an unfounded (but understandable) fear of being held liable for the violations of the seller, even when acquisitions would be socially and economically beneficial and likely could be accomplished without FCPA successor liability through an asset purchase"); Lindsey, "More than You Bargained For: Successor Liability under the U.S. Foreign Corrupt Practices Act" ("The cost of an expensive and time-consuming investigation, a decrease in share value and a tarnished reputation are among the consequences for companies that hastily enter into a deal without assessing potential FCPA liabilities and without putting a plan in place to mitigate any such liabilities."). *See, e.g.*, Shearman and Sterling LLP, *FCPA Digest January 2013*, pp. 20–23.
59. Schubert et al., "At Siemens, Bribery Was Just a Line Item."
60. United States v. Sharef, 11-cr-1056 (S.D.N.Y. 2011); US Securities and Exchange Commission v. Sharef, 924 F. Supp. 2d 539 (S.D.N.Y. 2013).
61. *See* Samatas "The SAIC-Siemens 'Super-panopticon' in the Athens 2004 Olympics as a Case of 'McVeillance': The Surveillance-Industrial Complex's Unscrupulous Global Business," p. 70, citing Telloglou (2009).
62. Bouras, "Greek Court Indicts 64 in Siemens-OTE Bribery Case."
63. Fisse, "Reconstructing Corporate Criminal Law," pp. 1159–1167; Arlen and Kraakman, "Controlling Corporate Misconduct."
64. *Cf.* Arlen and Kraakman, "Controlling Corporate Misconduct," pp. 699–707 (referring to prevention and policing but defining policing more narrowly to exclude imposition of private sanctions).
65. Sentencing Memorandum, pp. 18–19.
66. Sentencing Memorandum, p. 17.

67. In the United States this complaint has been expressed most vociferously in connection with the failure to prosecute individuals in the aftermath of the financial crisis of 2008. *See, e.g.*, Rakoff, "The Financial Crisis: Why Have No High Level Executives Been Prosecuted?"; Keefe, "Why Corrupt Bankers Avoid Jail."
68. OECD Working Group on Bribery, *Germany: Follow-Up to the Phase 3 Report & Recommendations*, p. 3 (note that this document does not explicitly identify Siemens as the case which involved sixty-one individuals being sanctioned). *See also Phase 3 Report on Implementing the OECD Anti-Bribery Convention in Germany*, pp. 9–10, 17, paras. 19–22, 39.
69. Examining Enforcement of the Foreign Corrupt Practices Act, Hearing Before the Subcommittee on Crime and Drugs of the Committee on the Judiciary United States Senate, One Hundred Eleventh Congress, Second Session, Nov. 30, 2010 Serial No. J–111–115.
70. United States v. Sharef, 11-cr-1056 (S.D.N.Y. 2011); US Securities and Exchange Commission v. Sharef, 924 F. Supp. 2d 539 (S.D.N.Y. 2013).
71. US Department of Justice, "Former Chief Financial Officer of Siemens Argentina Pleads Guilty to Role in Multimillion Dollar Foreign Bribery Scheme."
72. US Securities and Exchange Commission, "SEC Concludes Its Case Against Former Siemens Executives Charged with Bribery in Argentina, Obtaining Judgments over $1.8 Million.";.
73. US Department of Justice, "Siemens AG and Three Subsidiaries Plead Guilty to Foreign Corrupt Practices Act Violations and Agree to Pay $450 Million in Combined Criminal Fines"; US Securities and Exchange Commission, "SEC Charges Seven Former Siemens Executives with Bribing Leaders in Argentina."
74. These figures are based on a search of the Shearman and Sterling FCPA database for cases whose disposition was categorized as "acquittal," "dismissal," or "conviction." The cases involving corporate defendants were: United States v. Harris Corp., 3:90-cr-456 (N.D. Cal. Mar. 20, 1991) and United States v. Noriega, 10-cr-1031 (C.D. Cal. 2010).
75. *Compare* the ruling in United States v. Hoskins, 902 F.3d 69 (2d Cir. 2018) (holding that nonresident foreign national cannot be liable under the FCPA solely as a co-conspirator in the absence of other ties to the United States) to the negotiated resolutions of the actions against Snamprogetti and JGC, two of the defendants in the Bonny Island case discussed in chapter 10. *See* Information, United States v. Snamprogetti Netherlands B.V., 10-cr-460 (S.D. Tex. filed July 7, 2010); Deferred Prosecution Agreement, United States v. Snamprogetti Netherlands B.V., 10-cr-460 (S.D. Tex. filed July 7, 2010); Deferred Prosecution Agreement, United States v. JGC Corporation, 11-cr-260 (S.D. Tex. filed Apr. 6, 2011); Information, United States v. JGC Corp., 11-cr-260 (S.D. Tex. filed Apr. 6, 2011). *See also* Koehler, "Significant dd-3 Development in Africa Sting Case" (comparing outcomes of corporate settlements predicated on expansive definition of the FCPA's territorial jurisdiction to ruling in United States v. Patel, 9-cr-338 (D.D.C. Dec. 11, 2009)).
76. *See* Shearman and Stearling LLP, *FCPA Digest January 2012* (Jan. 3, 2012), *FCPA Digest January 2013* (Jan. 2, 2013), *FCPA Digest January 2014* (Jan. 6, 2014), *FCPA*

Digest January 2015 (Jan. 5, 2015), *FCPA Digest January 2016* (Jan. 4, 2016), *FCPA Digest January 2017* (Jan. 3, 2017), and *FCPA Digest January 2018* (Jan. 2, 2018).

77. Stephenson, "Beware Blowback: How Attempts to Strengthen FCPA Deterrence Could Narrow the Statute's Scope."
78. Priest and Klein, "The Selection of Disputes for Litigation."
79. *Compare* 15 U.S.C. § 78ff(c)(1)(A) (corporate criminal liability under issuer provision) *with* § 78ff(c)(2)(A) (individual criminal liability under issuer provision); *compare* 15 U.S.C. § 78dd-2(g)(1)(A) (corporate criminal liability under domestic concern provision) *with* § 78dd-2(g) (2)(A) (individual criminal liability under issuer provision); *compare* 15 U.S.C. § 78dd-3(e)(1)(A) (corporate criminal liability for territorial provision) *with* § 78dd-3(e)(2)(A) (individual criminal liability for territorial provision). However, companies still must act corruptly. *See* Section 30A(a), 15 U.S.C. § 78dd-1(a); 15 U.S.C. § 78dd-2(a), 78dd-3(a).
80. *See, e.g.*, Fed. R. Civ. Pro. 801(d)(2)(D).
81. Yates, "Individual Accountability for Corporate Wrongdoing."
82. Arlen, "The Potentially Perverse Effects of Corporate Criminal Liability."
83. Arlen, "Potentially Perverse Effects"; Arlen and Kraakman, "Controlling Corporate Misconduct."
84. Arlen and Kahan, "Corporate Governance Regulation through Non-Prosecution," pp. 354–357.
85. Coffee, "'No Soul to Damn: No Body to Kick': An Unscandalized Inquiry into the Problem of Corporate Punishment," pp. 413–424. For criticism, *see* Fisse, "Reconstructing Corporate Criminal Law," pp. 1235–1237, and Metzger, "Corporate Criminal Liability for Defective Products: Policies, Problems, and Prospects," pp. 69–70 (emphasizing collateral impact on innocent shareholders and that managers may be beyond shareholders' control).
86. Olken and Pande, "Corruption in Developing Countries" (describing negative correlation between income and measures of corruption).
87. Sentencing Memorandum, p. 21; Schubert et al., "At Siemens, Bribery Was Just a Line Item."
88. Sentencing Memorandum, p. 21; Peter Löscher, "The CEO of Siemens on Using a Scandal to Drive Change How I Did It."
89. For a comparison of US law on these points to the law of several other jurisdictions, *see* Arlen and Buell, "The Global Expansion of Corporate Criminal Liability: Effective Enforcement Policy Across Legal Systems."
90. *See* Hecker, Kucher, Shvets, Maximenko, and Melekhina, "Between a Rock and a Hard Place: Anti-Corruption Compliance and Antitrust Law in Russia."
91. *Resource Guide*, pp. 60–61.
92. *See* Seeger, C. Smith, Maximenko, and Shvets, "Russia: Recent Developments Bearing Upon Counterparty Selection Process and Data Domestication," citing Recommendations on development and application of commercial policies of business entities occupying a dominant position on the pharmaceutical and medical devices market, issued on June 30, 2015.
93. Barboza, "Drug Giant Faced a Reckoning as China Took Aim at Bribery."

94. Sng, Tang, and S. Huang, "China: Internal Investigations."
95. Sng, Tang, and S. Huang, "China: Internal Investigations, The Asia-Pacific Investigations Review 2016," pp. 29–30.
96. Palazzolo, "FCPA Inc.: The Business of Bribery: Corruption Probes Become Profit Center for Big Law Firms"; Koehler, "FCPA Inc. and the Business of Bribery."
97. Curtin and Senden, "Public Accountability of Transnational Private Regulation: Chimera or Reality?"
98. *See generally* K. Davis, "Legal Universalism: Persistent Objections"; Siems, *Comparative Law*, pp. 236–241.

Chapter 9

1. Odebrecht S.A, *Annual Report 2015*.
2. Braskem, *2014 Annual Report*, p. 32.
3. Connors and Kiernan, "Behind the Fall of Marcelo Odebrecht, Brazil's Construction 'Prince.'"
4. Nicholson, "Petrobras Raises $70 Billion in Share Issue."
5. Forero, "Brazil Building More Dams across Amazon."
6. Segal, "Petrobras Oil Scandal Leaves Brazilians Lamenting a Lost Dream."
7. Londoño, "Brazil Shuts Down Successful Corruption-Fighting Task Force"; Kaiser, "Brazil's President Temer Avoids a New Corruption Trial."
8. Ministério Público Federal, "MPF firma acordos de leniência com Odebrecht e Braskem" (Brazilian Federal Prosecution Service (MPF) enters into leniency agreements with Odebrecht and Braskem); US Department of Justice, "Odebrecht and Braskem Plead Guilty and Agree to Pay at Least $3.5 Billion in Global Penalties to Resolve Largest Foreign Bribery Case in History"; US Securities and Exchange Commission, "Petrochemical Manufacturer Braskem S.A. to Pay $957 Million to Settle FCPA Charges"; Office of the Attorney General of Switzerland, "Petrobras-Odebrecht Affair: The Office of the Attorney General of Switzerland Convicts Brazilian Companies and Demands Payment of over CHF 200 million."
9. Although plea bargaining is incompatible with the inquisitorial model of criminal procedure that has historically been prevalent in civil law countries, several civil law countries, besides Brazil, have adopted versions of plea bargaining. *See* Langer, "From Legal Transplants to Legal Translations: The Globalization of Plea Bargaining and the Americanization Thesis in Criminal Procedure."
10. OECD, Latin American and Caribbean Competition Forum Session II, p. 6.
11. Lei No. 12.846 de 1 de Agosto de 2013, D.O.U. de 2.8.2013 (Clean Companies Act); Lei No. 12.850 de 2 de Agosto de 2013, D.O.U. de 5.8.2013 (Criminal Organizations Enforcement Act).
12. *See, e.g.*, STF., Pet. 7.265/DF, Relator: Min. Ricardo Lewandowski, 14.11.2017 (Braz.); Appeal Nº 5023972-66.2017.4.04.0000/PR—TRF-4 (Aug. 22, 2017).
13. Plea Agreement, United States v. Odebrecht S.A., 16-cr-643 (E.D.N.Y. filed Dec. 21, 2016).

14. Plea Agreement, United States v. Braskem S.A., 16-cr-644 (E.D.N.Y. filed Dec. 21, 2016).
15. Odebrecht S.A., "Odebrecht Signs Agreement with Authorities in Brazil, United States and Switzerland."
16. Sentencing Memorandum, United States v. Odebrecht S.A., 16-cr-643 (E.D.N.Y. filed Apr. 11, 2017).
17. Department of Justice, "Odebrecht and Braskem Plead Guilty and Agree to Pay at Least $3.5 Billion in Global Penalties to Resolve Largest Foreign Bribery Case in History."
18. Sentencing Memorandum, United States v. Odebrecht S.A., 16-cr-643 (E.D.N.Y. filed Apr. 11, 2017); "Odebrecht tenta mudar imagem com 'compliance'" (Odebrecht tries to change its image through compliance).
19. Odebrecht, "Odebrecht Engenharia e Construção Posts Net Income of R$ 890 Million in 2015" (reporting on the hiring of Michael Munro).
20. Odebrecht, "Emílio Announces Exit and Changes in the Board of Directors of Odebrecht."
21. Ministério Público Federal, "A Lava Jato em números no Paraná" (The Numbers of Lava Jato).
22. Agostini, "Odebrecht tem R$ 1,5 bi bloqueado pelo BNDES por obras no exterior."
23. Administrative Council for Economic Defense, "CADE Investigates Bid Rigging in Infrastructure and Road Transport Bids in São Paulo."
24. Department of Justice, "Odebrecht and Braskem Plead Guilty and Agree to Pay at Least $3.5 Billion in Global Penalties to Resolve Largest Foreign Bribery Case in History."
25. Office of the Attorney General of Switzerland, "Petrobras-Odebrecht Affair: The Office of the Attorney General of Switzerland convicts Brazilian companies and demands payment of over CHF 200 million."
26. Department of Justice, "Odebrecht and Braskem Plead Guilty and Agree to Pay at Least $3.5 Billion in Global Penalties to Resolve Largest Foreign Bribery Case in History"; US Securities and Exchange Commission, "Petrochemical Manufacturer Braskem S.A. to Pay $957 Million to Settle FCPA Charges."
27. Office of the Attorney General of Switzerland, "Petrobras-Odebrecht Affair: The Office of the Attorney General of Switzerland convicts Brazilian companies and demands payment of over CHF 200 million."
28. "Panama to Cancel Odebrecht Contract Amid Corruption Scandal."
29. OECD, "Is Foreign Bribery an Attractive Investment in Some Countries?"
30. OECD, Convention on Combating Bribery of Foreign Public Officials in International Business Transactions, art. 3.1.
31. Pieth et al., *Commentary*, pp. 276–277 (describing provisions of Council of Europe Convention on Extradition and extradition treaties concluded by Argentina, South Korea, and the United States).
32. Pieth et al., *Commentary*, pp. 259–269 (art. 3, II).
33. UN Convention, arts. 30:1, 30:5.
34. UN Convention, art. 37.

35. OECD Convention, art. 5; OECD, "Commentaries on the Convention on Combating Bribery of Foreign Public Officials in International Business Transactions," p. 27; OECD Working Group on Bribery, *Recommendation of the Council*, Annex I.D.
36. UN Convention, art. 30:3.
37. OECD, "Is Foreign Bribery an Attractive Investment in Some Countries?"
38. OECD, "Is foreign bribery an attractive investment in some countries?"
39. Ibid., p. 211.
40. *See* OECD, "Is Foreign Bribery an Attractive Investment in Some Countries?"
41. This provision is actually found in a separate statute from the FCPA, namely, the Alternative Fines Act, 18. U.S.C. § 3571.
42. Lei No. 12.846 de 1 de Agosto de 2013, D.O.U. de 2.8.2013, art. 6 (Clean Companies Act); Decreto No. 8.420, de 18 de Marco de 2015, D.O.U. de 19.3.2015, art. 17–22.
43. OECD, "The Legal Framework for the Treatment of Proceeds of Active Bribery."
44. Department of Justice, *Justice Manual*, 9.27.760.
45. OECD, *Resolving Foreign Bribery Cases with Non-Trial Resolutions*, pp. 24, 28-31
46. OECD, *Resolving Foreign Bribery Cases with Non-Trial Resolutions*, pp. 141-142.
47. UN Convention, art. 54.
48. UN Convention, art. 23.2(c).
49. European Union, Directive 2014/24/EU of the European Parliament and of the Council of 26 February 2014 on public procurement, art. 57, http://eur-lex.europa.eu/legal-content/EN/ALL/?uri=CELEX:32014L0024.
50. Agreement on Mutual Enforcement of Debarment Decisions by and among the Asian Development Bank, the European Bank for Reconstruction and Development, Inter-American Development Bank, and the World Bank, Apr. 9, 2010, http://lnadbg4.adb.org/oai001p.nsf/0/F77A326B818A19C548257853000C2B10/$FILE/cross-debarment-agreement.pdf.
51. At least seventeen out of thirty-seven members of the OECD Convention were criticized for failing to provide adequate statistical data on enforcement during their Phase 3 peer reviews.
52. Based on analysis of recommendations compiled in OECD Working Group on Bribery, *Compilation of Recommendations*.
53. OECD Working Group on Bribery, *2016 Data on Enforcement of the Anti-Bribery Convention*. Note that at p. 4 the report states that 441 individuals were sanctioned criminally but a different figure, 443, appears at pp. 1, 3, and 6.
54. Ibid.
55. Ibid.
56. This trend is documented and criticized in Arlen and M. Kahan, "Corporate Governance Regulation Through Non-Prosecution."
57. R. v. Innospec Ltd., [2010] 3 WLUK 784, [2010] Crim. L.R. 665 (In the Crown Court at Southwark).
58. Corruption Watch UK, "Out of Court, Out of Mind: Do Deferred Prosecution Agreements and Corporate Settlements Fail to Deter Overseas Corruption."
59. *See generally* Arlen, "Prosecuting Beyond the Rule of Law: Corporate Mandates Imposed through Deferred Prosecution Agreements."

60. STF., Pet. 7.265/DF, Relator: Min. Ricardo Lewandowski, 14.11.2017 (Braz.).
61. Corruption Watch UK, "Out of Court, Out of Mind: Do Deferred Prosecution Agreements and Corporate Settlements Fail to Deter Overseas Corruption"; Transparency International, *Can Justice Be Achieved Through Settlements*; UNCAC Coalition, "Making UNCAC Work: Coalition Statement Ahead of the 6th Conference of States Parties in St. Petersburg."
62. *See* Letter from Corruption Watch UK.
63. Dell and McDevitt, *Exporting Corruption* (classified just seven countries as active enforcers in 2018).
64. Pieth et al. suggest the OECD Convention's "effective, proportionate and dissuasive" standard actually is interpreted by the Working Group to mean effective deterrence and proportionality and that little attention has been paid to the proportionality requirement. Pieth et al., *Commentary*, pp. 279–280, 290, 295.
65. The classic modern exposition of this theory is found in Becker, "Crime and Punishment: An Economic Approach." For applications to bribery and corruption, *see* Rose-Ackerman and Palifka, *Corruption and Government*, ch. 6; Søreide, *Corruption and Criminal Justice*), ch. 4.
66. For a general discussion of this point, *see* De Geest and Dari-Mattiacci, "The Rise of Carrots and the Decline of Sticks."
67. *See* the discussion in chapter 4 of World Duty Free Co. v. Republic of Kenya, ICSID Case No. Arb/00/7, Award, paras. 138–157, 172 (Sept. 25, 2006), and Metal-Tech Ltd. v. The Republic of Uzbekistan, ICSID Case No. ARB/10/3, Award (Oct. 4, 2013). For further analysis of the incentive effects of the "zero-tolerance" approach adopted in these cases, *see* K. Davis, "Contracts Procured Through Bribery: Zero Tolerance versus Proportional Liability."
68. Lambsdorff, "Who Accepts Bribery? Evidence from a Global Household Survey"; Hernandez and McGee, "A Demographic Study of African Attitudes on Bribery."
69. There is an extensive literature on the need to account for nonlegal sanctions in determining the deterrent effects of legal sanctions. Important contributions to the literature include: Zimring and Hawkins, *Deterrence*; Andenaes, *Punishment and Deterrence*); Fisse, "Reconstructing Corporate Criminal Law: Deterrence, Retribution, Fault, and Sanctions," pp. 1152–1159; Karpoff and Lott, Jr., "The Reputational Penalty Firms Bear from Committing Criminal Fraud"; Rasmusen, "Stigma and Self-fulfilling Expectations of Criminality"; C. Alexander, "On the Nature of the Reputational Penalty for Corporate Crime: Evidence"; D. Kahan and Posner, "Shaming White-Collar Criminals: A Proposal for Reform of the Federal Sentencing Guidelines"; Cooter and Porat, "Should Courts Deduct Nonlegal Sanctions from Damages?"
70. Braithwaite, *Crime, Shame and Reintegration*, ch. 9.
71. Andenaes, "The General Preventive Effects of Punishment," p. 966; Rasmusen, "Stigma and Self-Fulfilling Expectations of Criminality"; Iacobucci, "On the Interaction between Legal and Reputational Sanctions"; Mungan, "A Generalized Model for Reputational Sanctions and the (Ir)Relevance of the Interactions between Legal and Reputational Sanctions."

72. This point has been emphasized repeatedly by criminologists interested in the policy implications of deterrence theory. *See generally* Pickett, Loughran, and Bushway, "Consequences of Legal Risk Communication for Sanction Perception Updating and White-collar Criminality." For recent reviews of the literature suggesting gaps between perceived and actual probabilities of detection, *see* Apel, "Sanctions, Perceptions, and Crime: Implications for Criminal Deterrence"; Nagin, "Criminal Deterrence Research at the Outset of the Twenty-First Century."
73. Karpoff, Lee, and Martin make a creative but ultimately unpersuasive effort to overcome this difficulty and estimate the probability that a bribe-paying firm will be sanctioned. They use a statistical model to identify the characteristics of firms caught paying foreign bribes by US authorities between 1978 and May 2013. They then, effectively, assume that the firms caught were randomly selected from all the firms in the population with similar observable characteristics. They calculate the probability of detection by examining the entire population of firms to determine what proportion of firms that have the characteristics of bribe payers were actually caught. This exercise is interesting but the results cannot be taken too seriously, for one simple but fundamental reason: the assumption that firms that resemble those caught paying bribes also paid bribes may not be valid. Enforcement agencies might select to investigate and prosecute based on information that is not observable to the researchers. For example, suppose that over a three-year period, out of 1,000 firms, 5 are sanctioned for paying bribes, and all 5 are large multinationals operating in the oil and gas sector. Suppose that another 95 large multinational oil and gas firms were not sanctioned. Is it reasonable for a researcher to infer that all or virtually all large multinational oil and gas firms paid bribes, that no other types of firms paid bribes, and that the probability of detection during the relevant period is 5/100 = 5%? The answers to these questions are no, no, and no. The enforcement agency may have received information unobservable to the researcher—such as complaints from victims or competitors—that allowed them to target the only 5 oil and gas firms that paid bribes, implying that the probability of detection, at least for oil and gas firms, was 100%. At the same time, there may have been 10 petrochemicals firms that paid bribes and escaped liability entirely. For those firms the probability of detection was 0%. *See* Karpoff, Lee, and Martin, "Foreign Bribery: Incentives and Enforcement."
74. This issue is explored at greater length in K. Davis, "Multijurisdictional Enforcement Games: The Case of Anti-Bribery Law."
75. Pickett, Loughran, and Bushway, "Consequences of Legal Risk Communication."
76. OECD Working Group on Bribery, *Compilation of Recommendations.*
77. These theories are surveyed in N. Smith, Simpson, and C.Y. Huang, "Why Managers Fail to Do the Right Thing: An Empirical Study of Unethical and Illegal Conduct."
78. For discussions of the effects of socialization on willingness to engage in deviant behavior in organizational contexts, *see* Vikas, Ashforth, and Joshi, "Business as Usual: The Acceptance and Perpetuation of Corruption in Organizations."
79. For surveys of research on how individual differences in moral reasoning explain misconduct in organizational settings, *see* Treviño, den Nieuwenboer, and

Kish-Gephart, "(Un)Ethical Behavior in Organizations"; Treviño, Weaver, and Reynolds, "Behavioral Ethics in Organizations: A Review."

80. Tyler, *Why People Obey the Law*.
81. Bottoms and Tankebe, "Beyond Procedural Justice: A Dialogic Approach to Legitimacy in Criminal Justice"; Tankebe, "Viewing Things Differently: The Dimensions of Public Perceptions of Police Legitimacy."
82. Tyler, *Why People Obey the Law*.
83. On the idea of punishment as a means of moral education, *see* Braithwaite, *Crime, Shame and Reintegration*, pp. 141–143, and Garland, *Punishment and Modern Society*, pp. 41–46, 251–276.
84. Department of Justice, "Odebrecht and Braskem Plead Guilty and Agree to Pay at Least $3.5 Billion in Global Penalties to Resolve Largest Foreign Bribery Case in History," quoting Deputy Assistant Attorney General Suh and Assistant Director (FBI) Richardson.
85. For discussion of hybrid models of compliance behavior which lead to proposals to combine deterrence (by both legal sanctions and shame) and appeals to morality, *see*: Ayres and Braithwaite, *Responsive Regulation*; Paternoster and Simpson, "Sanction Threats and Appeals to Morality: Testing a Rational Choice Model of Corporate Crime."
86. On the advantages and disadvantages of these types of sanctions, *compare* Fisse, "Reconstructing Corporate Criminal Law," pp. 1237–1243, and Arlen and Kahan, "Corporate Governance Regulation Through Non-Prosecution."
87. Brandt, Affonso, Macedo, Vassallo, and Serapião, "Governo reduz equipe da Lava Jato e corta verba da PF" (Government Reduces Lava Jato Team and the Federal Police budget); Ministério Público Federal, "Equipe de Investigação no Ministério Público Federal" (Brazilian Federal Prosecution's Investigation Team).
88. Department of Justice, "Odebrecht and Braskem Plead Guilty and Agree to Pay at Least $3.5 Billion in Global Penalties to Resolve Largest Foreign Bribery Case in History."
89. Odebrecht S.A., *Annual Report 2015*, p. 5; Odebrecht S.A., *Annual Report 2017*, p. 50.
90. Alvarenga, "Impacto da Lava Jato no PIB pode passar de R$ 140 bilhões, diz estudo" (The Impact of the *Lava Jato* on GDP Can Be Greater than R$140 Billion, Says Study).
91. Lopes and Miroff, "A Corruption Scandal Wrecked Brazil's Economy. Now, Workers Face the Consequences ."
92. BMI Research, "Brazil Infrastructure Report Q4," pp. 27–32, 55.
93. Nolen, "Corruption beyond Brazil: Where the 'Car Wash' Scandal Has Splashed across Latin America"; BCR, "Odebrecht tendría un impacto negativo de hasta 0,6% en el PBI ."
94. Jelmayer and Pearson, "Brazil Corruption Scandal Has Companies Rushing to Bulk Up Compliance Ranks."
95. Andrew Spalding has objected to FCPA enforcement strategy on these grounds. *See* Spalding, "Unwitting Sanctions: Understanding Anti-Bribery Legislation as Economic Sanctions Against Emerging Markets."

96. *See, e.g.*, Heimann and Pieth, *Confronting Corruption*, p. 14 ("Corruption hurts all parts of society, but its most devastating effect is on the poor . . .").
97. Justesen and Bjørnskov, "Exploiting the Poor: Bureaucratic Corruption and Poverty in Africa." *But see* Hunt and Laszlo, "Is Bribery Really Regressive? Bribery's Costs, Benefits, and Mechanisms."
98. Cuervo-Cazurra, "Who Cares About Corruption?"
99. Oré, "Stalled Brazilian Odebrecht Projects Decay in Venezuela."
100. For similar critiques of the broader anti-corruption regime see Goodwin and Rose-Sender, "Linking Corruption and Human Rights" and Rajagopal, "Corruption, Legitimacy and Human Rights."
101. One prominent retributive theorist, Michael Davis, recommends ranking all the possible forms of misconduct in terms of harm, then ranking all the possible legal sanctions in terms of severity, and then connecting each type of misconduct with a sanction of the same rank. M. Davis, "How to Make the Punishment Fit the Crime." It is not difficult to rank most legal sanctions in terms of severity because they are expressed in ordinal terms—*x* years in prison or *y* dollars in fines. The most challenging analytical step will be to rank sanctions of different types, e.g., fines versus imprisonment.

Chapter 10

1. Deferred Prosecution Agreement paras. 21, 24, 36, 43, United States v. Marubeni Corp., 12-cr-22 (S.D. Tex. filed Jan. 17, 2012).
2. Iriekpen, "Nigeria: Leaked Files Link Abdulsalami Abubakar, Chris Garba to U.S.$182 Million Halliburton Bribery Scandal"; Garuba, "NIGERIA: Halliburton, Bribes and the Deceit of 'Zero-Tolerance' for Corruption https://perma.cc/X5Q3-NB8R."
3. Henley, "French Sleaze Inquiry Targets US Oil Subsidiary."
4. US Department of Justice, "Marubeni Corporation Resolves Foreign Corrupt Practices Act Investigation and Agrees to Pay a $54.6 Million Criminal Penalty."
5. Ibid.
6. U.K. Securities Fraud Office, "MW Kellogg Ltd to Pay £7 million in SFO High Court Action."
7. "Italy Court Upholds Saipem Fine and Seizure Order in Nigeria Case."
8. "French Court Fines two for Bribing Nigerians."
9. African Development Bank, "AfDB Levies US $17 Million in Financial Penalties in Corruption Case"; African Development Bank, "AfDB Charges Snamprogetti Netherlands B.V. US $5.7 Million in Monetary Sanction for Corrupt Practices."
10. Cour de cassation, crim., Jan. 17, 2018, N0. 16/86491 (Fr.).
11. "Blanchiment: 8 millions d'euros d'amende pour un ex-ministre nigérian du Pétrole"; Onanuga, "French Govt Pardons Former Petroleum Minister Etete"; "Former Nigeria State Governor James Ibori Receives 13-year Sentence"; "Nigeria's Ex-oil minister 'Arrested in London' "; Roberts, "Diepreye Alamieyeseigha, Nigerian Notorious for Corruption, Dies at 62."

12. For discussion, *see* Wouters, Ryngaert, and Coots, "The International Legal Framework Against Corruption: Achievements and Challenges," pp. 45–47.
13. UN Convention, art. 41:1.
14. OECD Convention, art. 4.1, cmt. n.1.
15. UN Convention, art. 42:2.
16. Ibid.
17. UN Convention, art. 42:2(c).
18. UN Convention, arts. 42:3, 42:4. The OECD Convention makes the exercise of jurisdiction obligatory for states that rely on the personality principle for other offences. OECD Convention, art. 4.2.
19. Ryngaert, *Jurisdiction in International Law*, pp. 82–84.
20. United Nations, *Report of the International Law Commission*, para. 16; *Restatement (Fourth) of the Foreign Relations Law of the United States—Jurisdiction*, § 217.
21. Kokott, "States, Sovereign Equality," para. 21.
22. Kokott, "States, Sovereign Equality," paras. 50–54.
23. The domaine réservé of a state, meaning the zone not governed by international law, has traditionally included the organization of its government. Ziegler, "Domain Réservé," paras. 4, 5. *But see* Dann, *Law of Development Cooperation*, p. 254 (claiming that anti-corruption measures are now so thoroughly internationalized that they can no longer be considered part of the domaine réservé).
24. McDonnell v. United States, 136 S. Ct. 2355 (2016) (citation omitted).
25. Fox and Webb, *The Law of State Immunity*, pp. 25–31; Kokott, "States, Sovereign Equality," paras. 35–39; Akande and Shah, "Immunities of State Officials, International Crimes, and Foreign Domestic Courts," pp. 824–825, 827 (suggesting that status-based official immunity is designed to give effect to principles of sovereign equality and non-intervention, while conduct-based immunity is designed to prevent states from circumventing state immunity).
26. International Law Commission, *Fifth report on immunity*, paras. 117, 230–234, and cases cited therein.
27. Wouters et al., "The International Legal Framework Against Corruption," p. 49.
28. 15 U.S.C. § 78 dd-3.
29. *See* Koehler, "Significant dd-3 Development in Africa Sting Case" (reporting on ruling in United States v. Pankesh Patel, 9-cr-338 (D.D.C. Dec. 11, 2009)). *See also* Hecker and Laporte, "Should FCPA 'Territorial' Jurisdiction Reach Extraterritorial Proportions?"
30. 15 U.S.C. § 78 dd-1.
31. 15 U.S.C. § 78 dd-2(h)(1).
32. US federal courts generally do not insist on proof that a defendant had notice of elements of an offense that are prescribed solely to confer jurisdiction on the federal government. *See* United States v. Feola, 420 U.S. 671, p. 677 (1975); United States v. Yermian, 468 U.S. 63, p. 68 (1984). Some courts examine whether a defendant knew or should have known that they were acting within US jurisdiction in order to determine whether the Constitution's due process requirement is satisfied. *See, e.g.*, United States v. Davis, 905 F.2d 245, p. 249 (9th Cir. 1989).

33. *Resource Guide*, p. 11 ("placing a telephone call or sending an e-mail, text message, or fax from, to, or through the United States involves interstate commerce—as does sending a wire transfer from or to a U.S. bank or otherwise using the U.S. banking system"); Information, United States v. ABB Vetco Gray, Inc., 04-cr-279 paras. 39, 41 (S.D. Tex. filed June 22, 2004) (In a settled case, asserting that foreign non-issuer violated FCPA while in US territory by causing agents to wire funds to a US bank account while outside the United States and by receiving an email sent from the United States to Scotland).
34. *Compare Resource Guide*, p. 12 ("A foreign national or company may also be liable under the FCPA if it aids and abets, conspires with, or acts as an agent of an issuer or domestic concern, regardless of whether the foreign national or company itself takes any action in the United States) with United States v. Hoskins, 902 F.3d 69 (2d Cir. 2018) (holding that nonresident foreign national cannot be liable under the FCPA solely as a co-conspirator in the absence of other ties to the United States).
35. Information, United States v. Marubeni Corp., 12-cr-022 (S.D. Tex. filed Jan. 17, 2012).
36. Information, United States v. Snamprogetti Netherlands B.V., 10-cr-460 (S.D. Tex. filed July 7, 2010); Deferred Prosecution Agreement, United States v. Snamprogetti Netherlands B.V., 10-cr-460 (S.D. Tex. filed July 7, 2010); Deferred Prosecution Agreement, United States v. JGC Corp., 11-cr-260 (S.D. Tex. filed Apr. 6, 2011); Information, United States v. JGC Corp., 11-cr-260 (S.D. Tex. filed Apr. 6, 2011).
37. 15 U.S.C. §§ 78dd-1(g), 78dd-2(i).
38. Laundering of Monetary Instruments, 18 U.S.C. § 1956(f). The provision that applies to less serious forms of money laundering, 18 U.S.C. § 1957, also applies to permanent residents of the United States as well as "a sole proprietorship, partnership, company, or association composed principally of nationals or permanent resident aliens of the United States." 18 U.S.C. § 1957(d).
39. Bribery Act 2010, § 12.
40. Bribery Act 2010, §§ 7, 12(5).
41. Wouters et al., "The International Legal Framework Against Corruption: Achievements and Challenges," p. 256.
42. For examples of national laws on state immunity, *see* International Law Commission, *Fifth report on immunity*, para. 44. For an example of a case in which a state—Nigeria—relied on sovereign immunity to escape liability for corruption, *see* Adler v. Federal Republic of Nigeria, 219 F. 3d 869 (9th Cir. 2000).
43. *See* European Community v. RJR Nabisco, 764 F.3d pp. 129, 140 (2d Cir. 2014), rev'd, 136 S. Ct. 2090 (2016) (mail and wire fraud statutes do not rebut the presumption against extraterritoriality). A court can also arrive at this conclusion by deploying other principles of statutory interpretation that rely on the same policy considerations as the presumption against extraterritoriality. For instance, in United States v. Giffen, 326 F. Supp. 2d 497 (S.D.N.Y. 2004), the court cited the void-for-vagueness doctrine and the principle of comity as grounds for concluding that bribery of a Kazakh public official did not violate the portion of the federal fraud statute that makes it an offence to participate in a scheme to deprive a person of another person's honest services.

44. Morrison v. National Australia Bank, 561 U.S. 247 (2010).
45. RJR Nabisco, Inc. v. European Communities, 136 S. Ct. 2090 (2016).
46. *See* United States v. Hoskins, 902 F.3d 69 (2d Cir. 2018).
47. This language is found in both the Fifth and Fourteenth amendments to the US Constitution. The former applies to the federal government; the latter applies to the states.
48. Licci v. Lebanese Canadian Bank, 732 F.3d 161, p. 174 (2d Cir. 2013); US Securities and Exchange Commission v. Sharef, 924 F. Supp. 2d 539 (S.D.N.Y. 2013); US Securities and Exchange Commission v. Straub, 921 F. Supp. 2d 244 (S.D.N.Y. 2013).
49. *See* US Securities and Exchange Commission v. Sharef, 924 F. Supp. 2d 539 (S.D.N.Y. 2013); United States v. Sidorenko, 102 F. Supp. 3d 1124, pp. 1132–1133 (N.D. Cal. 2015).
50. *See, e.g.*, Brown, "Extraterritorial Jurisdiction Under the 1998 Amendments to the Foreign Corrupt Practices Act: Does the Government's Reach Now Exceed its Grasp," pp. 241; Ashe, "The Lengthening Anti-Bribery Lasso of the United States: The Recent Extraterritorial Application of the U.S. Foreign Corrupt Practices Act"; Leibold, "Extraterritorial Application of the FCPA under International Law."
51. Song, "Pirates and Torturers: Universal Jurisdiction as Enforcement Gap-Filling."
52. K. Davis, "Self-interest and Altruism in the Deterrence of Transnational Bribery"; Stephan, "Regulatory Competition and Anticorruption Law."
53. Leslie Green offers this definition of authority and claims that all modern states' exercises of coercion through law are "gilded with the claim of authority." *See* L. Green, *The Authority of the State*, pp. 60, 75.
54. Brilmayer, *Conflict of Laws*, p. 236.
55. Brilmayer, *Conflict of Laws*, p. 241.
56. For an intellectual history of efforts to justify territoriality on this ground, beginning in seventeenth century Europe, *see* Ryngaert, *Jurisdiction in International Law*, pp. 54–60.
57. As Brilmayer points out, it is difficult to infer consent if this intuition is not shared by the foreigner. *Conflict of Laws*, pp. 248–249.
58. Brilmayer, *Conflict of Laws*, pp. 248–249. Relatedly, Jeremy Waldron argues that there is a natural duty to support institutions whose existence is necessary to avoid injustice and for practical reasons this will normally require supporting the institutions with nominal jurisdiction over a given territory. *See* Waldron, "Special Ties and Natural Duties." Chehtman takes a similar position. *See* Chehtman, *Philosophical Foundations*, pp. 56–58.
59. *See* Brilmayer, *Conflict of Laws*, 241; R.A. Duff, *Answering for Crime*, pp. 49–51. For critical surveys of the relevant arguments, *see* Chehtman, *The Philosophical Foundations of Extraterritorial Punishment*, and Ryngaert, *Jurisdiction in International Law*, pp. 106–107.
60. R.A. Duff, *Answering for Crime*, pp. 49–51.
61. Watson, "Offenders Abroad: The Case for Nationality-Based Criminal Jurisdiction," pp. 68; Arnell, "The Case for Nationality Based Jurisdiction," pp. 960 (referring to the

need to balance rights and responsibilities as part of an effort to strengthen the relationship between the state and its citizens).

62. *See, e.g.*, Buchanan, "Political Legitimacy and Democracy." For a survey of the literature on democracy as a source of political legitimacy, *see* Peter, "Political Legitimacy."
63. Arnell, "The Case for Nationality Based Jurisdiction," p. 959 (due process); Ryngaert, *Jurisdiction in International Law*, p. 106 (effectiveness); Chehtman, *Philosophical Foundations*, pp. 62–65.
64. Locke, *Second Treatise of Government*, § 119.
65. As Brilmayer puts it, to ground territorial jurisdiction on a consent-based theory a connecting factor "must reflect the aggrieved party's voluntary submission to the law that is chosen." Brilmayer, *Conflict of Laws*, p. 253.
66. In some quarters, there is reflexive skepticism about whether people have any interest—in the sense of an interest worth protecting—in regulating conduct that takes place outside the borders of their state, so-called extraterritorial conduct. This skepticism is at least superficially attractive when we think about laws motivated by peoples' interests in avoiding bodily harm. As a practical matter, there is little that German law can do to prevent a German citizen from being mugged in a dark alley in Buenos Aires, or even to provide meaningful condemnation or compensation. Alejandro Chehtman uses this example to support his argument that people generally only have an interest in their state's criminal laws being applied to conduct that takes place in their territory. *See* Chehtman, *Philosophical Foundations*, p. 68. Chehtman defines the interests protected by criminal law as the "interest of individuals in having a legal system in force containing rules that prohibit murder, rape, torture, and other wrongs" because such a system "contributes to our sense of being right-bearers, and that the legal system takes the protection of our rights seriously," or in other words, "contributes to our sense of dignity and security." Ibid., p. 40. This strikes me as an unnecessarily narrow specification of the interests protected by criminal law. Furthermore, the claim that a system of criminal law that is in force necessarily provides "security" seems to rest on an unacknowledged assumption that such a legal system has preventive effects. Chehtman fails to explain why those preventive effects do not affect conduct overseas. *See also* Binder, "Authority to Proscribe and Punish International Crimes."
67. *See generally* K. Davis, "Self-interest and Altruism"; Stephan, "Regulatory Competition and Anticorruption Law"; Perlman and Sykes, "The Political Economy of the Foreign Corrupt Practices Act: An Exploratory Analysis ."
68. H.R. Rep. No. 95-640, p. 4 (1977).
69. H.R. Rep. No. 95-640, p. 4–5 (1977).
70. S. Comm. on Banking, Housing and Urban Affairs, *Report of the Securities and Exchange Commission on Questionable and Illegal Corporate Payments and Practices*, pp. 39–40 (analyzing information provided by ninety-five companies that voluntarily disclosed questionable or illegal foreign payments and describing thirty-nine companies that reported questionable domestic activities).
71. *Cf.* Kant, *Perpetual Peace*, p. 113 ("the bad example which one free person gives another, (as *scandalum acceptum*) does no injury to the latter").

72. Burke, *Writings and Speeches VIII*, p. 96 (quoting Marshall at p. 30).
73. K. Davis, "Why Does the United States Regulate Foreign Bribery: Moralism, Self-Interest or Altruism?."
74. Cocks and Brock, "Special Report: Anatomy of Nigeria's $20 Billion 'Leak' "; Nossiter, "Governor of Nigeria's Central Bank Is Fired After Warning of Missing Oil Revenue."
75. "Corruption: The Only Thing that Works."
76. World Bank, *Nigeria Economic Report.*
77. "Corruption in Nigeria: The $20-billion Hole in Africa's Largest Economy" (quoting Andrew S. Nevin, PwC).
78. Chapter 5, citing views of Blake, Nagel, Pogge, and Rawls.
79. For an extension of this argument to multinational enterprises, *see* Hsieh, "Does Global Business Have a Responsibility to Promote Just Institutions?." Jeremy Waldron extends this argument to defend a worldwide duty to support all just institutions, a term which encompasses all institutions necessary to achieve Rawls's particular conception of fairness, "at least when this can be done without too much cost to ourselves." Waldron, "Special Ties and Natural Duties," p. 4.
80. Rawls, *Law of Peoples*, p. 106.
81. Pogge, *World Poverty and Human Rights*, pp. 148–149. Pogge devotes most of his attention to situations in which states support or enable the corrupt practices of foreign officials in other ways besides failing to regulate bribe payers.
82. In "Special Ties and Natural Duties," Jeremy Waldron seems to argue that the duty to support just institutions extends to countries like New Zealand. At the end of the article, however, he notes that an agent's duty of support is only triggered when it is necessary to achieve justice, which implies, among other things, that there will be no other effective action.
83. Tesler v. Government of the USA, [2011] EWHC (Admin) 52 (Eng.).
84. UN Convention, art. 51.
85. UN Convention, arts. 31, 57.3.
86. Jacinta Anyango Oduour et al., World Bank, *Left Out of the Bargain*, p. 73.
87. For a similar assessment of how divergent conceptions of criminal justice create the potential for disagreement in the enforcement of universally adopted prohibitions, *see* Müller, "Universal Jurisdiction, Pirates and Vigilantes."
88. *Cf.* Carson, "Bribery, Extortion, and 'The Foreign Corrupt Practices Act.'"
89. Jones, "Is the FCPA Standing in the Way of Haiti's Recovery?."
90. Pereira and Melo, "Reelecting Corrupt Incumbents in Exchange for Public Goods: Rouba mas faz in Brazil." The data in this study come from mayoral elections held in 2000 and 2004 in the state of Pernambuco as well as reports on irregularities issued by the Audit Court. Effectiveness is measured by per capita public expenditures on public goods at the municipal level. The study controls for measures of voters' access to information in an effort to reject the hypothesis that their behavior is explained by inability to distinguish clean politicians from dirty ones. The authors acknowledge that their findings do not rule out the possibility that corrupt mayors attract support through provision of private goods, in other words, through patronage.

91. United States v. Alcatel-Lucent France, SA, 668 F.3d p. 1301 (11th Cir. 2012); Republic of Iraq v. ABB AG, 920 F. Supp. 2d 517 (S.D.N.Y. 2013).
92. *See generally* Spahn, "Multijurisdictional Bribery Law Enforcement: The OECD Anti-Bribery Convention"; Stephan, "Regulatory Competition and Anticorruption Law"; K. Davis, "Multijurisdictional Enforcement Games."
93. Convention Implementing the Schengen Agreement of 14 June 1985 Between the Governments of the States of the Benelux Economic Union, the Federal Republic of Germany and the French Republic on the Gradual Abolition of Checks at Their Common Borders, art. 54; Charter of Fundamental Rights of the European Union, art. 50.
94. Code pénal, art. 113-9; Code de procédure pénale, art. 692.
95. Eurojust, *Guidelines for Deciding "Which Jurisdiction Should Prosecute"?*
96. Council of the European Union, Council Framework Decision of 13 June 2002 on joint investigation teams (2002/465/JHA).
97. OECD Convention, art. 4.3; UN Convention, art. 42.5.
98. UN Convention, Chapter IV—International Cooperation.
99. These meetings were formally recommended in the OECD Working Group on Bribery in International Business Transactions, *Recommendation of the Council*, para. XIV(iv).
100. *See, e.g.*, F. Davis, "International Double Jeopardy: U.S. Prosecutions and the Developing Law in Europe."
101. Cour de cassation, crim., Jan. 17, 2018, N0. 16/86491 (Fr.); C.A. Paris, Pole 5—Ch. 13, no. 14/06723, 21 September 2016.
102. United States v. Allen, 864 F.3d 63 (2d Cir. 2017).
103. *See* Watson, "Offenders Abroad: The Case for Nationality-Based Criminal Jurisdiction," pp. 45, 47; Ryngaert, *Jurisdiction in International Law*, pp. 62–63.
104. Jiewuh Song takes a similar position in arguing that principles of universal jurisdiction ought to be qualified by the principle of complementarity. She says that even when states have agreed to adopt universal norms they should have discretion to adjudicate them "through different procedures, with different consequences" because "the capacity to choose among procedures can be important for societies realizing the kinds of social relation that their members value." *See* Song, "Pirates and Torturers: Universal Jurisdiction as Enforcement Gap-Filling," p. 489.
105. Burke, "Opening of Impeachment," *Writings and Speeches VI*, p. 346 (quoting from *Journal of the House of Lords*, p. 56).
106. Ibid.
107. African Development Bank, "AfDB Levies US $17 Million in Financial Penalties in Corruption Case."
108. *See, e.g.*, Wolf, *The Case for an International Anti-corruption Court*; Lebedev, "A World Corruption Police."

Chapter 11

1. World Bank, "Personal remittances, received (% of GDP)—Haiti (2002–2004)."

2. "Elephant and the Blind Men."
3. The OECD Working Group's approach to participation seems to reflect an assumption that the only parties affected by its activities are the state parties to the Convention. For an analysis of the legitimacy of the OECD Convention along these lines, *see* Rose, *International Anti-Corruption Norms*.

References

Bibliography

Abbott, Kenneth W. "The Transnational Regime Complex for Climate Change." *Environment and Planning C: Government and Policy* 30, no. 4 (2012): 571–590.

Abbott, Kenneth W. and Duncan Snidal. "Values and Interests: International Legalization in the Fight Against Corruption." *Journal of Legal Studies* 31, no. S1 (2002): S141–S171.

ADB/OECD Anti-Corruption Initiative for Asia and the Pacific. *The Criminalisation of Bribery in Asia and the Pacific*. Organisation for Economic Co-operation and Development, Asian Development Bank, 2010.

Administrative Council for Economic Defense. "CADE investigates bid rigging in infrastructure and road transport bids in São Paulo." http://en.cade.gov.br/cade-investigates-bid-rigging-in-infrastructure-and-road-transport-bids-in-sao-paulo, December 28, 2017.

African Development Bank. "AfDB charges Snamprogetti Netherlands B.V. US $5.7 million in monetary sanction for corrupt practices." Press release, May 28, 2014, http://www.afdb.org/en/news-and-events/article/afdb-charges-snamprogetti-netherlands-b-v-us-5-7-million-in-monetary-sanction-for-corrupt-practices-13233.

African Development Bank. "AfDB Levies US $17 Million in Financial Penalties in Corruption Case." Press release, March 21, 2014, http://www.afdb.org/en/news-and-events/article/afdb-levies-us-17-million-in-financial-penalties-in-corruption-case-12923/.

Agostini, Renata. "Odebrecht tem R$ 1,5 bi bloqueado pelo BNDES por obras no exterior." *Folha de São Paolo*, October 2, 2017.

Akande, Dapo and Sangeeta Shah. "Immunities of State Officials, International Crimes, and Foreign Domestic Courts." *European Journal of International Law* 21, no. 4 (2010): 815–852.

Akerlof, George A. and Rachel E. Kranton. "Economics and Identity." *Quarterly Journal of Economics* 140 (2000): 715–753.

Ala'i, Padideh. "The Legacy of Geographical Morality and Colonialism: A Historical Assessment of the Current Crusade Against Corruption." *Vanderbilt Journal of Transnational Law* 33, no. 4 (2000): 877–932.

Alemanno, Alberto. "Is There a Role for Cost-Benefit Analysis Beyond the Nation-State? Lessons from International Regulatory Cooperation." In *The Globalization of Cost-Benefit Analysis in Environmental Policy*, edited by Michael A. Livermore and Richard L. Revesz, 104–122. New York: Oxford University Press, 2013.

Alexander, Cindy R. "On the Nature of the Reputational Penalty for Corporate Crime: Evidence." *Journal of Law and Economics* 42, no. S1 (1999): 489–526.

Alexander, Michael C. *Trials in the Late Roman Republic, 149 BC to 50 BC*. Toronto, University of Toronto Press, 1990.

Alschuler, Albert W. "Two Ways to Think About the Punishment of Corporations." *American Criminal Law Review* 46, no. 4 (2009): 1359–1392.

Alter, Karen J. and Kal Raustiala. "The Rise of International Regime Complexity." *Annual Review of Law and Social Sciences* 14 (2018): 329–349.

Alvarenga, Darlan. "Impacto da Lava Jato no PIB pode passar de R$ 140 bilhões, diz estudo." Accessed March 3, 2018. http://g1.globo.com/economia/noticia/2015/08/impacto-da-lava-jato-no-pib-pode-passar-de-r-140-bilhoes-diz-estudo.html.

Ambraseys, Nicholas and Roger Bilham. "Corruption Kills." *Nature* 469, no. 7329 (January 13, 2011).

"Ananya Sengupta, Khaleda son sentenced to 6 years in jail for graft." *The Telegraph*, June 24, 2011. Available online at https://www.telegraphindia.com/1110624/jsp/foreign/story_14154323.jsp.

Andenaes, Johannes. "The General Preventive Effects of Punishment." *University of Pennsylvania Law Review* 114, no. 7 (1966): 949–983.

Andenaes, Johannes. *Punishment and Deterrence*. Ann Arbor: University of Michigan Press, 1974.

Anderson, Christopher J. and Yuliya V. Tverdova. "Corruption, Political Allegiances, and Attitudes toward Government in Contemporary Democracies." *American Journal of Political Science* 47, no. 1 (2003): 91–109.

"Angola Due to Move Toward Marxist Rule." *New York Times*, December 5, 1977.

Apel, Robert. "Sanctions, Perceptions, and Crime: Implications for Criminal Deterrence." *Journal of Quantitative Criminology* 29, no. 1 (2013): 67–101.

Arlen, Jennifer. "The Potentially Perverse Effects of Corporate Criminal Liability." *Journal of Legal Studies* 23, no. 2 (1994): 833–867.

Arlen, Jennifer. "Prosecuting Beyond the Rule of Law: Corporate Mandates Imposed through Deferred Prosecution Agreements." *Journal of Legal Analysis* 8, no. 1 (2016): 191–234.

Arlen, Jennifer and Samuel W. Buell. "The Global Expansion of Corporate Criminal Liability: Effective Enforcement Policy Across Legal Systems" (unpublished draft dated November 16, 2018).

Arlen, Jennifer and Marcel Kahan. "Corporate Governance Regulation Through Non-Prosecution." *University of Chicago Law Review* 84, no. 1 (2017): 323–387.

Arlen, Jennifer and Reinier Kraakman. "Controlling Corporate Misconduct: An Analysis of Corporate Liability Regimes." *New York University Law Review* 72, no. 4 (1997): 687–779.

Arnell, Paul. "The Case for Nationality Based Jurisdiction." *International and Comparative Law Quarterly* 50, no.4 (2001): 955–962.

Ashe, Daniel Patrick. "The Lengthening Anti-Bribery Lasso of the United States: The Recent Extraterritorial Application of the U.S. Foreign Corrupt Practices Act." *Fordham Law Review* 73, no. 6 (2005): 2897–2945.

Ayres, Ian and John Braithwaite. *Responsive Regulation: Transcending the Deregulation Debate*. New York: Oxford University Press, 1992.

Bacon, Kenneth H. "Amnesty Gap." *Wall Street Journal*, September 9, 1975.

Baer, Miriam Hechler. "Governing Corporate Compliance." *Boston College Law Review* 50 (2009): 949–1019.

Barboza, David. "Drug Giant Faced a Reckoning as China Took Aim at Bribery." *New York Times*, November 1, 2016.

Bardhan, Pranab. "Corruption and Development: A Review of Issues." *Journal of Economic Literature* 35, no. 3 (1997): 1320–1346.

Barnett, Randy E. "Restitution: A New Paradigm of Criminal Justice." *Ethics* 87, no. 4 (1977): 279–301.

Basu, Kaushik. "Why, for a Class of Bribes, the Act of Giving a Bribe Should Be Treated as Legal." *MPRA Paper No.* 50335 (2011), http://www.kaushikbasu.org/Act_Giving_Bribe_Legal.pdf.

BCR. "Odebrecht tendría un impacto negativo de hasta 0,6% en el PBI." *El Commercio*, September 13, 2017.

Beale, Sara Sun. "A Response to the Critics of Corporate Criminal Liability." *American Criminal Law Review* 46, no. 4 (2009): 1481–1505.

Becker, Gary. "Crime and Punishment: An Economic Approach." *Journal of Political Economy* 76, no. 2 (1968): 169–217.

Beetham, David. *The Legitimation of Power* 2d ed. New York: Palgrave Macmillan, 2013.

Bertelsmann Stiftung, *Transformation Index of the Bertelsmann Stiftung 2018: Codebook for Country Assessments* (2018).

Bertrand, Marianne, Simeon Djankov, Rema Hanna, and Sendhil Mullainathan. "Obtaining a Driver's License in India: An Experimental Approach to Studying Corruption." *Quarterly Journal of Economics* 122, no. 4 (2007): 1639–1676.

Binder, Guyora. "Authority to Proscribe and Punish International Crimes." *University of Toronto Law Journal* 63, no. 2 (2013): 278–309.

Blackstone, Sir William. *Commentaries on the Laws of England*. Oxford: Clarendon Press, 1765–1769.

Blake, Michael. "Distributive Justice, State Coercion, and Autonomy." *Philosophy & Public Affairs* 30, no. 3 (2001): 257–296.

"Blanchiment: 8 millions d'euros d'amende pour un ex-ministre nigérian du Pétrole." *Jeune Afrique*, March 18, 2009.

Blanco, Kenneth A. "Remarks at Foreign Corrupt Practices Act/Organization for Economic Cooperation and Development Anniversary Conference at the NYU School of Law." November 9, 2017. https://www.justice.gov/opa/speech/acting-assistant-attorney-general-kenneth-blanco-delivers-remarks-foreign-corrupt.

BMI Research. "Brazil Infrastructure Report Q4." 2017.

Bogdan, Michael. "International Trade and the New Swedish Provisions on Corruption." *American Journal of Comparative Law* 27, no. 4 (1979): 665–677.

Boisson de Chazournes, Laurence and Edouard Fromageau. "Balancing the Scales: The World Bank Sanctions Process and Access to Remedies." *European Journal of International Law* 23, no. 4 (2012): 963–989.

Boister, Neil. "'Transnational Criminal Law'?" *European Journal of International Law* 14, no. 5 (2003): 953–976.

Bottoms, Anthony and Justice Tankebe. "Beyond Procedural Justice: A Dialogic Approach to Legitimacy in Criminal Justice." *Journal of Criminal Law and Criminology* 102, no.1 (2012): 119–170.

Bouras, Stelios. "Greek Court Indicts 64 in Siemens-OTE Bribery Case." *Wall Street Journal*, March 9, 2015.

Bowen, H.V. "A Question of Sovereignty? The Bengal Land Revenue Issue, 1765–67." *Journal of Imperial and Commonwealth History* 16, no. 2 (1988): 155–176.

Braithwaite, John. "Restorative Justice: Assessing Optimistic and Pessimistic Accounts." *Crime and Justice* 25 (1999): 1–127.

Braithwaite, John. *Crime, Shame and Reintegration*. New York: Cambridge University Press, 1989.

Brandt, Ricardo, Julia Affonso, Fausto Macedo, Luiz Vassallo, and Fábio Serapião. "Governo reduz equipe da Lava Jato e corta verba da PF." *Estadão*, May 21, 2017. http://politica.estadao.com.br/blogs/fausto-macedo/governo-reduz-equipe-da-lava-jato-e-corta-verba-da-pf/.

Braskem. *2014 Annual Report*. Accessed December 31, 2018, http://www.braskem-ri.com.br/annual-reports/2014.

Brewster, Rachel. "Enforcing the FCPA: International Resonance and Domestic Strategy." *Virginia Law Review* 103, no. 8 (2017): 1611–1682.

Brewster, Rachel and Samuel W. Buell. "The Market for Global Anticorruption Enforcement." *Law and Contemporary Problems* 80 (2017): 193–214.

Brilmayer, Lea. *Conflict of Laws.* New York: Little, Brown & Company, 1995.

Brown, H. Lowell. "Extraterritorial Jurisdiction Under the 1998 Amendments to the Foreign Corrupt Practices Act: Does the Government's Reach Now Exceed Its Grasp." *North Carolina Journal of International Law and Commercial Regulation* 26, no. 2 (2001): 239–360.

Buchanan, Allen. "Political Legitimacy and Democracy." *Ethics* 112, no. 4 (2002): 689–719.

Buchanan, Allen and Robert O. Keohane. "The Legitimacy of Global Governance Institutions." *Ethics & International Affairs* 20, no. 4 (2006): 405–437.

Buell, Samuel W. "Culpability and Modern Crime." *Georgetown Law Journal* 103, no. 3 (2015): 547–603.

Buell, Samuel W. "The Upside of Overbreadth." *New York University Law Review* 83, no. 5 (2008): 1491–1564.

Burke, Edmund. *The Writings and Speeches of Edmund Burke: Vol. VI, India: The Launching of the Hastings Impeachment 1786–1788*, ed. P.J. Marshall. New York: Oxford University Press, 1991.

Burke, Edmund. *The Writings and Speeches of Edmund Burke: Vol. VII, India: The Hastings Trial 1789–1794*, ed. P.J. Marshall. New York: Oxford University Press, 2000.

Burke, Edmund. "Motion Relative to the Speech from the Throne, 14 June 1784." In *The Works of Edmund Burke Vol. 2.* London: Henry G. Bohn, 1855.

Burke, Edmund. "Speech on the Sixth Article of Charge: Fourth Day: Thursday, May 7, 1789." In *The Works of the Right Honorable Edmund Burke*, 8th ed., Vol. X. Boston: Little, Brown, 1884.

Buttonwood. "What Is the OECD?" *The Economist*, July 6, 2017.

"Buying Favor: United Brands Paid Bribe of $l.25 Million to Honduran Official Cut in Banana-Tax Rate Was Goal; SEC Probes Affair; Other Payoffs Conceded Suicide Sparked the Inquiry." *Wall Street Journal*, April 9, 1975.

Canache, Damarys and Michael E. Allison. "Perceptions of Political Corruption in Latin American Democracies." *Latin American Politics and Society* 47, no. 3 (2005): 91–111.

Caney, Simon. "Cosmopolitan Justice and Equalizing Opportunities." *Metaphilosophy* 32, nos. 1–2 (2001): 113–134.

Caney, Simon. *Justice Beyond Borders: A Global Political Theory*. New York: Oxford University Press, 2005.

Carp, Benjamin L. *Defiance of the Patriots: The Boston Tea Party and the Making of America.* New Haven: Yale University Press, 2010.

Carson, Thomas L. "Bribery, Extortion, and 'The Foreign Corrupt Practices Act.'" *Philosophy & Public Affairs* 14, no. 1 (1985): 66–90.

Chayes, Sarah. *Thieves of State: Why Corruption Threatens Global Security.* New York: W.W. Norton & Company, 2015.

Chehtman, Alejandro. *The Philosophical Foundations of Extraterritorial Punishment.* London: Oxford University Press, 2011.

Chen, Feng. "The Dilemma of Eudaemonic Legitimacy in Post-Mao China." *Polity* 29, no. 3 (1997): 421–439.

"China Mobile executive gets death in bribery case." *Shanghai Daily*, June 21, 2011. Available online at http://www.china.org.cn/china/2011-06/21/content_22831176.htm.

Cicero. *On Obligations*, ed. Peter G. Walsh. New York: Oxford University Press, 2000.

Cicero. *The Republic*. In *Cicero, The Republic and the Laws*, trans. Niall Rudd; ed. Jonathan G. F. Powell. New York: Oxford University Press, 2009.

Cicero. *Verrine Orations*, trans. L.H.G. Greenwood. Cambridge: Harvard University Press, 1928.

Clinard, Marshall B. *Corporate Corruption: The Abuse of Power*. New York: Praeger, 1990.

CNBC Squawkbox, May 15, 2012, 7:30 a.m. ET, at 14:15–19:24. Available online at http://video.cnbc.com/gallery/?video=3000089630&play=1.

Cocks, Tim and Joe Brock. "Special Report: Anatomy of Nigeria's $20 billion 'leak.'" *Reuters*, February 6, 2015.

Coffee, John C. "'No Soul to Damn: No Body to Kick': An Unscandalized Inquiry into the Problem of Corporate Punishment." *Michigan Law Review* 79, no. 3 (1981): 386–459.

Coffee, Jr., John C. "Beyond the Shut-Eyed Sentry: Toward a Theoretical View of Corporate Misconduct and an Effective Legal Response." *Virginia Law Review* 63, no. 7 (1977): 1099–1278.

Cohen, Joshua and Charles Sabel. "Extram Republicam Nulla Justitia?" *Philosophy & Public Affairs* 34, no. 2 (2006): 147–175.

Coleman, Jules L. *Markets, Morals, and the Law*. New York: Oxford University Press, 1988.

Committee on Banking, Housing and Urban Affairs, United States Senate, 94th Congress, *Report of the Securities and Exchange Commission on Questionable and Illegal Corporate Payments and Practices* 39–40 (Committee Print 1976).

Connors, Will and Paul Kiernan. "Behind the Fall of Marcelo Odebrecht, Brazil's Construction 'Prince.'" *Wall Street Journal*, December 17, 2015.

Cooter, Robert and Ariel Porat. "Should Courts Deduct Nonlegal Sanctions from Damages?" *Journal of Legal Studies* 30, no.2 (2001): 401–422.

"Corruption: The only thing that works." *Economist*, June 20, 2015.

"Corruption in Nigeria: The $20-billion hole in Africa's largest economy," *Economist*, February 2, 2016 (quoting Andrew S. Nevin, PwC).

Corruption Watch UK. "Out of Court, Out of Mind: Do Deferred Prosecution Agreements and Corporate Settlements Fail to Deter Overseas Corruption." March 2016. https://www.cw-uk.org/single-post/2016/03/10/Out-of-Court-Out-of-Mind-%E2%80%93-do-Deferred-Prosecution-Agreements-and-Corporate-Settlements-deter-overseas-corruption.

Costa Rica. *Corrupción y daño social: Presentado por el Gobierno de Costa Rica* (13 October 2011) CAC/COSP/2011/CRP.6.

Criminal Division of the US Department of Justice and the Enforcement Division of the US Securities and Exchange Commission. *A Resource Guide to the U.S. Foreign Corrupt Practices Act* (2012).

Cuéllar, Mariano-Florentino. "The Tenuous Relationship between the Fight against Money Laundering and the Disruption of Criminal Finance." *Journal of Criminal Law and Criminology* 93, no. 2 (2003): 311–466.

Cuervo-Cazurra, Alvaro. "Who Cares About Corruption?" *Journal of International Business Studies* 37, no. 6 (2006): 807–822.

Curtin, Dierdre and Linda Senden. "Public Accountability of Transnational Private Regulation: Chimera or Reality?" *Journal of Law and Society* 38, no. 1 (2011): 163–188.

D'Souza, Anna. "The OECD Anti-Bribery Convention: Changing the Currents of Trade." *Journal of Development Economics* 97, no. 1 (2012): 73–87.

Danila Serra and Leonard Wantchekon eds. *New Advances in Experimental Research on Corruption*. Bingley, UK: Emerald, 2012.

Dann, Philipp. *The Law of Development Cooperation: A Comparative Analysis of the World Bank, the EU and Germany*. New York: Cambridge University Press, 2013.

Davis, Frederick T. "International Double Jeopardy: U.S. Prosecutions and the Developing Law in Europe." *American University International Law Review* 31, no. 1 (2016): 57–101.

Davis, Kevin E. "Contracts Procured Through Bribery: Zero Tolerance versus Proportional Liability." *New York University Journal of International Law & Politics* 50, no. 4 (2018): 1261–1319.

Davis, Kevin E. "Does the Globalization of Anti-Corruption Law Help Developing Countries?" In *International Economic Law, Globalization and Developing Countries*, edited by Julio Faundez and Celine Tan, 283–306. Cheltenham: Edward Elgar, 2010.

Davis, Kevin E. "Legal Universalism: Persistent Objections." *University of Toronto Law Journal* 60, no. 2 (2010): 537–553.

Davis, Kevin E. "Multjurisdictional Enforcement Games." In *Research Handbook on Corporate Crime and Financial Misdealing*, edited by Jennifer Arlen, 151–174. Cheltenham: Edward Elgar, 2018.

Davis, Kevin E. "Self-interest and Altruism in the Deterrence of Transnational Bribery." *American Law and Economics Review* 4, no. 2 (2002): 314–340.

Davis, Kevin E. "The Limits of Evidence-Based Regulation: The Case of Anti-Bribery Law" (unpublished draft).

Davis, Kevin E. "Why Does the United States Regulate Foreign Bribery: Moralism, Self-Interest or Altruism?" *New York University Annual Survey of American Law* 67, no. 3 (2012): 497–512.

Davis, Kevin E., Guillermo Jorge, and Maíra R. Machado. "Transnational Anticorruption Law in Action: Cases from Argentina and Brazil." *Law & Social Inquiry* 40, no. 3 (2015): 664–699.

Davis, Michael. "How to Make the Punishment Fit the Crime." *Ethics* 93, no. 4 (1983): 726–752.

De Búrca, Gráinne, Robert O. Keohane, and Charles Sabel. "Global experimentalist governance." *British Journal of Political Science* 44, no. 3 (2014): 477–486.

De Geest, Gerrit and Giuseppe Dari-Mattiacci. "The Rise of Carrots and the Decline of Sticks." *University of Chicago Law Review* 80, no. 1 (2013): 341–393.

de Sousa, Luís, Peter Larmour, and Barry Hindess eds. *Governments, NGOs and Anti-corruption: The New Integrity Warriors*. New York: Routledge, 2009.

Debevoise & Plimpton. "Anti-Corruption Enforcement in 2017: A Return to Normalcy." *FCPA Update*, 9, no. 6 (January 2018).

Dell, Gillian and Andrew McDevitt. *Exporting Corruption: Progress Report 2018: Assessing Enforcement of the OECD Anti-Bribery Convention*. Berlin: Transparency International, 2018.

Dirks, Nicholas B. *The Scandal of Empire*. Cambridge, MA: Harvard University Press, 2006.

Dolan, Kerry A. and Rafael Marques de Morais. "How An African 'Princess' Banked $3 Billion in a Country Living on $2 a Day." *Forbes*, September 2, 2013.

Dreher, Axel and Martin Gassebner. "Greasing the Wheels? The Impact of Regulations and Corruption on Firm Entry." *Public Choice* 155, no. 3–4 (2013): 413–432.

Dressler, Joshua. "Duress." In *The Oxford Handbook of Philosophy of Criminal Law*, edited by John Deigh and David Dolinko. New York: Oxford University Press, 2011.

Dube, Ryan. "Odebrecht Bribery Scandal Shakes Up Latin America." *The Wall Street Journal*, December 22, 2016.

Duff, Antony and Zachary Hoskins. "Legal Punishment." *The Stanford Encyclopedia of Philosophy* (Fall 2017 Edition), Edward N. Zalta (ed.), https://plato.stanford.edu/archives/fall2017/entries/legal-punishment/.

Duff, R.A. *Answering for Crime: Responsibility and Liability in the Criminal Law.* London: Hart, 2007.

Duff, R.A. *Punishment, Communication, and Community*. New York: Oxford University Press, 2001.

"Elephant and the Blind Men." Accessed December 31, 2018. http://www.jainworld.com/education/stories25.asp.

Esper, George. "Communists Take Over Saigon; U.S. Rescue Fleet Is Picking Up Vietnamese Who Fled in Boats." *New York Times*, May 1, 1975.

Fédération Internationale de Football Association. *FIFA Statutes*. April 26, 2016.

Feng, Yi. "Democracy, Political Stability and Economic Growth." *British Journal of Political Science* 27, no. 3 (1997): 391–418.

Financial Accounting Standards Board. "Topic 810, Consolidation." *Accounting Standards Codification* (2009).

Financial Action Task Force. *Mutual Evaluation Report: Anti-Money Laundering and Combating the Financing of Terrorism: Germany* (February 19, 2010).

Financial Action Task Force on Money Laundering. "Annual Report." (July 2, 1999).

Financial Services Authority. *Banks' Management of High Money-Laundering Risk Situations* (June 2011).

Financial Services Authority. "FSA publishes results of money laundering investigation." Press release, FSA/PN/029/2001. March 8, 2001.

Fisse, Brent. "Reconstructing Corporate Criminal Law: Deterrence, Retribution, Fault, and Sanctions." *University of Southern California Law Review* 56, no. 6 (1983): 1141–1246.

Fisse, Brent and John Braithwaite. *Corporations, Crime and Accountability.* New York: Cambridge University Press, 1993.

Fletcher, William M. et al. *Fletcher Cyclopedia of Law of Private Corporations* (rev. vol. 2008).

Forero, Juan. "Brazil building more dams across Amazon." *Washington Post*, February 9, 2013.

"Former Nigeria state governor James Ibori receives 13-year sentence." *The Guardian*, April 17, 2012.

Fox, Hazel and Philippa Webb. *The Law of State Immunity, 3rd ed.* New York: Oxford University Press, 2015.

Franck, Thomas. *Fairness in International Law and Institutions*. Oxford: Clarendon Press, 1995.

"French Court Fines Two for Bribing Nigerians." *AFP*, January 30, 2013.

Frick, Shane. "'Ice' Capades: Restitution Orders and the FCPA." *Richmond Journal of Global Law and Business* 12, no. 3 (2013): 433–452.

Garland, David. *Punishment and Modern Society: A Study in Social Theory*. Chicago: University of Chicago Press, 1990.

Garuba, Dauda. "NIGERIA: Halliburton, Bribes and the Deceit of 'Zero-Tolerance' for Corruption." Natural Resource Governance Institute, April 9, 2009, http://archive.resourcegovernance.org/news/nigeria-halliburton-bribes-and-deceit-zero-tolerance-corruption.

Gilbert, Jo-Anne and J.C. Sharman. "Turning a Blind Eye to Bribery: Explaining Failures to Comply with the International Anti-corruption Regime." *Political Studies* 64, no. 1 (2014): 74–89.

Gilby, Nicholas. *Deception in High Places: A History of Bribery in the Britain's Arms Trade*. London: Pluto Press, 2014.

Gingerich, Daniel W., Virginia Oliveros, Ana Corbacho, and Mauricio Ruiz-Vega. "When to Protect? Using the Crosswise Model to Integrate Protected and Direct Responses in Surveys of Sensitive Behavior." *Political Analysis* 24, no. 2 (2016): 132–156.

Gitlin, Sarah. "Beyond Sextortion: How Corruption Uniquely Affects Women." *The Global Anticorruption Blog*. January 2, 2015. https://globalanticorruptionblog.com/2015/01/02/beyond-sextortion-how-corruption-uniquely-affects-women/.

Goodwin, Morag and Kate Rose-Sender. "Linking Anti-Corruptionism and Human Rights: A Dangerous Addition to the Development Discourse." In *Corruption & Human Rights: Interdisciplinary Perspectives*, edited by Martine Boersma and Hans Nelen, 221–240. Portland: Intersentia, 2010.

Green, Leslie. *The Authority of the State*. New York: Oxford University Press, 1988.

Green, Stuart P. "Official and Commercial Bribery: Should They Be Distinguished?" In *Modern Bribery Law: Comparative Perspectives*, edited by Jeremy Horder and Peter Alldridge, 39–66. New York: Cambridge University Press, 2013.

Greenwood, L.H.G. "Introduction" to *Cicero, The Verrine Orations: Volume I*, trans. L.H.G. Greenwood. Cambridge: Harvard University Press, 1928.

Grosse, Scott D. "How much does IQ raise earnings." *Implications for Regulatory Impact Analyses. Association of Environmental and Resource Economists (AERE) Newsletter* 27, no. 2 (2007): 17–21.

Gulf Oil Corporation. "Report of the Special Review Committee of the Board of Directors of Gulf Oil Corporation." Filed with the Securities and Exchange Commission as an exhibit to Form 8-K, December 30, 1975.

Gutterman, Ellen. "Banning Bribes Abroad: US Enforcement of the Foreign Corrupt Practices Act." *Osgoode Hall Law Journal* 53, no. 1 (2015): 31–65.

Halliday, Terence C. and Gregory Shaffer. "Transnational Legal Orders." In *Transnational Legal Orders*, edited by Terence C. Halliday and Gregory Shaffer, 3–72. Cambridge: Cambridge University Press, 2015.

Hastings, Esq., Warren. "Address of Warren Hastings, Esq. in his Defence Upon the Several Articles of the Charge, 2d June 1791." In *Speeches of the Managers and Counsel in the Trial of Warren Hastings, Vol. II*, edited by E.A. Bond. London: Longman, Green, Longman & Roberts, 1860.

Hecker, Sean, Alyona N. Kucher, Jane Shvets, Anna V. Maximenko, and Alisa Melekhina. "Between a Rock and a Hard Place: Anti-Corruption Compliance and Antitrust Law in Russia." *FCPA Update*, 6, no. 8 (March 2015), http://www.debevoise.com/~/media/files/insights/publications/2015/03/fcpa_update_march_2015.pdf.

Hecker, Sean and Margot Laporte. "Should FCPA 'Territorial' Jurisdiction Reach Extraterritorial Proportions?" *International Law News* 42, no. 1 (2013).

Heimann, Fritz, Ádám Földes, and Sophia Coles. *Exporting Corruption, Progress Report 2015: Assessing Enforcement of the OECD Convention on Combatting Foreign Bribery*. Berlin: Transparency International, 2015.

Heimann, Fritz and Mark Pieth. *Confronting Corruption: Past Concerns, Present Challenges, and Future Strategies*. New York: Oxford University Press, 2018.

Henley, Jon. "Dumas spreads Elf blame to ministers." *The Guardian*, June 18, 2001.

Henley, Jon. "French sleaze inquiry targets US oil subsidiary." *The Guardian*, October 10, 2003.

Henley, Jon. "Gigantic sleaze scandal winds up as former Elf oil chiefs are jailed." *The Guardian*, November 12, 2003.

Henning, Peter J. "The Mounting Costs of Internal Investigations." *New York Times*, March 5, 2012.

Hernandez, Teresa and Robert W. McGee. "A Demographic Study of African Attitudes on Bribery." *Journal of Accounting, Ethics and Public Policy* 15, no. 2 (2014): 542–596.

Hess, David and Cristie L. Ford. "Corporate Corruption and Reform Undertakings: A New Approach to an Old Problem." *Cornell International Law Journal* 41 (2008): 307–346.

Hines, Jr., James R. "Forbidden Payment: Foreign Bribery and American Business After 1977." NBER Working Paper No. 5266 (1995).

Hinsch, Wilfried. "Legitimacy and Justice: A Conceptual and Functional Clarification." In *Political Legitimization Without Morality*, edited by Jörg Kühnelt, 39–52. Dordrecht: Springer, 2008.

Holmes, Oliver Wendell. *Ralph Waldo Emerson*. New York: Houghton Mifflin, 1884.

"Honduras Plans to Buy Operating Facilities of U.S. Banana Firms." *Wall Street Journal*, August 18, 1975.

Hornsby, Jennifer. "On What's Intentionally Done." In *Action and Value in Criminal Law*, edited by Stephen Shute, John Gardner, and Jeremy Horder, 55–74. Oxford: Clarendon Press, 1993.

House of Commons of Great Britain. *First Report from the Select Committee Appointed to Take into Consideration the State of the Administration of Justice in the Provinces of Bengal, Bihar, and Orissa* (London: 1782).

Hsieh, Nien-hê. "Does Global Business Have a Responsibility to Promote Just Institutions?" *Business Ethics Quarterly* 19, no. 2 (April 2009): 251–273.

http://lnadbg4.adb.org/oai001p.nsf/0/F77A326B818A19C548257853000C2B10/$FILE/cross-debarment-agreement.pdf.

Hunt, Jennifer and S Laszlo. "Is bribery really regressive? Bribery's costs, benefits, and mechanisms." *World Development* 40, no. 2 (2012): 355–372.

Huntington, Samuel P. *Political Order in Changing Societies*. Yale University Press, 1968.

Iacobucci, Edward M. "On the Interaction between Legal and Reputational Sanctions." *Journal of Legal Studies* 43, no. 1 (2014): 189–207

Idemudia, Uwafiokun and Uwem E. Ite. "Demystifying the Niger Delta Conflict: Towards an Integrated Explanation." *Review of African Political Economy* 33, no. 109 (2006): 391–406.

International Accounting Standards Board. "IFRS 10: Consolidated Financial Statements." *International Financial Reporting Standards* (2018).

International Accounting Standards Board. "IFRS 12: Disclosure of Interests in Other Entities." *International Financial Reporting Standards* (2018).

Iriekpen, Davidson. "Nigeria: Leaked Files Link Abdulsalami Abubakar, Chris Garba to U.S. $182 Million Halliburton Bribery Scandal." *allAfrica*, February 10, 2015, http://allafrica.com/stories/201502100935.html.

"Italian Court Believes Politician Got Bribe from Lockheed Corp." *Wall Street Journal*, August 6, 1979.

"Italy court upholds Saipem fine and seizure order in Nigeria case." *Reuters*, February 19, 2015.

Ivory, Radha. *Corruption, Asset Recovery, and the Protection of Property in Public International Law: The Human Rights of Bad Guys.* New York: Cambridge University Press, 2014.

Jackson, Jonathan, Ben Bradford, Mike Hough, Andy Myhill, Paul Quinton, and Tom R. Tyler. "Why Do People Comply with the Law? Legitimacy and the Influence of Legal Institutions." *British Journal of Criminology* 52, no. 6 (2012): 1051–1071.

Jelmayer, Rogerio and Samantha Pearson. "Brazil Corruption Scandal Has Companies Rushing to Bulk Up Compliance Ranks." *Wall Street Journal*, February 23, 2017.

Jensen, Nathan and Edmund J. Malesky. "Nonstate Actors and Compliance with International Agreements: An Empirical Analysis of the OECD Anti-Bribery Convention." *International Organization* 72, no. 1 (2018): 33–69.

Jessup, Philip C. *Transnational Law*. New Haven: Yale University Press, 1956.

Jones, Ashby. "Is the FCPA Standing in the Way of Haiti's Recovery?" *Wall Street Journal Law Blog*, March 16, 2010, 4:10 p.m.

Justesen, Mogens K. and Christian Bjørnskov. "Exploiting the Poor: Bureaucratic Corruption and Poverty in Africa." *World Development* 58, issue C (2014): 106–115.

Kahan, Dan M. and Eric A. Posner. "Shaming White-Collar Criminals: A Proposal for Reform of the Federal Sentencing Guidelines." *Journal of Law and Economics* 42, no. S1 (1999): 365–392.

Kaiser, Anna Jean. "Brazil's President Temer Avoids a New Corruption Trial." *Washington Post*, October 25, 2017.

Kamisher, Byeliyahu. "Five Senior Israel Electric Company Employees Sentenced in Massive Siemens Bribery Case." *Jerusalem Post*, June 13, 2017.

Kant, Immanuel. *Perpetual Peace: A Philosophical Essay*, trans. M. Campbell Smith. New York: Macmillan, 1917 (1795).

Karpoff, Jonathan M., D. Scott Lee, and Gerald S. Martin. "Foreign Bribery: Incentives and Enforcement." April 7, 2017, https://ssrn.com/abstract=1573222 or http://dx.doi.org/10.2139/ssrn.1573222.

Karpoff, Jonathan M. and John R. Lott, Jr. "The Reputational Penalty Firms Bear from Committing Criminal Fraud." *Journal of Law and Economics* 36, no. 2 (1993): 757–802.

Keefe, Patrick Radden. "Limited Liability: Why don't corporate wrongdoers get charged?" *The New Yorker*, July 31, 2017.

Kihss, Peter. "44-Story Plunge Kills Head of United Brands." *New York Times*, February 4, 1975.

Klaw, Bruce W. "State Responsibility for Bribe Solicitation and Extortion: Obligations, Obstacles, and Opportunities." *Berkeley Journal of International Law* 33, no. 1 (2015):60–113.

Koehler, Mike. "FCPA Inc. and the Business of Bribery." *FCPA Professor,* February 21, 2012. http://fcpaprofessor.com/fcpa-inc-and-the-business-of-bribery/.

Koehler, Mike. "Significant dd-3 Development in Africa Sting Case." *FCPA Professor,* June 9, 2011. http://www.fcpaprofessor.com/significant-dd-3-development-in-africa-sting-case.

Koehler, Mike. "The Story of the Foreign Corrupt Practices Act." *Ohio State Law Journal* 73, no. 5 (2012).

Kokott, Juliane. "States, Sovereign Equality." In *Max Planck Encyclopedia of Public International Law*, Oxford Public International Law. Accessed December 31, 2018.

Kornhauser, Lewis A. "A Guide to the Perplexed Claims of Efficiency in the Law." *Hofstra Law Review* 8, no. 3 (1980): 591–640.

Kraay, Art and Peter Murrell. "Misunderestimating Corruption." Policy Research Working Paper 6488, World Bank, Washington, D.C. (June, 2013).

Krueger, Anne O. "The political economy of the rent-seeking society." *American Economic Review* 64, no. 3 (1974): 291–303.

Lambsdorff, Johann Graf. "Who Accepts Bribery? Evidence from a Global Household Survey." *Passau University Discussion Paper*, 61–10, October 2010.

Langer, Máximo. "From Legal Transplants to Legal Translations: The Globalization of Plea Bargaining and the Americanization Thesis in Criminal Procedure." *Harvard International Law Journal* 45, no. 1 (2004): 1–64.

Laufer, William S. "The Missing Account of Progressive Corporate Criminal Law," *New York University Journal of Law & Business* 14, no. 1 (2017): 71–142.

Lebedev, Alexander. "A World Corruption Police." *New York Times*, February 26, 2014.

Leff, Nathaniel H. "Economic development through bureaucratic corruption." *American Behavioral Scientist* 8, no. 3 (1964): 8–14.

Leibold, Annalisa. "Extraterritorial Application of the FCPA under International Law." *Willamette Law Review* 51, no. 2 (2015): 225–268.

Leroy, Anne-Marie and Frank Fariello. *The World Bank Group Sanctions Process and Its Recent Reforms*. Washington D.C.: World Bank, 2012.

Letter from Corruption Watch UK, Transparency International. UNCAC Coalition and Global Witness to Angel Gurría regarding Global Standards for Corporate Settlements in Foreign Bribery Cases (March 10, 2016). http://uncaccoalition.org/files/OECD-Ministerial-letter.pdf.

Levi, Michael and Peter Reuter. "Money Laundering." *Crime and Justice* 34, no. 1 (2006): 289–375.

Lewinsohn, Jed. "Paid on Both Sides: *Quid Pro Quo* Exchange and the Doctrine of Consideration" (unpublished draft dated October 16, 2018).

Leys, Colin. "What Is the Problem about Corruption?" *Journal of Modern African Studies* 3, no. 2 (1965): 215–230.

Lindsey, Carolyn. "More than You Bargained For: Successor Liability under the U.S. Foreign Corrupt Practices Act." *Ohio Northern University Law Review* 35, no. 3 (2009): 959–986.

Lintott, Andrew. *Cicero as Evidence: A Historian's Companion*. New York: Oxford University Press, 2008.

Liscow, Zachary. "Is Efficiency Biased?" *University of Chicago Law Review* 85, no.7 (2018): 1649–1718.

Locke, John. *Second Treatise of Government: An Essay Concerning the True Original, Extent and End of Civil Government*, edited by Richard H. Cox. Wheeling: Harlan Davidson, 1982 (1698).

Lockheed. "Report of the Special Review Committee of the Board of Directors of Lockheed Aircraft Corporation." Filed with the Securities and Exchange Commission as an exhibit to Form 8-K, May 15, 1975.

"Lockheed Executive Dies." *Wall Street Journal*, August 25, 1975.

Lohr, Steve. "Tanaka Is Guilty in Bribery Trial." *New York Times*, October 12, 1983.

Londoño, Ernesto. "Brazil Shuts Down Successful Corruption-Fighting Task Force." *New York Times*, July 7, 2017.

Long, George. "Repetundae." In William Smith, *A Dictionary of Greek and Roman Antiquities*, 986–987. London: John Murray, 1875. Accessed December 31, 2018. http://penelope.uchicago.edu/Thayer/E/Roman/Texts/secondary/SMIGRA*/Repetundae.html.

Lopes, Marina and Nick Miroff. "A corruption scandal wrecked Brazil's economy. Now, workers face the consequences." *Washington Post*, June 19, 2017.

Löscher, Peter. "The CEO of Siemens on Using a Scandal to Drive Change." *Harvard Business Review* (November 2012): 39–42.

Malesky, Edmund et al. *The Vietnam Provincial Competitiveness Index: Measuring Economic Governance for Private Sector Development, 2015 Final Report*. Labour Publishing House, 2016.

Manion, Melanie. *Corruption by Design: Building Clean Government in Mainland China and Hong Kong*. Cambridge: Harvard University Press, 2004.

Marshall, P.J. *The Impeachment of Warren Hastings*. London: Oxford University Press, 1965.

Marshall, P.J. ed. *The Writings and Speeches of Edmund Burke: Vol. VI, India: The Launching of the Hastings Impeachment 1786–1788*. New York: Oxford University Press, 1991.

Marshall, P.J. ed. *The Writings and Speeches of Edmund Burke: Vol. VII, India: The Hastings Trial 1789–1794*. New York: Oxford University Press, 2000.

Méon, Pierre-Guillaume and Laurent Weill. "Is Corruption an Efficient Grease?" *World Development* 38, no. 3 (2010): 244–259.

Metzger, Michael B. "Corporate Criminal Liability for Defective Products: Policies, Problems, and Prospects." *Georgetown Law Journal* 73, no. 1 (1984): 1–88.

Ministério Público Federal. "A Lava Jato em números no Paraná." Accessed January 14, 2018. http://www.mpf.mp.br/para-o-cidadao/caso-lava-jato/atuacao-na-1a-instancia/resultado.

Ministério Público Federal. "Equipe de Investigação no Ministério Público Federal." Accessed January 2, 2018. http://www.mpf.mp.br/para-o-cidadao/caso-lava-jato/equipe-no-mpf.

Ministério Público Federal. "MPF firma acordos de leniência com Odebrecht e Braskem." Accessed December 21, 2016. http://www.mpf.mp.br/pgr/noticias-pgr/mpf-firma-acordos-de-leniencia-com-odebrecht-e-braskem.

Morrell, Kit. *Pompey, Cato, and the Governance of the Roman Empire*. Oxford: Oxford University Press, 2017.

Müller, Luise K. "Universal Jurisdiction, Pirates and Vigilantes." *Critical Review of International Social and Political Philosophy* (2017). DOI: 10.1080/13698230.2017.1390660.

Multinational Corporations and United States Foreign Policy: Hearings Before the Subcomm. on Multinational Corps. of the S. Comm. on Foreign Relations, 94th Cong., Part 12 (1975).

Mungan, Murat C. "A Generalized Model for Reputational Sanctions and the (Ir) Relevance of the Interactions between Legal and Reputational Sanctions." *International Review of Law and Economics* 46 (2016): 86–92.

Muzila, Lindy et al. *On The Take: Criminalizing Illicit Enrichment to Fight Corruption.* Washington D.C.: World Bank, 2012.

Nagel, Thomas. "The Problem of Global Justice." *Philosophy & Public Affairs* 33, no. 2 (2005): 113–147.

Nagin, Daniel S. "Criminal Deterrence Research at the Outset of the Twenty-First Century." *Crime and Justice* 23 (1998): 1–42.

Naik, Asmita. "Protecting Children from the Protectors: Lessons from West Africa." *Forced Migration Review* 15 (2002): http://www.fmreview.org/sites/fmr/files/FMRdownloads/en/FMRpdfs/FMR15/fmr15.7.pdf.

Naylor, R.T. "Wash-Out: A Critique of Follow-the-Money Methods in Crime Control Policy." *Crime, Law and Social Change* 32, no. 1 (1999): 1–57.

Newcomb, Danforth. *Digests of Cases and Review Releases Relating to Bribes to Foreign Officials Under the Foreign Corrupt Practices Act of 1977 (as of January 31, 2002).* New York: Shearman & Sterling, 2002. Accessed December 31, 2018. https://www.justice.gov/sites/default/files/criminal-fraud/legacy/2012/12/03/response2-appx-a.pdf.

Nichols, Philip M., George J. Siedel, and Matthew Kasdin. "Corruption as a Pan-Cultural Phenomenon: An Empirical Study in Countries at Opposite Ends of the Former Soviet Empire." *Texas International Law Journal* 39, no. 2 (2004): 215–256.

Nicholson, Chris V. "Petrobras Raises $70 billion in Share Issue." *New York Times*, September 24, 2010.

"Nigeria's ex-oil minister 'arrested in London.'" *BBC News*, October 2, 2015.

Nolen, Stephanie. "Corruption beyond Brazil: Where the 'Car Wash' scandal has splashed across Latin America." *Globe and Mail*, June 7, 2017 (updated November 12, 2017).

Noon, Chris. "OECD Concerned by U.K. Move on BAE." *Forbes*, January 18, 2007. https://www.forbes.com/2007/01/18/bae-oecd-uk-markets-equity-cx_cn_0118markets04.html#56cb53bf2eb3.

Noonan, John T. *Bribes.* New York: Macmillan, 1984.

Norris, Pippa, Andrea Abel van Es, and Lisa Fennis. *Checkbook Elections: Political Finance in Comparative Perspective—Executive Report.* Sydney: Money, Politics and Transparency, 2015. Accessed December 31, 2018. https://www.dropbox.com/s/9f2c5sxxd6mh9wc/Checbook%20Elections%2C%20MPT%2C%202015%20-%20final%20spreads.pdf?dl=0.

Nossiter, Adam. "Governor of Nigeria's Central Bank Is Fired After Warning of Missing Oil Revenue." *New York Times*, February 20, 2014.

Nye, J.S. "Corruption and Political Development: A Cost-Benefit Analysis." *American Political Science Review* 61, no. 2 (1967): 417–427.

Obama, Barack. "Remarks by the President at the Millennium Development Goals Summit in New York." (speech, New York, NY, September 22, 2010), http://www.whitehouse.gov/the-press-office/2010/09/22/remarks-president-millennium-development-goals-summit-new-york-new-york.

Odebrecht S.A. *Annual Report 2015*, accessed March 2, 2018, https://www.odebrecht.com/sites/default/files/ra_odebrecht_2015_en_0.pdf.

Odebrecht. "Odebrecht signs agreement with authorities in Brazil, United States and Switzerland." December 21, 2016, https://www.odebrecht.com/en/communication/releases/odebrecht-signs-agreement-authorities-brazil-united-states-and-switzerland.

Odebrecht. *Annual Report, 2015.*

Odebrecht. *Annual Report, 2017.*

Odebrecht. "Emílio announces exit and changes in the Board of Directors of Odebrecht." Press release, December 15, 2017.

Odebrecht. "Odebrecht Engenharia e Construção posts net income of R$ 890 million in 2015." Press release, June 6, 2016.

"Odebrecht tenta mudar imagem com 'compliance' *Época Negócios*, April 15, 2017, https://epocanegocios.globo.com/Empresa/noticia/2017/04/epoca-negocios-odebrecht-tenta-mudar-imagem-com-compliance.html.

Oduour, Jacinta Anyango et al. *Left Out of the Bargain: Implications of Settlements on Asset Recovery.* Washington D.C.: World Bank, 2014.

OECD Anti-Corruption Network for Eastern Europe and Central Asia. *Foreign Bribery Offence and its Enforcement in Eastern Europe and Central Asia*. OECD, 2016.

OECD Committee on International Investment and Multinational Enterprises. *Commentaries on the Convention on Combating Bribery of Foreign Public Officials in International Business Transactions* (1997), https://www.justice.gov/sites/default/files/criminal-fraud/legacy/2012/11/14/combatbribe2.pdf.

OECD Working Group on Bribery. *2015 Data on Enforcement of the Anti-Bribery Convention*. November 2016. Accessed December 31, 2018, http://www.oecd.org/daf/anti-bribery/WGB-Enforcement-Data-2015.pdf.

OECD Working Group on Bribery. *2016 Data on Enforcement of the Anti-Bribery Convention*. November 2017. Accessed December 31, 2018, https://www.oecd.org/daf/anti-bribery/Anti-Bribery-Convention-Enforcement-Data-2016.pdf.

OECD Working Group on Bribery. *Annual Report 2006.*

OECD Working Group on Bribery. *Australia: Phase 2 Report on the Application of the Convention on Combating Bribery Of Foreign Public Officials In International Business Transactions and the 1997 Recommendation on Combating Bribery In International Business Transactions.* January 4, 2006.

OECD Working Group on Bribery. *Compilation of Recommendations made in the Phase 3 Reports.* December 2014.

OECD Working Group on Bribery. *Germany: Follow-Up to the Phase 3 Report & Recommendations.* April 2013.

OECD Working Group on Bribery. *Greece: Phase 2: Report on The Application of The Convention on Combating Bribery of Foreign Public Officials In International Business Transactions and the 1997 Revised Recommendation on Combating Bribery in International Business Transactions*. April 2005.

OECD Working Group on Bribery. *Implementing the OECD Anti-Bribery Convention: Phase 4 Report: Czech Republic.* June 2017.

OECD Working Group on Bribery. *Phase 1 Report on Implementing the OECD Anti-Bribery Convention in the Russian Federation*. March 2012.

OECD Working Group on Bribery. *Phase 2 Report on Implementing the OECD Anti-Bribery Convention in the Slovak Republic*. November 2005.

OECD Working Group on Bribery. *Phase 3 Report on Implementing the OECD Anti-Bribery Convention in Australia*. October 2012.

OECD Working Group on Bribery. *Phase 3 Report on Implementing the OECD Anti-Bribery Convention in Canada*. March 2011.

OECD Working Group on Bribery. *Phase 3 Report on Implementing the OECD Anti-Bribery Convention in the Czech Republic*. March 2013.

OECD Working Group on Bribery. *Phase 3 Report on Implementing the OECD Anti-Bribery Convention in Denmark*. March 2013.

OECD Working Group on Bribery. *Phase 3 Report on Implementing the OECD Convention in Germany*. March 2011.

OECD Working Group on Bribery. *Phase 3 Report on Implementing the OECD Anti-Bribery Convention in Ireland*. December 2013.

OECD Working Group on Bribery. *Phase 3 Report on Implementing the OECD Anti-Bribery Convention in the Norway*. June 2011.

OECD Working Group on Bribery. *Phase 3 Report on Implementing the OECD Anti-Bribery Convention in Portugal*. June 2013.

OECD Working Group on Bribery. *Phase 3 Report on Implementing the OECD Anti-Bribery Convention in the Slovak Republic*. June 2012.

OECD Working Group on Bribery. *Phase 3 Report on Implementing the OECD Anti-Bribery Convention in Slovenia*. June 2014.

OECD Working Group on Bribery. *Phase 3 Report on Implementing the OECD Anti-Bribery Convention in Spain*. December 2012.

OECD Working Group on Bribery. *Phase 3 Report on Implementing the OECD Anti-Bribery Convention in the United Kingdom*. March 2012.

OECD Working Group on Bribery. *Portugal: Follow-Up to the Phase 3 Report & Recommendations*. November 2015.

OECD Working Group on Bribery. *Portugal: Phase 2: Report on The Application of The Convention on Combating Bribery of Foreign Public Officials In International Business Transactions and the 1997 Revised Recommendation on Combating Bribery in International Business Transactions*. March 2007.

OECD Working Group on Bribery. *Resolving Foreign Bribery Cases with Non-Trial Resolutions: Settlements and Non-Trial Agreements by Parties to the Anti-Bribery Convention*. 2019. Accessed April 16, 2019, http://www.oecd.org/daf/anti-bribery/Resolving-foreign-bribery-cases-with-non-trial-resolutions.htm

OECD Working Group on Bribery. *Slovak Republic: Phase 2: Report on The Application of The Convention on Combating Bribery of Foreign Public Officials In International Business Transactions and the 1997 Revised Recommendation on Combating Bribery in International Business Transactions*. November 2005.

OECD Working Group on Bribery. *Slovenia: Follow-Up to the Phase 3 Report & Recommendations*. July 2016.

OECD Working Group on Bribery. *Slovenia: Phase 2: Report on The Application of The Convention on Combating Bribery of Foreign Public Officials In International Business Transactions and the 1997 Revised Recommendation on Combating Bribery in International Business Transactions*. June 2007.

OECD Working Group on Bribery. *Spain: Follow-Up to the Phase 3 Report & Recommendations*. March 2015.

OECD Working Group on Bribery. *Spain: Phase 2: Report on The Application of The Convention on Combating Bribery of Foreign Public Officials In International Business Transactions and the 1997 Revised Recommendation on Combating Bribery in International Business Transactions.* March 2006.

OECD Working Group on Bribery. *United Kingdom Review of Implementation of the Convention and 1997 Recommendation.* 1999.

OECD. "Is foreign bribery an attractive investment in some countries?" *OECD Business and Finance Outlook 2016.* Accessed December 31, 2018, http://www.oecd.org/daf/anti-bribery/BFO-2016-Ch7-Bribery.pdf.

OECD. "The legal framework for the treatment of proceeds of active bribery." In OECD/The World Bank, *Identification and Quantification of the Proceeds of Bribery. A joint OECD-StAR analysis. Revised edition,* 15–28. OECD, February 2012.

OECD. Latin American and Caribbean Competition Forum Session II: Leniency Programmes in Latin America and the Caribbean—Recent Experiences and Lessons Learned—Contribution from Brazil—DAF/COMP/LACF (2016) 6 (March 14, 2016).

OECD. *The Liability of Legal Persons for Foreign Bribery: A Stocktaking Report.* 2016. Accessed December 31, 2018, https://www.oecd.org/daf/anti-bribery/Liability-Legal-Persons-Foreign-Bribery-Stocktaking.pdf.

Office of the Attorney General of Switzerland. "Petrobras-Odebrecht Affair: The Office of the Attorney General of Switzerland convicts Brazilian companies and demands payment of over CHF 200 million." December 21, 2016. Accessed December 31, 2018. https://www.admin.ch/gov/en/start/documentation/media-releases.msg-id-65077.html.

Olken, Benjamin A. and Patrick Barron. "The Simple Economics of Extortion: Evidence from Trucking in Aceh." *Journal of Political Economy* 117, no. 3 (June 2009): 417–452.

Olken, Benjamin A. and Rohini Pande. "Corruption in developing countries." *Annual Review of Economics* 4, no. 1 (2012): 479–509.

Onanuga, Adebisi. "French govt pardons former Petroleum Minister Etete." *The Nation,* March 31, 2014.

Oré, Diego. "Stalled Brazilian Odebrecht projects decay in Venezuela." *Reuters,* May 31, 2017.

"Our Organisation—FAQs on Corruption." Transparency International. Accessed July 26, 2016, http://www.transparency.org/whoweare/organisation/faqs_on_corruption.

Palazzolo, Joe. "FCPA Inc.: The Business of Bribery: Corruption Probes Become Profit Center for Big Law Firms." *Wall Street Journal,* October 2, 2012.

"Panama to cancel Odebrecht contract amid corruption scandal." *Reuters,* December 28, 2016, https://www.reuters.com/article/us-panama-corruption/panama-to-cancel-odebrecht-contract-amid-corruption-scandal-idUSKBN14H072.

Paternoster, Raymond and Sally Simpson. "Sanction Threats and Appeals to Morality: Testing a Rational Choice Model of Corporate Crime." *Law & Society Review* 30, no. 3 (1996): 549–584.

Pavarala, Vinod. "Cultures of Corruption and the Corruption of Culture: The East India Company and the Hastings Impeachment." In *Corrupt Histories,* edited by Emmanuel Kreike and William Chester Gordon, 291–336. Rochester, NY: University of Rochester Press, 2004.

"Payments Ordered in Italy." *Wall Street Journal,* July 24, 1980.

Pereira, Carlos and Marcus André Melo. "Reelecting Corrupt Incumbents in Exchange for Public Goods: Rouba mas faz in Brazil." *Latin American Research Review* 50, no. 4 (2015): 88–115.

Perlman, Rebecca L. and Alan O. Sykes. "The Political Economy of the Foreign Corrupt Practices Act: An Exploratory Analysis." *Journal of Legal Analysis* (2018) lay001, https://doi.org/10.1093/jla/lay001.

"Peru Expropriates Gulf Oil Subsidiary." *New York Times*, May 14, 1975.

Peter, Fabienne. "Political Legitimacy." In *The Stanford Encyclopedia of Philosophy* (Edward N. Zalta ed., 2016), http://plato.stanford.edu/archives/sum2016/entries/legitimacy.

Phillips, Taylor. "The Federal Common Law of Successor Liability and the Corrupt Practices Act." *William & Mary Business Law Review* 6, no .1 (2015): 89–136.

Pickett, Justin T., Thomas A. Loughran, and Shawn Bushway. "Consequences of legal risk communication for sanction perception updating and white-collar criminality." *Journal of Experimental Criminology* 12, no. 1 (2016) 75–104.

Pieth, Mark and Radha Ivory eds. *Corporate Criminal Liability: Emergence, Convergence, and Risk.* New York: Springer, 2011.

Pieth, Mark, Nicola Bonucci, and Lucinda A. Low eds. *The OECD Convention on Bribery: A Commentary 2d ed.* New York: Cambridge University Press, 2014.

Pogge, Thomas. *World Poverty and Human Rights: Cosmopolitan Responsibilities and Reforms 2d ed.* Cambridge, UK: Polity Press, 2008.

"Political Finance Database." Data & Tools, International IDEA, updated November 2018, accessed November 23, 2018, https://www.idea.int/data-tools/data/political-finance-database.

Porto, Mauro P. "The Media and Political Accountability." In *Corruption and Democracy in Brazil: The Struggle for Accountability*, edited by Timothy J. Power and Matthew M. Taylor, 103–126. Notre Dame: University of Notre Dame Pres, 2011.

Priest, George L. and Benjamin Klein. "The Selection of Disputes for Litigation." *Journal of Legal Studies* 13, no. 1 (1984): 1–55.

Protess, Ben and Jessica Silver-Greenberg. "On Defensive, JP Morgan Hired China's Elite." *New York Times*, Dec. 29, 2013, http://dealbook.nytimes.com/2013/12/29/on-defensive-jpmorgan-hired-chinas-elite/.

Rajagopal, Balakrishnan. "Corruption, Legitimacy and Human Rights: The Dialectic of the Relationship." *Connecticut Journal of International Law* 14, no. 2 (1999): 495–507.

Rakoff, Jed S. "The Financial Crisis: Why Have No High Level Executives Been Prosecuted?" *The New York Review of Books*, January 9, 2014.

Ran, Liao. "Sexual Favours Are Not Considered Corruption in China." *Transparency International—Space for Transparency*, July 16, 2013, http://blog.transparency.org/2013/07/16/sexual-favours-are-not-considered-corruption-in-china/.

Rasmusen, Eric. "Stigma and self-fulfilling expectations of criminality." *Journal of Law and Economics* 39, no. 2 (1996): 519–543.

Raustiala, Kal. "Compliance & Effectiveness in International Regulatory Cooperation." *Case Western Reserve Journal of International Law* 32, no. 3 (2000): 387–440.

Rawls, John. *Justice as Fairness: A Restatement*. Cambridge: Harvard University Press, 2001.

Rawls, John. *The Law of Peoples: With "The Idea of Public Reason Revisited."* Cambridge: Harvard University Press, 1999.

Reeder, Matt. "Estop That! Defeating a Corrupt State's Corruption Defense to ICSID BIT Arbitration." *American Review of International Arbitration* 27, no. 3 (2016): 311–325.

Restatement (Fourth) of the Foreign Relations Law of the United States—Jurisdiction (Tentative Draft No. 2, 2016), St. Paul, MN: American Law Institute.

Restatement (Second) of the Law of Contracts, 12 vols. St. Paul, MN: American Law Institute, 1979.

Reyes, Jessica Wolpaw. "Lead Exposure and Behavior: Effects on Antisocial and Risky Behavior among Children and Adolescents." *Economic Inquiry* 53, no. 3 (2015): 1580–1605.

Ripstein, Arthur. "Authority and Coercion." *Philosophy & Public Affairs* 32, no. 1 (2004): 2–35.

Roberts, Sam. "Diepreye Alamieyeseigha, Nigerian Notorious for Corruption, Dies at 62." *New York Times*, October 14, 2015.

Rose, Cecily. *International Anti-Corruption Norms: Their Creation and Influence on Domestic Legal Systems*. New York: Oxford University Press, 2015.

Rose-Ackerman, Susan and Bonnie J. Palifka. *Corruption and Government: Causes, Consequences, and Reform 2d ed.* New York: Cambridge University Press, 2016.

Ryngaert, Cedric. *Jurisdiction in International Law 2d ed.* New York: Oxford University Press, 2015.

Salbu, Steven R. "Extraterritorial Restriction of Bribery: A Premature Evocation of the Normative Global Village." *Yale Journal of International Law* 24, no. 1 (1999): 223–255.

Salbu, Steven R. "The Foreign Corrupt Practices Act as a Threat to Global Harmony." *Michigan Journal of International Law* 20, no. 3 (1998): 419–449.

Samatas, Minas. "The SAIC-Siemens 'super-panopticon' in the Athens 2004 Olympics as a case of 'McVeillance': The surveillance-industrial complex's unscrupulous global business." In *The Surveillance-Industrial Complex: A Political Economy of Surveillance*, edited by Kirstie Ball and Laureen Snider, 61–77. New York: Routledge, 2013.

Schubert, Siri, and Christian T. Miller. "At Siemens, Bribery Was Just a Line Item." *New York Times*, December 30, 2008.

"SEC Files Charges on United Brands." *New York Times*, May 22, 1975.

Seeger, Karolos, Colby A. Smith, Anna V. Maximenko, and Jane Shvets. "Russia: Recent Developments Bearing Upon Counterparty Selection Process and Data Domestication." *FCPA Update* 7, no. 2 (September 2015), http://www.debevoise.com/~/media/files/insights/publications/2015/09/fcpa_update_september_2015.pdf.

Segal, David. "Petrobras Oil Scandal Leaves Brazilians Lamenting a Lost Dream." *New York Times*, August 7, 2015.

Seligson, Mitchell A. "The Impact of Corruption on Regime Legitimacy: A Comparative Study of Four Latin American Countries." *Journal of Politics* 64, no. 2 (2002): 408–433.

Sharman, J.C. *The Despot's Guide to Wealth Management: On the International Campaign against Grand Corruption*. Ithaca: Cornell University Press, 2017.

Shavell, Steven. *Foundations of Economic Analysis of Law*. Cambridge: Harvard University Press, 2004.

Shearman & Stearling LLP. *FCPA Digest* (2012–2018).

Shearman & Sterling. *FCPA Case Digest 2002*, available online at https://www.justice.gov/sites/default/files/criminal-fraud/legacy/2012/12/03/response2-appx-a.pdf.

Siemens. *Siemens Annual Report 2009*.

Siemens. *Siemens Annual Report 2015*.

Siems, Mathias. *Comparative Law 2d ed.* New York: Cambridge University Press, 2018.

Sills, Deborah S. "The Foreign Emoluments Clause: Protecting Our National Security Interests." *Journal of Law and Policy* 26, no. 1 (2018): 63–121.

Smith, N. Craig, Sally S. Simpson, and Chun-Yao Huang. "Why managers fail to do the right thing: An empirical study of unethical and illegal conduct." *Business Ethics Quarterly* 17, no. 4 (2007): 633–667.

Sng, Melvin, Justin Tang, and Shanshan Huang. "China: Internal Investigations." In *The Asia-Pacific Investigations Review 2016*, 29–33. Global Investigations Review, 2015. Accessed December 31, 2018. https://globalinvestigationsreview.com/benchmarking/the-asia-pacific-investigations-review-2016/1024355/china-internal-investigations.

Song, Jiewuh. "Pirates and Torturers: Universal Jurisdiction as Enforcement Gap-Filling." *Journal of Political Philosophy* 23, no. 4 (2015): 471–490.

Søreide, Tina. *Corruption and Criminal Justice: Bridging Economic and Legal Perspectives.* Cheltenham: Edward Elgar, 2016.

Spahn, Elizabeth K. "Multijurisdictional Bribery Law Enforcement: The OECD Anti-Bribery Convention." *Virginia Journal of International Law* 53, no.1 (2012): 1–52.

Spalding, Andrew B. "Corruption, Corporations, and the New Human Right." *Washington University Law Review* 91, no. 6 (2014): 1365–1428.

Spalding, Andrew B. "Deconstructing Duty Free: Investor-State Arbitration as Private Anti-Bribery Enforcement." *University of California Davis Law Review* 49 (2015): 443–496.

Spalding, Andrew B. "Unwitting Sanctions: Understanding Anti-Bribery Legislation as Economic Sanctions Against Emerging Markets." *Florida Law Review* 62, no. 2 (2010): 351–427.

Spencer, Jennifer and Carolina Gomez. "MNEs and Host Country Corruption." *Strategic Management Journal* 32, no. 3 (2011): 280–300.

Sporkin, Stanley. "The Worldwide Banning of Schmiergeld: A Look at the Foreign Corrupt Practices Act on Its Twentieth Birthday." *Northwestern Journal of International Law & Business* 18, no. 2 (1998): 269–281.

Stephan, Paul B. "Regulatory Competition and Anticorruption Law." *Virginia Journal of International Law* 53, no. 1 (2012): 53–70.

Stephenson, Matthew C. "Beware Blowback: How Attempts to Strengthen FCPA Deterrence Could Narrow the Statute's Scope." In *Research Handbook on Corporate Crime and Financial Misdealing*, edited by Jennifer Arlen, 175–194. Cheltenham: Edward Elgar, 2018.

Stewart, Richard B. "Remedying Disregard in Global Regulatory Governance: Accountability, Participation and Responsiveness." *American Journal of International Law* 108, no. 2 (2014): 211–270.

Sullivan, Bob. "Reformulating Bribery: A Legal Critique of the Bribery Act 2010." In *Modern Bribery Law, Comparative Perspectives*, edited by Jeremy Horder and Peter Alldridge, 13–38. New York: Cambridge University Press, 2013.

Surrey, Walter Sterling. "The Foreign Corrupt Practices Act: Let the Punishment Fit the Crime." *Harvard International Law Journal* 20, no. 1 (1979): 293–304.

"Mr. Tanaka and Lockheed," *Washington Post*, August 21, 1976.

Tankebe, Justice. "In Search of Moral Recognition? Policing and Eudaemonic Legitimacy in Ghana." *Law & Social Inquiry* 38, no. 3 (2013): 576–597.

Tankebe, Justice. "Viewing Things Differently: The Dimensions of Public Perceptions of Police Legitimacy." *Criminology* 51, no. 1 (2013): 103–135.

Tarullo, Daniel K. "The Limits of Institutional Design: Implementing the OECD Anti-Bribery Convention." *Virginia Journal of International Law* 44, no. 3 (2004): 665–710.

Teachout, Zephyr. *Corruption in America: From Benjamin Franklin's Snuff Box to Citizens United*. Cambridge, MA: Harvard University Press, 2014.

The Wire. "Lessons." Directed by Gloria Muzo, written by David Sumon, HBO, July 21, 2002.

Theobald, Robin. "So What Really Is the Problem About Corruption?" *Third World Quarterly* 20, no. 3 (1999): 491–502.

Transparency International. "Bribe Payers Index: Overview." Accessed December 31, 2018. http://www.transparency.org/research/bpi/overview.

Transparency International. *Can Justice Be Achieved Through Settlements*. Policy Brief 01/2015, July 28, 2015. Accessed December 31, 2018. https://www.transparency.org/whatwedo/publication/can_justice_be_achieved_through_settlements.

Transparency International. *Civil Society Participation, Public Accountability and the UN Convention Against Corruption*. December 2015. Accessed December 31, 2018. https://www.transparency.org/whatwedo/publication/civil_society_participation_public_accountability_and_the_uncac.

Transparency International. "Corruption Perceptions Index 2016: Short Methodology Note." Accessed December 31, 2018. https://www.transparency.org/news/feature/corruption_perceptions_index_2016.

Transparency International. "Global Corruption Barometer: Overview." Accessed December 31, 2018. http://www.transparency.org/research/gcb.

Treisman, Daniel. "What Have We Learned About the Causes of Corruption from Ten Years of Cross-National Empirical Research?" *Annual Review of Political Science* 10, no.1 (2007): 211–244.

Treviño, Linda Klebe, Niki A. den Nieuwenboer, and Jennifer J. Kish-Gephart. "(Un)Ethical Behavior in Organizations." *Annual Review of Psychology* 65, no. 1 (2014): 635–660.

Treviño, Linda K., Gary R. Weaver, and Scott J. Reynolds. "Behavioral ethics in organizations: A review." *Journal of Management* 32, no. 6 (2006): 951–990.

Turk, Matthew C. "A Political Economy Approach to Reforming the Foreign Corrupt Practices Act." *Northwestern Journal of International Law & Business* 33, no. 2 (2013): 325–391.

Tyler, Tom R. *Why People Obey the Law*. New Haven: Yale University Press, 1990.

U.K. Securities Fraud Office. "MW Kellogg Ltd to pay £7 million in SFO High Court action." Press release, February 16, 2011.

"United Brands Pleads Guilty to Plotting Honduran Bribe; $15,000 Fine Ends Case." *Wall Street Journal*, July 20, 1978.

United Nations, International Law Commission, *Fifth report on immunity of State officials from foreign criminal jurisdiction, by Concepción Escobar Hernández, Special Rapporteur*, A/CN.4/701, June 4, 2016.

United Nations, International Law Commission, *Draft Articles on Responsibility of States for Internationally Wrongful Acts*, Rep. of the Int'l Law Comm'n, 53rd Sess., Apr. 23–Jun. 1 and Jul. 2–Aug. 10, U.N. GAOR, 56th Sess., Supp. No. 10, A/56/10 (2001).

US Congress, House. "*The Activities of American Multinational Corporations Abroad: Hearings Before the Subcomm. on Int'l Econ. Policy of the H. Comm. on Int'l Relations.*" 94th Cong. 1–3 (1975).

US Congress, Senate. "*Lockheed Bribery: Hearings Before the S. Comm. on Banking, Hous. & Urban Affairs.*" 94th Cong. (1975).

US Congress, Senate. "*Multinational Corporations and United States Foreign Policy: Hearings Before the Subcomm. on Multinational Corps. of the S. Comm. on Foreign Relations.*" 94th Cong., Part 12 (1975).

US Congress, Senate. "*Prohibiting Bribes to Foreign Officials: Hearing on S. 3133, S. 3379 and S. 3418 Before the S. Comm. on Banking, Hous. & Urban Affairs.*" 94th Cong. 43 (1976).

US Congress, Senate. *The Final Report of the Select Committee*, 93rd Cong., 2d sess., S. REP. NO. 93-981 (1974).

US Department of Justice. "Former Chief Financial Officer of Siemens Argentina Pleads Guilty to Role in Multimillion Dollar Foreign Bribery Scheme." Press release, September 30, 2015, https://www.justice.gov/opa/pr/former-chief-financial-officer-siemens-argentina-pleads-guilty-role-multimillion-dollar.

US Department of Justice. "Former Haitian Government Official Sentenced to Nine Years in Prison for Role in Scheme to Launder Bribes." Press release, May 21, 2012, https://www.justice.gov/opa/pr/former-haitian-government-official-sentenced-nine-years-prison-role-scheme-launder-bribes.

US Department of Justice. *Justice Manual*, updated February 2018, https://www.justice.gov/usam/usam-9-27000-principles-federal-prosecution#9-27.760.

US Department of Justice. "Executive Sentenced to 15 Years in Prison for Scheme to Bribe Officials at State-Owned Telecommunications Company in Haiti." Press release, October 25, 2011, https://www.justice.gov/opa/pr/executive-sentenced-15-years-prison-scheme-bribe-officials-state-owned-telecommunications.

US Department of Justice. "Florida Telecommunications Company, Two Executives, an Intermediary and Two Former Haitian Government Officials Indicted for Their Alleged Participation in Foreign Bribery Scheme." Press release, July 13, 2011, https://www.justice.gov/opa/pr/florida-telecommunications-company-two-executives-intermediary-and-two-former-haitian.

US Department of Justice. "Former Haitian Government Official Sentenced to Prison for His Role in Money Laundering Conspiracy Related to Foreign Bribery Scheme." Press release, June 2, 2010, https://www.justice.gov/opa/pr/former-haitian-government-official-sentenced-prison-his-role-money-laundering-conspiracy.

US Department of Justice. "Marubeni Corporation Resolves Foreign Corrupt Practices Act Investigation and Agrees to Pay a $54.6 Million Criminal Penalty." Press release, January 17, 2012, https://www.justice.gov/opa/pr/marubeni-corporation-resolves-foreign-corrupt-practices-act-investigation-and-agrees-pay-546.

US Department of Justice. "Odebrecht and Braskem Plead Guilty and Agree to Pay at Least $3.5 Billion in Global Penalties to Resolve Largest Foreign Bribery Case in History." Press release, December 21, 2016, https://www.justice.gov/opa/pr/odebrecht-and-braskem-plead-guilty-and-agree-pay-least-35-billion-global-penalties-resolve.

US Department of Justice. "Oil Services Companies and a Freight Forwarding Company Agree to Resolve Foreign Bribery Investigations and to Pay More Than $156 Million in Criminal Penalties." Press release, November 4, 2010, https://www.justice.gov/opa/pr/oil-services-companies-and-freight-forwarding-company-agree-resolve-foreign-bribery.

US Department of Justice. "Siemens AG and Three Subsidiaries Plead Guilty to Foreign Corrupt Practices Act Violations and Agree to Pay $450 Million in Combined Criminal Fines." Press release, December 15, 2008, https://www.justice.gov/archive/opa/pr/2008/December/08-crm-1105.html.

US Environmental Protection Agency. *Regulatory Impact Analysis of the Proposed Revisions to the National Ambient Air Quality Standards for Lead* (Research Triangle Park, North Carolina: Office of Air Quality Planning and Standards, 2008).

US Securities and Exchange Commission. "SEC Charges BNY Mellon with FCPA Violations." Press release, August 18, 2015, https://www.sec.gov/news/pressrelease/2015-170.html.

US Securities and Exchange Commission. Press Release, "SEC Charges Seven Former Siemens Executives with Bribing Leaders in Argentina." Press release, December 11, 2011, https://www.sec.gov/news/press/2011/2011-263.htm.

US Securities and Exchange Commission. *Report of the Securities and Exchange Commission on Questionable and Illegal Corporate Payments and Practices*, submitted to the Senate Committee on Banking, Housing and Urban Affairs. May 19, 1976.

US Securities and Exchange Commission. *Report on Questionable and Illegal Corporate Payments and Practices*, submitted to the S. Comm. on Banking, Hous., & Urban Affairs, 94th Cong., 2nd Sess. Comm. Print 1976.

US Securities and Exchange Commission. "Petrochemical Manufacturer Braskem S.A. to Pay $957 Million to Settle FCPA Charges." Press release, December 21, 2016, https://www.sec.gov/news/pressrelease/2016-271.html.

US Securities and Exchange Commission. "SEC Charges Texas-Based Layne Christensen Company with FCPA Violations." Press release, October 27, 2014, https://www.sec.gov/news/press-release/2014-240#.VE7t7_nF-iM.

US Securities and Exchange Commission. "SEC Concludes Its Case Against Former Siemens Executives Charged with Bribery in Argentina, Obtaining Judgments over $1.8 Million." Litigation Release No. 22923, February 10, 2014, https://www.sec.gov/litigation/litreleases/2014/lr22923.htm.

UNCAC Coalition. "Making UNCAC Work: Coalition Statement Ahead of the 6th Conference of States Parties in St. Petersburg," May 21, 2015, http://uncaccoalition.org/files/UNCAC-Coalition-Statement-6th-COSP-English.pdf.

United Nations Office of Drugs and Crime. "Country Profiles." Accessed December 31, 2018. https://www.unodc.org/unodc/en/treaties/CAC/country-profile/index.html.

United Nations Office on Drugs and Crime, *Corruption in Nigeria, Bribery: Public Experience and Response*. July 2017.

United Nations Office on Drugs and Crime, *Country Review Report of Armenia*, Review Cycle: 1. Vienna: United Nations Office, 2013.

United Nations Office on Drugs and Crime, *Country Review Report of Bulgaria*, Review Cycle: 1. Vienna: United Nations Office, 2013.

United Nations Office on Drugs and Crime, *Country Review Report of Latvia*, Review Cycle: 1. Vienna: United Nations Office, 2014.

United Nations Office on Drugs and Crime, *Country Review Report of Ukraine*, Review Cycle: 1. Vienna: United Nations Office, 2013.

United Nations Office on Drugs and Crime, *State of Implementation of the United Nations Convention against Corruption: Criminalization, Law Enforcement and International Cooperation, 2d ed.* Vienna: United Nations Office, 2017.

United Nations Office on Drugs and Crime, *Travaux Préparatoires of the Negotiations for the Elaboration of the United Nations Convention against Corruption*. New York: United Nations, 2010.

United Nations. *Report of the International Law Commission*, 58th Sess., U.N. Doc. A/61/10 (2006).

Vagts, Detlev F., Harold Koh, William S. Dodge, and Hannah L. Buxbaum. *Transnational Business Problems*. St. Paul, MN: Foundation Press, 2015.

Vikas, Anand, Blake E. Ashforth, and Mahendra Joshi. "Business as usual: The acceptance and perpetuation of corruption in organizations." *The Academy of Management Executive* 18, no. 2 (2004): 39–53.

Viscusi, Kip. "The Value of Risks to Life and Health." *Journal of Economic Literature* 31, no. 4 (1993): 1912–1946.

Viswanatha, Aruna, Joshua Robinson, Andrew Morse, and Christopher M. Matthews. "FIFA Rocked as U.S. Charges 14 in Corruption Investigation." *Wall Street Journal*, May 27, 2015.

Viswanatha, Aruna, Joshua Robinson, and John Revill. "U.S. Indicts 16 New Suspects in FIFA Corruption Case." *Wall Street Journal*, December 3, 2015.

Von Bogdandy, Armin, Matthias Goldmann, and Ingo Venzke. "From Public International to International Public Law: Translating World Public Opinion into International Public Authority." *European Journal of International Law* 28, no. 1 (2017): 115–145.

Waldron, Jeremy. "Special Ties and Natural Duties." *Philosophy & Public* Affairs 22, no. 1 (1993): 3–30.

Watson, Geoffrey R. "Offenders Abroad: The Case for Nationality-Based Criminal Jurisdiction." *Yale Journal of International Law* 17, no. 1 (1992): 41–84.

Watts, Jonathan. "Brazil: Insider claims Rousseff coalition took funds from Belo Monte mega-dam." *The Guardian*, April 8, 2016.

Wei, Shang-jin. "How Taxing Is Corruption on International Investors." *Review of Economics and Statistics* 82, no. 1 (2000): 1–11.

Weigend, Thomas. "Societas delinquere non potest? A German Perspective." *Journal of International Criminal Justice* 6, no. 5 (2008): 927–945.

Weinraub, Bernard. "Dutch Prince Quits Posts as Inquiry Board Assails His Links with Lockheed." *The New York Times*, August 27, 1976.

Weinrib, Ernest J. *The Idea of Private Law*. Cambridge: Harvard University Press, 1995.

Weissmann, Andrew and Alixandra Smith. *Restoring Balance: Proposed Amendments to the Foreign Corrupt Practices Act*. US Chamber Institute for Legal Reform, 2010.

Williams, Glanville. "Oblique Intention." *Cambridge Law Journal* 46, no. 3 (1987): 417–438.

Windsor, Duane and Kathleen A. Getz. "Multilateral Cooperation to Combat Corruption: Normative Regimes Despite Mixed Motives and Diverse Values." *Cornell International Law Journal* 731, no. 3 (2000): 731–772.

Wolf, Mark L. *The Case for an International Anti-corruption Court*. Brookings Institution, 2014.

Wolfensohn, James D. "People and Development. Annual Meetings Address." Washington, D.C., October 1, 1996.

Wolff, Jacqueline C. "Voluntary Disclosure Programs." *Fordham Law Review* 47, no. 6 (1979): 1057–1082.

World Bank. "Control of Corruption." Accessed December 31, 2018, http://info.worldbank.org/governance/wgi/#doc.

World Bank. "CPIA Criteria 2017. September 1, 2017." Accessed December 31, 2018, http://pubdocs.worldbank.org/en/203511467141304327/CPIA-Criteria-2017v2.pdf.

World Bank. *Helping Countries Combat Corruption: The Role of the World Bank.* The World Bank, 1979. Accessed December 31, 2018, http://www1.worldbank.org/publicsector/anticorrupt/corruptn/corrptn.pdf.

World Bank. *Nigeria Economic Report No. 2.* Washington, D.C.: World Bank, July 2014.

World Bank. "Personal remittances, received (% of GDP)—Haiti (2002–2004)." World Bank Open Data. Accessed December 31, 2018, https://data.worldbank.org/.

World Bank. "Population, total." World Bank Open Data. Accessed December 31, 2018, https://data.worldbank.org/.

World Bank. *World Bank Enterprise Survey: Manufacturing Module* (2018). Accessed December 31, 2018, http://www.enterprisesurveys.org/Data.

World Bank. *World Bank Group Sanctions System. Annual Report FY18.* World Bank Group, 2018.

World Justice Project. *Rule of Law Index 2017–2018* (2018). Accessed April 15, 2019, https://worldjusticeproject.org/our-work/wjp-rule-law-index.

Wouters, Jan, Cedric Ryngaert, and Ann Sofie Coots. "The International Legal Framework Against Corruption: Achievements and Challenges." 14 *Melbourne Journal of International Law* 14, no. 1 (2013): 1–76.

Yackee, Jason Webb. "Investment Treaties and Investor Corruption: An Emerging Defense for Host States?" *Virginia Journal of International Law* 52, no. 3 (2012): 723–745.

Yates, Sally Quillian. "Individual Accountability for Corporate Wrongdoing." US Department of Justice, Office of the Deputy Attorney General. September 9, 2015.

Young, Oran R. "Effectiveness of international environmental regimes: Existing knowledge, cutting-edge themes, and research strategies." *Proceedings of the National Academy of Sciences* 108, no. 50 (2011): 19853–19860.

Young, Oran R. *Governance in World Affairs.* Ithaca: Cornell University Press, 1999.

Ziegler, Katja S. "Domain Réservé." In *Max Planck Encyclopedia of Public International Law*, edited by Rüdiger Wolfrum, Oxford Public International Law, accessed December 31, 2018.

Zimring, Franklin E. and Gordon Hawkins. *Deterrence: The Legal Threat in Crime Control.* Chicago: University of Chicago Press, 1973.

International and Intergovernmental Instruments

African Union, African Union Convention on Preventing and Combatting Corruption, July 11, 2003, 43 I.L.M. 5.

Agreement on Mutual Enforcement of Debarment Decisions by and among the Asian Development Bank, the European Bank for Reconstruction and Development, Inter-American Development Bank, and the World Bank, April 9, 2010, http://lnadbg4.adb.org/oai001p.nsf/0/F77A326B818A19C548257853000C2B10/$FILE/cross-debarment-agreement.pdf.

Charter of Fundamental Rights of the European Union, Dec. 7, 2010, 2010 O.J. (C 83/02).

Convention Implementing the Schengen Agreement of 14 June 1985 Between the Governments of the States of the Benelux Economic Union, the Federal Republic of Germany and the French Republic on the Gradual Abolition of Checks at Their Common Borders, art. 54, June 14, 1985, 2000 O.J. (L 239) 19.

Council of Europe, Criminal Law Convention on Corruption, Jan. 27, 1999, Eur. T.S. No. 173.

Council of Europe, Civil Law Convention on Corruption, Nov. 4, 1999, Eur. T.S. No. 174.
Council of the European Union, Council Framework Decision of 13 June 2002 on joint investigation teams (2002/465/JHA).
Eurojust, Guidelines for Deciding "Which Jurisdiction Should Prosecute"? Revised 2016.
FATF, International Standards on Combating Money Laundering and the Financing of Terrorism & Proliferation (Paris: FATF, 2012–2018), http://www.fatf-gafi.org/recommendations.html.
International Covenant on Civil and Political Rights, G.A. res. 2200A (XXI), 21 U.N. GAOR Supp. (No. 16) at 52, U.N. Doc. A/6316 (1966), 999 U.N.T.S. 171, entered into force Mar. 23, 1976.
OECD Convention on Combating Bribery of Foreign Public Officials in International Business Transactions, 37 I.L.M. 1 (1998).
OECD Working Group on Bribery in International Business Transactions, Recommendation of the Council for Further Combating Bribery of Foreign Public Officials, November 26, 2009 (with amendments adopted by Council 18 February 2010 to reflect the inclusion of Annex II, Good Practice Guidance on Internal Controls, Ethics and Compliance).
United Nations Convention against Corruption, Oct. 31, 2003, 2349 U.N.T.S. 41.
United Nations Convention against Illicit Traffic in Narcotic Drugs and Psychotropic Substances, Dec. 19, 1988, 1582 U.N.T.S. 95.
United Nations Convention against Transnational Organized Crime, Nov. 15, 2000, 2237 U.N.T.S. 319.
United Nations General Assembly. Work of the Statistical Commission pertaining to the 2030 Agenda for Sustainable Development. G.A. Res. 71/313 (July 6, 2017).

Legislative Materials

Belgium

Code Pénal, art. 246(3).

Brazil

Decreto No. 8.420, de 18 de Marco de 2015, D.O.U. de 19.3.2015.
Lei No. 12.846 de 1 de Agosto de 2013, D.O.U. de 2.8.2013 (Clean Companies Act).
Lei No. 12.850 de 2 de Agosto de 2013, D.O.U. de 5.8.2013 (Criminal Organizations Enforcement Act).

Canada

Corruption of Foreign Public Officials Act, S.C. 1998, ch. 34.

Colombia

L. 1778/2016, febrero 2, 2016, D.O. art. 2.

European Union

European Union, Directive 2014/24/EU of the European Parliament and of the Council of 26 February 2014 on public procurement, art. 57, http://eur-lex.europa.eu/legal-content/EN/ALL/?uri=CELEX:32014L0024.

France

Code pénal, art. 113-9.

Code de procédure pénale, art. 692.

Loi 2016-1691 du 9 décembre 2016 relative à la transparence, à la lutte contre la corruption et à la modernisation de la vie économique, J.O., Dec. 10, 2016.

Germany

Gesetz zur Bekampfund Internationaler Bestechung [IntBestG], Sept. 10, 1998, Bundesgesetzblatt, Teil II [BGBL II] at 2327, as amended.

Strafgesetzbuch, §§ 299, 334.

Singapore

Prevention of Corruption Act (Cap. 241, 1993 Rev. Ed.).

Switzerland

Schweizerisches Strafgesetbuch, Code pénal suisse, Codice penale svizzero, art. 322septies.

United Kingdom

Bribery Act 2010, ch. 23.

The East India Company Act, 1772, 13 Geo. 3 ch. 63

The East India Company Act, 1784, 24 Geo. 3 sess. 2 ch. 25.

United States of America—Federal

18 U.S.C. § 201.

18 U.S.C. §§ 1341, 1343.

Alternative Fines Act, 18. U.S.C. § 3571.

Articles of Confederation of 1781.

Bank Secrecy Act, 12 U.S.C. §§ 1730(d), 1829b, 1951–59 (1970); 31 U.S.C. §§ 1051–1122 (1970).

Customer Due Diligence Requirements for Financial Institutions, 31 C.F.R. §§ 1010, 1020, 1023, 1024, 1026 (May 11, 2016).

Exchange Act § 20(a) (codified at 15 U.S.C. §78t).

Fed. R. Civ. Pro. 801(d)(2)(D).

Foreign Corrupt Practices Act of 1977, Pub. L. No. 95-213, 91 Stat. 1494 (1977) (codified as amended at 15 U.S.C. §§ 78dd-1, 78dd-2, 78dd-3, 78ff, 78m(b), (d)(1), (g)–(h) (2012)), amended by Foreign Corrupt Practices Act Amendment of 1988, Pub. L. No. 100-418, 102 Stat. 1107, 1415 (1988) (codified at §§ 78dd-1 to 78dd-3, 78ff (2006)) and International Anti-Bribery and Fair Competition Act of 1998, Pub. L. No. 105-366, 112 Stat. 3302 (1998) (codified at §§ 78dd-1 to 78dd-3, 78ff (2012)).

Foreign Corrupt Practices Act Opinion Procedure, 28 C.F.R. § 80.4 (2009).

Hobbs Act, 18 U.S.C. § 1951 (1946).

Laundering of Monetary Instruments, 18 U.S.C. § 1956(f), 1957.

Omnibus Trade and Competitiveness Act of 1988, Pub. L. No. 100-418, 102 Stat. 1107 (codified as amended at 19 U.S.C. § 2901, pt. 3 (2006)), §§ 5001–5003.

Racketeer Influenced and Corrupt Organizations, 18 U.S.C. §§ 1961–1968.

Sarbanes-Oxley Act of 2002, Pub. L. No. 107-204, 116 Stat. 745 (enacted July 30, 2002).
Travel Act, 18 U.S.C. § 1952.

United States—State and other laws

11 Delaware Code § 1202.
Model Penal Code § 240.1 and Explanatory Note for §§ 240.1–240.7 American Law Institute, 1962.
New York Penal Law § 200.05.
Oregon Revised Statutes § 162.035.

Table of Cases

Adler v. Federal Republic of Nigeria, 219 F.3d 869 (9th Cir. 2000).
Appeal N° 5023972-66.2017.4.04.0000/PR—TRF-4 (August 22, 2017) (Braz.)
Cour de cassation, crim., Jan. 17, 2018, N0. 16/86491 (Fr.); C.A. Paris, Pole 5—Ch. 13 (Fr.).
District of Columbia v. Trump, 315 F. Supp. 3d 875 (D. Md. 2018).
European Community v. RJR Nabisco, 764 F.3d 129, 140 (2d Cir. 2014), rev'd, 136 S. Ct. p. 2090 (2016).
Evans v. United States, 504 U.S. 255 (1992).
Federal Constitutional Court, Second Senate, June 23, 2010, Doc. Nos. 2 BvR 2559/08, 2 BvR 105/09, 2 BvR 491/09.
Fehl v. S. W. C. Corp., 433 F. Supp. 939 (D. Del. 1977).
Jacobellis v. Ohio, 378 U.S. 184, 197 (1964).
Licci v. Lebanese Canadian Bank, 732 F.3d 161 (2d Cir. 2013).
LG Munchen, I, 10 December 2013 (5 HK O 1387/10).
McCormick v. United States, 500 U.S. 257 (1991).
McDonnell v. United States, 136 S. Ct. 2355 (2016).
McNally v. United States, 483 U.S. 350 (1987).
Melrose Distillers v. United States, 79 S. Ct. 763 (1959).
Meridian Global Funds Management Asia Ltd. v. Securities Commission [1995] 2 A.C. 500.
Metal-Tech Ltd. v. The Republic of Uzbekistan, ICSID Case No. ARB/10/3, Award (Oct. 4, 2013).
Morrison v. National Australia Bank, 561 U.S. 247 (2010).
Oscanyan v. Arms Co., 103 U.S. 261 (1880).
STF., Pet. 7.265/DF, Relator: Min. Ricardo Lewandowski, 14.11.2017 (Braz.)
R. v. Innospec Ltd., Sentencing Remarks of Lord Justice Thomas, [2010] 3 WLUK 784, [2010] Crim. L.R. 665 (In the Crown Court at Southwark).
R.C.M. Executive Gallery Corp. v. Rols Capital Co. 901 F. Supp. 630 (S.D.N.Y. 1995).
Ray v. Alad Corp., 560 P.2d p. 3 (1977).
Republic of Iraq v. ABB AG, 920 F. Supp. 2d 517 (S.D.N.Y. 2013).
Republic of Iraq v. ABB AG, 768 F.3d 145, pp. 160-169 (2d Cir. 2015), cert. denied, 135 S. Ct. 2836 (2015).
RJR Nabisco, Inc. v. European Communities, 136 S. Ct. 2090 (2016).
Skilling v. United States, 561 U.S. 358 (2010).
Stichting Ter Behartiging v. Schreiber, 327 F.3d 173, 182 (2d Cir. 2003).
Tesco Supermarkets Ltd. v. Nattrass, [1972] A.C. 153 HL.

Tesler v. Government of the USA, [2011] EWHC (Admin.) 52 (Eng.).
United States v. Alamo Bank of Texas, 880 F.2d 828 (5th Cir. 1989).
United States v. Alcatel-Lucent France, SA, 688 F.3d 1301 (11th Cir. 2012).
United States v. Alfisi, 308 F.3d 144 (2d Cir. 2002).
United States v. All Assets Held at Bank Julius, 251 F. Supp. 3d 82 (D.D.C. 2017).
United States v. Allen, 864 F.3d 63 (2d Cir. 2017).
United States v. Bestfoods, 524 U.S. 51 (1998).
United States v. Carson, 09-cr-77, 2011 WL 5101701 (C.D. Cal. May 18, 2011).
United States v. Castle, 925 F.2d 831 (5th Cir. 1991).
United States v. Davis, 905 F.2d 245, 249 (9th Cir. 1989).
United States v. Feola, 420 U.S. 671, 677 (1975).
United States v. Giffen, 326 F. Supp. 2d 497 (S.D.N.Y. 2004).
United States v. Hanson, 2 F.3d 942 (9th Cir. 1993).
United States v. Harris Corp., 3:90-cr-456 (N.D. Cal. Mar. 20, 1991).
United States v. Hoskins, 902 F.3d 69 (2d Cir. 2018).
United States v. Jennings, 160 F.3d 1006, 1015 n.4 (4th Cir. 1998).
United States v. Jensen, 532 F. Supp. 2d 1187 (N.D. Cal. 2008).
United States v. Kay, 359 F.3d 738 (5th Cir. 2004).
United States v. Kay, 513 F.3d 432 (5th Cir. 2007).
United States v. Kozeny, 582 F. Supp. 2d 535 (S.D.N.Y. 2008).
United States v. Kozeny, 664 F. Supp. 2d 369 (S.D.N.Y. 2009), aff'd, 667 F.3d 122 (2d Cir. 2011).
United States v. Lazarenko, 564 F.3d 1026 (9th Cir. 2009).
United States v. Liebo, 923 F.2d 1308 (8th Cir. 1991).
United States v. Liu, 960 F.2d 449 (5th Cir. 1992).
United States v. Gonzalez, 13-cr-901 (S.D.N.Y. Jan. 19, 2016).
United States v. Muldoon, 931 F.2d 282 (4th Cir. 1991).
United States v. Noriega, 10-cr-1031 (C.D. Cal. 2010).
United States v. Patel, 9-cr-338 (D.D.C. Dec. 11, 2009).
United States v. Polizzi, 500 F.2d 856 (9th Cir. 1974).
United States v. Shields Rubber Corp., 732 F. Supp. 569 (W.D. Pa. 1989).
United States v. Sidorenko, 102 F. Supp. 3d 1124 (N.D. Cal. 2015).
United States v. Strand, 574 F.2d 993 (9th Cir. 1978).
United States v. Sharef, 11-cr-1056 (S.D.N.Y. 2011)
United States v. West, 746 F. Supp. 2d 932 (N.D. Ill. 2010).
United States v. Yermian, 468 U.S. 63, 68 (1984).
US Securities and Exchange Commission v. Jackson, 908 F. Supp. 2d 834 (S.D. Tex. 2012).
US Securities and Exchange Commission v. Mattson, 01-cv-3106 (S.D. Tex. Sept. 9, 2002).
US Securities and Exchange Commission v. Sharef, 924 F. Supp. 2d 539 (S.D.N.Y. 2013).
US Securities and Exchange Commission v. Straub, 921 F. Supp. 2d 244 (S.D.N.Y. 2013).
US Securities and Exchange Commission v. World-Wide Coin Investments, 567 F. Supp. 724 (N.D. Ga. 1983).
World Duty Free Co. v. Republic of Kenya, ICSID Case No. Arb/00/7, Award (Sept. 25, 2006).

Settlements

In the Matter of Diagnostics Products Corp., Admin. Proc., File No. 51724, 2005 WL 1211548 (May 20, 2005).
United States v. Snamprogetti Netherlands B.V., 10-cr-460 (S.D. Tex. filed July 7, 2010).
US Securities and Exchange Commission v. ENI, S.p.A., 4:10-cv-2414 (S.D. Tex. filed July 7, 2010).
US Securities and Exchange Commission v. Oracle Corp., 3:12-cv-4310 (N.D. Cal. Aug 13, 2012).
US Securities and Exchange Commission v. United Brands Co., Litigation Release No. 6827 (D.C. Cir. 1975).
In re United Industrial Corp., Exchange Act Release No. 60005, 2009 WL 1507586 (May 29, 2009).
United States v. ABB Vetco Gray, Inc., 04-cr-279 (S.D. Tex. filed June 24, 2004).
United States v. Vassiliev, 14-cr-341 (N.D. Cal. filed June 26, 2014).
United States v. Braskem S.A., 16-cr-644(E.D.N.Y. filed Dec. 21, 2016).
United States v. Esquenazi, 09-cr-21010 (S.D. Fla. filed Dec. 4, 2009).
United States v. JGC Corp., 4:11-cr-260 (S.D. Tex. filed Apr. 6, 2011).
United States v. Marubeni Corp., 12-cr-22 (S.D. Tex. filed Jan. 17, 2012).
United States v. Odebrecht S.A., 16-cr-643 (E.D.N.Y. filed Dec. 21, 2016).
United States v. Siemens Aktiengesellschaft, 08-cr-367 (D.D.C. filed Dec. 12, 2008).
United States v. Vasconez Cruz, 09-cr-21010 (S.D. Fla. filed Jan. 19, 2012).

Index

For the benefit of digital users, indexed terms that span two pages (e.g., 52–53) may, on occasion, appear on only one of those pages.

Note: Figures are indicated by an *f* following the page number.

Between Impunity and Imperialism. Kevin E. Davis.